CAMBRIDGE

CB135024

Official Cambridge Exam Preparation

COMPLETE

ADVANCED

Student's Book with answers

WITH DIGITAL PACK

Third edition

C1

Greg Archer, Guy Brook-Hart, Sue Elliot and Simon Haines

CAMBRIDGE
UNIVERSITY PRESS & ASSESSMENT

Shaftesbury Road, Cambridge CB2 8EA, United Kingdom

One Liberty Plaza, 20th Floor, New York, NY 10006, USA

477 Williamstown Road, Port Melbourne, VIC 3207, Australia

314–321, 3rd Floor, Plot 3, Splendor Forum, Jasola District Centre, New Delhi – 110025, India

103 Penang Road, #05–06/07, Visioncrest Commercial, Singapore 238467

Cambridge University Press & Assessment is a department of the University of Cambridge.

We share the University's mission to contribute to society through the pursuit of education, learning and research at the highest international levels of excellence.

www.cambridge.org
Information on this title: www.cambridge.org/9781009162319

First published 2009
Second edition 2014
Third edition 2023

20 19 18 17 16 15 14 13 12 11 10 9 8 7 6 5 4 3 2

Printed in Poland by Opolgraf

A catalogue record for this publication is available from the British Library

ISBN 978-1-009-16231-9 Student's Book with Answers with Digital Pack

Additional resources for this publication at www.cambridge.org/complete

Contents

Map of the units

Unit title	Reading and Use of English	Writing	Listening
1 People like us	**Part 8:** 'You can choose your friends' **Part 4:** Key word transformation	**Part 1:** An essay: Methods schools use to help students find jobs	**Part 4:** Five people talking about a close friend
2 More than words	**Part 3:** 'You'll always have your accent – or will you?' **Part 6:** 'Using movies to help learn a language'	**Part 2:** A report: Foreign language learning in your country	**Part 1:** Three short conversations about language and communication
Vocabulary and grammar review Units 1 and 2			
3 Mind, body and soul	**Part 5:** 'Living with synaesthesia' **Part 2:** 'The importance of music' 'Forest bathing'	**Part 1:** An essay: How schools can ensure students don't suffer too much stress	**Part 2:** Personality quiz
4 Career paths	**Part 1:** 'Zero-hours contracts' **Part 8:** 'What do you bring to the table?'	**Part 2:** An email: Young people, migration and opportunities	**Part 3:** An interview with two business leaders about an open salary policy
Vocabulary and grammar review Units 3 and 4			
5 Events to remember	**Part 4:** Key word transformation **Part 7:** 'A cycle ride'	**Part 2:** A proposal: Identifying someone who should be honoured	**Part 1:** Three short conversations about dramatic past experiences
6 Creative pursuits	**Part 5:** 'The camera never lies' **Part 2:** 'Live or recorded?' 'The timeless appeal of the selfie'	**Part 2:** A review: A film you didn't expect to like but did	**Part 2:** A talk offering career advice by a professional artist
Vocabulary and grammar review Units 5 and 6			
7 In your free time	**Part 7:** 'Young film actors' **Part 1:** 'The power of art galleries'	**Part 2:** An informal letter: Replying to a friend's dilemma	**Part 4:** Five people talking about the experience of going to a concert to listen to a band
8 Sound and vision	**Part 3:** 'The future of TV' **Part 6:** 'Bring a social media influencer'	**Part 2:** A proposal: Identifying what should be included in a TV programme	**Part 3:** An interview about student media organisations
Vocabulary and grammar review Units 7 and 8			
9 Invention and innovation	**Part 7:** 'A welcome/unwelcome visit' **Part 4:** Key word transformation	**Part 1:** An essay: Online safety An essay: How technology has benefited society	**Part 1:** Three short conversations about technology
10 Learning for life	**Part 1:** 'The candle problem' **Part 8:** 'A first time for everything'	**Part 2:** A report: Improving an education establishment	**Part 2:** A presentation on 21st century skills
Vocabulary and grammar review Units 9 and 10			
11 Globetrotters	**Part 5:** 'Into the desert' **Part 2:** 'Caretakers wanted' 'Living in a castle'	**Part 2:** A review: Two hotels in your area	**Part 1:** Three short conversations about travel
12 Our planet	**Part 7:** 'The dramatic life – so far – of *Birdgirl*' **Part 3:** 'What drives an eco-warrior?'	**Part 2:** A proposal: An environmental campaign	**Part 2:** A podcast about living and working in Antarctica
Vocabulary and grammar review Units 11 and 12			
13 A healthy lifestyle	**Part 8:** 'Sports and me!' **Part 3:** 'The joy of a warm bath'	**Part 2:** A letter: Suggesting how council funds should be best spent	**Part 3:** A radio interview about sleep
14 A new land	**Part 6:** 'The psychology of emigration' **Part 4:** Key word transformation	**Part 1:** An essay: Problems arising from large-scale migration from the countryside to cities	**Part 4:** Five people talking about their reasons for moving to another country
Vocabulary and grammar review Units 13 and 14			

Speaking	Vocabulary	Grammar
Part 1: Responding to questions about yourself, your friends and family	Collocations with *give* and *make*	Verb forms to talk about the past
Part 2: Talking about how people explain things Talking about intergenerational conversations	Collocations with *make*, *get* and *do*	Expressing purpose, reason and result
Part 3: Discussing actions that help people prevent or cope with stress	Multi-word verbs Verb collocations	*no*, *none*, *not* The passive
Part 4: Talking about people's opinion regarding satisfaction at work	Dependant prepositions Adjective-noun collocations (1)	Expressing possibility, probability and certainty
Part 2: Talking about people doing dangerous activities	Idiomatic language	Verbs followed by *to* + infinitive or the *-ing* form
Part 3: Discussing factors that affect people's enjoyment of a movie Discussing what motivates a person to take a course in a creative activity	Adjective-noun collocations (2)	Avoiding repetition
Part 4: Discussing ways to get to know other people	Complex prepositions Money words and idioms	Linking ideas: relative and participle clauses Linking ideas: apposition
Part 3: Discussing how people's ideas are affected by media influence	Prefixes and suffixes Reporting verbs	Reported speech Transitive and intransitive verbs
Part 2: Talking about how people use technology	Multi-word verbs *action*, *activity*, *event* and *programme*	Future perfect and continuous *be* + *to* infinitive Objects, reflexives and reciprocals
Part 4: Discussing opinions on different styles of learning	*chance*, *occasion*, *opportunity* and *possibility*	Expressing ability, possibility and obligation
Part 1: Responding to questions about travel	Fixed phrases *at*, *in* and *on* to express location	Conditionals *wish* and *if only*
Part 3: Discussing how environmental issues affect people's lives	Prepositions following verbs Word formation	Countable and uncountable nouns Articles
Part 2: Discussing the effectiveness of and qualities needed for different physical activities	Prepositions following adjectives	Ways of contrasting ideas The language of comparison
Part 4: Discussing issues regarding moving to another country	Comment adverbials and intensifying adverbs *learn*, *find out* and *know* *provide*, *offer* and *give*	Emphasis

Introduction

Who this book is for

Complete Advanced is a stimulating and thorough preparation course for learners who wish to take the **C1 Advanced exam** from **Cambridge Assessment English**. It helps them to develop the necessary reading, writing, listening and speaking skills for the exam, as well as teaching essential grammar and vocabulary. For those who are not planning to take the exam in the near future, the book provides skills and language based around engaging topics, all highly relevant for learners moving towards a C1 level of English.

What the Student's Book contains:

- **14 units for classroom study.** Each unit comprises:
  - an authentic exam task taken from each of the four papers (Reading and Use of English, Listening, Speaking and Writing) in the C1 Advanced exam.
  - Exam advice boxes containing essential information on what each part of the exam involves, and the best way to approach each task.
  - a wide range of enjoyable speaking activities designed to increase learners' fluency and ability to express themselves.
  - a step-by-step approach to doing C1 Advanced Writing tasks.
  - grammar activities and exercises for the grammar that learners need to know for the exam; grammar exercises with the symbol are based on research from the **Cambridge Learner Corpus** and deal with the areas which often cause problems for candidates in the exam.
  - vocabulary activities and exercises for the vocabulary that learners need to know for the exam; vocabulary exercises with the symbol feature words which C1 Advanced candidates often confuse or use wrongly in the exam.
- **Seven unit reviews** comprised of exercises which revise the grammar and vocabulary in each unit.
- **Speaking and Writing banks.** These explain the possible tasks students may have to do in the Speaking and Writing papers, and provide examples and models together with additional advice on how best to approach these Speaking and Writing exam tasks.
- A **Grammar reference section** which clearly explains, unit by unit, all the main areas of grammar which you will need to know for the **C1 Advanced exam**. There are also practice exercises for all grammar points.
- **Cambridge One Digital Pack** For more information about the Digital Pack, please scan the QR code.

Also available

- A Student's **Workbook** containing 14 units for homework and self-study. Each unit contains further exam-style exercises to practise the reading, listening and writing skills needed in the **C1 Advanced exam**. In addition, they provide further practice of grammar and vocabulary, using information about C1 Advanced candidates' common errors from the Cambridge Learner Corpus .
- **Downloadable audio** containing all the listening material for the Workbook.
- A **Teacher's Book** containing:
  - **step-by-step guidance** for teaching activities in the Student's Book
  - a number of suggestions for **alternative treatments** of activities in the Student's Book listening material.
  - **complete answer keys** including audioscripts for all the listening material.
  - **access to extra photocopiable materials online** to practise and extend language abilities beyond the requirements of the **C1 Advanced exam**.
- **A Test Generator** containing:
  - a **Grammar and Vocabulary Test** at 'standard' and 'plus' levels of each of the 14 units in the Student's Book.
  - three **Term Tests** including grammar, vocabulary and C1 Advanced Reading and Use of English, Writing, Speaking and Listening exam tasks.
  - an **End of Year Test** including grammar, vocabulary and Advanced Reading and Use of English, Writing, Speaking and Listening exam tasks.

C1 Advanced content and overview

PART/TIMING	CONTENT	EXAM FOCUS
Reading and Use of English 1 hour 30 minutes	**Part 1** A modified cloze containing eight gaps followed by eight 4-option multiple-choice items. **Part 2** A modified cloze test containing eight gaps. **Part 3** A text containing eight gaps. Each gap corresponds to a word. The stems of the missing words are given beside the text and must be changed to form the missing word. **Part 4** Six separate items, each with a lead-in sentence and a gapped second sentence to be completed in three to six words, one of which is a given 'key' word. **Part 5** A text followed by six 4-option multiple-choice questions. **Part 6** Four short texts, followed by multiple-matching questions. Candidates must read across texts to match a prompt to elements in the texts. **Part 7** A text from which paragraphs have been removed and placed in jumbled order after the text. Candidates must decide from where in the text the paragraphs have been removed. **Part 8** A text or several short texts preceded by multiple-matching questions. Candidates must match a prompt to elements in the text.	Candidates are expected to demonstrate their knowledge of vocabulary and grammar in parts 1–4, and their reading comprehension skills in parts 5–8. Candidates are also expected to show understanding of specific information, text organisation features, tone, attitude, opinion, and text structure throughout the exam.
Writing 1 hour 30 minutes	**Part 1** Candidates are required to write an essay, between 220 and 260 words, based on two points given in the input text. They will be asked to explain which of the two points is more important and to give reasons for their opinion. **Part 2** Candidates have a choice of task. The tasks provide candidates with a clear context, topic, purpose and target reader for their writing. The task types are: • letter/email • proposal • report • review	Candidates are expected to demonstrate their ability to write at a C1 level. They should be able to demonstrate awareness of style and tone, as well as functions such as describing, evaluating, hypothesising, persuading, expressing opinion, comparing, giving advice, justifying and judging priorities.
Listening Approximately 40 minutes	**Part 1** Three short extracts from exchanges between interacting speakers with two multiple-choice questions on each extract. **Part 2** A monologue lasting approximately three minutes. Candidates are required to complete the sentences with information heard on the recording. **Part 3** A conversation between two or more speakers of approximately four minutes. There are six multiple-choice questions, each with four options. **Part 4** Five short themed monologues, of approximately 30 seconds each. Each multiple-matching task requires selection of the correct options from a list of eight.	Candidates are expected to be able to show understanding of agreement, attitude, course of action, detail, feeling, function, genre, gist, opinion, purpose, situation, specific information, etc.
Speaking 15 minutes	**Part 1** A short conversation between the interlocutor and each candidate (spoken questions). **Part 2** An individual 'long turn' for each candidate with a response from the second candidate. In turn, the candidates are given three photographs and asked to talk about any two of them. **Part 3** A two-way conversation between the candidates. The candidates are given spoken instructions with written stimuli, which are used in a discussion and a decision-making task. The conversation is divided into a discussion phase (2 minutes) and a decision phase (1 minute). Candidates are given approximately 15 seconds to initially read the task before starting to speak. **Part 4** A discussion on topics related to the collaborative task (spoken questions).	Candidates are expected to demonstrate competence at organising a large unit of discourse through comparison, description, speculation and expressing opinion. Candidates are also expected to demonstrate an ability to sustain interaction through their use of social language and their ability to exchange ideas, express and justify opinions, agree and disagree, suggest, speculate, evaluate and negotiate.

1 People like us

Starting off

1 **Work in small groups. How do you think these things reflect our personality? (Give examples.)**

- the job we choose
- the subject(s) we choose to study
- our free-time interests
- the clothes we wear
- the friends we choose

2 **What sort of personalities do you imagine the people in the photographs have?**

3 **Look at the statements below and say if they are true (T) or false (F) for you.**

1 My close friends tend to be people who are very similar to me.
2 People tell me I take after a particular person in my family.
3 I'd describe myself as a fairly outgoing person.
4 I find it easy to get on with most people I meet.
5 People would probably say I'm hard-working.
6 There's one thing I wish I could change about myself!
7 The number of friends and followers I have on social media is very important to me.

4 **These adjectives can be used to describe personality. Complete the table by writing each adjective in the correct column.**

chaotic competent conscientious considerate genuine hilarious idealistic imaginative insecure insensitive naïve open-minded outgoing protective self-centred supportive thoughtful unconventional well-organised

Personality attributes		
Usually positive	**Usually negative**	**Could be either**

5 **Choose adjectives from Exercise 4 and talk to your partner.**

1 Explain how three of the adjectives form part of your personality.
2 Use three different adjectives to describe someone you know.

Listening Part 4

- In Listening Part 4, you hear five short monologues on related subjects and you do two listening tasks.
- You have to choose one answer for each speaker in each task, from a list of eight options.
- You hear each speaker twice.
- This part tests your ability to identify the gist of what the speakers say, their attitude or the main points, and to interpret the context they are speaking in.

Exam info

1 **Work in pairs. You will hear five short extracts in which people are talking about a close friend. Before you listen, look at the list of ways in which each speaker's friendship began (A–H) in Task One. Look at each option and think about what you might hear.**

2 **Now look at Task Two (A–H). The options are about what the speaker has learnt about friendship. Talk about each statement with a partner. How important do you think they are in friendships?**

3 **Now listen to the five speakers and do Tasks One and Two.**

02

4 **Compare your answers with a partner. Do you agree? Listen to the recording again, paying particular attention to the items where your answers were different.**

02

TASK ONE

For questions **1–5**, choose from the list (**A–H**) how each speaker's relationship with their close friend began.

A through attending a pre-arranged meeting

B through a mutual friend

C through an unavoidable commitment

D through having an interest in common

E as a result of an unfortunate incident

F as a result of being at an unusual social gathering

G through a family connection

H as a result of having a similar sense of humour

Speaker 1	**1**
Speaker 2	**2**
Speaker 3	**3**
Speaker 4	**4**
Speaker 5	**5**

TASK TWO

For questions **6–10**, choose from the list (**A–H**) what each speaker says they have learnt about friendship as a result of their relationship with their close friend.

A True friends will always be supportive.

B Friends are bound to fall out at times.

C An ability to tolerate people's behaviour is necessary.

D Initial impressions aren't always valid.

E It's important to adapt to friends' situations.

F Friendships are more easily damaged than family relationships.

G Shared experiences are extremely important.

H Complete honesty isn't always advisable.

Speaker 1	**6**
Speaker 2	**7**
Speaker 3	**8**
Speaker 4	**9**
Speaker 5	**10**

5 **Look at the following verbs and verb phrases from the recording. Match each phrase with its meaning.**

1	bump into	**A**	keep thinking or talking about
2	let down	**B**	disintegrate
3	put up with	**C**	become friends quickly
4	dwell on	**D**	like
5	hit it off	**E**	tolerate
6	fall out	**F**	disappoint
7	fall apart	**G**	meet by chance
8	take to	**H**	argue and stop being friends

6 **Use suitable phrases from Exercise 5 to complete the sentences. Make any changes necessary. There are two phrases that you do not need to use.**

1. Our friendship .... for a while following an argument, but we're OK again now!
2. My sister always borrows my clothes, but I don't really mind. I just .... it.
3. Pablo tends to .... things, instead of just forgetting about them.
4. I .... Sarah in the supermarket. It was a nice surprise!
5. Ben and I .... straightaway. We got on well immediately.
6. I didn't .... James when I first met him, but now I really like him.

1

Grammar

Verb forms to talk about the past

The COMPLETE grammar reference
▶ Scan the QR code, watch the video, then turn to page 162

1 **Look at these extracts 1–6 from Listening Part 4. Match the underlined verb forms with the explanations A–F.**

1 I'd known Nigel for years – we'd done the same course at uni, but had never really hung out.

2 I bumped into her after locking myself out of our apartment block one night.

3 During the interval I ran into Amara and it turned out we'd had the same opinion of him.

4 The costume she was wearing was so astonishing that I simply had to ask her about it.

5 We've had our ups and downs, too, over the years, and fallen out.

6 We'd meet occasionally at parties.

A something that happened at a specific time in the past

B a repeated action or habit in the past which doesn't happen now

C an activity that was in progress around a particular past time

D something which happened before another situation in the past

E a longer action or situation which had continued up to a specified moment in the past

F a recurring action or event that started in the past and has continued until now

2 **Put the verbs in brackets into the simple or continuous form of the past, past perfect or present perfect. (In some cases more than one answer is possible.)**

1 Chen .... (work) in Singapore since he .... (leave) university two years ago, but next year he expects to be transferred to Hong Kong.

2 Alexander takes university life very seriously. He .... (study) here for six months and he still .... (not go) to a single party!

3 Maria .... (come) round to dinner last night. She .... (start) telling me her life story while I .... (make) the salad and .... (continue) telling it during dinner.

4 Ivana .... (have) a splitting headache yesterday evening because she .... (work) in the sun all day and she .... (not wear) a hat.

5 I .... (grow) up in a house which .... (belong) to my great-great-grandfather. We .... (sell) it now because it was too big for our small family.

3 **Choose the correct option in *italics* in each of the following sentences.**

a My teachers **(1)** *were often getting / often used to get* annoyed with me when I was at school because I **(2)** *never used to bring / had never brought* a pen with me and I **(3)** *would always ask / have always asked* someone if I could borrow theirs.

b The village **(4)** *used to be / would be* very quiet and remote until they **(5)** *built / had built* the motorway two years ago. In those days everybody **(6)** *would know / used to know* everyone else, but since then, a lot of new people **(7)** *came / have come* to live in the area and the old social structures **(8)** *gradually changed / have gradually been changing*.

c When I was a child, both my parents **(9)** *used to go / were going* out to work, so when they **(10)** *would be / were* out, my grandparents **(11)** *were looking / would look* after me.

4 **Work in pairs. Student A: Ask questions 1–3 to Student B. Student B: Ask questions 4–6 to Student A. Give detailed answers and ask follow-up questions.**

What was the last …

1 television series / film you watched?
2 present you received?
3 post you liked on social media?
4 celebration you attended?
5 book/article you read?
6 holiday you went on?

5 **Exam candidates often make mistakes with present perfect, past simple and past perfect tenses. In the sentences below, circle the correct alternative in *italics*.**

1 In recent times people *had / have had* more contact with their friends through email and mobile phones than they did in the past.
2 The feedback we received from our clients meant we *have been / were able* to provide excellent advice to the people developing the product, which they then acted on.
3 The party was great and the best bit for me *has been / was* the jazz band.
4 We should have had a really good holiday for what we paid, but unfortunately, we discovered that they *didn't organise / hadn't organised* any activities or local food, so it was rather a disappointment.
5 While I was studying in England, I *haven't taken / didn't take* an examination because it was not offered to me or to any of my fellow students.
6 Are you going to the dinner on Saturday? A lot of my other friends *were invited / have been invited* and I know they'd love to meet you.
7 I *have only lived / have only been living* in Geneva for the past few months, though Madeleine, who you met yesterday, *lived / has lived* here all her life.
8 Petra looks after my children very well. I *haven't noticed / didn't notice* any weaknesses in her character, so I'm sure you'll be happy to offer her a job.

Reading and Use of English Part 8

Exam info

- In Reading and Use of English Part 8, you must match ten questions or statements with a text divided into four sections or four to six separate short texts.
- This task tests your ability to read quickly and understand details, opinions and attitudes and to locate specific information.

1 **Work in small groups and discuss the questions below.**

- What are teenagers' lives like in your country?
- How important is it to spend time with family?
- What kinds of things can cause difficulties between teenagers and their families?

2 **Read through the questions in Exercise 3, to familiarise yourself with them before you read the four texts. Underline the key words in the sentences, so that you know what information to look for in the texts, then paraphrase each one as if you were the person speaking.**

3 You are going to read an article in which young people give their views on their siblings during their teenage years. For questions 1–10, choose from the people A–D. The people may be chosen more than once.

Which person

1 mentions a downside of seeking an honest opinion from a family member? 1 ___

2 is grateful to a family member for providing a place of escape whenever needed? 2 ___

3 jokingly accuses a family member of displaying exactly the behaviour they're claiming to protect the writer from? 3 ___

4 understands that they tend to incorporate a feature of their upbringing into their current lifestyle? 4 ___

5 expresses appreciation for what the writer feels is undeserved support from a family member? 5 ___

6 admits that a family member has remained over-protective of the writer? 6 ___

7 has finally come to recognise the advantages of their upbringing? 7 ___

8 mentions that a family member had an irritated response to something apparently insignificant? 8 ___

9 missed having an ally in the family? 9 ___

10 acknowledges a family member's positive role in their own development? 10 ___

4 Look at the multi-word verbs in the extracts from Reading Part 8. What does each one mean?

1 … people tend to come out with all the usual assumptions, like whether everyone looks on me as the baby of the family.

2 … he's been the one who's always known exactly how to wind me up.

3 But none of that gets in the way of my close relationships with either of them.

4 … I've become determined to catch up with her.

5 … the rest of the family have always tolerated [her bad moods] and put them down to her frustration …

6 … chaos is now something I can't do without, …

7 … one of my older brothers, the only other one left at home, headed off for uni, …

8 … he's finally settled down in his own flat …

9 it's … a relief to just turn up to unannounced …

5 Work with a partner. Which of the four people do you feel you have the most in common with? Why?

You can choose your friends

Four young people talk about their teenage years, and their siblings.

A Sarah (18)

When I mention I'm the youngest of five, people tend to come out with all the usual assumptions, like whether everyone looks on me as the baby of the family. I've always hotly denied that. Admittedly, though, my older sister will still warn me a car's coming as we cross busy roads – but with the best of intentions, I know. And thankfully, she's been considerate enough to never once mention in front of my friends the time, aged six, I decorated my face with her makeup. Until recently, too, my brother had a tendency to judge whatever I was watching as far too violent – only to grab the remote off me in what I can only describe as a rather rough manner! And I guess, of my two siblings, he's been the one who's always known exactly how to wind me up – typical older brother! But none of that gets in the way of my close relationships with either of them. Underneath it all, they are both incredibly thoughtful and always make time for me. I'm really lucky to have them.

B Andrew (21)

People assume that growing up with a high-achieving sister might have been demoralising somehow, but nothing could have been further from the truth. In fact, if anything, she's been so well organised and conscientious in her approach to studying that it's been hugely motivating for me, as I've become determined to catch up with her. Admittedly, she's often got into bad moods over the years, but I think the rest of the family have always tolerated them and put them down to her frustration in trying to get where she wanted to be, but seeing her ambitions obstructed in some way. Having said that, though, the trigger for her kicking off could just be as simple as my attempting to set the table for dinner while she'd got all her books laid out on it! Anyway, the thing is, she's sometimes seen me at my absolute worst, which she really shouldn't have had to put up with, and yet, she's still stuck by me no matter what! You really can't put a price on that.

Growing up surrounded by an incredibly diverse range of people (my father's family are from South America and my step-mother's Swedish) I always felt that family life for me and my brother, Tom, was slightly chaotic – always travelling, never settling anywhere. But as a result, we've experienced a huge range of languages, lifestyles and cultures, so our lives have been by no means limited. And I don't know about Tom, but while I've personally reached a point where I can now appreciate what a privileged life that's been, I also know that chaos is now something I can't do without, to the point where I approach my studies and my personal life in quite a disorderly way – but it seems to work! My ambition's to become a professional artist, but I'm constantly looking for reassurance that my work's worth something. As a last resort, I might even ask my brother, but his response has sometimes been far from what I was hoping to hear. But there you go – flattery's overrated, in my view!

C Isabella (19)

D Ibrahim (23)

Being the youngest child was great – until the day that one of my older brothers, the only one left at home, headed off for uni, leaving me alone at home with just my parents, and no-one to complain to or roll my eyes at secretly across the table when there was some discussion going on that we'd heard a million times before! But my brother still sided with me whenever he came back from uni – and he and I still maintained our very effective cheaters' partnership in family card games! We don't always see eye to eye, but it's clear he's always had my best interests at heart – and I've always tried to return that kindness. And even now that he's finally settled down in his own flat nearby, it's still a kind of open house – and a relief to just turn up to unannounced when life with my parents gets a bit too much. So, despite any miscommunication and frustrations over the years, we're still there for each other.

Vocabulary
Collocations with *give* and *make*

1 **Look at this sentence from Reading and Use of English Part 8. Write the correct verb (A–D) in the gap.**

Underneath it all, they are both incredibly thoughtful and always .... time for me.

A do **B** give **C** make **D** take

2 **Exam candidates often confuse the verbs *give* and *make*. In most of the sentences below, the underlined verb is wrong. Replace the underlined verb with *give* or *make*, or write *correct* if you think there is no mistake.**

1 When you print the article, we also expect you to give an apology.
2 Her report on the trip did not give accurate information so we were quite confused.
3 I have some suggestions to give before the forthcoming trip.
4 I hope your company will give me at least a partial refund.
5 I'm so grateful that you have made me the chance to attend the course.
6 In my boss's absence, I give telephone calls to customers, clean desks, and write emails.
7 Installing modern technology will give a good impression of the college.
8 Our evening lectures were made by 'experts' who knew nothing about the subject.
9 There is another recommendation I would like to give concerning the club.

3 **Words which are often used together (e.g. *make an apology*) are called collocations. Which verb often forms a collocation with these nouns? Write *give* or *make* in each gap.**

1 .... a speech, lecture, talk, performance
2 .... (someone) information, details, advice, instructions
3 .... a(n) recommendation, comment, apology, suggestion
4 .... someone a(n) chance, opportunity
5 .... someone a refund, their money back
6 .... a phone call
7 .... an impression on someone
8 .... someone an impression
9 .... time for someone
10 .... something a miss

Reading and Use of English Part 4

Exam info

- In Reading and Use of English Part 4, you complete six sentences with between three and six words so that they mean the same as the sentences printed before them.
- You must use a word given in CAPITALS without changing it in any way.
- This part tests your ability to manage grammar, vocabulary and collocations.

1 **Work in pairs. Study the exam instruction below. Then, for questions 1–4, read some answers that different students gave for each question. Decide which answer (A–C) is correct and say why the other answers are wrong.**

For questions 1–4, complete the second sentence so that it has a similar meaning to the first sentence, using the word given. Do not change the word given. You must use between three and six words, including the word given.

1 His actions were based on what his uncle advised him to do.

ADVICE

The basis for his actions .... him.

A was some advice that his uncle gave
B was the advice his uncle gave
C was what his uncle advised

2 Alba made every effort to arrive at the meeting on time.

BEST

Alba .... to the meeting on time.

A did her best to get
B made the best to arrive
C tried very hard to make it

3 Unless the product is in perfect condition, we cannot return your money.

REFUND

We will be unable .... the product is not in perfect condition.

A to pay you a refund unless
B to refund the money you paid if
C to give you a refund if

4 Otto's teachers were favourably impressed by the presentation he gave to the class.

IMPRESSION

Otto's presentation to the class .... his teachers.

A gave a favourable impression to
B made a favourable impression on
C made an impression which was found very favourably by

2 **For questions 1–6, complete the second sentence so that it has a similar meaning to the first sentence, using the word given. Do not change the word given. You must use between three and six words, including the word given.**

1 Kate is both considerate and conscientious.
ONLY
Kate is .... also conscientious.

2 Dan didn't go to the match with Paul because of their argument several days previously.
OUT
Dan didn't go to the match with Paul because they .... few days previously.

3 My sister is far better organised than me.
NEARLY
I .... as my sister.

4 Everyone considers me to be an expert on photography – but I'm not, really!
LOOKS
Everyone .... an expert on photography – but I'm not, really!

5 Being completely honest about your opinions isn't always advisable.
IDEA
It isn't .... completely honest about your opinions.

6 I often used to go walking through the forest with my parents when I was younger.
WOULD
My parents .... take walks through the forest when I was younger.

Speaking Part 1

▶ **Page 205 Speaking bank**
Speaking Part 1

Exam info

- In Speaking Part 1, the examiner asks you questions about yourself. These may include questions about your life, your work or studies, your plans for the future, your family and your interests, etc.
- This part is intended to break the ice and tests your ability to interact with the examiner and use general social language.

1 **Work in pairs. Read the questions below from Speaking Part 1. Which questions are**
a mainly about the present?
b mainly about the past?

1 What do you most enjoy doing with your friends?
2 Have you ever had the opportunity to really help a friend? How?
3 Would you prefer to spend your holidays with your family or your friends?
4 What is the best way for people visiting your country to make friends?
5 Who do you think has influenced you most? Why?
6 What is your happiest childhood memory?
7 Who is the best teacher you've ever had?
8 Tell me about a friend of yours and how you got to know him or her.

2 03 **Listen to two students, Marta and Lukas. Which question does each of them answer?**

Marta: .... Lukas: ....

3 04 **Now listen to them again, with the examiner's questions, and say if the following statements are true (T) or false (F).**

1 They both give very brief answers.
2 They give some details or reasons to support their answers.
3 They use a range of tenses appropriately.
4 They speak in a relaxed, natural way.

4 **Think about how you could answer each of the questions in Exercise 1. Then work in pairs and take turns to ask and answer the questions.**

Writing Part 1: An essay

▶ **Page 193 Writing bank**
An essay

- In Writing Part 1, you write an essay in which you discuss a question or topic.
- You are given three areas to consider and you must discuss two of them.
- You are given three opinions which you can use if you wish.
- This part tests your ability to develop an argument or discussion, express your opinions clearly and support your ideas with reasons and examples.

Exam info

1 Work in pairs. Discuss the questions.

How do people decide on a career to follow?

How does the education system in your country help students find a career?

In your own experience, how helpful or useful is the system for helping students find a career?

2 Underline the key ideas in the writing task below.

Your class has taken part in a seminar on whether education systems do enough to help young people to find jobs which fit their abilities and interests. You have made the notes below.

Ways in which schools can help students with their future careers

- offering a wide variety of courses
- work experience programmes
- careers advice departments within schools

Some opinions expressed in the seminar:

'We study lots of things which we'll never use in any future job.'

'Without work experience you'd have no idea which career you would or wouldn't like to do.'

'Some of my teachers can't give me advice because they've never done any job other than teaching.'

Write an **essay** discussing **two** of the methods in your notes. You should explain **which method is more effective**, giving **reasons** in support of your answer.

You may, if you wish, make use of the opinions expressed in the seminar, but you should use your own words as far as possible.

Write your **essay** in 220–260 words in an appropriate style.

3 Work in small groups.

- Discuss each of the methods and whether or not you agree with the opinions expressed in the seminar.
- During your discussion, express your own opinions on the methods and give reasons for your opinions.
- Take notes on the main ideas which arise during the discussion.

4 Read the writing task in Exercise 2 again. Do you think the following sentences are true (T) or false (F)? Why?

1. You must discuss all three methods.
2. You must decide which is the best method.
3. You must say whether you agree or disagree with the opinions expressed.
4. If you use any of the opinions, you should express them in a more formal style.
5. When you express your opinion, you should say why you hold that opinion.
6. You can expand the topic to talk about other issues related to work that interest you.
7. You can write your answer using a bulleted list of points instead of formal paragraphs.
8. The task contains a word limit, but if you write 300 words, you will get higher marks.

5 **Read Cristina's essay. Then complete the plan she wrote beforehand by matching the notes (a–e) with the paragraphs.**

For many young people it is hard to find the sort of job they aspire to. [1]<u>This</u> is in part due to a mismatch between what education provides and what employers believe [2]<u>they</u> require.

Schools and universities should offer students a range of courses which provide [3]<u>them</u> with qualifications which will attract potential employers. However, employers often complain that courses are too theoretical and do not teach students the practical skills [4]<u>they</u> will need in the workplace.

While I understand [5]<u>this viewpoint</u>, I do not entirely share [6]<u>it</u>. I believe that the purpose of education is primarily to develop critical thinking skills, including the ability to analyse and solve problems. [7]<u>These</u> abilities will be useful throughout people's working lives. To achieve [8]<u>this</u>, I do not think it matters whether someone studies history or theoretical physics as long as the right teaching methods are used. Students will then pick up the specific job skills they require very quickly once they are in full-time employment.

It is often suggested that young people need to gain work experience in order to make an informed choice of university course and career. Although I believe [9]<u>this</u> helps to focus students' minds on what working life will be like, generally speaking it is not possible for students to get a wide enough range of experience to be able to choose [10]<u>their</u> career wisely.

I would therefore argue that the best way to help young people find suitable jobs is to give them an excellent general education while ensuring that employers realise how valuable [11]<u>it</u> is.

Plan

Paragraph 1: intro ....

Paragraph 2: ....

Paragraph 3: ....

Paragraph 4: ....

Paragraph 5: conclusion ....

a education should teach students to think – useful for every job

b provide a good all-round education + persuade employers of its importance

c employers say courses not practical enough

d difficulty finding jobs – education vs. employers' needs

e work experience often too limited for students to make informed choices

6 **Work in pairs. Discuss these questions.**

1. Why is it important to underline the key ideas in the writing task?
2. Why should you write a plan before you write your essay?
3. Did Cristina follow her plan exactly?
4. Has she dealt completely with the instructions in the writing task?
5. What words and phrases does she use in her essay to introduce her opinions?
6. To what extent do you agree with Cristina's point of view?
7. Why is it important to make your opinions clear in an essay?

7 **When you write, it is important that each paragraph should cover a different aspect of the subject and that sentences should be linked together using clear references. What do the underlined reference words in Cristina's essay refer to?**

8 **Write your own plan for the writing task in Exercise 2. When you have finished, compare your plan with a partner's.**

9 **Read Christina's essay in Exercise 5 and highlight any words you would like to use in your essay.**

10 **Copy the words and phrases you highlighted into your plan.**

11 **Write your essay following the plan.**

2 More than words

People tend to be **(1)** .... – they speak the regional and the national language and they **(2)** .... between languages with ease.

I think it's due to globalisation, but lots of **(3)** .... are coming into the language, particularly from English, so my **(4)** .... is not at all the same as it was, say, fifty years ago.

My English has got **(5)** .... because I don't use it very often.

Living in a different country, you just **(6)** .... the local language naturally and that may well be the best way to learn it.

I'm aiming to achieve **(7)** .... of English, which means becoming **(8)** .... and being able to use the language **(9)** .... and effortlessly.

I wouldn't consider accuracy to be as important as **(10)** .... when learning a foreign language.

It's all very well being able to say what you think and feel, but you've got to be able to sell yourself, sell your product, achieve your **(11)** ....

Starting off

1 (05) **Work in pairs. Read the following seven people's remarks and write a word or phrase from the box in each gap. Then check your answers by listening to the speakers.**

a bit rusty	accurately	aims	an excellent command	bilingual	fluency	highly articulate	loanwords	mother tongue	pick up	switch

2 (05) **Work in pairs. Listen again. Which of the speakers' opinions do you agree with? Which do you disagree with? Why?**

Listening Part 1

Exam info

- In Listening Part 1, you hear three short conversations on different themes.
- You have to answer two multiple-choice questions with three options about each conversation.
- This part tests your ability to identify both the gist and specific details in the conversation and to identify the speakers' attitudes and opinions and how they agree or disagree.

1 **Work in pairs. Read and discuss the following questions. Give reasons for your answers.**

a What do people enjoy about learning another language?

b Would you consider doing a course on the origins of your first language?

c Do you enjoy reading great works of literature?

d Is it important to study literature at school?

e What are your three most common reasons for sending emails?

f Are there any differences in the language people use for face-to-face conversation and for texting?

2 (06) You will now hear the first part of Extract One. Try to answer the question below in your own words, then check your ideas with a partner. Which aspect of studying languages do the friends disagree on?

3 (07) Now listen to the second part of Extract One and repeat the task from Exercise 2. What does the woman believe is the main benefit of doing the course?

4 (08) Listen to Extract One in full and choose the correct answers from options A–C. You hear two people talking about an evening class the woman is doing.

1 Which aspect of studying languages do the friends disagree on?
  - A It is difficult to learn without an effective teacher.
  - B It is rare to take a course in expectation of financial reward.
  - C It is important to engage with the content of a course in a personalised way.

2 The woman believes that the main benefit of doing the course is
  - A applying its content to the understanding of wider issues.
  - B recognising its relevance to global communication.
  - C learning about history through the lyrics of old songs.

5 (09) Choose the correct answers, A–C, for Extracts Two and Three. Use the same approach as in Exercises 2–4:
1) read the question only, 2) listen, 3) match what you hear to the correct option.

Extract Two

You hear two literature students talking about the relevance of their subject.

3 According to the woman, the main value of literature of the past is
  - A the way in which it reflects eternal human concerns.
  - B the detail it presents when describing past ways of life.
  - C the opportunity it brings to evaluate modern culture.

4 Why does the man believe that literature should be studied at school?
  - A It impacts positively on a student's ability to write essays.
  - B It improves students' understanding of the lesson content in other classes.
  - C It provides students with a potential source of emotional support.

Extract Three

You hear two friends discussing different styles of writing.

5 When talking about the response to his job application, the man suggests that
  - A the accepted conventions of writing should be more flexible.
  - B an awareness of context is more important than writing skills.
  - C humour is an important part of communication.

6 What is the woman doing?
  - A suggesting that all text messages should not be written in a particular style
  - B illustrating older people's objections to the informal style of text messages
  - C evaluating the effect of the style of text messages compared to spoken conversation

6 Discuss these questions.

- Which aspects of your language would you enjoy teaching someone about? Why?
- Do you believe that an appreciation or understanding of literature can impact positively on other areas of study? Why? / Why not?
- Do you think it's easy for people to misjudge the tone or intention of a text message or email? How can we avoid this?

Vocabulary

Collocations with *make*, *get* and *do*

1 **Form collocations with the words in bold by writing the correct form of *make*, *get* or *do* in the gaps in the sentences below.**

1. I'm .... **a course** on the origins of the English language.
2. It .... **sense** to study a language you're already fluent in.
3. I .... **the impression** that people generally prefer to learn a new language, hoping it might help their future earning potential.
4. I think that's a bit short-sighted, but I do .... **their argument**.
5. Apparently, I .... **an unsuitable comment** in my application.

2 **Exam candidates often use the wrong verb with the words and phrases in the box. Write each word or phrase in the correct column of the table below. Three words/phrases can be written in more than one column.**

a comment a course a decision a job
a mistake a point a proposal a qualification
a suggestion an activity an apology
an effort an improvement business
changes complaints exercise
friends further information harm
household chores one's best one's money back
some shopping sport the cooking
the right choice use of something

make	get	do
a comment	a job	a course

3 **Each of the sentences below contains a mistake or an uncommon collocation. Replace a word in each sentence with *make*, *get* or *do*.**

1. Before working in our shop you first make a one-week course in developing photos.
2. A lot of my time was wasted, so I think I should receive some of my money back.
3. She did everything possible to turn the trip more pleasant
4. We were made to work very hard at school and that certainly didn't make me any harm.
5. We need to reduce the time taken to achieve all the tasks mentioned above.
6. Other members of the club have given suggestions about a quiz or karaoke night to form part of our social programme.
7. We'd be very grateful if you'd make your best to solve this problem.
8. You can spend lots of time at this holiday camp practising exercise and having a great time!

Reading and Use of English Part 3

- In Reading and Use of English Part 3, you read a text of 150–170 words with eight gaps and one example (0).
- In each gap you write the correct form of the word given in CAPITALS at the end of the line.
- This part tests your knowledge of vocabulary and your ability to form words by adding prefixes and suffixes and making other changes.

Exam info

1 **Listen to five people speaking in English. Which part of the UK are they from?**

10

Scotland Northern Ireland Northern England
Southern England Wales

Speaker 1: ....
....

Speaker 2: ....
....

Speaker 3: ....
....

Speaker 4: ....
....

Speaker 5: ....
....

2 **Look at the transcript of what was said. How many words can you make from each of the underlined words?**

My best <u>friend</u> is from another <u>part</u> of the country to me and I absolutely <u>love</u> her accent; it's really <u>different</u> from mine.

friend: friendship(s), friendly, unfriendly, unfriendliness, friendless(ness), befriend(ed), defriend(ed), unfriend(ed)

3 What prefixes and suffixes did you use in your answers to Exercise 2? Can you think of more prefixes and suffixes, and words they attach to?

4 In the Advanced exam, correct spelling is extremely important. In Reading and Use of English Part 3, you will lose a mark if you spell your answer incorrectly. Find and correct the spelling mistakes in the sentences below.

My friend's accent is much softer, so even when she's iritated or having an arguement she sounds like she's entirly relaxed. I find it really fasinating that two people who are essencially from the same part of the country can have such disimilar accents.

5 Work in pairs and look at the text in Exercise 6. Student A: quickly read the first paragraph; Student B: quickly read the second paragraph. When you have finished, turn away from the text and summarise your paragraph to your partner.

6 For questions 1–8, read the text again. Use the word given in capitals at the end of some of the lines to form a word that fits in the gap in the same line. There is an example at the beginning (0).

You'll always have your accent – or will you?

For centuries, people existed in isolated **(0)** *communities* far from	**COMMUNE**
one another. Rarely was there any spoken **(1)** .... between	**ACT**
groups, so regional accents became established because they were only used by a finite number of people. **(2)** ...., there have	**HISTORY**
been long periods when one might barely detect a single change in pronunciation. Through time, however, an accent would develop as a result of migrants arriving from other regions, bringing with them some distinct **(3)** .... in	**DIFFERENT**
the way they spoke the language.	
How long it takes for an accent to change is difficult to assess and largely **(4)** ....,	**MEASURE**
although we can certainly work from the general **(5)** .... that	**ASSUME**
it happens more quickly than it used to. In today's world, there are many factors that determine a person's accent, such as class, education and **(6)** .... The latter has	**ETHNIC**
certainly had a hugely **(7)** .... effect on the	**INFLUENCE**
way in which modern languages are spoken, particularly in cities and larger towns, where multicultural populations are more **(8)** .... than elsewhere.	**NUMBER**

7 Work in small groups to discuss the following questions.

- How widely do accents vary in your country?
- Are there any accents in your language that you find difficult to understand?
- Have you ever wanted to change your accent in some way? Why? / Why not?
- How important is it for you to develop a 'native' accent in the language you are studying?

Reading and Use of English Part 6

Exam info

- In Reading and Use of English Part 6, you read four short extracts from texts on the same subject.
- You must answer four questions.
- This part tests your ability to identify similarities, differences and connections between opinions and attitudes expressed in the extracts.

1 **You are going to read four extracts from articles in which academics give their views about using movies to help learn a language. Before you read, complete the questionnaire below by placing a cross on each dotted line to indicate how far you agree or disagree. Then work in small groups and compare and explain your answers.**

I much prefer to watch movies in my own language than in English.

Disagree - - - - - - - - - - - - - - - - - - - Agree

I believe it is possible to become fluent in a language solely by watching films and TV series.

Disagree - - - - - - - - - - - - - - - - - - - Agree

I generally choose subtitles in my own language when watching movies produced overseas.

Disagree - - - - - - - - - - - - - - - - - - - Agree

I enjoy the challenge of watching an English-language film without any on-screen subtitles.

Disagree - - - - - - - - - - - - - - - - - - - Agree

I often make notes of new vocabulary when I am watching a movie with English subtitles.

Disagree - - - - - - - - - - - - - - - - - - - Agree

I prefer watching movies with the dialogue dubbed into my language to having subtitles provided on-screen.

Disagree - - - - - - - - - - - - - - - - - - - Agree

2 **Work with a new partner. Imagine that you are giving advice to Paola, a student who is learning English and considering using movies to help her improve. What would you say in answer to her questions below?**

- Do movie scripts provide good examples of how people speak to each other in real life?
- Should I watch movies with subtitles on? If so, should they be in my language or in English?
- What notes should I make when I'm watching a movie? How much time should I set aside for reviewing them?
- How important is it to memorise what you hear in movies if you want to learn a language?

3 **Read Extract A and answer the following questions.**

a What does the writer say about movie scripts providing good examples of how people speak to each other in real life?

b Does the writer agree with your advice to Paola?

c What do the other writers in Extracts B, C and D have to say on this idea?

d Who agrees with Extract A?

A If the key to engaging fully with language learning is for a student to find something they identify with, movies are perfect resources for learning. Script writers today are exceptionally skilled in reproducing genuine discussions, so it makes sense to note down unknown phrases while watching a film, take them away and investigate how they are used by proficient speakers in different contexts. These days, this can easily be done with the help of the internet and, although it takes patience and concentrated effort to become familiar and confident with the language as it is spoken on screen, it certainly brings rewards. Conversely, if the student reads the subtitles in their mother tongue – translated from the original – this minimises any potential for improvement as the viewer relaxes into the role of passive consumer, rather than active learner.

B There is widespread agreement that bringing movies into the language learning process can be extremely valuable. That said, learners should avoid the temptation to repeat the carefully chosen language of a screenplay with the intention of communicating in an entirely natural way. The act of remembering and reciting phrases from films is unlikely to take a language learner very far. Furthermore, despite many tales I have heard of someone becoming proficient by spending hours on end passively watching one full movie after another, I always have my doubts. 'How did you manage it?' I ask. 'I listen in English and read subtitles in my language,' comes the reply. With the aid of a translation on screen, it is too easy to drift into enjoying the film on its own merits instead of focusing on the task at hand. As such, success seems improbable. Instead, allocating a little time each day to interpreting and understanding short sections of dialogue would seem to be the optimal route to achievement.

C First-language subtitles allow the viewer to connect the known language (the one they are reading) to the unknown speech (the one they are hearing), with the result that they become more open to learning opportunities. Movie dialogue is perfectly capable of capturing the patterns of everyday speech, so a vocabulary notebook can be filled with examples of useful and authentic dialogue for the learner to adopt as their own. And, just as one would never expect to make huge improvements through sitting down and reading a dictionary from cover to cover, this notebook should be similarly treated as a reference tool for ongoing practice. A regular review of one's notes is the way forward, as the 'little-and-often' method creates the ideal conditions for learning. After all, becoming fluent in a language is essentially about being able to remember a huge range of set phrases and structures, and delivering them in conversation.

D Many people devote hours on end to repeated viewings of the same film in order to build their ability to quote whole sections of dialogue by heart. This is a solid idea, if the only aim is to impress and entertain one's fellow film enthusiasts, rather than being able to converse with somebody else in an authentic way. While a belief did exist for many years among language learners that this type of 'rote learning' through repetition and, principally, memorisation, was an effective route to proficiency, this idea has since been rejected as entirely false. So too has the notion that reading subtitles is always a means for successful language development. This certainly can be the case, but studies have shown there is little effect on the learning process if these are displayed in the language of the viewer, rather than as spoken by the actors.

4 **Now do the exam task. For questions 1–4, choose from the extracts A–D. The extracts may be chosen more than once.**

Which extract …

1 shares C's view of the extent to which movie scripts effectively imitate real-life conversation? **1** ____

2 expresses a different belief from the others about the helpfulness of reading subtitles in one's first language? **2** ____

3 expresses a similar view to B about the value of setting aside time for frequent study? **3** ____

4 takes a similar position to D when considering how memory impacts on language learning? **4** ____

Speaking Part 2

▶ **Page 207 Speaking bank**
Speaking Part 2

- In Speaking Part 2, you are each given three photos and are asked to choose two of the photos to speak about. You must speak on your own for one minute.
- You have to compare the two photos you have chosen.
- You have to answer two questions connected with the photos, which are printed on the task sheet.
- When the other candidate is speaking, you need to listen and then answer a brief question about the photos.
- This part tests your ability to speak at length, organise your ideas, compare, describe and express opinions, and speculate about things connected with the photos.

Exam info

1 Look at the photos and read the examiner's instructions. What are the three parts to the task?

'In this part of the test, I'm going to give each of you three pictures. I'd like you to talk about two of them on your own for about a minute, and also to answer a question briefly about your partner's pictures. Here are your pictures. They show people explaining things. I'd like you to compare two of the pictures and say what the speakers might be explaining and what problems the speakers might have.'

2 In the Speaking test you will get higher marks if you use a range of appropriate vocabulary. Decide which of these phrases you could use with each photo. (Some can be used with more than one photo.)

argue a case   boost morale
defend a client
decide on / discuss / explain tactics
encourage the team   give a demonstration
influence the outcome   persuade the judge/jury
reach a verdict   take people through the steps

3 Listen to Daniel doing the Speaking task.

11

1 Which phrases from Exercise 2 does he use?
2 When he compares the photos, does he just point out differences or does he also mention similarities?
3 Does he answer both of the examiner's questions?

1

2

3

4 Complete each of these sentences about the photos Daniel chose. You can use your own or Daniel's ideas.

1 The coach looks as if …
2 The boys give the impression that … judging by …
3 The lawyer seems …
4 She appears …
5 In both photos I imagine …
6 The coach wants … while the barrister wants …

5 **Work in pairs.**

- Take turns to talk for a minute to do the Speaking task in Exercise 1. You can choose which two photos you wish to speak about.
- When your partner has finished speaking, briefly answer this question about the photos your partner chose: *Which of the two speakers do you think has the harder task?*

6 **Work in pairs. Look at the photos and read the examiner's instructions. Then answer questions 1 and 2 below.**

'Here are your pictures. They show adults and children talking to each other. I'd like you to compare two of the pictures and say why they might be talking to each other and how each of them might benefit from this.'

1. Do you think you should choose the two easiest photos to talk about, or the two most difficult? Why?
2. When you answer the second question, should you just talk about how the children might benefit?

7 **Work in pairs. Which of these phrases could you use with each of the photos?**

bond with each other cheer someone up
give encouragement look through an album
put a brave face on things
remember good times
share family history
spend quality time together
teach someone basic skills

8 **Work in pairs.**

1. Student A: Follow the examiner's instructions in Exercise 6.
2. Student B: When Student A has finished, follow the examiner's instructions in Exercise 6 using the photo Student A didn't use and one of the others.
3. When your partner has finished speaking, briefly answer this question: *Which situation do you think the adult would find most rewarding?*

1

2

3

Grammar

Expressing purpose, reason and result

The COMPLETE grammar reference
▶ Scan the QR code, watch the video, then turn to page 164

1 **The following sentences appeared in the Reading and Use of English Part 6 task on pages 22–23. Match the beginnings of sentences 1–4 with their endings (A–D) and correctly connect them with one of the words/phrases from the box. Then check your answers in the text.**

1 Conversely, if the student reads the subtitles in their mother tongue – translated from the original – this minimises any potential for improvement
2 Many people devote hours on end to repeated viewings of the same film
3 Learners should avoid the temptation to repeat the carefully chosen language of a screenplay
4 First-language subtitles allow the viewer to connect the known language (the one they are reading) to the unknown speech (the one they are hearing),

A communicating in an entirely natural way.
B they become more open to learning opportunities.
C the viewer relaxes into the role of passive consumer, rather than active learner.
D build their ability to quote whole sections of dialogue by heart.

as in case in order to otherwise so to
with the intention of with the result that

2 **Use the remaining four words/phrases from the box to connect the sentence halves below.**

1 I thought I should pick the language up while I was there,
2 They used to give us dictations in class
3 I always write new vocabulary down in my notebook
4 You'll need to use a microphone,

A make sure we knew things like putting a double 'p' in 'approve'.
B there is very little chance I will remember it.
C the people at the back can't hear you.
D I immersed myself in the life of the local community.

3 **Answer the following questions.**

1 Which of the words/phrases from the box in Exercise 1 express …
  a a purpose?
  b a reason?
  c a result?
2 Which of the words/phrases are followed by …
  a an infinitive?
  b a noun / verb + *-ing*?
  c a clause?

4 **Exam candidates often make mistakes with words and phrases to express reason, purpose and result. Circle the correct alternative in *italics* in each of the following sentences.**

1 My Italian is excellent *because / due to* I lived in Italy for four years.
2 *By / For* technical reasons, the flight was delayed for several hours.
3 Over the last decade, our lives have changed a lot *because of / by* computers.
4 Could you please send us a brochure *so as / so that* we can see exactly what you are offering?
5 I hope the organisation's efficiency will improve *for not to / in order not* to waste people's time and money.

Writing Part 2: A report

▶ **Page 200 Writing bank**
A report

Exam info

- In Writing Part 2, you do one writing task from a choice of three.
- The possible tasks are an email/letter, a proposal, a report or a review.
- You must write between 220 and 260 words.

1 **Read the following writing task and answer the questions below.**

> You work for an education technology company which is developing an app to help English language students learn new vocabulary. You have done some research with language students at a local college. Write a report for your manager on your findings. Describe some of the methods students use to learn new vocabulary and explain which methods they find the most effective. Your report should also include recommendations for any useful features to include in the app.

1 Who is expected to read this report?
2 Is it more appropriate to write in a formal or an informal style?
3 What are the main points you should deal with?
4 In what order would you deal with them?

2 **Read the sample report and decide which word or phrase best fits each gap.**

accounting for · the aim · as a consequence · due to · means · resulted · so as · the effect

Introduction

(1) .... of this report is to outline the main methods employed by a group of 25 English language students to increase their vocabulary, to explain the perceived effectiveness of these methods, and to recommend features for a new learning app.

Main methods used

Three methods were uncovered in the research. Keeping a notebook was mentioned by 90% of students, with a digital notebook **(2)** .... the highest proportion of users. Eighteen respondents stated that they repeated new words and phrases to themselves, while sixteen students regularly used flashcards.

Effect on learning

The students who mentioned vocabulary notebooks felt this was the most efficient way to learn. Typically, students would collect words with translations, examples and pronunciation notes. This has **(3)** .... that students build their own dictionary. It should be noted, however, that many only did this **(4)** .... their teachers' suggestion.

Those who stated they rely heavily on the repetition of new words and phrases believed the approach had **(5)** .... in a better ability to learn new vocab. Repeating words out loud was beneficial, with many doing it **(6)** .... to improve their pronunciation skills.

Students who used flashcards liked the visual aspect. They also liked the fact that the cards could be used to create games, which, **(7)** .... , motivated further use.

Recommendation

I would recommend that any new app should be based on the principle of users being able create their own library of flashcards. Set repetition exercises could additionally be built into each page. This **(8)** .... that students could use the cards to self-test new vocabulary at home.

3 **Read the report again and answer these questions.**

1 How is the layout of a report different from other types of writing?
2 Has the writer included all the points in the writing task? Where are they dealt with in the report?
3 Is the style appropriate for the target readers?

4 **Read the following writing task. You should …**

- underline the points you must deal with
- identify who will read the report
- decide what style you will need to use
- decide what title to give your report and what sections and section headings you will need.

You work for a leading educational publisher who wants to produce schoolbooks in your country. The company wants to learn more about the people who will use its books and has asked you to write a report on foreign language learning in your country. Write a report explaining what languages people learn and why, describing the ways in which they learn these languages and making recommendations on how language learning could be improved in your country.

5 **Write the report, using the sample report in Exercise 2 as a model.**

1 Vocabulary and grammar review

Vocabulary

1 **Complete each of the sentences below by writing the correct form of *give* or *make* in each gap.**

1. The minister .... a rousing speech at the end of the conference.
2. Carrie sat through the entire meeting without .... a single suggestion to solve the problem.
3. We .... our students plenty of opportunities to speak to ensure they become fluent.
4. Fergus .... a pretty bad impression in Saturday's match, so the manager is .... him just one last chance or he'll be dropped from the team.
5. If you'd just .... me the details, I'll take a note of them and pass them to the person responsible.
6. I never expected to see you at the concert because the last time we met, you .... me the impression that you didn't like classical music.
7. If you're not completely satisfied with the result, we'll .... you a full refund.
8. Imani is just .... a phone call at the moment, so she'll be with us in a second.
9. My teacher is great. She always .... time for me even though she's incredibly busy.
10. I'm not feeling very well so I'll have to .... the concert a miss tonight.

Grammar

2 **For questions 1–6, complete the second sentence so that it has a similar meaning to the first sentence, using the word given. Do not change the word given. You must use between three and six words, including the word given.**

1. I received some very useful advice from Gustavo.
   FOUND
   I .... me very useful.
2. Jason moved to Berlin in 2020.
   BEEN
   Jason .... since 2020.
3. The first time Carla went skiing was last Monday.
   NEVER
   Carla .... last Monday.
4. We were all favourably impressed with Paola's lecture.
   FAVOURABLE
   The lecture .... on all of us.
5. Students don't spend their free time in the same way as they did fifty years ago.
   CHANGED
   The way students spend their free time .... fifty years.
6. I couldn't find my receipt and they wouldn't give me a refund.
   HAD
   They wouldn't give me a refund because ....

3 **Choose the correct option in *italics*.**

1. We got to the park quite soon after lunch and fortunately the rain *stopped* / *had stopped* by then.
2. *We'd stand* / *We'd been standing* in the rain for at least twenty minutes before the bus arrived, by which time we *were feeling* / *had been feeling* pretty cold and wet, as you can imagine.
3. *I've driven* / *I've been driving* along this road a thousand times – I could almost do it with my eyes shut!
4. You'd expect Yuriko to be looking tired because *she's studied* / *she's been studying* for her final exams for the last three weeks.
5. Maisie *ate* / *had been eating* sweets all evening, so it was not surprising she didn't want any supper!
6. I think people *used to work* / *would work* much harder in the past than they do nowadays.
7. So much noise *had come* / *had been coming* from our flat all afternoon that eventually the neighbours complained, and we had to explain that we *repaired* / *were repairing* the heating and that we'd be finishing soon.
8. We always used to go to the Mediterranean for our holidays when I was a child. I think we *went* / *used to go* to Ibiza at least five times.

Vocabulary and grammar review 2

Vocabulary

1 Complete each of these sentences with a word/phrase relating to language (the number of letters in each word is given at the end of the sentence).

1. You've got to be able to write .... for this job. We can't afford to have people making mistakes. (10 letters)
2. Amina expresses her ideas very clearly – but then she's a highly .... young woman. (10)
3. Having lived in Chile for seven years, Philippe has a perfect .... of Spanish. (7)
4. It takes a great deal of practice to achieve .... in a language. (7)
5. I prefer to .... the language while I'm visiting the country rather than going to classes. (4, 2)
6. Maria's English is virtually perfect although her .... is Greek. (6, 6)
7. With a Japanese father and a French mother, Motoko is completely .... (9)
8. I apologise. My French is a little bit .... It's been years since I've had to use it. (5)

2 Complete these sentences by writing the correct form of *make*, *get* or *do* in the gaps.

1. Lee has been working hard because he needs to .... better professional qualifications.
2. The new principal is planning on .... quite a few changes to the way this college is run.
3. How long have you been .... your current job?
4. It was a difficult decision, but I think you .... the right choice.
5. I don't understand you. What point are you trying to ....?
6. It wouldn't .... you any harm to take a bit more exercise!
7. It's been a long time, but I finally .... an apology from my aunt.
8. Look, we can't ask any more of you other than that you .... your best.
9. Despite it being a competitive field, my cousin has managed to .... a name for herself as a talented actor.
10. Stop running with those scissors. You could really .... yourself some serious harm acting like that.

Grammar

3 Complete each of these sentences with a word or phrase from the box.

as	in case	otherwise	to	with the intention of	with the result that

1. I caught an earlier train .... finishing the report before my boss arrived in the office.
2. Natalie delivered the parcel herself .... make sure it arrived safely.
3. If I were you, I'd take your bank card .... your money runs out.
4. You really should write new vocabulary in your notebook, ... you'll forget it.
5. Services on North-East Trains were cancelled today .... there was a train drivers' strike.
6. I overslept and missed my train, ... I was late for the interview.

4 Find and correct the mistake in each of these sentences.

1. I phoned my internet provider with the intention for cancelling my contract.
2. My brother always carries a portable charger with him case his phone runs out of battery while he's out.
3. My car broke down this morning as the result that I was late to work.
4. You need to pass all your exams other than you won't be able to graduate from university.
5. I didn't have a ticket for the final, as I had to watch the match on TV instead.
6. The company plans to move their headquarters out of the capital city in order save money.

3 Mind, body and soul

Starting off

1 **Discuss these questions.**

- Do you believe it is possible to measure a person's intelligence accurately? Why? / Why not?
- Even if you believe it is possible, do you think we should measure intelligence? Why? / Why not?

2 **Below are nine different intelligences that, it is argued, measure our strengths and abilities. Look at the intelligences below and give yourself a score of 0–5 for each statement (0 = completely untrue for you, 5 = absolutely true for you).**
Compare yourself with other students. How similar or different are you?

Type of intelligence	Characteristics	Score 0–5
Logical/ Mathematical	You analyse issues logically, looking for patterns and relationships between things in order to find solutions. You're an excellent problem solver and have an intuitive grasp of numbers and figures.	
Linguistic	You are able to express yourself through written and spoken language without difficulty. You analyse written information from different sources with ease and enjoy stories and plots. You may also find it easy to learn other languages.	
Interpersonal	Building relationships with other people is important to you. You find it easy to understand and interact with friends, family and colleagues and are sensitive to others' moods and body language.	
Intrapersonal	You know yourself well. You are aware of your own moods, desires, motivations and intentions and are able to use this awareness to inform your behaviour and achieve your life goals.	
Musical	You experience the world through sound and rhythm. You listen to music wherever you go and may even play an instrument. You recognise different tones and identify audio patterns and might compose your own music or find it easy to copy what you hear.	
Naturalistic	You enjoy spending time in nature, learning more about the natural world. You're sensitive to environmental changes, such as changes in the seasons. You may also not feel comfortable in large crowds or spending long periods of time indoors.	
Pedagogical	You are a natural teacher. You find it easy to convey information to other people in a clear and easy-to-understand manner and are able to make people see things differently.	
Spatial	You see patterns all around you and find it easy to visualise pathways through a physical world. You may enjoy interpreting data through charts and graph or designing solutions through plans and drawings. You know where things are, are sensitive to changes around you, and rarely get lost.	
Kinaesthetic	Your body and mind work as one and your experience of the world is mostly physical. You have excellent control of your body and find it easy to conduct practical tasks. You have good hand-eye coordination and often do well at sports.	

3 What intelligences do you think these famous people possess? Focus on their occupations and use some of the expressions below.

I imagine someone like … would be …
… probably has both … and … intelligences, don't you think?
I think it's reasonable to suggest that … has …
What are your thoughts on …?
Would you agree?
That's just my opinion.
It's difficult/impossible to tell.

Ai Wei Wei, artist, China

Tim Berners-Lee, computer scientist, UK

Oprah Winfrey, actress, talk-show host, businesswoman, USA

Rihanna, singer, Barbados

Greta Thunberg, climate activist, Sweden

Steve McQueen, filmmaker, UK

Bill Gates, businessman, USA

Vivianne Miedema, footballer, Netherlands

4 What is your opinion of attempts to categorise people like this?

Listening Part 2

- In Listening Part 2, you hear a monologue lasting about three minutes. You hear the recording twice.
- You have to listen and complete eight sentences with information you hear, using 1–3 words.
- You must write the actual words that the speaker uses.
- This part tests your ability to identify specific information and the opinions expressed.

Exam info

1 Work in pairs. Which three adjectives do you think best describe your personality?

2 It's believed that the colours you prefer can reveal something about your personality.
Look at the four colours below – which of the four particularly catches your eye?

3 Read what your choice says about you. Then discuss with a partner how accurate you think the assessment is.

Red:

You're active and energetic, and generally hit it off with new people you meet. You like to co-operate with others and are happy to take on responsibility.

Workwise: you need a job that isn't repetitive, with the freedom to be creative.

Blue:

You'd like to settle down, and enjoy being with family and friends. You like a sense of order in your life, and dislike anything unpredictable.

Workwise: you'd be successful as a manager, because you're trustworthy and reliable.

Yellow:

You're cheerful, but also a bit of a perfectionist. You're fun to be around, and quite impulsive. Although you have many friends, you're also happy being on your own.

Workwise: you'd do well in jobs involving working outdoors.

Green:

You're sincere and caring, and a great listener, but tend not to hide your feelings. You're good at understanding the big picture rather than getting distracted by details.

Workwise: you'd be successful in jobs involving research.

4 **Look at the sentences in the listening task below. What kinds of words could fill the gaps? Can you guess any words?**

You will hear a radio programme in which a woman called Kate Walsh is talking about doing a personality quiz based on colour preferences. For questions 1–8, complete the sentences with a word or short phrase.

Personality quiz

Kate wondered initially whether her background in **(1)** .... (1 word) might be a problem when doing the quiz.

Kate fully expected to be described as **(2)** .... (1 word) in the analysis of her personality.

Kate was surprised that the word **(3)** .... (1 word) was included in her results.

Kate reports that people's **(4)** .... (1 word) can apparently be suggested by the colours they dislike.

Kate mentions that the colour red commonly represents **(5)** .... (1 word) in Chinese culture.

Kate personally thinks that people who favour red might do well in a career in **(6)** .... (1 word).

Kate believes people's **(7)** .... (2 words) is the most revealing indicator of personality.

Kate describes herself as **(8)** .... (1 word) when talking about how she finally felt about the quiz.

5 **Listen and fill in as many answers as you can. Compare your answers with a partner.** 12

6 **Now listen again. Complete any answers you didn't hear the first time, and check the answers you've already completed. Make sure your answer makes sense in the sentence.** 12

Vocabulary
Multi-word verbs

1 **Look at these examples of multi-word verbs from the programme in Listening Part 2.**

1. Whenever my bike *breaks down*, I always need to find a mechanic.
2. I was rather *taken aback* by one of the terms the quiz generated.
3. I was determined not to be *put off* by that.

Work with a partner. What does each verb mean?

2 **Look at the following sentences and decide what the multi-word verb in each one means.**

1. Will this new fashion ever *catch on* with young people?
2. He *comes across as* very shy, but I'm not sure he is.
3. How did you first *get into* badminton?
4. Management have *put forward* interesting proposals.
5. It's never good to *rush into* an important decision.
6. If a university place *comes up*, I'll take it.
7. Luckily, my school *did away with* uniforms before I started there.

3 **Complete the sentences with multi-word verbs from Exercise 2. Change the verbs into the correct form for the contexts.**

1. Elijah .... some good suggestions for the publicity campaign.
2. It's best not to .... anything – take your time.
3. I .... classical music while working in a music shop.
4. My boss can .... very strict, but he's actually not like that.
5. A great job opportunity has .... , so I might go for it!
6. One designer's making flared trousers again, but they'll never .... People just won't buy them!
7. Some businesses are proposing .... cash altogether, and just using cards for payments.

Grammar
no, none, not

The COMPLETE grammar reference Turn to page 165

1 **Complete these sentences with *no*, *none* or *not*.**

1. You're a great listener, but tend .... to hide your feelings.
2. I have .... great aptitude for fixing things that have broken.
3. Luckily, the results included .... of my more negative characteristics!

2 **Five of these sentences contain mistakes that exam candidates have made in expressing negation. Correct the mistakes. (One sentence is correct.)**

1. It was difficult to get around last weekend as there was not public transport.
2. Most students were no satisfied with the standard of food in the school canteen.
3. We've had hardly no communication from management for over a week.
4. As far as I can see, there's not much difference between Spanish grammar and Italian grammar.
5. I'm afraid I don't know nothing about psychology.
6. We couldn't get treated for two hours because none doctors were available.

Grammar

The passive

The COMPLETE grammar reference

▶ Scan the QR code, watch the video, then turn to page 166

1 **How are passive verbs formed? Compare these two sentences.**

Active:

The quiz includes an analysis of your personality, together with career suggestions.

Passive:

An analysis of your personality, together with career suggestions, is included in the quiz.

2 **Underline the passive verbs in these sentences.**

- **a** It's widely believed that your colour preference may reveal something about your personality.
- **b** Personality quizzes have been found to be quite accurate indicators of what you're really like.
- **c** The speaker was relieved that some of her character traits were omitted by the quiz analysis.

3 **Focus on the passive verbs in Exercise 2 and discuss these questions.**

1. In which of the sentences above is the doer of the action (the 'agent') mentioned?
2. Who or what could be the agent if the doer of the action *isn't* mentioned?
3. Why is the agent not mentioned? (There are several possible reasons.)
4. Would you be more likely to find passive verbs

- in an email to a friend or an essay?
- in a scientific report or a magazine story?
- in a personal anecdote or a job application?

4 **Change these active sentences into the passive form. Only include an agent if you think it is important.**

1. Over a million people have watched this YouTube clip.
2. They made the film over twenty years ago.
3. At the time no one had seen anything like it.
4. Apparently, they are making a new version of the film at the moment.
5. They are going to release it next year.

5 **In formal writing, we often begin sentences with *It* + passive, especially if we want to focus attention on ideas and arguments. Work in pairs to complete these beginnings with your own ideas. Choose any subject you find interesting.**

1. It is commonly believed that …
2. It has been reported in the last few days that …
3. It has been proved beyond doubt that …

6 **Rewrite this text using passive verbs to replace the underlined active verbs. Only include an agent if you think it is important. Use one verb with *it*, as in Exercise 5.**

A new study on Albert Einstein has been completed …

An expert **(1)** has completed a new study on Albert Einstein and she **(2)** will publish it next month in a journal on neurology. The study suggests that a uniquely shaped brain **(3)** may have influenced Einstein's extraordinary genius. When anthropologist Dean Falk and her team made a comparison with 85 'normal' human brains, **(4)** they found that Einstein's brain possessed some remarkable features. Notably, that the left and right hemispheres of his brain were well connected compared to the control group.

The researchers were using 14 photos of the genius's brain which people **(5)** had only recently rediscovered. With permission from his family, scientists **(6)** removed and photographed Einstein's brain after his death in 1955. The National Museum of Health and Medicine **(7)** holds the photographs, but people **(8)** had never fully investigated them before.

Reading and Use of English Part 5

- In Reading and Use of English Part 5, you have to read a text of 650–750 words.
- You answer six questions about it by choosing A, B, C or D.
- This part tests your ability to understand the main ideas and purpose of the text and the writer's opinions or attitude, and to understand text organisation features such as exemplification.

Exam info

1 **You are going to read an article about people who have a condition called synaesthesia. Read the article quickly and find what synaesthesia is, and one or two examples of the way in which people are affected by it. Compare your answers with a partner.**

Living with synaesthesia

Saturdays are yellow, and Thursdays are dark blue: that's always been so apparent to me that, for most of my life, I didn't think it was even worth making a point of mentioning it. I also didn't consider it unusual to imagine that the word 'courage' had a texture like iron, and 'wisdom' was purple in colour. It's not that I thought everyone else saw Thursdays as specifically blue; I just thought everyone processed information in that way. It wasn't until university that it began to dawn on me that that was far from the case, when I spotted a poster asking: 'What colour is Monday? If you can answer that question, you might have synaesthesia,' with an invitation to participate in a neurological study. I stared at the poster, then messaged a friend, asking her the same question. She had absolutely no idea what I was talking about.

In fact, sources suggest that approximately 2–4% of people are thought to have the condition. However, when I asked on social media for any fellow synaesthetes to contact me, a surprising number of people began sharing similar experiences. One person first had suspicions as a child that he understood things differently from other people when explaining to his initially slightly puzzled mum that because green was his favourite colour, it followed that seven must be his favourite number – because it was also green. He now finds it relatively easy to remember things like phone numbers, but runs into issues if the 'real life' number on something such as a sign has its own colour that's in conflict with the colour in his head. As for prose, it's a multi-coloured thing for him, with literary features – such as the same sounds being used at the beginnings of a string of words, or neighbouring syllables with the same sounds – leaping out as being all the same colour, to the extent that they may even present a distraction at times.

While the effects of synaesthesia are becoming well documented, its origins remain obscure. The brain regions responsible for processing language and colours may have accidentally grown too many neural connections between each other, a possibility that could explain why grapheme-colour synaesthesia – the association between colours and words, like knowing that Thursdays are blue – is the most common form. In fact, brain scans show there's activity in both regions when synaesthetes hear words. It's an explanation people with the condition may feel drawn to, as is another possibility that's been proposed, which goes by the catchy name of 'disinhibited feedback'. Decisions are constantly being made by our brains about which type of information is important and which can be selectively ignored – otherwise we'd be too distracted by what's going on around us to properly function. And that includes any associations we might have made about the information. For example, when meeting someone for the first time, we might make associations based on information such as someone we know who resembles them or the colour of their clothes that strikes us. However, in order to keep functioning normally, we shut down most of those associations without attending to them – inhibiting our feedback, in other words. Synaesthesia is an example of what occurs when that shutdown doesn't happen.

For many synaesthetes, this can actually help rather than negatively affect them. I remember spellings of words after only seeing them once because they immediately have powerful colour combinations I can't forget. Similarly, I remember long strings of unconnected numbers fairly easily because of their colours – despite my maths skills leaving much to be desired. And if, as some of us do, you effectively see dates, numbers and time in 3D, diaries become almost unnecessary.

In fact, one feature that certain extremely gifted mathematicians may share is that they also have synaesthesia – a particular subset of the condition which allows them to do seemingly impossible calculations at lightning speed. They perceive numbers as shapes, which then come together and morph into other complex combinations and somehow give them the answers. Synaesthetes can also experience a mixture of more than one subset. There's 'lexical-gustatory synaesthesia', for instance, where words have tastes, or 'ordinal-linguistic personification,' where letters have personalities.

However, for non-synaesthetes vaguely wishing they had the condition, it seems you can trick your brain into developing similar skills by forcing associations (always picturing words beginning with T as red, for instance). Meanwhile, a small percentage of us will continue to avoid numbers with particular personalities and notice letters jumping off the page in vivid colours. It might sound extraordinary to the majority of the population, but for people like me who know the number four is aquamarine and has an easy-going personality, it's a life-enhancing kind of gift.

2 Read the article again and for questions 1–6, choose the answer (A, B, C or D) which you think fits best according to the article.

1 What does the writer say about her attitude to synaesthesia?
- **A** She was puzzled by the associations the condition presented her with.
- **B** She assumed her perceptions were identical to other people's.
- **C** She was largely unaware of its existence for some time.
- **D** She felt it enriched her impressions of words she came across.

2 One fellow synaesthete on social media suggested that the condition
- **A** can have drawbacks in certain situations.
- **B** enhances his appreciation of written language.
- **C** is responsible for his level of creativity.
- **D** has given his family considerable cause for concern.

3 What is the writer doing in the third paragraph?
- **A** summarising results of research into the condition
- **B** putting forward conflicting views of the cause of the condition
- **C** outlining the recent expansion of research into the condition
- **D** examining appealing theories that could account for the condition

4 What does the writer imply about her maths skills by referring to them as 'leaving much to be desired' in line 79?
- **A** She envies other people's maths skills.
- **B** She's worked hard to improve her maths skills.
- **C** She feels the level of her maths skills is inadequate.
- **D** She realises her maths skills are rather unconventional.

5 What point is made about synaesthesia in the fifth paragraph?
- **A** It may exist in various forms within a single individual.
- **B** It indicates a higher level of intelligence than in the general population.
- **C** It may be more widespread than previously thought.
- **D** It presents comparable traits in different contexts.

6 In the final paragraph, what feeling does the writer express about having synaesthesia?
- **A** surprise at the reactions of others to the condition
- **B** a sense of privilege in having an alternative view of the world
- **C** a keenness to share the advantages of the condition with others
- **D** sympathy towards people who regret being unable to experience it

3 Discuss these questions in pairs.

1 Have you experienced any of the signs of synaesthesia that are mentioned in the text?

2 How would having synaesthesia affect your life, do you think? Would it be a problem or would it make it more interesting?

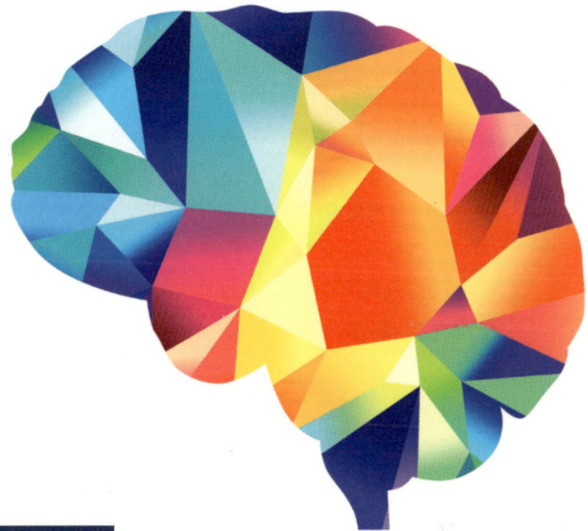

Vocabulary
Verb collocations

1 Match the verbs in A with the words in B to make common verb collocations. You will need to use some of the verbs more than once. Look at the example to help you.

A	B
make	things as they come
take	into problems
run	a point of
catch	your eye
	your time
	ends meet
	up with

2 Complete the sentences with the verb collocations from Exercise 1. Change the pronouns and tenses where necessary.

1 The red dress in the window really .... , so I bought it!

2 I always .... remembering family members' birthdays.

3 There's no need to hurry – we can ....

4 It must be hard to .... if you only have a part-time job.

5 I'll have to work hard to .... the other students after my holiday.

6 I .... difficulties as soon as I set off to drive home in the snow.

7 Harry's very laid back and relaxed – he just ....

Reading and Use of English Part 2

1 **You are going to read an article about the importance of music in our lives.**

1 Read the article *The importance of music* quickly. What examples does the article mention of music featuring in our lives? Work in pairs and compare your answers.

2 Discuss with a partner the importance of music in your life. What would your life be like without any music at all?

3 Work in pairs to complete the text. Use the list below to help you think of the type of word you need for each gap.

adjective   adverb (x3)   determiner   preposition   pronoun (x2)

The importance of music

It's easy to underestimate the extent **(0)** ....to.......... which music affects our lives. Some people may maintain that they have very **(1)** .... time for music, and never listen to any, **(2)** .... than the kind of background music they encounter in a restaurant, say. **(3)** .... so, we're all born with a degree of musical appreciation, and most people could probably follow the rhythm of a tune.

In fact, **(4)** .... from being an insignificant aspect of our lives, music can actually be an important presence. For example, it can influence **(5)** .... our reactions might be to amusing or frightening scenes in films, or to new products in advertisements. And regardless **(6)** .... musical taste, certain types of music can help people feel calmer in difficult situations. Furthermore, learning to play a musical instrument is believed to enhance ability in areas such as maths.

(7) .... fact, one of the most positive benefits may be for patients suffering from memory loss, for **(8)** .... music can bring back long-forgotten memories and assist with the recovery of verbal skills.

Exam info

- In Reading and Use of English Part 2, there is a text with eight gaps. You have to write one word in each gap.
- Most missing words are 'grammar words', e.g. articles (*the, a*) auxiliary or modal verbs (*are, is, can*) pronouns (*he, us*) conjunctions (*but, although*) possessive adjectives (*my, our*) prepositions (*at, to*)
- A few may be 'meaning' words, e.g. nouns, verbs, adjectives.
- You must spell your answers correctly.

2 **Now do the task below with no assistance. For questions 1–8, read the text and think of the word which best fits each gap. Use only one word for each gap. There is an example at the beginning.**

Forest bathing

I recently joined a group to participate in **(0)** ....what.......... is known as forest bathing, a practice involving spending time in a forest to improve one's mood and general wellbeing.

The forest we visited was absolutely glorious. But before we actually **(1)** .... foot in it, we were invited to remove our boots and walk barefoot, presumably so as **(2)** .... to disturb the wildlife. For a city-dweller like me, that was a big ask. It did mean, though, that I couldn't think about anything aside **(3)** .... where to place my feet. And **(4)** .... my initial resistance, I soon began to enjoy it, **(5)** .... the point where I declined to put my boots back on again, even after finally **(6)** .... given the option.

Then we sat and listened to the sounds of the forest – and mentally slowed down. Admittedly, before the visit, I'd been **(7)** .... two minds about participating, but when the session finished, I was reluctant to go back to the city. And no sooner had I arrived home afterwards **(8)** .... I started making plans for my return to the forest.

3 **Discuss these questions.**

1 Do you find spending time in nature beneficial? Why? / Why not?

2 Would you considering joining a group and trying forest bathing?

Speaking Part 3

▶ **Page 211 Speaking bank**
Speaking Part 3

Exam info

- In Speaking Part 3, you and the other candidate discuss a situation or issue together.
- The examiner gives you instructions and a set of written prompts.
- You have about 15 seconds to think about the task and then two minutes to discuss your ideas.
- The examiner then asks you another question, which requires you to come to a decision. You have one minute to do this.
- This part tests your ability to interact with your partner by exchanging ideas, expressing and justifying opinions, agreeing and disagreeing, speculating, evaluating and reaching a decision through discussion. It is important that you keep talking.

1 **Do the following tasks related to the causes of stress in today's society.**

1 Make a list of things that make people feel stressed, for example, overwork, difficult relationships, etc.
2 Compare lists with a partner. How many causes of stress are in both your lists?
3 Explain to your partner how you cope with stressful situations.

2 13 **Listen to two people discussing stress and how they cope with it. Does either of the speakers mention any of the causes of stress that you have discussed?**

3 13 **To make sure you don't speak too much in the discussion, ask your partner questions. Listen to the conversation again and complete these questions which the speakers ask to involve their partner.**

1 Do you know what I .... ?
2 That's one of the worst effects of stress, ... ?
3 So what .... if you're feeling stressed?
4 What .... you?
5 Have you .... that?

4 **Read the examiner's instructions. Then look at the written prompts below and prepare what you are going to say.**

'Here are some of the actions that people take to prevent or cope with stress and a question for you to discuss.'

What are the advantages and disadvantages of these actions in preventing or coping with stress?

- avoiding stressful situations
- expressing your feelings
- having an active social life
- taking regular exercise
- practising relaxation techniques

5 **Now talk to your partner about what the advantages and disadvantages of these actions might be in helping people to prevent or cope with stress.**

Your discussion should last for about two minutes.

6 **After your discussion, the examiner will give you a final instruction, like this:**

'Now you have about a minute to decide which action would be the most effective in helping people prevent or deal with stress.'

Try to reach agreement with your partner.

Writing Part 1: An essay

▶ **Page 193 Writing bank**
An essay

- Read the question and notes carefully, underlining key words so that you know exactly what you have to do.
- Make sure that you answer the question, dealing with two of the three topic areas listed.
- Use your own words if you decide to make use of any of the opinions expressed.
- Start by making a paragraph plan to ensure that you cover all the points in the question.

Exam advice

1 Discuss these questions in pairs or groups and note down your ideas while you are talking.

- What are the main distractions for students when they are studying?
- Which aspects of their studies can cause students to feel stressed?
- How can teachers, friends and family members help students who are struggling with their studies?

2 Read the essay task below and discuss these questions:

- Why can it be hard to prioritise things in your life?
- How best can students organise their time?
- In what ways can other people help students find a good work/life balance?
- Do you strongly agree or disagree with any of these opinions?

Your class has listened to a debate about the factors which help students achieve a good work/life balance when studying. You have made the notes below:

Factors which help students achieve a good work/life balance when studying

- understanding good study habits
- planning free-time activities
- having a support network

Some opinions expressed in the debate:

'Planning my college work is really helpful.'

'Having something to look forward to at the weekend helps me focus on my studies.'

'My friends support me with help and advice.'

Write an **essay** in 220–260 words discussing **two** of the factors in your notes that are important for students in achieving a good balance between studying hard and enjoying other things in their lives. You should **explain which factor you think is more important**, **giving reasons** to support your opinion.

You may, if you wish, make use of the opinions expressed in the debate, but you should use your own words as far as possible.

3 Read the following essay on the task in Exercise 2. Then discuss these questions with a partner.

1 Has the writer
   a discussed two factors from the task?
   b provided reasons for their opinion?
   c used their own words?
2 Is the style of the essay appropriate?
3 Is the essay roughly the correct length?

Most students have come up against situations when it has been difficult to balance the need to study hard with other aspects of life, like socialising with friends or taking time out to follow their leisure pursuits. To become fully rounded individuals, we should all be able to take time off from our work or studies in order to relax and enjoy ourselves. But how can we achieve this balance?

Teachers can give advice about how best to research a project or which sources will be useful to use for an essay. This helps students to save time which might otherwise have been wasted. Similarly, parents can help their children by providing a quiet environment for them to work in and by not reprimanding them when they want to relax or go out. In this way, other people can definitely help students find that essential balance between studying and life.

It's also vital for students to be able to plan their time, organise their schedules sensibly and keep to them. Being realistic about how much time it will take to finish a project, and then building in sufficient time to unwind and maybe go out with friends afterwards, shows that a person can take on responsibilities yet still have time to relax.

Both these factors are significant in reaching that necessary balance between life and study. However, in my experience, it is effective time management that is the most important of all because with this you can feel satisfied that you are successful in different areas of your life.

4 **Look at the structure of the sample essay and discuss the following.**

1 Summarise the purpose of each of the four paragraphs, like this:
Para 1: Introduction showing the writer's general approach to the topic
Para 2: One of the factors ...
2 How do the paragraphs relate to the essay task?
3 In which paragraph(s) does the writer express their opinions?

5 **Read the essay task below.**

1 Discuss the topic of the essay with a partner, using your own experience of schools or universities.
2 Do you agree with any of the opinions expressed?

You have taken part in a seminar discussing how schools can help to make the exam period less stressful for students. You have made the notes below.

How can schools help to ensure that students do not suffer from stress during the exam period?

- support from teachers
- a structured revision timetable prior to exams
- time for relaxation and leisure activities

Some opinions expressed in the seminar

'Students need to remember that there is more to life than exam success.'

'Revising for 24 hours a day before exams doesn't necessarily lead to success.'

'You won't do well on the day if you feel stressed.'

Write an essay discussing **two** of the methods in your notes. You should **explain which method you think is more important** for schools to adopt, **providing reasons** to support your answer.

You may, if you wish, make use of the opinions expressed in the seminar, but you should use your own words as far as possible.

6 **Consider how you can adapt the paragraph structure in Exercise 4 for the new essay task. Discuss this question.**
Which of the following paragraph openings would be appropriate for this essay and in which paragraph (1–4) would each of these fit best?

1 One way in which schools can help is ...
2 Both of these methods ...
3 I feel incredibly stressed out when ...
4 Firstly, ...
5 For many students, exams are ...
6 Another method ...
7 Exams don't bother me much ...
8 In my opinion, the more important ...
9 Exam stress is a problem which ...
10 In addition, ...

7 **Plan and write your essay on the task in Exercise 5. Start by making a paragraph plan which is clearly related to the essay task, as in Exercise 4.**

4 Career paths

Starting off

1 **Look at the photos of people in jobs. What aspects of work do you associate with each job?**

This person is probably a high-flying executive in a large multinational company. She is likely to be involved in high-level decision-making, so she has a lot of power, high status and a large salary. I'd imagine she works long hours and has to deal with a lot of stress.

2 **Which of these aspects of work appeal to you?**

working under pressure · being creative · working with the public · working as part of a team · working independently · being your own boss · having managerial responsibilities · problem solving and troubleshooting · quick promotion · working set hours each day

Reading and Use of English Part 1

Exam info

- In Reading and Use of English Part 1, you read a short text with eight gaps and one example (0). You must choose the best option, A, B, C or D, for each gap.
- This part tests your knowledge of the meanings of words, how they are used, collocations and the grammar connected with particular words.

1 Work in pairs and discuss the following questions.

1. Which jobs are more likely to employ people on hourly, rather than permanent, contracts?
2. Why might someone decide to take a job that pays them an hourly rate rather than an annual salary?
3. How important is it for students to work in order to support themselves through their studies?
4. If somebody offered you a day's work, but couldn't guarantee the job would still be available when you arrived for your shift, would you accept?

2 For questions 1–8, read the text and decide which answer (A, B, C or D) best fits each gap. There is an example at the beginning (0). Use the clues to help you (in the exam there are no clues).

Zero-hours contracts

Under the (0) ....terms.......... of a zero-hours contract, employers and employees both have a limited degree of commitment. An employer is not required to offer any (1) .... of working hours to their employees, while employees can (2) .... their own working patterns by deciding which hours they work (or not). These types of contracts are attractive to students, who don't necessarily want to feel (3) .... to work during busy periods of study. Zero-hours workers are also able – theoretically, at least – to take time off spontaneously without first having to seek their manager's (4) .... to do so.

However, while the flexibility of zero-hours work is not in (5) ...., managers often put huge amounts of pressure on staff to be on (6) .... to go into work at a moment's notice. Refusal to do so can often lead to an extremely negative (7) .... – not being given any more shifts. What's more, the unpredictability of this type of employment eventually (8) .... many people to seek something more permanent so that they have a steady income to rely on.

0 A needs B provisions (C) terms D instructions

1 A policy B declaration C commitment D assurance

Clue: You need a word that is similar in meaning to 'promise' and takes the dependent preposition 'of'.

2 A conclude B determine C resolve D settle

Clue: Which verb is closest in meaning to 'select'?

3 A compelled B supposed C imposed D constrained

Clue: This word means 'doing something because you feel forced to or you feel it is necessary'.

4 A acceptance B consent C understanding D authority

Clue: This word refers to a decision made by one person who is in a superior position to another.

5 A discussion B debate C disagreement D dispute

Clue: The word you need refers to doubt and uncertainty, rather than differing opinions. Also, look at the word before the gap – 'in', not 'under'.

6 A orders B request C call D demand

Clue: This is a phrase that means 'to be available to work'.

7 A outcome B ending C product D finish

Clue: Which noun collocates most naturally with the verb 'lead (to)'.

8 A drives B urges C directs D thrusts

Clue: If something .... someone to do something, it forces or motivates them to do it.

3 Work in pairs.

- Why do you think zero-hours jobs are more common than they used to be?
- Some people suggest that zero-hours work is representative of an 'imbalance of power'. What do you think they might mean?

Reading and Use of English Part 8

Exam advice

- Before you read the sections, read the questions carefully, underlining the key ideas.
- Read the first section and find which questions it seems to answer.
- Deal with each section in turn in this way.
- Go back and check whether each potential answer corresponds *exactly* with the wording of the question.

1 **Work in small groups and discuss the questions below.**

In your country

- how easy is it for young people to find jobs?
- what are the most common methods of job hunting?
- what is the most effective way to find a job?
- how well do universities prepare students for the world of work?

2 **You are going to read an article. Read the title and sub-heading. What do you think the article is about?**

3 **Read section A. Which of the questions, 1–10 in Exercise 6, can you rule out as a possible answer for A? Why?**

4 **On first reading, question 1 might seem to correspond to the following part of section A. Discuss with a partner why the answer to question 1 is *NOT* section A.**

'… far too many managers still think that young people just need to toughen up and accept antiquated, dying industry practice as "the way it is" …'

5 **Now compare question 2 with the following part of section A. Discuss with a partner how this might give you the correct answer.**

'For any business to prosper, … a true understanding of the cultural shifts that have taken place in the workplace over the past decade is vital.'

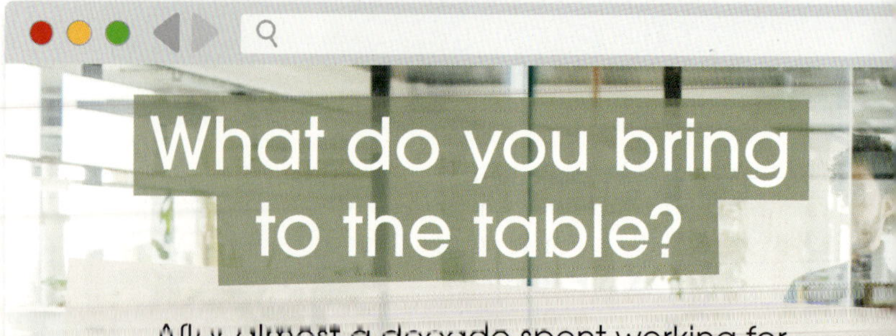

What do you bring to the table?

After almost a decade spent working for companies across the UK and Europe, Shantel Williams reflects on the ways in which young people are valued – or not – in today's workplace.

A For any business to prosper, both now and into the future, a true understanding of the cultural shifts that have taken place in the workplace over the last few decades is vital. During that time, the companies that have found success in the face of one financial or health crisis after another have often done so by opening their doors to youth. They have understood that if a business doesn't go out of its way to fully engage with the talent of the future, that talent will end up looking elsewhere. Despite this, far too many managers still think that young people just need to toughen up and accept antiquated, dying industry practice as 'the way it is', oblivious to the major drawback of this type of mindset: it prevents them from attracting the most promising candidates. Most jobs are likely to look very different in a few short years, so doesn't it make sense to fill them with people who can continually develop and upgrade themselves?

6 **Now do the exam task. For questions 1–10, choose from the sections (A–D). The sections may be chosen more than once.**

In which section does the writer …

explain how a management strategy has become increasingly redundant?	1
recommend an evaluation of long-term developments?	2
describe a modern means of assessing a person's suitability for a post?	3
illustrate a refusal to adapt to a widely held view?	4
emphasise the work ethic of a particular group of people?	5
detail a contemporary application of a traditional process?	6
predict the end of a form of communication?	7
mention conflicted feelings that job seekers may have about a certain practice?	8
criticise a belief that unintentionally imposes limits on recruitment?	9
specify ways in which younger staff could be supported by those in charge?	10

B One word, for me, sums up young people in today's workforce: dynamic. Perhaps because we are conscious of the difficulties faced by the generation immediately before us, we are coming to the workplace better prepared. Realistic, rather than optimistic, with the hope that our managers will empower us in our daily duties, embrace our digital dependence, and allow us to demonstrate how the business can be improved by our contributions. In many companies, there is still a reliance on the increasingly stale tactic of trying to keep staff happy with office perks that are designed to take their minds off the daily grind of work. While we wouldn't necessarily steer clear of the bean-bag chairs, foosball tables and pizza Fridays that seemingly kept people happy for so long, they hold far less appeal for young employees these days. We don't want distraction. We want to focus on our tasks entirely and wholeheartedly, accepting long hours as part of what we have to do to be successful.

C Meanwhile, our instinctive bond with new technology is frequently overlooked. I have one friend whose boss insists that she take a notebook and pen to every meeting, even though she has a perfectly good note-taking app designed to integrate all aspects of her work. It astonishes me that such devotion to an outdated routine is still alive. Why go out of your way to dispute the consensus in business around the world, that advanced digital know-how is increasingly imperative and brings only benefits to a company? Any effective manager should jump at the chance to take advantage of our substantial digital intelligence, not to mention our keenness to share our expertise. Instead, younger staff seem to be evaluated on our ability to use a spreadsheet program designed in the 1980s. It's time to move things forward. People of my age much prefer to get our work done through instant messaging rather than sending emails. Yet so many businesses are still entirely dependent on this latter medium, which anyone with any sense knows is bound to become obsolete soon. Over time – and some people would do well to accept this – everything changes.

D In one area in particular, businesses are investing in innovation to attract today's bright-eyed job-hunters. Paper-based job applications have been on their way out for a while, and forward-thinking employers are now partnering with software companies to create company-specific, mobile-based games that all potential candidates must play. Such a game might collect data on how well candidates solve problems, for example, or use algorithms to predict whether they would be a good fit within the company. Some companies even use games to determine whether the user was state or privately educated, or if their parents went to university (instead of having to ask these questions directly at interview). Millions of young people today are desperate for society to become more inclusive, and would undoubtedly welcome any initiative centred on improving the employment prospects of less privileged applicants. That said, it might sit uncomfortably with those who are keen to be picked purely for their talent and qualifications, however much they recognise the need for increased diversity in the workplace.

7 Work in small groups. Discuss these questions.

- Would you say that these days, having 'advanced digital know-how' is crucial in getting a good job?
- What is more important to you, colleagues you get on well with or a boss who values your skills and talents?
- What are the dangers of excessive reliance on technology in the workplace?

Vocabulary

Dependent prepositions

▶ **Page 188 Dependent prepositions**

1 Complete these extracts from Reading and Use of English Part 8 by writing a preposition in each gap.

1. … oblivious to the major drawback of this type of mindset: it prevents them .... attracting the most promising candidates.
2. Perhaps because we are conscious .... the difficulties faced by the generation immediately before us, we are coming to the workplace better prepared.
3. In many companies, there is still a reliance .... the increasingly stale tactic of trying to keep staff happy with office perks that are designed to take their minds off the daily grind of work.
4. We want to focus .... our tasks entirely and wholeheartedly, accepting long hours as part of what we have to do to be successful.
5. In one area in particular, businesses are investing .... innovation to attract today's bright-eyed job-hunters.
6. … forward-thinking employers are now partnering .... software companies to create company-specific, mobile-based games that all potential candidates must play.
7. Millions of young people today are desperate .... society to become more inclusive.

2 Correct the mistake with the preposition in each of these questions. Then discuss the questions with a partner.

1. Do you think that a job application that focuses of candidates playing games rather than sending a paper-based application is a good way to determine a candidate's suitability for a role? Why / Why not?
2. A low salary is the biggest reason that prevents candidates for applying for a job. Do you agree?
3. Do you think it's necessary for companies to invest money on office perks, like foosball tables and pizza Fridays, to keep people motivated at work? Why / Why not?

Adjective–noun collocations (1)

1 Look at these sentences from Reading and Use of English Part 8. Which of the words in *italics* form collocations with the words in bold that follow them?

1 … oblivious to the *large/major* **drawback** of this type of mindset …

2 … accepting *long/many* **hours** as part of what we have to do to be successful.

2 Exam candidates often make mistakes forming collocations with the words in bold in the following sentences. Which adjective from each set is not correct?

1 Karl has *wide* / *extensive* / *vast* **experience** in software troubleshooting.

2 Gustav's report made a(n) *huge* / *extreme* / *powerful* **impact** on his managers.

3 Our staff enjoy a *high* / *big* / *great* **degree** of flexibility in their working hours.

4 People working here have to work under *heavy* / *constant* / *large* **pressure**.

5 The company I work for has a(n) *excellent* / *big* / *unrivalled* **reputation** for quality.

6 There has been *severe* / *fierce* / *intense* **competition** for the manager's job.

7 We have had a *high* / *large* / *wide* **number** of applicants for this job.

8 There's been a *strong* / *huge* / *considerable* **increase** in the number of job applicants.

9 With her *expert* / *high* / *specialist* **skills**, Suzy is bound to get the job.

10 With Mei's *vast* / *extensive* / *strong* **knowledge** of statistical theory, I'm sure she'll get the job.

Listening Part 3

Exam info

- In Listening Part 3, you will hear an interview or conversation between two or more speakers.
- It lasts about four minutes.
- It has six multiple-choice questions, each with four options.
- This part tests your ability to understand attitude and opinion.

1 You will hear an interview with two business leaders about their open salary policy and their attempts to make their workplace more democratic. Before you listen, discuss the questions with a partner.

- What do you think an 'open salary' policy is?
- In which ways could a company make its workplace more democratic?

2 14 You will now hear the first part of the interview. Try to answer the questions below in your own words, then compare your ideas with a partner.

1 What does Patricia say about:
   a other companies?
   b staff interaction?
   c consistency in her and Tom's company?
   d industry research?

2 In which of these areas does Patricia express a reason for taking a decision?

3 15 **Listen to the whole interview. For questions 1–6, choose the answer (A, B, C or D) which fits best according to what you hear.**

1 Patricia says her company decided to introduce an open salary policy
- **A** to apply the findings of industry research
- **B** to ensure consistency within their company
- **C** to distinguish their company from its competitors
- **D** to encourage honest interaction between staff

2 In Patricia's view, what is the main benefit of the salary charts?
- **A** They help increase levels of respect between colleagues.
- **B** They are compiled in an exhaustive level of detail.
- **C** They enable the company to publicise employees' achievements.
- **D** They improve internal communication between departments.

3 Ahmad mentions experiencing a sense of satisfaction from
- **A** controlling the distribution of company budgets.
- **B** overseeing the company's plans for development.
- **C** addressing inequality in the workplace.
- **D** encouraging colleagues to push themselves to succeed.

4 What reason does Patricia give for rejecting her salary increase?
- **A** She thought it was too soon after her previous pay rise.
- **B** She believed the money should be distributed elsewhere.
- **C** She felt embarrassed to accept the amount she was offered.
- **D** She detected strong opposition to the proposal from some employees.

5 The recruitment policy at Oyay aims to attract employees who are
- **A** eager to participate in taking company decisions.
- **B** keen to put their academic qualifications to practical use.
- **C** comfortable negotiating salary expectations with their manager.
- **D** determined to lead change in the workplace.

6 When Patricia and Ahmad reflect on the changes they have made, they disagree on
- **A** the extent to which they have introduced new practices.
- **B** the importance of promoting inexperienced staff.
- **C** the value of analysing decisions taken in the past.
- **D** the need to explain their philosophy to other companies.

4 **Work in pairs. Discuss the questions.**
- Which personal qualities do you think would be most useful for anyone wanting to work at Oyay?
- Would you like to be an employee at Oyay, or would you prefer a more traditional working environment? Why?

Grammar

Expressing possibility, probability and certainty

The COMPLETE grammar reference
▶ Scan the QR code, watch the video, then turn to page 167

1 **Read the underlined phrases in these pairs of sentences. Which sentence in each pair expresses a stronger possibility?**

1 **a** Any candidate could well come in with a first-class degree, but for us, attitude is everything.
  b Any candidate could come in with a first class degree, but for us, attitude is everything.

2 **a** For example, it's unlikely we'd ever employ someone who wasn't happy to join in with day-to-day discussions about how the business is run.
  b For example, it's highly unlikely we'd ever employ someone who wasn't happy to join in with day-to-day discussions about how the business is run.

3 **a** We had a lot of new faces in the office, and I suspected they might easily have thought they had to vote it through simply because I'm on the management team.
  b We had a lot of new faces in the office, and I suspected they might have thought they had to vote it through simply because I'm on the management team.

2 **What do you think you will be doing in five years' time? Write five sentences about yourself, using the phrases underlined in Exercise 1.**

In five years' time I could well be working for an international company.

When you have finished, compare and discuss your sentences in pairs. Give reasons for your statements.

3 **The sentences below all contain mistakes made by exam candidates. Find and correct the mistakes.**

1 By reaching an advanced level of English, I am more probably to succeed in business.
2 If you come here for your holiday in July, you bound to enjoy it.
3 If you also watch television and films, then you're most likely to learn the language faster than if you just go to class.
4 I've studied the three posible options to try to solve the problem.
5 I'd like to recommend Grey's Academy as one of the possibly best schools in Barnsley.
6 This was the worst trip I probably have ever experienced.
7 That may be the possible reason why you're having such problems.

4 **For questions 1–6, complete the second sentence so that it has a similar meaning to the first sentence, using the word given. Do not change the word given. You must use between three and six words, including the word given.**

1 Madeleine felt sure that she would be offered the job.
BOUND
Madeleine felt she .... offered the job.

2 Boris is unlikely to win the prize.
LIKELIHOOD
There is little .... the prize.

3 There's a good chance that Takesi has seen your message.
WELL
Takesi .... your message.

4 I'm sure you didn't remember to post the letter.
MUST
You .... post the letter.

5 If you arrive late, the teacher may well get angry with you.
LIKELY
The teacher .... his temper with you if you arrive late.

6 Do you think you might be able to help me with the essay?
CHANCE
Is .... me with the essay?

Speaking Part 4

▶ **Page 213 Speaking bank**
Speaking Part 4

Exam info

- In Speaking Part 4, the examiner asks both candidates questions to find out their opinions on general topics related to Part 3. You may both be asked the same question, or each asked different questions.
- The examiner may also ask you to react to ideas and opinions which the other candidate expresses, so it is important to listen carefully to what they say.
- This part tests your ability to express and justify opinions, agree and disagree.

1 **Work in pairs. Before working on Speaking Part 4, follow the examiner's instructions for the first part of this Speaking Part 3 task.**

'Now, I'd like you to talk about something together for about two minutes. Here are some things that companies can do to make their employees' working lives more pleasant. Talk to each other about how effective these things might be in making employees' lives more pleasant.'

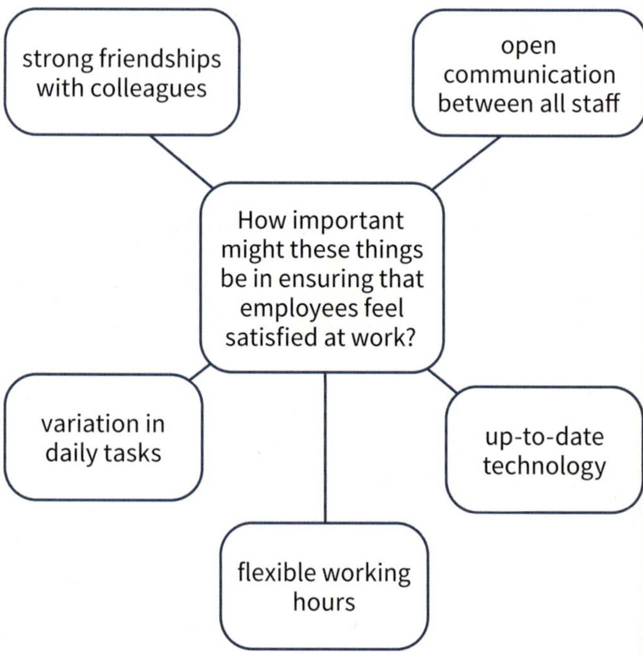

2 **Follow the examiner's instruction for the second part of the Part 3 task.**

> 'Now you have about a minute to decide which two things would be most likely to ensure employees' contentment.'

3 **Work in pairs. Look at these Part 4 questions and decide which of them you should answer by**

a **expressing just one point of view and a reason(s) for it**

b **giving a number of different ideas and perhaps reasons for them.**

1 Should the salaries for certain types of jobs be set by the government?

2 What do you think are the advantages and disadvantages of working from home?

3 Some people believe that people should continue working as long as they can, while other people believe that everyone should retire at 60 or 65. What is your view?

4 Which do you think is more important in a job: friendly colleagues or a good salary?

5 What types of skills are most useful for young people entering the job market for the first time?

6 Many people complain about their managers. What qualities would you look for in a perfect manager, and why?

4 **Work in pairs. Discuss and make brief notes on how you could answer questions 1–6 in Exercise 3.**

5 **In which answers to questions 1–6 could you use these words/phrases?**

achieve a good work–life balance commute
feel valued give praise a good communicator
a feeling of isolation a job vacancy
motivate/motivation
a reasonable/heavy/light workload
recruit take somebody on a trainee
a work environment a workplace

6 **Listen to Daniel and Laura answering three of the questions.**

16

1 Which words/phrases from Exercise 5 did they use?

2 Which answers do you agree with?

7 **Say if the following statements are true (T) or false (F).**

1 Daniel and Laura suggest several different ideas to answer each question.

2 They give general answers to the questions.

3 They occasionally mention their personal situation but don't answer the question entirely with that.

4 They answer the question but also add other ideas which are not relevant.

5 When they agree with their partner, they add extra ideas.

6 When they disagree with their partner, they explain why.

8 **Work in pairs. Take turns to ask and answer questions 1–6 in Exercise 3.**

Writing Part 2: An email

Page 196 Writing bank
An email

1 **Read the exam task and the sample answer. Then answer the questions below.**

1 Does Charlie write in a formal or informal style?
2 Is this appropriate for the task?
3 Does Charlie use an equal amount of space on the page to reply to each of Ariel's questions?
4 Is he likely to lose marks because of this?

You have received an email from a friend.

> Hi, Charlie,
>
> How's it going? I'm starting a project about employment opportunities for young people today, and was wondering what your thoughts are on these questions:
>
> When young people in your area have completed their education, do they tend to stay living in the same region or move to a new area?
>
> What, in your view, influences their choices about whether to stay or go?
>
> Any help you could give me would be great,
>
> Ariel

Write your **email** in reply.

Hey Ariel,

Good to hear from you. I'm more than happy to spell out a few of my thoughts on this subject.

Going by what my friends and people at college say about their plans for the future – and given my own ambitions, as well – there won't be anyone of my age left here once we've all finished our degrees! We're all off to find our fortunes in the big city.

If I'm being bit more realistic about it, though, there's no arguing with the fact that, each year, there is always a sizeable number of people who stay here. Not necessarily because they want to, but because for some, the idea of moving away permanently can often feel quite scary, so they shy away from leaving home for good.

To give another example for the second question, it's all about what type of qualification you end up with. There are quite a few engineering and tech companies on the outskirts of town here, and they're always a big draw if you've got a good science degree. They pay really well, too, which is certainly a good enough reason to stay put.

On the flip side, if you're not a scientist, that doesn't really apply. Plus, there isn't that much for young people to do outside of work here. So, since the capital city is only 25 km away, and apparently has a far wider range of jobs available (and let's not forget the social life and culture), that's where most of us are desperate to live.

Anyway, this is my take on the situation. Hope it helps.

Speak soon,

Charlie

Exam info & advice

- Writing an email tests your ability to write in a style which is consistently appropriate for the specified target reader. This could be a friend or peer, or the editor of a newspaper or a blog, or a school principal, and so on.
- You will need to write in a more- or less- formal style, depending on who the target reader is.

2 **Compared to the previous email from Charlie, should the answer to this question be written in a more, less or equally formal style? Why?**

You read this notice on the home page of a local government website:

> We are planning a series of articles about education opportunities for young people and are inviting comments from our residents in answer to the following questions:
>
> When young people in your area have completed their education, do they tend to stay living in the same region or move to a new area?
>
> What, in your view, influences their choices about whether to stay or go?

Write an **email** to the editor of the website, giving your responses and reasons.

3 **Read the opening of Lola's response to the editor of the local government website. Choose the most appropriate option to complete the sentence.**

Dear Editor,

After reading the invitation on your website for comments, …

a I'm more than happy to spell out a few of my thoughts on this subject.
b I would like to offer my opinions on the subject of where and why young people decide to relocate after completing their education.
c I'd like to run through one or two things I've noticed about where young people end up living once they're done with college or university.

4 Read the rest of Lola's email and answer the questions A and B.

From:

Subject:

(1) Going by what my friends and people at college say, when the time comes to enter the world of work, we would ideally like to move away from our home town. With luck, **(2)** we're all off to find our fortunes in the big city.

In reality, however, **(3)** there's no arguing with the fact that each year there is always a sizeable number of people who stay here. This is not necessarily through choice but because for many people **(4)** the idea of moving away permanently can often feel quite scary, and so they continue living here.

Turning to the second question, **(5)** it's all about what type of qualification you end up with. There are a considerable number of engineering and technology companies on the outskirts of town here which are always hugely attractive to those with a good science degree. They also tend to offer highly competitive salaries, which is often enough to convince potential employees to continue living here.

Aside from that, for those in my age group who aren't scientists, options both inside and outside of work in this town are quite limited. As such, the majority of us are hugely attracted to life in the capital city, which is only 25 km away and can offer a far wider range of jobs (not to mention the attraction of its social life and culture).

I hope my interpretation of the situation in this area will be of interest to you.

Thank you for your time,

Lola Prince

A) Match sentences 1–5 with their more appropriate options, a–f. There is one option that you do not need to use.

- **a** the unavoidable truth is that
- **b** which leads many people to decide against doing so
- **c** the concept of relocating can often feel intimidating
- **d** everyone will be able to secure rewarding employment offers elsewhere
- **e** this very much depends on what type of qualification a person has gained
- **f** There is a general consensus among my friendship and peer groups that

B) Complete the table with the language used in Charlie's and Lola's emails.

	More formal language (Lola's email)	Less formal language (Charlie's email)
1	a considerable number of	
2		because they want to
3		a big draw
4	not to mention	
5		pay really well
6		stay put
7	Aside from that,	
8		So,
9		my take on

3 Vocabulary and grammar review

Vocabulary

1 **Use the correct form of the verbs *make*, *take*, *run* or *catch* to complete the sentences below.**

1. The bracelet in the shop window ………………………… my eye so I went in to buy it.
2. The drawing John did was successful because he ………………………… his time instead of rushing it.
3. I've always ………………………… a point of remembering close friends' birthdays.
4. Robert was absent from college classes last week, but he very quickly ………………………… up with the work he'd missed.
5. If you don't earn enough to cover your bills and expenses each month, then you're not ………………………… ends meet.
6. Joel ………………………… into problems when he realised he'd left his passport at home.
7. Sam's always been quite laid-back. He's always just ………………………… things as they come.

2 **Use the correct form of the multi-word verbs in the box to complete the sentences. There are two verbs you do not need to use.**

catch on   come across   come up
do away with   get into   hit it off   put forward
rush into   settle down   take on

1. The fashion for wearing mini-skirts ………………………… really quickly in the 1960s.
2. The art teacher at my old school, Mr James, always ………………………… as being really strict, but once you got to know him, you could see he was very kind.
3. When I first met Jane, we ………………………… immediately – and we've been close friends ever since.
4. Tom ………………………… a decision about which university course to study, instead of thinking about it carefully.
5. I need to thank John for ………………………… some great ideas for our project.
6. My workplace has recently ………………………… the usual formal dress code, so no-one wears suits any more.
7. An opportunity to study abroad ………………………… unexpectedly, so Harry applied. He leaves tomorrow!
8. Sarah's been ………………………… folk music much more recently. She's playing it all the time at the moment.

Grammar

3 **The words *no*, *none* and *not* and are used incorrectly in some of these sentences. Correct the mistakes.**

1. I've searched everywhere for my passport but there is not sign of it.
2. Most of my family love all kinds of sport, but no my sister – she thinks all sport is a waste of time.
3. The exam was so difficult that I didn't get none of my answers right.
4. Humans are basically no different from any other animal.
5. I thought we had plenty of coffee but I've just looked in the cupboard and there's no left.
6. Not one of Patrick's friends remembered his birthday.
7. Our rate of pay is no the point – it's the actual working conditions that are so awful.
8. The group left for the North Pole three weeks ago and so far we've had none news of their progress.

4 **Rewrite these short texts replacing active verbs with passive verbs where possible and appropriate.**

1 We use the term 'amnesia' to refer to a partial or complete loss of memory. It is usually a temporary condition which only affects a certain part of a person's experience. Specific medical conditions can cause amnesia.

2 We all know very well that our real experiences form our memory. But could someone put a false memory into our heads? Could they persuade us that we had experienced something that never actually took place?

3 We use our semantic memory to store our knowledge of the world. Everyone has this knowledge base, and normally we can access it quickly and easily. Our semantic memory includes the meanings of words and the names of people and places.

4 Our working memory is a very important part of our memory system. You can think of it as the ability to remember and use a limited amount of information for a short amount of time. Our working memory can help us to perform a task, like following a set of instructions. However, this information is erratic. If someone distracts you, you can lose the information and you have to start the task again.

Vocabulary and grammar review 4

Vocabulary

1 Complete the sentences with a preposition in each gap.

1. Try to remain conscious .... the amount of time each task takes to complete.
2. Sometimes, it's difficult to prevent things .... going wrong, but you can make the most .... any situation by using it as an opportunity to learn more.
3. I've had no success hunting .... jobs in the local area, so it's probably time to start applying .... jobs elsewhere.
4. Due to a lack of opportunities, many candidates are desperate .... the chance to gain experience and will work for very low wages.
5. It was only after looking again at the advert that I realised I hadn't paid attention .... the job description when writing my application letter.
6. This year I want to focus .... building up my skill set and making myself attractive to a new employer.
7. You should try to stay in touch .... your old colleagues once you've left. You never know when you may want to go back.
8. He didn't have any experience, so he relied .... his family connections to get him work in the industry.

2 Complete each of the sentences with an adjective from the box. In some cases more than one answer is possible.

constant	excellent	extensive	fierce	huge	powerful	specialist	vast

1. Malik's positive attitude and experience make him the best person for the job.
2. Almodóvar's film has made a(n) impact on audiences throughout the country.
3. This is a highly stressful job and we're under pressure to meet our targets.
4. The Paradise Hotel has a(n) reputation in this town.
5. I want to join the football team but there's extremely competition for places.
6. The increase in house prices has made it very difficult for young people to buy a first home.
7. Ivan's knowledge of the market is invaluable to our operations.
8. We need someone with language skills to work as part of our expert team.

Grammar

3 Circle the correct option in *italics* in each of these sentences.

1. It's by far the best film of the festival so far. I think it *must* / *could* easily win first prize.
2. The weather forecast isn't too good so the outing *might not* / *could not* take place tomorrow.
3. Jay had a sprained ankle so he *mightn't have* / *couldn't have* run very far!
4. It's just about *probable* / *possible* that the train has been delayed.
5. We're *highly* / *strongly* likely to see Fran at the concert tonight.
6. You look exhausted! You *mustn't* / *can't* have had a very relaxing holiday.
7. Why don't you call Marcos? He's *bound* / *liable* to have the information you need.

5 Events to remember

Hydro speeding

Hydrospeeding in Morzine, Switzerland, is not for everyone but the more adventurous will love it. Equipped with a float, helmet, flippers and wetsuit, you will float, plunge and scream your way down the River Dranse!

Interested? Click here ▶

York Skydiving Centre

Ready to **skydive?** We offer tandem skydiving, **parachuting** and **freefalling** at York Skydiving Centre.

Come and experience the exhilaration of jumping from an aeroplane at 4,000 metres at the closest full-time parachute centre to York.

Interested? Click here ▶

Wilderness Husky Safari

Quite simply, we love this and, judging by the feedback, so do our clients.

You will be provided with all the necessary equipment, including thermal clothing, and then taken to meet the dogs. You will be taught how to handle your team and the sled, and then you depart into Pallas-Yllästunturi National Park in Western Lapland, one of Europe's few remaining wilderness areas.

Interested? Click here ▶

Starting off

1. **You receive an email telling you that you have won an adventure activity competition. Which of these three activities would you choose?**
2. **Compare and discuss your choice of activity with other students.**
3. **Work in pairs. Discuss these quotations. What do they mean? Do you agree with them?**

   'Do one thing every day that scares you.' (Eleanor Roosevelt)
   'Distrust and caution are the parents of security.' (Benjamin Franklin)
4. **Work in small groups. Discuss these questions.**
   1. Would you consider yourself to be an adventurous person? Why? / Why not?
   2. What do you think the advantages and disadvantages of being adventurous are?
   3. Do you think doing adventurous activities is a good way of improving a person's character?

Listening Part 1

Exam advice

- Before you listen to the recording, read the questions and options and infer as much information as possible from them about the topic. This should help you to understand the recording when you hear it for the first time.
- The words you hear will usually be different from the words in the question, so listen for the meaning rather than for specific words.

1 **You will hear three people talking about dramatic past experiences. Before you listen, match 1–10 with a–j to make sentences which refer to frightening experiences.**

1	It seemed to go on …	**a**	nightmares about it.
2	Everything seemed to be happening …	**b**	in a flash.
3	It was as though time …	**c**	I'll never forget.
4	It was all over …	**d**	stood still.
5	Everything was …	**e**	as if it was yesterday.
6	I remember it …	**f**	jumped out of my skin.
7	It's an experience …	**g**	in slow motion.
8	I still have …	**h**	happening at once.
9	It's all …	**i**	forever.
10	I nearly …	**j**	a bit of a blur now.

2 **Now tell a partner about a dramatic experience that happened to you or someone you know. Use some of the sentences from Exercise 1 if possible.**

3 **Read the questions and options in Exercise 4. At this stage, think about what you can work out from the question and answers. Ask yourself questions like these:**

1 In Extract One, what might have happened to the farmer's tractor, do you think? From the options in question 2, do you think the story had a happy ending?

2 In Extract Two, what might have motivated the man to undertake such a challenge? Read carefully through question 4 and the options. Why might he have had those feelings?

3 In Extract Three, the woman is talking about learning to fly. What do you think might have happened with the other plane?

4 17 **Now listen and for questions 1–6, choose the answer (A, B or C) which fits the best according to what you hear.**

Extract One

You hear a man telling a friend a story that involves a local farmer and a runaway tractor.

1 During his explanation of what happened, the man reveals his
- **A** concern to reassure his friend about the outcome.
- **B** sympathy for the farmer and his situation.
- **C** regret for his lack of detailed information.

2 What is the woman's reaction to the story?
- **A** disbelief that such a thing could have happened
- **B** admiration for the farmer's heroic actions
- **C** relief at the limited extent of the injuries suffered

Extract Two

You hear part of an interview with a man who climbed up a very high mountain in order to ski down it again.

3 Why did the man think he could achieve his ambition?
- **A** He'd already coped with an extremely challenging climb in his area.
- **B** He'd been assured his skills were completely up to it.
- **C** He'd been able to study his target during another climb.

4 The man explains that before he set off, he
- **A** was reluctant to witness other people's reactions.
- **B** felt that a degree of nervousness was a useful thing to experience.
- **C** began to fear he might not be physically fit enough.

Extract Three

You hear a woman talking to a friend about her experiences flying a light plane.

5 What does the woman admit about her first solo flight?
- **A** She was fortunate to have been allowed to undertake it.
- **B** She was astonished at how well it went.
- **C** She was over-confident about her own capabilities.

6 When describing an incident with another plane, the woman
- **A** suggests that her calm attitude surprised her.
- **B** expresses doubts about whose fault it was.
- **C** wonders whether she'd handled it in the best possible way.

5 **How do you think you would have felt if you'd been involved in each of these situations? Would you have behaved in the same way as the people in each story, or differently? Which one do you think is the most frightening situation? Why?**

Vocabulary
Idiomatic language

1 Discuss these questions about words and phrases from Listening Part 1.

1 Are *flashbacks* pleasant or unpleasant? What kinds of events cause flashbacks?
2 What does *backed off* mean in this sentence?
… an absolute monster of a mountain, known to be deadly – other ski mountaineers had already *backed off*.
3 What does it mean if you *get off lightly* when something bad happens?
4 What do you do if you *jump the queue*?
5 If you were about to do something potentially risky with someone, how would you check they were *up to it*?

2 Discuss the meaning of the idiomatic expressions in these sentences, which all include parts of the body.

1 In the end all I could do was jump off and *keep my fingers crossed*.
2 I'm really scared of heights but if you *twist my arm*, I suppose I'll go climbing with you.
3 James may seem friendly but he's likely to *stab you in the back* when he has something to gain.
4 Lots of people use their work computers for personal reasons, but managers usually *turn a blind eye to it*.
5 He told me I'd won the lottery but I knew he was just *pulling my leg*.

Grammar
Verbs followed by *to* + infinitive or the *-ing* form

The COMPLETE grammar reference
▶ Scan the QR code, watch the video, then turn to page 168

1 Choose the correct verb form in these sentences from Listening Part 1. Compare your answers with a partner.

1 I somehow managed *to keep / keeping* my head.
2 I started taking on increasingly difficult climbs and descents, then considered *to tackle / tackling* the biggest climb close to home.
3 In fact, I didn't talk much about the trip to family and friends, to avoid *to see / seeing* how anxious I was making them.
4 What on earth was he intending *to do / doing*?
5 If I'd attempted *to land / landing*, I would've hit the other plane.

2 Are the verbs/phrases in the box followed by the *to* infinitive or the *-ing* form? Make two lists of verbs.

admit agree avoid can't afford can't help choose deny enjoy expect finish hope involve keep on mind offer pretend promise put off refuse resent risk suggest

3 Some verbs have different meanings depending on whether they are followed by the *-ing* form or the *to* infinitive. Discuss the differences in meaning between the verbs in *italics* in these pairs of sentences.

1 a I *remember* arriving home very late that evening.
b *Remember* to wake me up early tomorrow morning.
2 a I *tried* putting my foot on the brake, but the car simply went faster.
b I *tried* to hold on to the steering wheel, but it slipped out of my hand.
3 a I *forgot* to send Anabel a birthday card.
b I'll never *forget* opening that card on my birthday.
4 a I *regret* saying anything now.
b I *regret* to say that I won't be able to come to your wedding.
5 a Being a careful driver *means* paying attention to other road users.
b I'm sorry. I didn't *mean* to offend you.

4 The following sentences contain mistakes made by exam candidates. Correct the mistakes.

1 I suggest to take the overnight train to Vienna.
2 Part of my job is to help maintaining the machinery in good working order.
3 I would strongly recommend to sail rather than going by plane.
4 I never considered to do anything except being a teacher.
5 I told my department manager that I objected to work at weekends.
6 Despite not being able to afford going abroad, I am interested in diving in other countries.

5 Work in small groups. Discuss some of these topics.

- something I'm looking forward to
- things I'd like to give up
- things I put off doing
- jobs I'd refuse to do
- something I regret having done
- something I've tried to do, but failed

Reading and Use of English Part 4

Exam advice

- Use the word in CAPITALS without changing it.
- Count the words you have used to complete the gapped sentence. Contractions (*isn't*, *don't*, etc.) count as two words.
- Check that the words you have added are grammatically correct in the gapped sentence.
- Finally, read both sentences again to check that they have the same meaning.

1 Work in pairs. Look at this sample task for Reading and Use of English Part 4 and discuss the questions.

Tom and Jane were only able to see all the way to the mountains once the snow had stopped.

UNTIL

It was only after the snow had finally stopped that Tom and Jane were able to see all the way to the mountains

1. Does the completed second sentence have a similar meaning to the first sentence?
2. Is it grammatically correct?
3. Would this answer be correct in the exam?
4. If not, what should the answer be?

2 Read sentences 1–3 in Exercise 3 and discuss the clues under each one (you do not have clues in the exam).

3 Complete the second sentence in sentences 1–6 (sentences 1–3 have clues) with between three and six words, including the word given.

1 I don't think Ben ever intended to accompany me on the cycling trip.

INTENTION

I don't think Ben .... me on the cycling trip.

> Clue: Which preposition do you need after 'intention'? And what form should the following verb take?

2 I was expecting the route to be far harder than this.

TOUGH

The route isn't .... thought it would be.

> Clue: Which comparative structure uses the word 'as'? And what word is needed in order to include the idea of 'far harder' in your answer?

3 Hakim decided to start tackling climbs that increased in difficulty each time.

INCREASINGLY

Hakim decided to start taking .... climbs.

> Clue: What's a multi-word verb with 'take' that means 'to tackle'?

4 Maria was in a hurry to check out of the hostel, but immediately after leaving, she realised she'd forgotten her camera.

SOONER

Maria was in a hurry to check out of the hostel, but .... she realised she'd forgotten her camera.

5 'I should have turned back prior to the start of the storm,' said Aisha.

REGRETTED

Aisha .... the storm started.

6 Jiang was out of his tent earlier than usual this morning, so maybe the loud birdsong woke him up!

MIGHT

Jiang was out of his tent earlier than usual this morning, so he .... the loud birdsong!

4 Some questions in Part 4 test your knowledge of idiomatic expressions and multi-word verbs, such as those in *italics* below. Match the expressions in 1–6 with the meanings a–f.

1 After the meal we *settled up* and left.
2 It's *a wonder* that you got here at all.
3 *Keep an eye on* the weather.
4 I'm *tied up* until this afternoon.
5 Thank goodness, she's *on the mend*.
6 He's always trying to *pick a fight*.

a very busy
b start an argument
c get better
d surprising
e watch carefully
f pay what you owe

5 Write sentences of your own using the six expressions in Exercise 4.

Reading and Use of English Part 7

Exam info

- In Reading and Use of English Part 7, you read a text of 650–800 words from which six paragraphs have been removed and placed after the text. You have to decide which paragraph fits in each gap. There is one extra paragraph which does not fit into any of the gaps.
- This part tests your ability to understand the structure of a text, how an argument develops and how ideas link to one another.

1 Work in pairs. Discuss these questions.

1. Tell each other about an interesting place you have visited, either by bicycle or on foot. Where did you go? Did you encounter any problems during the trip?
2. Do you prefer visiting rural countryside areas, or more urban places?
3. Are there any wild areas, such as forests, deserts, lakes or mountains, that you would like to visit in the future? Why would you like to go there?

2 Read the exam task. Then follow the steps below to complete the task.

You are going to read an article about a cycle ride. Six paragraphs have been removed from the text. Choose from paragraphs A–G the one which fits each gap (1–6). There is one extra paragraph which you do not need to use.

Exam advice

- Read the main part of the text quickly to build up a picture in your mind of what is happening.
- Underline any reference words or phrases in the text which you think may refer to either the previous or the following missing paragraph. These may include pronouns, time expressions, conjunctions and other linking phrases.
- Read the missing paragraphs and look for subject matter and language links.
- Match any gaps and missing paragraphs that you are sure of first.

3 Discuss these questions in pairs or small groups. Give reasons for your answers.

1. If a friend suggested going on a long cycle ride lasting several days, would you be keen to accompany them?
2. If you had the chance to explore a cave, would you go inside? Why? / Why not?
3. What would it be like to cycle in snow, do you think?

Cycle ride

Despite being an enthusiastic amateur cyclist, I'd been stuck at home for a while due to bad weather. So once conditions improved slightly, I was keen to get out and explore. Early one morning, I hopped onto a train bound for the coast, with my bike. Once there, I jumped off, ready for an adventure – a visit to the beach, followed by a long cycle ride home again.

1 ....

Originally built to transport coal (by boat?) from the mines to the docks, it ran past a grey, decaying power station that had once formed part of a thriving industrial centre. As the path was so even, I was able to ride along at some speed – a good re-introduction to cycling.

2 ....

But once that level, more rural section of the route came to an end, so did the easy riding. My legs began to ache as, leaving the canal behind me, the path suddenly climbed upwards – I stopped briefly at the entrance to the last coal mine in the area, now closed but surrounded by new housing and leisure facilities. My route then took me up a narrow lane overlooking huge fields of crops to the top of a hill. From there I could make out the shapes of two great peaks on the horizon.

3 ....

Indeed, from my position high on the hilltop, I looked out across what would once have been an expanse of factory buildings, gradually being reclaimed by nature. By now, the temperature had dropped several degrees, and flakes of snow were beginning to drift towards me. However, I merely put on some extra clothes from my backpack, and carried on enjoying the view.

4 ....

That made the descent quite hazardous, so I was hoping I'd soon reach one landmark I was keen to visit – a deep cave. It was actually some way from the road and I had to get off my bike and push it, sliding around unsteadily down the path. By then there was quite a breeze blowing, and I was beginning to question whether the effort was worth it. However, eventually I spotted a sign confirming I'd arrived at the entrance to the cave.

5 ....

The fresh air seemed all the sweeter as I emerged to tackle the next leg of the journey – a traffic-free cycleway on a nearby bridge, over a steep valley. It offered a view of the massive drop below it that cyclists would find either totally thrilling or absolutely terrifying, depending on their attitude to heights – and I probably belonged to the latter category.

6 ....

The bridge was a stunning example of engineering. The cycling itself was nothing in comparison to the descent down the steep valley, following an old, winding railway line, and despite my initial misgivings about it, the bridge turned out to be one of the most memorable parts of my ride, before I finally cycled home.

A Beside me at the summit, a group of wind turbines at a small windfarm were spinning endlessly. They seemed to be keeping a silent watch over the deserted, chilly landscape below. I set off again, down what had become a slippery cycle path.

B I was beginning to realise that the many changes of scenery I'd been witnessing along the way were all part of the unique character of the area I was in, and could actually see evidence of that from where I was standing – industrial landscapes, vast open countryside and the mountains in the distance.

C I was relieved to get out of the wind, and began to prepare to explore further as I knew it went underground for several hundred metres. But the damp atmosphere put me off going too far in case I lost my way. I returned to the exit.

D However, the landscape I then entered further on, with grass and trees on either bank, couldn't have been more of a contrast to the run-down area I'd just passed. I heard a splash up ahead and watched as a swan took off from the surface of the water.

E The motivation to overcome that was the thought of the waterfalls and woodland, just waiting to be explored – if only I could steel myself to reach the other side, and onto the track that would take me to the bottom.

F In fact, on my map I'd spotted a few places similar to this that I wanted to visit. The only issue, as with this one, was that I hadn't properly checked their location in relation to my route, so I ended up making a detour for some distance.

G To ease myself back into cycling, I headed for the harbour, then onwards to a deserted sandy cove at the foot of some cliffs. I rested there before joining a cycleway going inland away from the shore, alongside a quiet canal.

Speaking Part 2

▶ **Page 207 Speaking bank**
Speaking Part 2

Exam advice

- Listen very carefully to the instructions you are given by the examiner, so that you answer the specific questions you are asked rather than talking vaguely or generally about the photos.
- You are asked two questions, which are printed on the page with the photos. Make sure you answer them both.
- Compare the photos in the context of the questions – don't make irrelevant comparisons. Spend about half your time comparing the photos and the other half answering the questions.
- You shouldn't try to describe the photos in detail.
- If you have time before starting to speak, spend a few seconds planning what you want to say.

1 **Answer these questions about Speaking Part 2. Then compare answers with a partner.**

1. How many photos is each candidate given by the examiner?
2. How many photos does each candidate have to talk about?
3. How long does each candidate have to speak for?
4. What happens after each candidate finishes talking about their photos?

2 **Read the examiner's instructions and look at the three photos. Write brief notes in answer to the questions below.**

'Here are your pictures. They show people doing dangerous jobs. I'd like you to compare two of the pictures and say what the dangers of the jobs might be and why people choose to do jobs like these.'

1. What are the three jobs? (If you don't know the job title, how can you describe it?)
2. In what way is each job dangerous?
3. What words might describe the sort of person who chooses each of these jobs?

3 **Work in pairs. Take turns to compare two of the three photos. You should each talk for about a minute. Time your partner, but don't interrupt while they are speaking.**

1

2

3

4 Listen to a student speaking about the photos and answer the questions. 18

1 Which two photos is he comparing?
2 Why does he use these words and phrases?
almost certainly, obviously, I suppose, It must be, he seems to be, probably, perhaps
3 What are the dangers of these jobs?
4 Why do people choose to do jobs like these?

5 Read the examiner's instructions and look at another set of three photos.

'Here are your pictures. They show people doing dangerous activities. I'd like you to compare two of the pictures and say what skills and personal qualities each activity involves, and how these activities make people feel.'

Before you start the task, consider the two questions you have to answer and decide which of these words/phrases are most suited to each question.

adrenaline rush concentration control courage daring excitement exhausted exhilarated fit proud satisfaction self-confident stamina steady nerves a sense of achievement strength terrified thrill

6 Work in pairs.

Student A: Choose photos 4 and 5.
Student B: Choose photo 4 or 5 and photo 6.
Now prepare what you are going to say about your two photos.

7 Take turns to speak for one minute about your photos. Incorporate some of the words and phrases from Exercises 4 and 5.

8 After your partner has spoken, ask them a question related to their photos.

4

5

6

Writing Part 2: A proposal

▶ **Page 202 Writing bank**
A proposal

Exam info

- In Writing Part 2, a proposal may be written for a superior, for example a boss or a teacher, or for a peer group, for example club members or work colleagues.
- You are expected to make suggestions, supported by factual information, to persuade your reader(s) that a certain course of action should be taken.
- A proposal should be clearly organised and may include headings.
- The style should be formal if you are writing for a superior, but may be more informal if your readers are colleagues or club members.

1 **Read the writing task and think about who you would choose as your local hero and make brief notes.**

You see this notice on the website for your town or city council.

> The Council is planning to honour a local hero connected with our area. The local hero can be someone well known or an ordinary citizen. He/She could still be alive or someone from history.
>
> Residents are invited to send in proposals identifying a deserving person, giving reasons for their choice and suggesting a suitable way in which this hero should be honoured.

Write your **proposal** in 220–260 words.

2 **Take turns to tell a partner about the person you would choose. Give at least two reasons for your choice. Answer your partner's questions about your nomination.**

3 **Read the example proposal without paying attention to the alternatives in *italics*. Answer these questions.**

1. How well does the writer know his local hero?
2. What did Helen Keane do?
3. What does the writer say she could have done instead?
4. What has Helen Keane shown people?
5. How does the writer suggest Helen Keane should be honoured?

In response to your invitation, I am writing to suggest a local hero who, [1]*in my opinion / I think*, deserves to be honoured. My hero is from my neighbourhood, but not someone I know personally.

My choice

My choice is Helen Keane, who, until recently, was just an ordinary working [2]*mother / mum*. One Friday last August, Helen was driving home, looking forward to a relaxing weekend. Suddenly, a lorry in front of her swerved and crashed into a bridge. Helen immediately stopped and went to help. When she [3]*got to / reached* the lorry, flames were coming from the cab but, without hesitating, Helen opened the door, pulled the unconscious driver out of his lorry and dragged him to safety. Helen herself [4]*was burnt / suffered burns* which kept her in hospital for two weeks.

Reasons for my choice

My main reason for choosing Helen is that she was an ordinary person going about her daily life. She could easily have [5]*gone off / driven home*, leaving the [6]*ambulance / emergency services* to deal with the accident. But instead, she stopped and saved a man's life. My other reason is that Helen has shown us all that special training is not necessarily required to help other people. Anyone can [7]*make a difference / help*.

Honouring my hero

If my choice of local hero is accepted, I suggest that the council should [8]*set up a fund / get together some money* which could be used for [9]*an annual prize / a prize every year* for someone who helps other people. This could be known as the Helen Keane Award.

I hope you will consider Helen Keane a suitable nominee who deserves to be honoured.

4 **Work in pairs.**

1. Read the proposal again and choose the most appropriate words and phrases in *italics*. Compare your choices with a partner and discuss the reasons for your choice.
2. Has the writer of this proposal covered all parts of the task appropriately?

5 **Underline the *-ing* forms in the sample proposal. Then work in pairs to discuss how these forms are used, choosing from this list.**

1. as an adjective
2. as part of a participle clause
3. as part of a main verb
4. after a preposition
5. as a noun

6 **Most of the following sentences contain one or more mistakes made by exam candidates. Correct all the mistakes you can find.**

1. We think we can solve this problem by opening the museum to the public and charge them an entrance fee.
2. In addition to keep up with their studies, university students often have to cope on very low budgets.
3. Within the next few weeks, a new sports centre will be opening in the north of the city.
4. A hardwork committee has recently put forward a set of interested proposals for improve the food and service be offered in the college canteen.
5. To bring in new health and safety regulations, the government has shown that it is concerned with improving the wellbeing of the whole population.
6. I knew my decision to work abroad would mean to leave my friends and family.
7. There's nothing preventing us to take action to ensure that the new facilities meet our needs.
8. The need to keep visited tourists happy means this is a scheme we should back.

7 **Which of the adjectives in this list could be used to describe a hero? (Some are negative and would not be appropriate.)**

cautious courageous creative enthusiastic exceptional extraordinary fearless generous greedy innovative inspiring kind narrow-minded passionate remarkable self-interested significant tireless

8 **Use the adverb form of some of the adjectives in Exercise 7 to complete these sentences. (In some cases, more than one answer is possible.)**

1. When the fire broke out, he acted quickly and ....
2. She works .... to promote green issues.
3. He was an .... gifted leader.
4. Her work has contributed .... to the welfare of our community.
5. He has been .... successful in achieving his aims.
6. He believes .... in what he is doing.
7. She treats everyone she meets .... and with respect.
8. He thinks .... about ways of solving social problems.
9. Residents have responded .... to the idea of naming the park after her.

9 **Now plan and write your proposal for the writing task in Exercise 1.**

- Use the example proposal in Exercise 3 as a model.
- If you cannot think of a real person to write about, your hero can be fictional.
- Write in an appropriately formal style.
- Try to include *-ing* forms to link ideas in your proposal.
- Use some interesting and appropriate adjectives and adverbs.

6 Creative pursuits

1

2

3

4

5

6

Starting off

1 Work in pairs. A class of art students were given an assignment to produce a self-portrait in a medium of their choice for display in an exhibition in their college. Look at these submissions to the assignment.

- Which picture gives you the strongest sense of the artist's personality?
- Which do you think shows the highest level of artistic ability? Why?

2 (19) Listen to three of the art students speaking about the self-portrait assignment they were given. Which of the images above is each student talking about?

Student A: ....

Student B: ....

Student C: ....

3 (19) Listen again and answer the questions. Which speaker (A, B or C) …

1 has produced pictures of other people in the past?

2 spent a long time working on their artwork?

3 often puts photo portraits on social media?

4 was influenced by their family's history?

5 used a different technique to their classmates?

6 was complimented by their classmates?

4 **Complete the sentences with the words and phrases from Exercise 3 in the box below. You don't need to use every word or phrase. Then, with a partner, ask and answer the questions.**

complimentary fiddle around fundamental
more often than not opted for self-assured
throwaway worked out well

1 How often do you .... with your photos to try and make them look better?
2 Does taking pictures of yourself make you feel more ....?
3 Are there any photos you've taken that your friends have been particularly .... about?
4 Do you feel that the photos you post on social media are just .... images, or do they have lasting value?
5 ...., is your first instinct to reach for your phone when you see something interesting?
6 Have you ever worked on something that you weren't sure about but which .... in the end?

Listening Part 2

Exam info

- In Listening Part 2, you will hear a talk, lecture or broadcast in which one person speaks.
- It lasts about three minutes.
- There are eight sentences with a gap to complete in each one.
- This part tests your ability to extract specific information and opinion from what you hear.

1 **Work in pairs. You will hear a talk by a professional artist called Akari, who is giving some career advice to students at an art college. Before you listen, discuss these questions.**

- Have you ever been to an art exhibition? If so, which one(s)? If not, would you like to go to one?
- How do you think artists might go about getting their work displayed at exhibitions?

2 **Look at question 1 below. Which type of word – noun, verb, adjective, adverb, singular, plural, etc. – will you need to write in the gap?**

Akari recommends helping out at **(1)** .... while still an undergraduate.

3 (20) **Listen to the first part of the talk. Make a note of all examples of that type of word you hear. Which gives you the correct answer to question 1? How do you know it is correct?**

4 (21) **Now listen to the whole talk. For questions 1–8, complete the sentences with a word or short phrase.**

Akari recommends helping out at **(1)** .... while still an undergraduate.

Akari advises new artists to ensure that their work caters to the **(2)** .... of the gallery curator or owner.

Akari believes that attending gallery **(3)** .... will bring useful networking opportunities.

Akari says that new artists should acknowledge their role as **(4)** .... when at another artist's exhibition.

Akari stresses the importance to new artists of **(5)** ...., despite any embarrassment they might feel.

According to Akari, having a distinct **(6)** .... increases the likelihood of being offered an exhibition.

When selling your art, Akari recommends accepting without complaint any **(7)** .... that a gallery sets.

Akari specifies fields such as **(8)** .... and teaching as other potential sources of income.

5 **Work in pairs. Discuss the questions.**

- What type of art would you consider having in your own home?
- How big would it be and where would you ideally like to put it?

Reading and Use of English Part 5

Exam advice

- First read the text quickly to get a general idea of what it is about.
- Read the first question and options A–D, and find the part of the text that they refer to, underlining any key words and phrases.
- Read each of the options A–D again carefully and choose the one which matches the meaning of the text.
- Deal with the other questions one by one in the same way.

1 **Work in pairs. Quickly read the article and then summarise the writer's views about photography apps and filters.**

2 **Read the first paragraph more closely and discuss your answers to the questions below.**
Does the writer:

a mention her feelings about how many photos exist of her mother's family holidays?
b offer any judgement on the process of amateur photography in the past?
c suggest how she feels about modern photo technology?
d make it clear how she feels about her grandparents' photography skills?

3 **Read the text again and <u>underline</u> where it answers the following four questions. Then work in pairs and summarise your answers in your own words.**

1 In the second paragraph, what point is being made about photography?
2 Which view does the writer put forward in the third paragraph?
3 In the fourth paragraph, what does the writer say is the main benefit of photo apps?
4 What is the writer's view of the latest photo apps in the fifth paragraph?

4 **For questions 1–6 below, choose the answer (A, B, C or D) which you think fits best according to the text.**

1 In the first paragraph, the writer is expressing her
A regret that so few photos exist of her mothers' family holidays.
B surprise at the lengthy process of amateur photography in the past.
C appreciation of the photo technology which is available today.
D amusement at her grandparents' limited photography skills.

2 In the second paragraph, what point is being made about photography?
A It is best left to the professionals.
B It reinforces a particular set of cultural stereotypes.
C It relies entirely on the possession of specialist equipment.
D It is a medium that has undergone a notable transformation.

3 In the third paragraph, the writer shows that she
A recognises how photo apps do not necessarily deliver the simplicity they claim.
B believes it is dishonest for experienced photographers to use apps and filters.
C approves of the widespread recognition of humorous photos found on the internet.
D doubts whether taking a photography course is likely to produce expert results.

4 In the fourth paragraph, the writer says that the main benefit of photo apps is that they
A inspire users to document their routines for others' enjoyment.
B allow users to deepen the connections they feel towards certain people.
C provide users with an opportunity to promote their online businesses.
D encourage users to be alert to the dangers of sharing personal details.

5 On the subject of the latest photo apps, the writer makes clear her view that
A any negative effects can be blamed on the greed of the designers.
B the improvements made to image quality have been remarkable.
C the pleasure she gains from them is not necessarily felt in every user.
D they are largely responsible for the problems of self-worth in today's society.

6 In the final paragraph, the writer suggests that people who use photo apps today
A are becoming entirely dependent on them as time passes.
B often do so to publicise idealistic opinions.
C tend to have an overly obsessive type of personality.
D are taking advantage of a historic societal development.

The camera never lies

Emily Colson takes a personal look at the rise of photo apps and filters.

My mum has often told me how, when she was a child and on a family holiday, my grandparents were perfectly satisfied to come home with a mere twenty-eight photos of the entire week, each one taken on a disposable plastic camera. Once home, this would be sent off in the post for the film to be developed. A full week later the pictures would eventually arrive through their letterbox, at which point they would excitedly flick through them, only for the inevitable anti-climax soon to follow, when everyone came to the agreement that only three or four were genuinely worth keeping. This whole experience is so far outside of my own frame of reference as to be utterly unthinkable – how vastly improved would my family's lives have been, given the chance to retake, filter and edit their pictures?

Photography – by which I'm referring to the sophisticated images taken by someone who genuinely knows what they're doing, rather than some blurred smudges of a beach taken by my grandad – has historically had a reputation for being a somewhat exclusive hobby. Not so much in the intense practice and expertise required to shoot that perfect shot, but more in the expense of obtaining the necessary, top-level gear: the cameras, lenses, flashes and rolls of film that always used to shut the average novice out. Yet, after manufacturers found they were able to bring to market the self-focusing digital cameras which require little technical know-how to operate, any remaining barriers began to be broken down, ultimately leading us to the photo apps that inhabit billions of smartphones today.

The unique selling point of photo apps and filters is that novices can quickly come up with a collection of stunning shots without having to spend serious amounts of time and effort carefully learning how to skilfully frame, capture and edit their work. (That said, I've probably used up as many long hours messing around with equipment as I could have spent attending a full-time photography course, so whether they are as easy to use as advertised is certainly questionable.) Of course, photo apps have also been adopted by the more skilled and knowledgeable enthusiasts who see filters as correction tools for their already accomplished photographs, but by and large, the most popular images online are those posted by rank amateurs who don't take their creations too seriously.

These days, I and millions of others like me are firm in our conviction that life is so much more with our photo apps. For both friends and unknown followers, we compile and share the images that populate our lives online; we detail, discuss and display. Doing so has meant both gaining self-confidence in the creation of our own individual brands, and cementing the emotional bonds we have with our friends, whose Instagram feeds we spend so much time on. In being more willing than ever to communicate aspects of our character with such vitality, colour and playfulness, perhaps we unknowingly reveal more about ourselves and our inner thoughts than we had intended.

Despite this, critics have not been slow to argue that, for every user of the latest photo apps as a fun addition to their social circle, there is another who takes things to the opposite extreme. App designers, for example, who supposedly make millions by promoting a laser-focused fixation on vanity. Or, indeed, anyone creating these hyper-real versions of themselves, who is supposedly contributing to our culture's obsession with image, betraying their true selves with face-altering filters, the function of which is to make teeth appear whiter, jawlines sharper, and to somehow remove imperfections. Or so the claim goes. Of course, I willingly accept that, while seeing celebrities' snaps next to my own on Instagram gives me an immense buzz of excitement, that might very well, in others, provide stimulation for negative self-comparison. Yet I would urge caution in anyone seeking to blame photo apps for all of society's ills.

We have witnessed the great democratisation of photography. In 2010, the year of its launch, Instagram saw over 150 million photos uploaded. This has since risen to around 100 million snaps a day. And that's just one app; our apparent need to retake, edit and filter is unlikely to fade any time soon. With any photo we take, armed with our favourite app and a preference for a particular style, it is clear that we find great difficulty in resisting the urge to interfere with it, edging hopefully towards our own, very personal, visual interpretation of perfection.

Grammar
Avoiding repetition

The COMPLETE grammar reference
▶ Scan the QR code, watch the video, then turn to page 170

1 Look at these extracts from Reading and Use of English Part 5 and write one word in each gap. Then check your answers by looking back at the text.

1 ... my grandparents were perfectly satisfied to come home with a mere twenty-eight photos of the entire week, each .... taken on a disposable plastic camera. Once home, ... would be sent off in the post for the film to be developed. (para 1)

2 ... the most popular images online are .... posted by rank amateurs who don't take their creations too seriously. (para 3)

3 ... we compile and share the images that populate our lives online; we detail, discuss and display. Doing .... has meant both gaining self-confidence in the creation of our own individual brands, and ... (para 4)

4 ... for every user of the latest photo apps as a fun addition to their social circle, there is .... who takes things to the opposite extreme. (para 5)

5 ... betraying their true selves with face-altering filters, the function of .... is to make teeth appear whiter, jawlines sharper, and to somehow remove imperfections. Or .... the claim goes. (para 5)

6 Of course, I willingly accept that, while seeing celebrities' snaps next to my own on Instagram gives me an immense buzz of excitement, ... might very well, in others, provide stimulation for negative self-comparison. (para 5)

2 Exam candidates often make mistakes when using pronouns and determiners. Correct the mistake in each of these sentences. In some cases, there is more than one possible answer.

1 I wasn't happy about my hotel room. I said it to the receptionist but she didn't do anything about it.

2 There are several umbrellas in the stand in the hall. I'd advise you to take it if you're going for a walk.

3 I'd always wanted a smartphone and when I was given it as a birthday present, I thought it was wonderful.

4 Some of the machines broke down quite often, but when things like these happened we just called a technician.

5 The lecturers will give you a detailed explanation of the subject. You may not be able to understand all, but you should be able to get a general idea.

6 There was a long queue at the ice cream parlour because most of the children wanted it.

7 We're looking for a new accountant and it is why I'm writing to you.

8 You should aim to arrive at any time that's convenient for yourself.

3 Rewrite the following to reduce the number of words and avoid repetition.

1 I enjoy learning about science as much as art. Science and art are equally interesting to me.

I enjoy learning about science as much as art. Both are equally interesting to me.

2 Fewer and fewer people listen to classical music these days. The fact that fewer and fewer people listen to classical music these days is a shame, as classical music offers something for everyone.

3 I spend a fair amount of my free time listening to podcasts. The podcasts I enjoy most are the podcasts about gaming and sports.

4 I'm hoping to get a ticket at some point for a show by my favourite artist/musician. Buying a ticket for a show by my favourite artist/musician would make me so happy.

5 Although I enjoy watching my favourite sports team, there are other sports teams that are better than the sports team I support.

6 I don't like spending a lot of money on clothes or trainers, so I tend to buy second-hand clothes or trainers I find in online stores.

7 I've never learnt how to play a musical instrument really well, and I really wish I had learnt to play a musical instrument really well.

8 Whenever I feel strongly about a particular topic or idea, I say I feel strongly about a particular topic or idea.

9 I don't like staying up late. If I had to stay up late, I would stay up late, but I prefer to go to bed early if I can go to bed early.

10 Whenever I meet someone new, I always seem to forget the person's name when I stop talking to the person, even if the person has mentioned the name to me three times.

4 Discuss with a partner whether you agree or disagree with statements 1–10 from Exercise 3.

Vocabulary
Adjective–noun collocations (2)

1 **Look at this sentence from Listening Part 2.**

Spend *a fair amount* of time each day on their social media pages.

One of the adjectives below cannot be used with the word *amount* to form a collocation. Which one?

fair large huge big small limited

2 **Candidates often make the mistake of using *big* with the nouns in bold in sentences 1–10. Which of the adjectives in the box can be used to form collocations with each noun? (In all cases several answers are possible.)**

amazing considerable endless good great heavy high huge large loud satisfactory terrible tremendous valuable wide

1 Pascual is very busy: he spends a(n) .... **amount** of time studying.
2 Our local supermarket sells a(n) .... **range** of coffees, so you should find what you're looking for.
3 I found it difficult to concentrate on the conversation because of the .... **noise** coming from the neighbours' television.
4 Your decision about whether to go to art school or study economics is of .... **importance**, so think it over carefully.
5 Magda was very late for the meeting because of the .... **traffic** on the motorway.
6 Meeting such a distinguished artist was a(n) .... **experience** and quite unforgettable.
7 Quite a(n) .... **percentage** of our students go on to become professional artists – in the region of 60%.
8 I think Jaroslaw has made .... **progress** with his drawing and is showing real talent.
9 Colin is a teacher with .... **experience** of teaching both adults and children.
10 The paintings in this gallery show a(n) .... **variety** of different styles.

3 **Work in pairs. Where there was more than one possibility in Exercise 2, do the different alternatives change the meaning of the sentence? If so, how?**

Reading and Use of English Part 2

Exam advice

- Read the text quite quickly to get a general idea of what it is about.
- Look at the words before and after the gap and decide what type of word you need (an article, pronoun, preposition, etc.).
- Check whether the word you need refers to some other part of the text.

1 **You will read a text about live and recorded music. Read the text quite quickly to get a general understanding. Then decide what type of word you will need to fill each gap (1–8).**

2 **For questions 1–8, read the text again and think of the word which best fits each gap. Use only one word in each gap.**

Live Is Life?

According to the best minds **(0)** ....*in*........ science, live music has enormously positive effects on a person's health. The exact neurological reason why is still **(1)** .... investigation but, essentially, it has something to **(2)** .... with the production of dopamine, and makes us feel alive. Who hasn't been at a gig or in a club and felt that primal, physical reaction to the bass coming through the floor and up into your chest? You have no option **(3)** .... to dance, to feel the excitement that comes by **(4)** .... of love for the music; for *all* live music.

It isn't for everyone, however. Amplified live music is loud, and venues' acoustics rarely bring **(5)** .... the best in the music; the sports arenas where top-selling artists perform are, to put it politely, **(6)** .... from ideal for anyone hoping to hear their idol's best performance. But, let's be honest, anyone who complains, **(7)** .... chosen to buy a ticket for a boisterous live show, should keep their protests to **(8)** .... Leave 'live' to the rest of us.

3 **Use these clues to check your answers to Exercise 2.**

1 a preposition which is used to mean 'in the process of'
2 a word which completes a fixed phrase meaning 'related to something but not in a way you understand completely'
3 part of a phrase used to say that there is no possibility of doing anything else
4 a word which completes a phrase that can mean 'through' or 'as a form of'
5 part of a multi-word verb which means 'produce a particular quality'
6 a preposition which completes a phrase that means 'certainly not'
7 an auxiliary that gives grammatical meaning to the main verb 'choose'
8 a pronoun used to refer back to the subject

4 **Work in small groups. Imagine you are arranging a one-day programme of events in your town. Put together a programme that you think might attract a large number of visitors (there is no limit to your budget).**

Suggestions to include

- musicians/bands
- outdoor/indoor exhibitions
- classes or tuition
- poetry/book readings
- food/drink options

5 **Compare your programme with that of another group. Combine the ideas of both groups and decide on the best programme for the day.**

6 **Work in pairs. Look at the pictures and the title of the article in Exercise 7. What ideas do you think the article will contain?**

7 **Read the text quickly and compare your predictions from Exercise 6 to what you read. Don't worry about the gaps for now.**

THE TIMELESS appeal of the selfie

While we often claim selfies as a uniquely modern phenomenon, the fact **(0)** .... is .... they aren't exactly new. Artists have, in one way or **(1)** .... , always been experts at using themselves as the main subject of their work, **(2)** .... through paint, pencil, or photography. Many critics argue that **(3)** .... was during the Renaissance that self-portraiture hit a high point, both through the application **(4)** .... ever more realistic techniques and brush strokes, and in how widespread its popularity became.

Fast forward to today and this popularity has extended into a stunning array of self-portraiture, one example of **(5)** .... is the 'mirror selfie', where the subject snaps themselves looking into a mirror. To create the impression of intimacy, this is often done in bedrooms or bathrooms, **(6)** .... the light can often make it difficult to create beautiful shots. Hence, many people are open **(7)** .... a little dishonesty: their picture is taken not in front of a mirror **(8)** .... by another photographer, or by a spare handset, the subject covering their face with a smartphone in a fake 'mirror selfie' pose.

8 **For questions 1–8, read the text and think of the word which best fits each gap. Use only one word in each gap.**

9 **Are selfies art or just a bit of fun? Discuss in small groups.**

Speaking Part 3

Page 211 Speaking bank
Speaking Part 3

1 (22) **Work in pairs. Read the examiner's instruction below and look at the task. Then listen to extracts from two pairs of students doing the task and tick the correct box for each question.**

'Now I'd like you to talk about something together for about two minutes. Here are some factors which might affect people's enjoyment of a film and a question for you to discuss. First, you have some time to look at the task.

Now, talk to each other about how these factors might affect people's enjoyment of a film and why.'

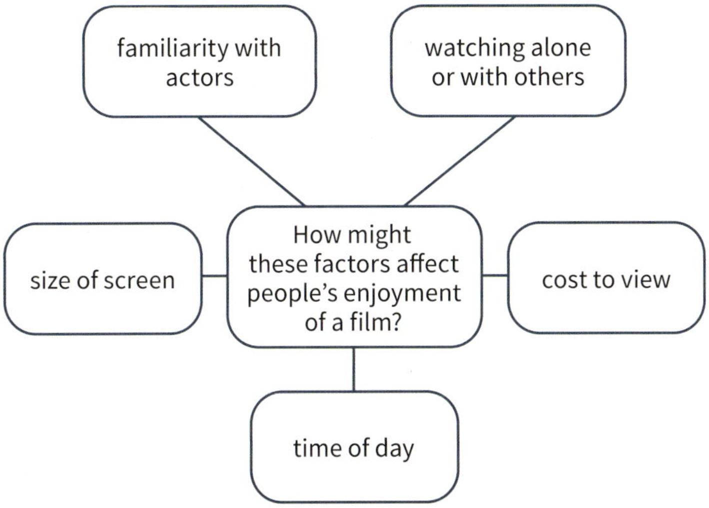

Which pair (Pair A, Pair B or both) …	A	B
1 doesn't start working on the task immediately?	☐	☐
2 deals with each prompt on the task sheet in order?	☐	☐
3 spends a lot of time on one or two prompts, so probably won't have time for all of them?	☐	☐
4 relates the prompts to themselves personally?	☐	☐
5 shows most interest in their partner's reactions to the prompts?	☐	☐

Exam advice

- When you discuss the first part of the task, you needn't talk about all of the options but you should make suggestions, ask your partner's opinion, listen carefully to what your partner says and respond to their ideas in order to have a natural conversation or discussion.
- When you discuss the second part of the task, it isn't necessary to reach agreement, but you should:
  - discuss which option(s) to choose and give reasons for these choice(s)
  - try to reach a decision.

2 **Work in pairs. Answer the questions.**

1 Which pair do you think deals with the task better? Why?
2 How do you think each pair could improve their performance?

3 **You will get higher marks in the exam if you use advanced vocabulary appropriately when speaking. Work in pairs. In what context did the candidates use each of these phrases? (You need not remember the exact words.)**

1 I'm hardly what you'd call
2 you'll often find me
3 the high point of my week
4 I don't think there's anything inherently wrong
5 get absorbed in
6 get distracted
7 get more involved
8 it's pretty expensive

4 **Work in pairs. Do the task in Exercise 1, following the examiner's instructions. Try to use some phrases from Exercise 3.**

5 **Work in pairs. Look at the examiner's instruction for the second part of Speaking Part 3 and the list of strategies below. Then decide together which strategies would be good for this part of the task. Write *Yes* or *No* for each strategy and give a reason.**

'Now you have about a minute to decide which factor has the greatest influence over people's enjoyment of a film.'

Strategies

1 Go over each of the options in turn again.

No. There isn't time – you need to reach a decision in one minute.

2 Suggest an option, give a reason and ask your partner's opinion.

3 Agree with the first option your partner suggests.

4 Disagree with the first option your partner suggests, give a reason, then suggest another option and give a reason.

5 Agree with the first option your partner suggests but then suggest an alternative and give a reason.

6 Disagree with everything your partner says in order to fill the time.

6 **Listen to Lukas and Anna doing the second part of the task. Which strategies do they use?**

23

7 **Work in pairs. Follow the examiner's instruction in Exercise 5, using one or two of the strategies from Exercise 5.**

8 **Work in pairs. Read the examiner's instruction below and do the first part of the Speaking task.**

'Now I'd like you to talk about something together for about two minutes. Here are some creative or artistic activities which young people can do a course in and a question for you to discuss. Talk to each other about what attracts young people to taking a course in these activities.'

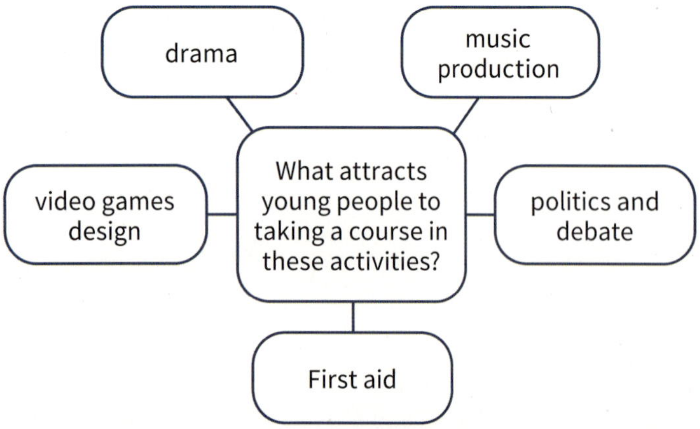

9 **Read the examiner's next instruction and do the second part of the Speaking task.**

'Now you have a minute to decide which activity it is most beneficial for young people to study at school.'

Writing Part 2: A review

▶ **Page 198 Writing bank**
A review

- Writing a review tests your ability to describe and give your opinions about something you have experienced (e.g. a book, a film, a café or restaurant, a language course) and to tell your readers whether or not you recommend it. You may be asked to compare two things of the same type in your review.
- When writing a review:
  - consider what information will be of interest to your readers (e.g. where is the language course? What are the teachers like? Is it good value for money?)
  - express your opinions of the different elements you decide to include in your review, so that your readers have a clear idea whether or not you are recommending what you are reviewing.

Exam info

1 **Read the writing task below and underline the key points you must include.**

You have seen this announcement on an entertainment blog.

From time to time, everyone watches a film that they were expecting not to like, only to end up loving it. With which film did this happen to you? Write us a review of the film explaining how the reality differed from your expectations of it and saying who you would recommend it to.

Write your **review**.

2 **Work in pairs. Decide which of these elements you should include in your review.**

a biographical information about the lead actors
b a summary of the whole plot
c a general synopsis of the plot and characters and why they appeal to you
d a description of the type of film, the setting and what it's about
e references to aspects of the film you particularly like
f recommendation(s) and supporting reasons for your readers
g a criticism of things you didn't like
h suggestions for other films that you think your readers would enjoy

3 **Read the review of *Banked* without paying attention to the *highlighting*. Complete the paragraph plan for this review.**

Plan

Para 1: 'scene-setting', establishing the writer as a keen cinema-goer

Para 2: ....

Para 3: ....

Para 4: ....

4 **Does the review give you a clear idea of what *Banked* is about? Having read the review, do you think you would enjoy the film? Why? / Why not?**

It was while watching the trailer for Banked that I [1]*resolved / promised* never to go near it. 'I can't stand **juvenile** road-trip comedies like this,' I said to my friend, sitting next to me in the cinema as we waited earnestly for the start of the serious, **bleak** drama we'd gladly paid to see.

But something about that trailer stayed with me, and when I gave Banked a try, I realised how wrong I'd been. Yes, it's a road-trip comedy, but not in the typical, [2]*cliché-ridden / predictable* sense. It tells the story of Margot, a twenty-something food blogger finding her way in the big city, and her long-lost brother, Mitchell, who's left his dead-end rural job to convince her to accompany him across the country, hoping to claim their [3]*large / sizeable* inheritance after the death of a distant, elderly relative.

We follow their [4]*interesting / absorbing* journey, set against the [5]*vivid / colourful* backdrop of the routes they follow. Both lead actors shine – Ariana Ducey gives her most **charismatic** performance yet, and Collins West is [6]*brilliant / dazzling* as Mitchell. The plot develops in [7]*riveting / fascinating* fashion, and their relationship is [8]*utterly / completely* compelling throughout. It was all I could do to stop myself from bursting into tears when, in the **emotional** final scene, they share a [9]*tender / loving* embrace.

As you might expect, the script is packed with [10]*clever / snappy* dialogue, but it's not often that you come across a comedy whose storyline is so **intricate**. This only added to my appreciation of the screenwriter's craft, and I have no doubt that anyone, young or old, would feel the same. While the tone of the film may be **light-hearted** in so many ways, it is one that will [11]*undoubtedly / definitely* stay with you for some time.

5 **You will score higher marks in the exam if you use a range of appropriate advanced vocabulary. Read the review again, choosing the adjectives and adverbs in *italics* which are more likely to gain credit from the examiner.**

6 **In the questions below, the words in bold have been taken from the review of *Banked*. Discuss with a partner how the meaning would change if one of the three other words were used instead (e.g. would you use them to express a positive or a negative opinion?)**

1 One thing that is particularly noteworthy is just how **intricate** the plot is.
- **A** complicated
- **B** far-fetched
- **C** complex

2 It may or may not surprise you to learn that this **juvenile** comedy was once an Academy Award nominee.
- **A** mindless
- **B** hilarious
- **C** wacky

3 The film takes a **light-hearted** look at life in France in the mid-20th century.
- **A** nostalgic
- **B** sentimental
- **C** cheery

4 Jamelia Tandy gives a **charismatic** performance as the protagonist.
- **A** compelling
- **B** implausible
- **C** charming

5 There can be no argument that, above all, this is a **bleak** drama.
- **A** gloomy
- **B** depressing
- **C** uplifting

6 There are so many **emotional** moments in the film that it is impossible to mention them all.
- **A** melodramatic
- **B** touching
- **C** heart-breaking

7 **Work in pairs. Which film could each of you write about? Tell each other a little about**

- the type of film, the setting and what it's about
- the plot and characters
- what you particularly liked – why you would recommend it.

8 **Plan and write your own answer in 220–260 words to the task in Exercise 1.**

5 Vocabulary and grammar review

Vocabulary

1 Read the sentences and choose the option (A, B, C or D) which best fits each gap.

1 No, don't worry. You're not in trouble. I was just .... your leg about the boss being angry.
A grabbing **B** pulling **C** making **D** joking

2 Yes, they let me .... the queue because they could see my injury was pretty bad.
A leap **B** cross **C** jump **D** pass

3 OK, you've .... my arm. Let's all go to Las Vegas for our holiday.
A sprained **B** turned **C** pulled **D** twisted

4 Although I wasn't registered at college, the professor .... a blind eye to my attendance at his lecture.
A turned **B** closed **C** kept **D** ignored

5 She thought he was her best friend, but then he .... her in the back and took all the money.
A cut **B** kicked **C** stabbed **D** speared

Grammar

2 Complete the second sentence so that it has a similar meaning to the first sentence, using the word given. Do not change this word. Use three to six words including the word given.

1 I can't wait to start my new job.
FORWARD
I'm really .... my new job.

2 Thank goodness we avoided the floods.
LUCKY
We .... the floods.

3 I wish I hadn't phoned my sister.
REGRET
I .... call to my sister.

4 We can't buy a new car – we don't have enough money.
AFFORD
We .... a new car.

5 He says he's never seen her before.
DENIES
He .... her before.

6 We paid our hotel bill when we checked out.
SETTLED
It wasn't until .... our hotel bill.

3 Complete these texts with the infinitive, *to* infinitive or *-ing* form of the verbs in brackets. One verb is in the passive.

Three of the people trapped on the third floor managed 1 .... (climb) out onto the roof of the hotel, where they jumped to safety. The other two refused 2 .... (leave) their room and waited 3 .... (rescue). The manager admitted 4 .... (wait) for 20 minutes before 5 .... (phone) the emergency services. He claimed that he had attempted 6 .... (put out) the fire himself before 7 .... (realise) the seriousness of the situation. He apologised to his colleagues for 8 .... (put) their lives at risk.

The climbers refused 9 .... (take) the weather forecast seriously and ended up 10 .... (get) lost when it started 11 .... (snow). Despite this, they went on 12 .... (climb), but were eventually forced 13 .... (admit) defeat. It was then that they tried 14 .... (phone) mountain rescue 15 .... (ask) for help. However, because there was no phone signal on the mountain, they could not 16 .... (contact) the team and spent the night on the mountain, 17 .... (regret) their decision 18 .... (ignore) the forecast.

Vocabulary and grammar review 6

Vocabulary

1 In each of the sentences below, cross out the adjective in *italics* which does not collocate with the noun in bold.

1. A *high* / *big* / *significant* **percentage** of accident victims coming to hospital have been doing DIY at home.
2. For me, visiting Paris is always a *great* / *wide* / *tremendous* **experience** – it really is my favourite city.
3. Jamal attaches *considerable* / *great* / *large* **importance** to the way he dresses, so he always gets up extra early.
4. I'm leaving for work early tomorrow to try to avoid the *deep* / *heavy* / *terrible* **traffic** on my route.
5. Martina is showing a lot of promise and she's made *high* / *considerable* / *satisfactory* **progress** with her English this term.
6. My brother has spent a *huge* / *heavy* / *considerable* **amount** of money renovating an old farmhouse – I don't know how he can afford it.
7. They're doing road works in the street and the **noise** is so *loud* / *terrible* / *big* that I can hardly hear myself think!
8. One of the attractions of this job is the *endless* / *high* / *wide* **variety** of different tasks I have to perform.

Grammar

2 Rewrite the following sentences in order to avoid repetition of words and phrases.

1. 'Do you think you'll get a holiday in July?' 'I hope I get a holiday in July!'
   'Do you think you'll get a holiday in July?' 'I hope so!'
2. When a child feels unhappy, the child will ask for the child's mother more often than the child will ask for the child's father.
3. Gustav bought a large house by the sea about ten years ago. Buying a large house by the sea turned out to be a good investment.
4. Leonardo lived in Canada as a child. The fact that he lived in Canada is the reason why he speaks such fluent English.
5. Svetlana spent several months trying to decide which car to buy and she finally bought a car last week.
6. Matthew likes reading novels. Matthew especially likes reading romantic novels.
7. Violeta bought apples in the market. Violeta put some of the apples in the fruit bowl. Violeta used the other apples to make an apple pie.
8. Narayan has had two jobs. The two jobs were in a bank. Unfortunately, the two jobs were not well paid.
9. There are five official languages in Spain and Manolo speaks all of the five official languages of Spain.
10. Pete had never spoken to Ann, although Pete had often wanted to speak to Ann.

3 Correct the mistake in each sentence

1. I watched the film. I didn't understand all, but what I did understand was interesting.
2. Despite finding the twins at the party, she forgot to give the book to both of them.
3. Sorry. We're always getting lost. When things like these happen, we normally find our way back.
4. Do it whenever you like. It's something you can do at a time that's convenient for yourself.
5. If you'd like a piece of cake, just take it on your way out.
6. We're still waiting for our meal. Maybe we should say it to the waiter.
7. I'm really annoyed at me. I saw my bank card on the table as I was leaving and forgot to pick it up.
8. I really like ice cream, but then again, everyone likes.

7 In your free time

Starting off

1 What do you enjoy doing in your free time? Look at the photos and choose which of these types of activities you like doing or would like to try.
Then compare your preferences with other students. Say what it is that you particularly enjoy about the activities you've chosen, or why you would like to try them. Also, think about why people might take up activities like these.

2 Discuss these questions.

1 What kind of leisure activities do you do that weren't available to your parents' generation? How did people use to spend their leisure time when they were young? Do you think you have more or less free time than your parents had when they were younger?

2 Do you combine work or study with leisure? For example, do you listen to music, text friends or spend time on social networking sites while you are working or studying?

Listening Part 4

Exam advice

- Before you listen, read both tasks, underlining the key ideas in each option.
- Listen for words and phrases which mean the same as the key ideas you have underlined. Listen for the answers to both tasks. You may hear the answer to Task Two before the answer to Task One.
- Wait until each speaker has finished talking before you choose your answer.

1 24 **You are going to hear nine extracts of music. Listen and match each with one of the types of music in the box. Which of these types of music do you enjoy listening to?**

classical dance music disco folk
jazz Latin pop rap rock

2 **How, when and where do you listen to music? Have you ever been to a live concert? If not, which band or artist would you most like to see live?**

3 **In Part 4, you have to choose which option most closely matches what each speaker says. You may also hear the speaker make reference to other options – but only one will be correct. Look at the transcript of a woman talking about listening to an album for the first time and the options below. Which option most closely matches what she says? The other three are distractors. Why are they wrong?**

On the recommendation of a friend, I'd downloaded an album by a solo female singer that I wasn't really familiar with. To be honest, I'd kind of categorised her as being more my dad's era than mine. He reckoned she'd been really innovative when she first started making albums, and that her appeal endured to this day. His tastes in music are sometimes quite at odds with mine, though, so I wasn't entirely sure what I was in for. Anyway, I remember eventually walking along listening to it – and then having to sit down. I was overwhelmed by the music – everything from her swooping voice through to the jazz piano. Breathtaking!

A It completely disproved what I'd been told about it.
B It was clear why it had been so ground-breaking.
C It greatly exceeded my expectations.
D It made me regret my negative attitude.

4 **You will hear five short extracts in which people are talking about the experience of going to a concert to listen to a band. Before you listen, read through Tasks One and Two. Discuss the options with a partner to make sure you clearly understand them.**

5 25 **Listen to the five speakers and do Tasks One and Two.**

TASK ONE

For questions **1–5**, choose from the list **(A–H)** what each speaker says about their impression of the band.

A They were stunningly dressed.
B They appeared uncomfortable on stage.
C They communicated well with the audience.
D They looked rather ordinary.
E They filled the entire stage.
F They created a lively party atmosphere.
G They didn't perform well to begin with.
H They were full of energy and confidence.

Speaker 1	1
Speaker 2	2
Speaker 3	3
Speaker 4	4
Speaker 5	5

TASK TWO

For questions **6–10**, choose from the list **(A-H)** what each speaker says they experienced during the concert.

A the enjoyment of great lyrics
B a desire to escape from everyday life
C a glimpse into someone else's life
D a determination to master an instrument
E the inspiration to be musically creative
F an appreciation of a top-quality performance
G an insight into the feelings music can express
H an admiration of the musicians' playing skills

Speaker 1	6
Speaker 2	7
Speaker 3	8
Speaker 4	9
Speaker 5	10

6 **Use the words and phrases in the box below to complete the questions.**

backing group blown away gigs musician
lively atmosphere lyrics master warm-up band

1 Do you enjoy going to .... ? Why? / Why not?
2 Who, in your opinion, is the greatest .... in your country?
3 What do you think creates a .... at a party?
4 How important do you think the .... are to the overall success of the song?
5 Why might a .... perform before the main act comes on stage?
6 When was the last time you were .... by a piece of music or a live event?
7 Would you prefer to be a famous artist or part of the .... ? Why?
8 Some people believe it takes 10,000 hours to .... a new skill, like learning an instrument. Do you agree?

Vocabulary
Complex prepositions

1 **Some prepositions can form part of a phrase, for example:**

The band I saw wasn't well known – *far from it*, in fact …
… *because of* my friend's great obsession with the band.

Complete these sentences with the correct prepositions.

1 Last night's concert was performed .... aid .... a charitable trust.
2 These remarkable sounds were produced .... means .... magnetic waves.
3 She's bought an electric guitar .... place .... her old acoustic one.
4 We couldn't sleep .... account .... the bright light outside our window.
5 .... behalf .... the whole family, I'd like to thank you for being with us today.
6 I am writing to you .... regard .... your recent enquiry.
7 His grandfather played music very much .... keeping .... folk traditions.
8 We worked for five hours a day .... exchange .... meals and accommodation.

2 **Match each three-word phrase from Exercise 1 with the correct meaning (a–h).**

a	because of	**e**	in return for
b	fitting appropriately with	**f**	representing
c	on the subject of	**g**	as a substitute for
d	in order to help	**h**	by using

3 **Look at the following statements. Correct any mistakes with prepositions in each sentence.**

1 Well-known bands have a responsibility to become involved in social issues by account of the amount of influence they have.
2 Most music fans would probably be willing to volunteer to work on the festival site for free in exchange of tickets.
3 It must be helpful for a band when one of its members always speaks from behalf of the rest of the band.
4 It can be disappointing if a different band performs in place from the one booked at a concert.
5 If possible, it's good to go to a concert that's held for aid of a charity, by raising money.

4 **Do you agree or disagree with each statement? Discuss each one with your partner.**

Reading and Use of English Part 7

Exam advice

- First, read the main body of the text carefully to familiarise yourself with the contents of each paragraph and how the whole text is structured.
- Then read each of the missing paragraphs one by one. Pay close attention to the content and place six of the paragraphs in a gap after you have read it.

1 **Work in pairs. You are going to read an article about young film actors.**

1 How many examples of young film actors can you think of? Which films have they starred in? If you saw the films, did you enjoy them?
2 What might be the advantages and disadvantages of becoming a young film star?

2 **Read the main part of the article (but not the missing paragraphs A–G).**

1 Is the writer positive or negative about young actors at the beginning of the text?
2 How was one young star particularly well looked after when travelling to another country to film?
3 What reaction did one mother have prior to signing a contract for her young son?
4 Is the writer positive or negative about young stars' futures at the end of the text?

3 **Read paragraphs A–G. Note down a phrase that summarises the main idea of each paragraph.**

Example: Para A: what casting directors are looking for

4 **Work in pairs. What do you think the phrases in *italics* from the article mean?**

1 … what happens to these young actors *further down the line*?
2 … these *painstaking searches* undertaken by casting directors …
3 'I was incredibly nervous for him and *what this was potentially unleashing* in his life.'
4 … she still feels *mixed emotions* …
5 … young actors today will *emerge unscathed* from the whole experience of early stardom.
6 … entering the profession so early *closed as many doors as it opened*.
7 … the actor always regretted *missing out on school*.
8 They may not all manage to *negotiate the transition into adult roles*.

5 **Now choose from the paragraphs A–G the one which fits each gap in the text. There is one extra paragraph which you do not need to use.**

Young film actors

Starring in an award-winning film, perhaps when you've barely reached your teens, may seem like a dream come true for many of us. But is it really the amazing experience it appears to be? There are a growing number of young actors coming into the profession, on whose shoulders may rest the responsibility for the success of multi-million-pound films. And perhaps more importantly, what happens to these young actors further down the line?

1 ______

What's more, some casting directors suggest that young actors are better now than they were in the past, possibly because they have access to far more films, and they watch them all the time. So how are they chosen for parts?

2 ______

It may be that these painstaking searches undertaken by casting directors are one reason for the quality of the actors turning up on screen. And another may be that directors are working differently with kids, encouraging these young actors to bring their own natural energy to their acting, and even carefully choreographing some scenes by bringing in specialists.

3 ______

Indeed, compared to the past, current young actors do seem to be amazingly well looked after during filming. One former young star recalls that, having been chosen for a major role in a film, she flew to another country, where filming would take place over several months. On arrival at the airport, the actor met her chaperone, the person assigned to keep an eye on her for the duration of the shoot. The young actor had spent very little time away from home, but despite her concerns, she says the chaperone that she was given helped her settle into her new life abroad – and the filming went brilliantly.

4 ______

And what effect does living with a young star have on the rest of the family? One young actor's mother explains that she suffered from sleepless nights before signing his contract for a major film. Her son had been spotted by a casting director at an after-school theatre group. 'I was incredibly nervous for him and what this was potentially unleashing in his life,' she says.

5 ______

However, she still feels mixed emotions about her son's acting, because of his age, which she considers to be an important developmental period for a young person. 'We haven't yet had to deal with a bad review,' she says. 'How are we going to handle that, if and when it happens?'

6 ______

On balance, though, and judging by the numbers who have made it through and become successful as adults, there's a good chance that young actors today will emerge unscathed from the whole experience of early stardom.

A One person responsible for finding young actors explained that she sometimes goes into schools. She does improvisations in which students make up scenes such as pretending one of them has had something stolen. 'I'm looking for clever, self-assured young people who can think on their feet,' she says.

B After all, not every film critic is going to love these young actors' work, which could be especially hard to take at such a young age. It's easy to imagine that the long-term effects could be damaging.

C Despite this, however, the actor believes entering the profession so early closed as many doors as it opened. Although she got to do many crazy things on screen, the actor always regretted missing out on school, and has now started a university degree, to help build a career away from film.

D Increasingly skilled people working in film, from agents through to film directors, are probably the secret behind why there are such good young actors around at the moment, receiving rave reviews.

E In fact, in one case this even included an ex-soldier, who mentored a young actor for a major role in an adventure film. He passed on a number of martial arts skills, teaching him the basics of kung fu, karate and judo. So young stars are generally finding their needs being taken far more seriously.

F To add to these worries, despite having been given permission to be on set during filming, there was still a reluctance on her part to observe the filming process, as she couldn't bear to see him make mistakes. However, she eventually found the courage – and it turned out to be a wonderful experience.

G They may not all manage to negotiate the transition into adult roles. But the financial returns for their work are astonishing, with some making it into the 'rich list' of the most highly paid celebrities.

6 **Discuss these questions.**

1. How many jobs can you think of connected with the film industry?
2. Would a job in the film industry appeal to you? Why? / Why not?

Grammar

Linking ideas: relative and participle clauses

The COMPLETE grammar reference
▶ Scan the QR code, watch the video, then turn to page 171

1 **Complete these extracts from Reading and Use of English Part 7 with a word or phrase from the list.**

encouraging in which teaching that
undertaken where which who

1 … she flew to another country, ………………… filming would take place …
2 [His mother is concerned] because of his age, ………………… she considers to be an important developmental period …
3 It may be that these painstaking searches ………………… by casting directors are one reason for the quality of the actors turning up on screen.
4 She does improvisations ………………… students make up scenes …
5 And another may be that directors are working differently with kids, ………………… these young actors to bring their own natural energy to their acting …
6 She says the chaperone ………………… she was given helped her settle in to her new life abroad.
7 'I'm looking for clever, self-assured young people ………………… can think on their feet.'
8 He passed on a number of martial arts skills, ………………… him the basics of kung fu, karate and judo.

2 **Discuss these questions on the sentences in Exercise 1.**

1 a Which sentences contain a relative clause?
b Which of these are defining clauses (containing essential information)?
c Which are non-defining clauses (containing additional, non-essential information)?
2 a Which sentences contain a participle clause?
b Which of these use a present participle and which use a past participle?
c In which sentences does the participle clause replace a relative clause?
3 In which of the sentences could the relative pronoun be left out? Why?

3 **The sentences below are about the comedy series, *Friends*. Complete these sentences with relative pronouns. You may also have to include a preposition.**

1 *Friends*, ………………… was filmed in the USA, was a long-running TV series.
2 The series centred around six friends, ………………… lived in Manhattan in New York City.
3 The series followed the lives of these friends, ………………… romantic adventures and career issues were both entertaining and funny.
4 One key place in the series was a cafe called Central Perk, ………………… the friends regularly met up.
5 The series finale, ………………… the characters were seen moving on with their lives, was broadcast in 2004.
6 Over 52 million viewers tuned in, ………………… made it one of the most-watched programmes on TV.
7 The cast members ………………… appeared in the series became among the highest-paid actors on TV, according to media reports.
8 The series had a huge number of loyal fans, ………………… the appeal was perhaps that the characters had become like their own personal friends.

4 **Discuss these points with a partner.**

- *Friends* is still widely shown on some TV channels. Have you ever seen it? What was your impression?
- Are there similar long-running series in your country? What are they like?
- Tell your partner about a TV programme that you enjoy watching. In your description, try to use sentences similar to those in Exercise 3, with relative pronouns.

5 **Choose the correct participles in these sentences.**

1 We came out of the cinema *quivered / quivering* with fright.
2 We'd seen a film *based / having based* on a science fiction short story.
3 *Reading / Having read* the story, I was interested to see how they would turn it into a film.
4 It was only the second film *made / having been made* by this director.
5 I'd read a review of the film in a magazine *specialising / specialised* in science fiction stories.

Linking ideas: apposition

6 **It is often possible to link information about someone/something by putting two nouns or noun phrases next to each other, with no relative pronoun.**

The actor met her chaperone, the person assigned to keep an eye on her for the duration of the shoot.

Join these sentences using phrases in apposition.

1 *Tenet* was released in 2020. It is a science fiction film.
2 The film follows the story of a secret agent. The agent is called The Protagonist.
3 Two stars of the film are John David Washington and Robert Pattinson. They are both well-known actors.
4 The title of the film is a palindrome. A palindrome is a word that reads the same forwards or backwards.

Reading and Use of English Part 1

- First read the title and the whole text quickly to get a general idea of what it is about.
- Study the gapped sentences one by one, reading carefully before and after the gap.
- The four words you have to choose from will be similar in meaning but only one will fit correctly into the gap. You should consider dependent prepositions and other grammatical structures.
- If you are not sure which option is correct, discard the options you think are wrong and choose from the others.

Exam advice

1 **Work in pairs. Discuss the questions.**

1 Do you do any painting or other creative art in your free time?
2 How often do you visit art galleries? How do you feel about the experience? Do you enjoy it? Why? / Why not?
3 Is seeing a print of a picture different from seeing the real thing? In what way?

2 **Quickly read the article about art galleries. Which of the ideas in it do you agree with?**

3 **For questions 1–8, read the article again and decide which answer (A, B, C or D) best fits each gap. There is an example at the beginning (0).**

THE POWER OF ART GALLERIES

Would you like to find out about someone's **(0)** .... on art? Then send them an invitation to a gallery and see how long they take to get **(1)** .... to you. Many people claim to enjoy looking at art, yet when it **(2)** .... to actually visiting a gallery, they may appear **(3)** .... to do so. But why?

Admittedly, entering large galleries can seem intimidating. Yet, **(4)** .... which ones you visit, you might get to see some of the finest art ever created. In smaller galleries, you can also purchase the work of new artists, before they achieve celebrity **(5)** .... and their work increases in price. What's more, the atmosphere there can really **(6)** .... your head as you quietly contemplate the artworks on display.

(7) ...., however we choose to engage with art, the important thing is what we take away from it – the sense of being part of something much larger than ourselves, for example. Moreover, there's nothing quite like being among a crowd of gallery-goers who completely share your **(8)** .... for art.

	A	B	C	D
0	insight	perspective	approach	overview
1	round	back	over	through
2	includes	arrives	involves	comes
3	reluctant	opposed	hostile	regretful
4	regarding	according to	concerning	depending on
5	prestige	capacity	status	grade
6	clear	lighten	refresh	calm
7	As it happens	In turn	As a consequence	In any event
8	appeal	passion	attraction	commitment

4 **Discuss these questions.**

1 What do you know about the major galleries in your country? Which are the most popular with visitors?
2 Why might some people find large galleries intimidating to visit?
3 Do you think art has become too big a business?

Vocabulary

Money words and idioms

1 **Complete these sentences with the correct form of the verbs in the box.**

borrow buy earn hire lend pay rent sell

1 I'm .... a room in London while I'm studying there next term.
2 Thousands of people .... their living by .... and .... things online.
3 Tom's .... a dance band for his graduation party in August.
4 I've asked my parents if they would .... me some money to buy a car. I'll .... it back when I can.
5 People say you shouldn't .... money from friends, but I don't agree.

2 **Complete the questions with ten of the verbs from the box. Then discuss the questions in pairs.**

afford borrow burn buy cost cover make meet pay raise sell shop take out

1 If you went for a job interview, how would you try to .... yourself?
2 What would you do if you wanted to .... a quick buck?
3 Do you believe that money can .... happiness?
4 When you go shopping, for example for clothes, how do you .... – by card or with your phone?
5 Is there anything you can't .... to buy because it .... a fortune?
6 If you were short of money, what would you do to make ends .... ?
7 Would you like to be able to .... a loan to buy a house or flat one day? Why? / Why not?
8 What is the first thing you would buy if you had money to .... ?
9 How would you .... money for a charity you wanted to support?

3 **Complete the money idioms in these sentences by choosing the correct noun in *italics*. Then discuss in pairs what each idiom means. The idioms are in bold.**

1 They say they want to help the disabled, but they should **put their money where their *mouth* / *pocket* is**.
2 You need to be a bit more careful with your money. **Money doesn't grow on *bushes* / *trees***, you know.
3 The shop wouldn't accept a cheque or a credit card. They insisted on **hard *cash* / *money***.
4 Flats in the city are always expensive but I had to **pay through the *hand* / *nose*** for the one I wanted.
5 I always prefer to **pay my own *road* / *way***, so you pay your bill and I'll pay mine.
6 I've no idea where he gets it from, but Martin's been **spending money like *air* / *water*** recently.
7 It's the local council that has to decide whether to build a new college. It **holds the *purse* / *wallet* strings**.
8 I can't afford a new car – I'm afraid it would **break the *savings* / *bank***.

4 **Each of these sentences contains one or more errors made by exam candidates. Correct the mistakes.**

1 I'm sure you'll enjoy the job – and don't forget, you'll be gaining good money.
2 As you will be using your own car and staying in hotels, the company will afford all your expenses and spend you a daily meal allowance.
3 You can pay your ticket here or on the bus.
4 I can borrow you some money, but please give it back tomorrow.
5 You can rent all the books you need from the college library – at no cost.
6 We offer free delivery if you buy more than $200.
7 In the last month we have earned over £2,000 for charity – most of it from public donations.

Speaking Part 4

Page 213 Speaking bank
Speaking Part 4

Exam advice

- Listen carefully to all the examiner's questions – you may be asked the same question as your partner.
- Listen to your partner's answers to questions, as you may have to respond to these.
- Try to use a range of expressions to express and justify opinions and to agree and disagree.

1 **Work in pairs. Read the examiner's instruction and the written prompts for a Part 3 task. Discuss the question.**

'Here are some team-building activities which have been suggested for new members of a social club. Talk to each other about how effective these activities would be in helping people to get to know one another better.'

How effective would each of these activities be in helping people to get to know each other better?

- playing a team sport
- rock climbing
- teaching others a new skill
- raising funds for the club
- playing computer games in teams

2 **Read these Part 4 questions that might follow the Part 3 task in Exercise 1. Which of the six questions would you most like to answer? Which would you find the most difficult to answer? Briefly exchange ideas in pairs.**

1 Some people say that team-building activities are a waste of time. Do you agree?
2 Does a person's character affect their ability to be a good team member?
3 Is it a manager's responsibility to make sure teams of employees work well together on a day-to-day basis? Why? / Why not?
4 Large clubs and organisations are more likely than small ones to organise team-building activities. Why do you think this is?
5 What problems can arise if individuals in a large organisation feel isolated or undervalued?
6 Is it always best for people to avoid conflict with others? Why? / Why not?

3 26 **Listen to two extracts from a Part 4 exam and answer the questions.**

1 Which two questions from Exercise 2 are the candidates answering?
2 In each dialogue, what is the first speaker's main point?
3 Does the second speaker agree, partly agree or disagree?
4 What opinion would you give?

4 **Now take turns with a partner to answer the questions in Exercise 2. After your turn, ask your partner's opinion about the question you have answered. Use some of the words in the boxes.**

Nouns: achievement a common goal cooperation incentive

Verbs: appreciate compete contribute cooperate share support respect

Adjectives: constructive creative productive supportive worthwhile

Writing Part 2: An informal letter

▶ **Page 196 Writing bank**
An email/letter

Before you start to write, think carefully about:

- the purpose of the letter or email (this will be stated in the task instruction)
- who the reader will be and what this person will expect to hear from you
- what information/advice/suggestions you need to include in your response
- how formal or informal the language should be (this will depend on your relationship with the reader and on the purpose of your letter or email).

Exam advice

1 Answer these questions individually. Then compare your answers with a partner.

1 How often do you write letters (not including emails)?
2 Why and when might you write a letter rather than sending a text or writing an email?

2 Read the extracts A–E from five letters. Number them 1–5 according to how formal they are (1 = very informal, 5 = very formal).

3 Read the extracts again and answer the questions.

1 What is the purpose of the letter each extract is taken from?
2 What can you deduce about the writers and recipients of each letter?
3 What features of informal language does each extract include?

4 Rewrite these formal expressions in more informal English. The first six expressions are from extracts B and E.

1 We can now confirm that …
2 your forthcoming vacation …
3 will be debited from your credit card …
4 the week following your departure …
5 Please accept my apologies for this …
6 We do make every effort …
7 Firstly, I raised the issue of …
8 Should you wish me to act on your behalf …
9 There is another factor that needs to be taken into account …
10 I am not in a position to provide advice on this matter …

5 Rewrite these openings to letters replying to extracts A and C. Use more appropriate language.

A: Thank you for your enquiry about sharing our home with us for five days in November. Unfortunately, the room will be occupied during that period, and I am therefore unable to comply with your request.

C: With reference to your letter of 24 May, I wish to express my appreciation of your invitation to attend the college function on 15 June and to inform you that I shall be very happy to attend.

A

… so am looking for a really tolerant family to put me up for a few days. As you seemed sorry we didn't manage to meet up last time I was over, I thought I'd give you first option this time. I'll be around from 7–11 November. Don't worry if it's inconvenient, there are loads of other people I can ask, but it'd be good to see you all.

B

We can now confirm that we have taken 1,490 euros from your credit card account, that being the total cost of your forthcoming vacation. Any agreed deductions for extras, breakages, cleaning, etc. will be debited from your credit card the week following your departure.

C

Secondly, we would like to try to get everyone together before they start their summer break – we're asking all the trainees and course tutors over for a barbecue in Junko's garden on 15 June. It's a Friday evening, so hopefully people shouldn't be going to work or doing anything too serious the next day.

D

Just a short note to thank you for the music on Saturday. Everyone seemed to have an excellent time and we have had some nice emails and notes back. Everyone really liked the dancing as well – I thought it set the evening up very nicely.

E

Please accept my apologies for this. We do make every effort to pack our books well and always use the best available courier company. Unfortunately, it only needs one employee in any of the various depots across the country to handle the package carelessly and the corners of books can be damaged. This can even happen when the delivery drops through your letterbox.

6 **Work in pairs. Read the following writing task and discuss these questions.**

1 What kind of tone or register would you use to reply to the letter?

2 What is the main question that Stevie wants advice about?

3 Which of Stevie's alternatives would you support and why?

4 What would you actually say to a friend in this situation?

You have received this letter from a friend.

> I'm currently attending a music college and some of the people on my course have asked me to play with them on a nationwide tour. They're really good musicians and it'll be an amazing experience, but actually I'm already in a band with some friends. If I go on this tour, I won't be able to play our upcoming show and I'm worried about letting them down. What should I do and why?
>
> Thanks
>
> Stevie

Write your **letter** in reply. You do not need to include postal addresses.

7 **Explain whether you would include the following ideas at the beginning, in the middle or at the end of your letter.**

1 hoping that the suggestions given have been helpful
2 asking how the dilemma is affecting Stevie
3 saying how pleased you are to have been asked for advice
4 giving your opinion on what Stevie should do
5 asking Stevie to let you know the outcome of the situation
6 referring to your own experience of such a dilemma

8 **Look at expressions 1–10 for making suggestions. Which of these are followed by**

a an infinitive without *to*?
b the *to* infinitive?
c the *-ing* form?

In one expression there are two possible answers.

1 It might be an idea …
2 What would you think about …?
3 Another possibility would be …
4 I suggest that you should …
5 What about …?
6 I'd say you ought …
7 You could consider …
8 You might feel like …
9 What I think you should do is …
10 I'd say your best option is …

9 **Write your answer to the task in Exercise 6 in 220–260 words. Remember to use informal language.**

8 Sound and vision

Starting off

1 Work in pairs. Look at the pictures below. Which of these sources of information do you use regularly?

2 What are the advantages and disadvantages of older and newer forms of media?

3 Are there some sources of information that are more difficult to look at on an electronic device?

4 Work in pairs and discuss. What are your favourite sources for the following types of information? If the source is online, which websites and platforms do you prefer?

- checking the results of a sporting event
- looking up information for a study project
- finding something special to wear for a special occasion
- booking tickets for a concert
- reading about a major news story – local, national, or international
- checking a word you don't understand

Listening Part 3

1 You are going to listen to an interview with two people who have both been involved in student media organisations. Before you listen, discuss th questions in pairs.

1 Are school and college newspapers and magazines common in your country? Does/Did your school or university have one? If so, did you read it? What kind of things did it feature? Who contributed to it?

2 Have you ever listened to local radio stations in your area? If so, what's your opinion of them? H popular are they?

2 27 **Now listen to the interview, in which university student Kate Evans and radio personality Harry Fielding talk about their experiences in student media organisations. For questions 1–6, choose the answer (A, B, C or D) which fits best according to what you hear.**

1 Kate decided to join her university student newspaper because she was

A reluctant to disappoint the person who introduced her to it.

B optimistic that it might offer great creative opportunities.

C confident that it would help her achieve her aim of working in the field of media.

D desperate to find some kind of a career path.

2 During her time at the newspaper, Kate has been

A surprised at the level of professionalism among people there.

B relieved to find herself in an atmosphere where she can develop as a person.

C impressed by the high-level training she's received.

D proud of the rapid progress she's made.

3 What does Kate say about producing printed copies of the newspaper?

A She's concerned about the environmental impact of the process.

B She emphasises their importance in raising initial awareness of the publication.

C She regrets the lack of opportunities for last-minute editorial changes.

D She acknowledges their vital role in raising revenue.

4 Harry explains that for him, getting involved in student radio

A was the result of a chance encounter.

B revealed talents he didn't realise he had.

C gave him valuable experience for his degree course.

D took him into an area of broadcasting he wasn't yet ready for.

5 What does Harry say about student radio when compared with professional organisations?

A Its broadcasting equipment can be almost as good.

B There's far less pressure on participants to take it seriously.

C There are opportunities for much greater creative freedom.

D It provides more opportunities for developing vocational skills.

6 Kate and Harry agree that student media organisations

A play a key role in preparing young people to become media professionals.

B help gather important data on how young people consume media.

C provide a unique service in informing young people about world affairs.

D introduce young people to the huge range of creative jobs available.

Exam advice

- Before you listen, read the questions, and underline the main idea in each one.
- Read each option carefully and think about its meaning.
- Listen for the general idea of what each speaker is saying.
- Wait until each speaker has finished before making your final decision about the answer.
- Listen for the same ideas to be expressed, not the same words.

3 **Work in pairs. Discuss the questions.**

1 In what ways did Kate and Harry benefit from joining student media organisations?

2 Do you think there might have been any downsides to doing the work while they were students?

3 Would a job in media appeal to you (e.g. in TV, radio or newspapers)? Why? / Why not?

4 **Use the correct form of the verbs in the box to complete the sentences from the recording.**

find	follow	get (x2)	map	meet	provide	push	run	take	work

1 I'd been feeling time was .... out …

2 My friends all had their futures .... out …

3 I really hoped that's how it'd be – and it's .... my expectations.

4 I soon .... my feet there …

5 … I .... my way up to being a presenter …

6 … it would have been harder to .... a foot on the ladder …

7 All that .... a great stepping stone for my subsequent career.

8 I also .... on the role of station manager …

9 For students considering .... in your footsteps, how does student radio compare …?

10 You get far more chances to really .... the boundaries of your imagination …

11 … an industry that depends on connections to .... you through the door.

Grammar
Reported speech

The COMPLETE grammar reference
▶ Scan the QR code, watch the video, then turn to page 173

1 **The following are reports of what was said during the interview in Listening Part 3. What were the speakers' actual words?**

1 The interviewer asked Harry and Kate how important student media organisations were.
2 Kate said she'd recently found a post with a national newspaper.
3 Kate said she couldn't see a day coming when content would be generated by automatic processes.
4 Harry explained that it was often said that young people didn't listen to the radio.
5 Harry said that we would always need writers and broadcasters to produce content.

2 **Now listen and check your answers.** 28

3 **Work in pairs. You are going to listen to four short dialogues between Latifa and Jake.** 29

Student A: Make brief notes about what Latifa says.
Student B: Make brief notes about what Jake says.

4 **Convert your notes into reported speech sentences using some of the verbs in the box. Then compare sentences with your partner.**

ask explain reply tell want to know wonder

Vocabulary
Prefixes and suffixes

1 **Work in pairs. Add prefixes to these adjectives to make them negative.**

1 .... popular
2 .... experienced
3 .... efficient
4 .... legal
5 .... satisfied
6 .... relevant
7 .... perfect
8 .... certain

Now change each negative adjective into a noun. How do you do this?

2 **Add prefixes to these verbs so that they have the meanings given.**

1 approve	feel something's bad or wrong
2 locate	move to another place e.g. because of work
3 act	talk and do things with other people
4 understand	understand something wrongly
5 estimate	rate something too low
6 construct	build something again

Now change each verb into a noun by using a suffix.

3 **Add prefixes to these words so that they have the meanings given.**

1 biography	when a person writes about themself
2 pilot	someone sharing the task of flying an aircraft with another person
3 fiction	not fictional
4 president	former president
5 detached	house joined to the one next door

Reading and Use of English Part 3

1 **What are your five senses? What senses do you use when you are:**

- making a meal?
- visiting an art gallery?
- swimming in a river?
- walking in the countryside?
- crossing a road?

2 **Read the text about the possible future of television, and answer these questions. (Don't try to fill in the gaps at this stage.)**

1 What was Sensurround?
2 What possible reasons does the writer give for the lack of appeal of sensory additions to TV programmes?

3 **Read the text again. For questions 1–8, use the word given in capitals at the end of some of the lines to form a word that fits in the gap in the same line. There is an example at the beginning (0).**

Exam advice

- Read the whole text quickly first for a general idea of what it is about.
- When looking at the gaps, decide:
  - what type of word you need (noun, adjective, etc.)
  - how you should change the word in capitals to form the word you need.
- These are some of the questions to ask yourself:
  - does the word need a negative prefix (*un-*, *in-*, etc.)?
  - if the word is a noun, should it be singular or plural?
  - if it is a verb, what form is needed (*-ed*, *-ing*, etc.)?

4 **Discuss these questions in pairs.**

1 Would you find the idea of watching TV with added sensory effects appealing? Why? / Why not?
2 How would you rate the kinds of programme broadcast on TV in your country? Which ones do you enjoy watching? Which do you most dislike? Why?

The future of TV

You might remember when Sensurround was **(0)** ......fashionable...... in cinemas up and down the land. Its aim was to **(1)** .... audiences' experiences of watching films, by providing them with sounds and sensations to match what was on screen. And recent research might soon lead to us experiencing similar entertainment at home – on our TVs. Researchers are studying the effects of using various **(2)** .... of smells and tastes. During programmes, viewers would be able to use scent sprays and drinks to simulate the tastes of onscreen dishes, for example – something which could be very **(3)** .... in getting viewers to participate in the shows themselves.

However, the appeal may prove to be a short-lived **(4)** ...., and it is also possible that certain **(5)** .... issues could arise. One problem might be that different tastes and smells, and people's **(6)** .... of them can be extremely **(7)** .... So what suggests a delicious dish to one person may suggest something totally inedible to another. Another issue may be the sheer **(8)** .... of the equipment required – not necessarily what people want when relaxing in front of the TV.

FASHION
RICH
COMBINE
PERSUADE
NOVEL
FORESEE
PERCEIVE
SUBJECT
COMPLEX

Speaking Part 3

▶ **Page 211 Speaking bank**
Speaking Part 3

1 Look at the photos and discuss the following questions.

1. How much do you think people are affected by the influences shown in the photos?
2. What other powerful influences shape people's ideas? How are people affected by them?

2 Read these written prompts for a Speaking Part 3 task. Briefly consider this task and note down a few ideas.

In what ways are people's ideas and behaviour affected by these powerful influences?

- celebrities
- political and environmental groups
- television and radio programmes
- social media
- newspapers

Exam advice

- The most important thing in this part of the exam is to demonstrate good communication skills. This involves:
  - keeping the conversation going and avoiding long pauses – giving your own opinion is important, but it is equally important to ask your partner for their opinion
  - listening carefully to what your partner says and responding – don't just say what you think.
- When speaking, look at the person you are talking to.

3 (30) **Listen to two candidates discussing the prompts, and answer these questions.**

1. Which of the influences do the speakers talk about?
2. Do they answer the question 'In what ways are people's ideas and behaviour affected by these powerful influences?'
3. Do they talk about the influences in sufficient depth?
4. Do they participate equally in the conversation?

4 (30) **Listen again. Which of these examples of imprecise language do the speakers use? (Imprecise language is used when being accurate is impossible, unnecessary, over-formal or too direct.)**

- *all sorts of, and so on, I guess, I mean, some kind, sort of, stuff, things like that*
- *a bit, (quite) a few, several, a lot, lots, loads of, plenty of two or three,*
- *almost, fairly, nearly, pretty much, probably, quite*
- the suffix *-ish*

Note: *-ish* can be added to words to make them less precise, e.g., *green* → *greenish* (a shade somewhere between blue and green or grey and green), *thirty* → *thirtyish* (about 30, between 27 and 33).

5 Work in pairs and do the task in Exercise 2.

- Make sure you both speak for roughly the same length of time.
- Use imprecise words and phrases from the list above where appropriate.

6 At the end of Part 3 you and your partner are asked to come to a decision. Follow the examiner's instruction below with your partner.

'Now you have about a minute to decide which two of these influences have the greatest effect on people.'

7 (31) **Listen to the last part of the interview, where the two candidates answer the question in Exercise 6.**

1. Do they make the same choices as you?
2. How well do they interact to reach their decision?

Vocabulary
Reporting verbs

1 Complete the gaps in this summary with the verbs in the box in the correct form. In some cases more than one answer is possible.

comment discuss say speak talk tell

In Part 3 of the Speaking test the examiner **(1)** .... the two candidates that they have to **(2)** .... to each other for about two minutes. In the conversation you listened to, the candidates **(3)** .... the comparative importance of a number of influences on people's ideas and behaviour. The first candidate started by **(4)** .... that celebrities have huge influence on people. They went on to **(5)** .... on the influential role played by social media. During their conversation the two candidates **(6)** .... for about the same length of time, and responded to each other's ideas.

2 Exam candidates sometimes make mistakes when using reporting verbs. Choose the correct verbs in *italics* in these sentences.

1 Many people believe that the mass media do not always *say* / *tell* the truth.
2 When I'm in China, I can understand what people are *speaking* / *saying* to me, but I can hardly *speak* / *talk* any Chinese myself.
3 This newspaper website doesn't even *say* / *mention* the economic crisis.
4 The spokesperson for the authorities *expressed* / *spoke* his thanks for people's understanding.
5 There's an article on this website which *says* / *writes* that people absorb information more quickly from the internet than from printed material.
6 When asked about the latest rumours, the minister refused to *comment* / *say*.
7 After Ben had used an online dictionary, he *said* / *told* everyone how great it was. He didn't *mention* / *tell* the fact that it had taken him an hour to find what he wanted.
8 If you feel strongly about something, you should *express* / *speak* your mind.

Reading and Use of English Part 6

1 Discuss these questions in pairs.

1 How much do you know about social media influencers? What is it that they do?
2 Are there any social media influencers that you might recommend?
3 Would you be more likely to buy something if you saw it advertised by someone well-known on the internet? Why? / Why not?
4 Do you think influencers might be open to exploitation by companies because of the work they do? If so, in what ways?

2 Read extracts A–D quickly. What do you understand by the following phrases?

Extract A:

1 *a collaborative process*
2 *thrash out*
3 *attract traffic to your site*

Extract B:

4 *take on everything you're offered*

Extract C:

5 *a polarising topic*
6 *mould themselves into*
7 *diluted their appeal*

Extract D:

8 *of the same mindset*
9 *quick to pick up on*

3 Decide what each of these sentences means. Choose either *a* or *b*.

1 *My work as an influencer has slowly grown over the years, to the point where it's now a full-time job.* (Extract A)
  - **a** I went into becoming an influencer with a view to it eventually being my main source of work.
  - **b** Being an influencer wasn't how I made a living when I started, but now it is.

2 *If you then start letting people down because you can't deliver, that's bad news for your followers.* (Extract B)
  - **a** Your readers may lose interest if you begin publishing negative material on your site.
  - **b** Your readers may no longer use your site if you're unable to supply what they're looking for.

3 *I only collaborate with those businesses that match my own profile, as I grew my following by being true to my values.* (Extract C)
  - **a** I've appealed to regular readers by restricting myself to working with firms I have a lot in common with.
  - **b** My regular readers tend to be attracted by the fact that I work with their preferred companies.

4 *People immediately assume the driving force behind what I do is trying to sell them stuff they don't really need, when actually, as I'm often at pains to point out, that's far from the truth.* (Extract D)
  - **a** I dislike the fact that people suspect me of publicising potentially useless goods, and make frequent efforts to deny this.
  - **b** There's a temptation as an influencer to advertise anything at all just to make some money – but it's one I've so far resisted.

Being a social media *influencer*

Four experienced influencers talk about their work, promoting brands on social media.

A

My work as an influencer has slowly grown over the years, to the point where it's now a full-time job. I work with lots of different companies, promoting their goods – but I've always insisted on it being a collaborative process. Even though you're being paid by them, your site will inevitably have its own particular flavour and feel, so it's important to thrash out with companies beforehand how your two brands might best fit together when creating content. I also like companies that actively support worthwhile causes – and not just because they feel an obligation to do so. On my site, I'm also about encouraging people to be happy and confident in themselves – to do otherwise seems irresponsible. If you handle that kind of thing carefully, it can attract traffic to your site. But if not, you risk losing some of your followers, who can be very judgemental.

B

I've operated as an influencer for a long time now, and I've reached a point in my work where I no longer say yes to everything – in fact, nowadays I tend to stick to firms that have clearly done their research beforehand and can say why they particularly want me to promote their brand. Otherwise, I'm likely to turn them down, whether their brand matches my site or not. I've been known to sometimes take on firms whose brands I'm not wholly in favour of because their recognition of my talents is the more important factor. Of course, the temptation's certainly there to take on everything you're offered, but if you then start letting people down because you can't deliver, that's bad news for your followers, who'll still expect to see regular new content – and they can unfortunately be brutal in their reactions. So you can find yourself under constant pressure.

C

It can be hard at times to maintain my own voice while still partnering with different brands. So as far as possible, I have discussions with companies about what they're looking for. I only collaborate with those businesses that match my own profile, as I grew my following by being true to my values. I'm very cautious not to promote anything just for the money that might then turn out to be a polarising topic for my followers – in the end, no-one wins in that situation. My whole take on this ever since I started was that no matter what, I needed to stay true to myself. I've seen plenty of people trying to mould themselves into what they thought others wanted them to be, and it really diluted their appeal and lost them their original readership. They're the ones who make you what you are and, in my experience, they will always value quality content. Hence, I owe them the best I can produce, even if it means there will be delays.

D

When I mention what I do for a living, I do feel that people immediately assume the driving force behind what I do is trying to sell them stuff they don't really need, when actually, as I'm often at pains to point out, that's far from the truth. I don't think I could live with myself if that's what I thought I was doing. I promote stuff that I genuinely think people could benefit from hearing about. I also try to focus on products that are likely to boost health and self-esteem alongside the fashion and cosmetics products that I feature – that's essential, as I'm in a position of considerable influence. And I've reached a point where I just don't collaborate with people that aren't of the same mindset as me – there's just no point in sacrificing my following, which I'd probably end up doing. They'd be quick to pick up on that kind of thing, and would be quite unforgiving.

Exam advice

- Read the questions one at a time and identify the aspect of the topic being focused on.
- To answer the questions, you will need to keep this topic in mind and then scan the texts as often as necessary, looking for the similarities or differences of opinion.

4 **For questions 1–4, choose from the extracts A–D. The extracts may be chosen more than once.**

Which influencer

has developed a different view from the others on how they select companies to work with? **1** ____

shares D's opinion on the importance of promoting positivity? **2** ____

has a different attitude from B towards their followers' expectations? **3** ____

expresses a similar view to C on the importance of maintaining personal authenticity? **4** ____

5 **Work in pairs and discuss these questions.**

1. Have you ever referred to social influencers' sites to find out about a product?
2. Do you follow any particular social influencers? Have you ever thought about becoming one yourself?
3. Are there any downsides to social influencers' presence on the internet?

Grammar

Transitive and intransitive verbs

The COMPLETE grammar reference Turn to page 175

1 Transitive verbs must be followed by an object.

- He persuaded me to leave. (*Persuade* is a transitive verb, which needs an object.)
- He decided to leave. (*Decide* is an intransitive verb, which has no direct object.)

Which of the verbs listed need an object to complete these sentences?

1 *agreed, allowed, arranged, instructed, refused, required, warned*
He .... to leave at 10 o'clock.

2 *admitted, convinced, informed, mentioned, recalled, reminded, told*
She .... that she was leaving at 10 o'clock.

2 Many verbs can be used both transitively and intransitively, sometimes with different meanings. Discuss the differences in meaning between the verbs in bold in these sentences.

1 **a** He promised he'd be at home, but he was out when I **called**.
b I was so annoyed that I **called** him a very rude name.

2 **a** Tarek **runs** every day before he goes to work.
b He works in London where he **runs** a small IT company.

3 **a** I'm fine thanks – I can usually **manage** on my own.
b I've applied for a job **managing** a bookshop.

4 **a** We need to **leave** in half an hour.
b You can't take your bike. You'll have to **leave** it here.

5 **a** We're planning to **move** next year.
b My car won't start – could you help me **move** it please?

3 Exam candidates often miss out objects after transitive verbs, especially verbs with a complex structure. Correct the mistakes in these sentences.

1 I can assure that we will do everything to resolve your case as quickly as we can.
2 I'd be very grateful if you could tell where to look for the information I need.
3 Do you like my new painting? Maria gave to me.
4 We have been taught special techniques that will allow to do well in our exams.
5 I didn't know anyone at Jo's party, so she introduced to some of her friends.
6 Your new job starts on Monday, doesn't it? We all wish the best of luck.

Writing Part 2: A proposal

Page 202 Writing bank
A proposal

Exam advice

- Think about who will read the proposal and how formal you need your writing style to be.
- If you decide to divide the proposal into sections, think about what sections you need and what section headings are appropriate.

1 Read the writing task below. What would you propose as the content for a programme about the cultural facilities available in the area where you live?

You see the following announcement on a website.

> A TV company is making a series of programmes about the cultural facilities available in different parts of your country. The company is asking members of the public for proposals suggesting places in their area that should feature in the programme.
>
> Write a proposal for the company outlining which cultural facilities ought to be included in a programme about your area. Include suggestions, with reasons, on where the company should film, who could be interviewed and how the programme could be made interesting for people of different ages.

Write your **proposal**.

2 Read the sample answer on page 93 and discuss these questions.

1 Has the writer followed the task instructions fully?
2 Is the style appropriately formal?
3 What expressions does the writer use in order to be positive and persuasive?

I welcome this opportunity to put forward ideas for the programme your company is intending to make about the cultural facilities in my area. As a young person interested in all aspects of the arts, I feel able to make some valuable suggestions.

The Phoenix Centre

I strongly recommend opening the programme with an exploration of our community arts centre, The Phoenix, which has become a hub of cultural activity for people of all ages in our area. From dance and drama classes to art-house film nights, this thriving facility consistently provides a diverse, exciting programme of activities and events for people with very different tastes. Full of fire and enthusiasm, director Helena Forsythe would make a great person to showcase everything The Phoenix has to offer.

City Museum

The programme could then move its focus to the newly renovated and refurbished museum in the heart of our city. Gone are the days of 'Don't touch' and 'Stay behind the line' notices. I feel that our museum encapsulates the modern approach to presenting artefacts and ideas by fully involving visitors in the learning process. Children are bound to be fascinated by the 'hands-on' trip through history from prehistoric times to the present day. I'd suggest speaking to a range of visitors and asking them to talk about their favourite museum object. I'm convinced this would be especially interesting for viewers.

These are just two of a number of places I'd recommend your programme should focus on and I hope very much that you will take my proposal into consideration.

3 **How could you change these sentences to make them more appropriate for a formal proposal?**

1 I reckon it would be cool to chat to people in the street.

2 A programme like this will go down really well with kids and teens.

3 You're sure to grab the audience's attention filming stuff like that.

4 You might want to take a look at the massive concert hall that's going up.

5 I'll be thrilled to bits if you go along with my ideas.

4 **The following sentences contain verbs that may be useful for writing a proposal. Complete them with the correct prepositions.**

1 Boys and girls alike would undoubtedly **benefit** .... a new dance studio.

2 Promising young musicians could also **contribute** .... the town's annual festival.

3 An opportunity to learn an instrument would **appeal** .... young people of all ages.

4 I'm convinced that the presenter should **focus** .... the benefits of painting.

5 Teenagers need to be **provided** .... ideas that they can personally **identify** ....

6 Everyone, whether amateur or professional, **responds** .... encouragement and praise.

7 If people **succeed** .... one area of the arts, this often **results** .... them following another artistic pursuit.

5 **Read this writing task and make notes in the plan.**

You see the following announcement on a website.

> An internet TV company is planning to produce a series of documentaries for young people to encourage participation in the arts. They would like people to send in proposals suggesting an art form to feature in the series. Say what art form you would suggest, describe what aspects of the art form they should include and explain how young people could benefit from participating in this activity.

Write your **proposal**.

Plan

Paragraph 1:	*Intro:*	....
Paragraph 2:	*Heading:*	....
	First idea:	....
	Reasons:	....
Paragraph 3:	*Heading:*	....
	Second idea:	....
	Reasons:	....
Paragraph 4:	*Conclusion:*	....

6 **Write your proposal in 220–260 words. Try to use some of the words and phrases from Exercise 4.**

7 Vocabulary and grammar review

Vocabulary

1 Complete the sentences with the correct form of the money verbs in the box.

afford buy cost earn hire
lend pay rent sell

1 I'd love to own a sports car, but I can't .... one.
2 I'll be working in Prague for two years. Hopefully we'll .... a flat near the city centre.
3 My brother works in a fast-food restaurant. He only .... £120 a week.
4 I've decided to .... my motorbike and get a car.
5 We've .... a jazz band to play at the party on Saturday.
6 I don't get paid until Friday. Could you .... me £30 until then?
7 Those jeans .... a fortune, but it's really the designer label you're .... for.
8 I didn't expect you to .... me a birthday present, but thank you very much!

2 Complete the text using the words in the box that best fit each gap. Use only one word in each gap. There are four words you do not need to use.

because place common account keeping means
exchange way behalf regard view aid

Learning to play a musical instrument

Have you ever tried to learn to play a musical instrument? It can be hugely rewarding, but on **(1)** .... of all the practice you have to put in to make any progress, it can also be hugely frustrating. Of course, if you have a keen musician as a friend, you could ask for some lessons in **(2)** .... for looking after his cats. However, you still have to practise outside of class and **(3)** .... of my propensity to procrastinate, I rarely found the time to practise.

Nevertheless, I joined a small orchestra, hoping I'd improve by performing with others. But it wasn't until we were asked to perform live that I got down to some serious practice. The concert, which was in **(4)** .... of a charity, was going to be a challenge. Our orchestra decided to shake things up a bit and decided to add some new songs. In **(5)** .... of our usual classical pieces, we suddenly had to play a series of jazz standards. While the music wasn't entirely in **(6)** .... with the venue, a wonderful old former palace, the audience loved it! And with **(7)** .... to the amount of money we raised, the charity was thrilled! In fact, we received a letter written by the charity on **(8)** ....of its many beneficiaries, thanking us for our efforts. That made it all worthwhile.

Grammar

3 Combine sentences in the following extracts from film reviews, using these ways of linking ideas:

- relative clauses
- participle clauses
- apposition

1 Libero

A boy tries to understand his family. He tries to stop it from breaking apart. At the same time he has to deal with his mother's absence. He finds all this very difficult. The boy is only eleven years old.

2 Be Kind Rewind

A man unintentionally destroys every tape in a video store. The man's name is Black. His brain becomes magnetised. The store is owned by Black's best friend. Black and his friend feel sorry for the store's most loyal customer. This customer is an elderly woman. She is losing her memory. The two men set out to remake the lost films. These films include *The Lion King* and *RoboCop*.

3 I Am Legend

A military scientist is left completely alone in New York. The city is deserted. A virus has wiped out the human race. The scientist is played by Will Smith. The film is based on a sci-fi novel by Richard Matheson.

Vocabulary and grammar review 8

Vocabulary

1 Complete these words to match the definitions.

1 ....**president** (n) someone who used to have the position of president
2 ....**understand** (v) understand something incorrectly
3 ....**legal** (adj) against the law
4 .... **satisfied** (adj) how you feel when you find something unsatisfactory
5 ....**biography** (n) a book about a person's life, written by that person
6 ....**build** (v) the act of building something again
7 ....**relevant** (adj) having nothing to do with the subject being talked about
8 ....**efficient** (adj) something/someone that's not producing the results it/they should

2 Complete the table with the related words. Use the suffixes in the box. In some cases, there is more than one possible answer.

dis- im- in- over- re- un- (x2) under

Positive adjectives	Negative adjectives
popular	1 ....
experienced	2 ....
perfect	3 ....
certain	4 ....

Verbs	Related verbs
approve	5 .... (dislike)
locate	6 .... (move to a different place)
act	7 .... (communicate with other people)
estimate	8 .... (think something is less than it is) 9 .... (think something is more than it is)

Grammar

3 Rewrite the following quotes in reported speech.

1 "You mustn't tell anyone what you've seen." (Roland to Joanna)
2 "It was a surprise seeing Tom last week. I hadn't seen him since we were at school together." (Clare)
3 "Shall I do the shopping this afternoon?" (Ben to Jerry)
4 "You must stop smoking if you want to get rid of your cough." (doctor to me)
5 "How many languages can you speak?" (Bogdan to me)

4 Rewrite the following as direct quotes.

1 The police officer wanted to know what I was doing out so late.
2 She asked if I had any plans for the following evening.
3 I said that was the worst programme I'd ever seen.
4 I promised I'd phone her as soon as I got home.
5 Jerry said he hoped he'd be going there the following day.

5 Complete the second sentence so that it has a similar meaning to the first sentence, using the word given. Do not change the word given. You must use between three and six words, including the word given.

1 Maria said, "I'll never do that again."
PROMISED
Maria .... do that again.

2 "I think you should apply for this job," Alexei said to me.
ADVISED
Alexei .... job.

3 Simon said, "Have you ever thought of starting your own business?"
ASKED
Simon .... ever thought of starting my own business.

4 "Let's meet tomorrow," said Svetlana.
SUGGESTED
Svetlana .... day.

5 "Don't drink if you're driving," the police officer said to the motorist.
WARNED
The police officer .... if he was driving.

6 Tom and Alexis said, "We're getting married in May."
ANNOUNCED
Tom and Alexis .... in May.

9 Invention and innovation

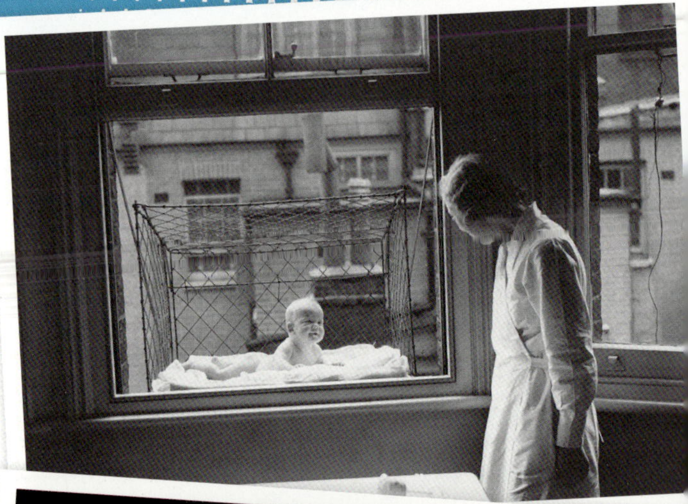

Starting off

1 **Work in pairs. Discuss these questions.**

1. Each of these photos shows an invention from the past that never became popular. What do you think they were called and what do you imagine was the thinking behind the design of each one?
2. Why do you think these inventions failed to become widely used? What could be done to improve them?

Listening Part 1

Exam advice

- Listen to the whole extract before you choose an option: the answer may depend on the general idea rather than a few words.
- If you are not sure about the answer after listening the first time, try to decide which answers you think are wrong before you listen the second time.

1 **You will hear three different extracts where people talk about technology. Extract One is a discussion about unsuccessful inventions. Before you listen, look at these words/phrases. Do they suggest agreement or disagreement?**

a I don't know. **b** Really?
c I suppose so. **d** Nor me.

2 32 **For question 1, listen to the first part of Extract One and choose the answer (A, B or C) which fits best according to what you hear.**

Extract One

1 The speakers agree that the concept of underwater buses

- **A** should be admired as being reflective of a powerful imagination.
- **B** could only have been conceived at a particular point in time.
- **C** might provide a means of dealing with a contemporary problem.

3 33 **Now listen to the second part of Extract One, in which the woman continues the conversation by using the example of augmented reality (AR) glasses. Discuss with a partner what you think her main point is.**

4 33 **Listen to the second part of Extract One again. Then discuss your answers to the questions below.**

- **a** What received 'a phenomenal amount of investment'?
- **b** What do you learn about the challenges of launching a new invention?
- **c** Who does the woman suggest should 'exercise a little more caution'?

For question 2, choose the answer (A, B or C) which fits best according to what you have heard.

2 The woman uses the example of augmented reality glasses to

- **A** criticise the amount of money wasted by technology companies.
- **B** illustrate the challenges of successfully launching a new invention.
- **C** question the man's ability to assess the potential of new inventions.

5 34 **Listen to Extract One in full to check your answers to the exam questions 1 and 2.**

6 35 **Now listen to Extract Two. For questions 3 and 4, choose the answer (A, B or C) which fits best.**

Extract Two

You hear two people discussing developments in technology.

3 What is the woman's main point about recent technological development?

- **A** It has caused understandable feelings of frustration.
- **B** It is reducing the costs of using a device.
- **C** It is becoming progressively accessible to the majority of people.

4 When giving his view on the subject, the man makes it clear he is

- **A** doubtful that technological advancements could ever be stopped.
- **B** certain about the destructive influence of online communication.
- **C** frustrated by people's lack of interest in changes occurring across the globe.

7 36 **Now listen to Extract Three. For questions 5 and 6, choose the answer (A, B or C) which fits best.**

Extract Three

You hear two friends discussing smart phone apps.

5 What is the girl's view of her new fitness app?

- **A** She is surprised at how visually appealing it is.
- **B** She is convinced it has an advantage over its competitors.
- **C** She is disappointed that it is not available for free.

6 When talking about apps he has previously downloaded, the man is

- **A** highlighting the usefulness of online app reviews.
- **B** describing the most reliable way to discover new apps.
- **C** demonstrating that suitable apps are often found by chance.

8 **In each of these extracts from the recordings, use a verb from the box in the correct form to form a collocation with the noun in bold.**

dream up exercise lose make present take undergo

1. How do people .... such absurd **ideas** and still get taken seriously?
2. Did life .... a massive **transformation**?
3. Could you imagine going online tomorrow and seeing some supposedly visionary inventor .... it as a **solution** to congestion in cities?
4. So it might be an idea to .... a little more **caution** before doubting someone else's judgement.
5. We need to .... **responsibility** now if we're to gain control of it all.
6. I've no idea how many times I've downloaded one and .... **interest** within minutes because it's unusable.
7. It's .... a huge **impact** on my playing.

Grammar

Future perfect and continuous; *be* + *to* infinitive

The COMPLETE grammar reference
▶ Scan the QR code, watch the video, then turn to page 175

1 In each of these sentences from Listening Part 1, choose the correct alternatives in *italics*.

1. *I'll have had / I'll be having* this phone for two years soon.
2. In the coming year or so, more than half the world's population will *be using / have been using* them.
3. By the year 2000, humans won't *be living / have been living* only on land – we will also *have settled / be settling* in the sea.
4. By the end of this decade, *we'll have been relying on / we'll be relying on* computers for about seventy years.
5. I bet *I'll have been spending / I'll be spending* more time on this app than any other when I upgrade my phone.
6. We need to take responsibility now if *we'll be gaining / we're to gain* control of it all.

2 Rearrange the words to form correct sentences. Include correct punctuation.

1. have / by / will / We / arrive / time / you / left / the
2. be / game / video / new / playing / his / all / will / brother / My / evening
3. for / we / will / been / have / years / English / May / In / learning / eight
4. 9.00 / after / have / Come / definitely / by / I'll / then / over / finished / work / my
5. it / since / Soon / Argentina / will / to / been / Angela / weeks / six / have / moved
6. later / speech / president / The / a / to / today / give / is

3 With a partner, decide which of the verbs in bold are correct. If they are not, correct them. Then discuss whether or not you think the predictions are likely to come true.

1. In ten years' time, we **will have been travelling** around in driverless cars, and taxi driving **will have ceased** to exist as a job.
2. In the future, the majority of the world's students **will be doing** most of their learning online.
3. By the end of the century, thousands of people **will have been offering** the chance to take a holiday on the moon.
4. It won't be long before most people **will be deciding** to switch to a plant-based diet.
5. In 2050, our devices **will have become** obsolete and we**'ll be plugging** our brains straight into the Cloud.

Reading and Use of English Part 7

Exam advice

- Read the text carefully, looking at the subject of each paragraph and the information before and after each gap.
- Work methodically through the paragraphs, reading them and placing them one by one.
- Pay attention to words and phrases in the missing paragraphs which may refer to something in the text.
- If you are not sure of an answer, read the paragraph before, then the option from A–G you have chosen, then the paragraph after, checking that they make complete, logical sense together.
- When you have finished, quickly read the text again to confirm your answers.

1 Work in pairs. You are going to read an article about a person who works in technology and computing. Before you read, discuss with a partner what the following jobs might involve.

- Ethical hacker
- Computational linguist
- Chief listening officer
- Digital overlord

2 Six paragraphs have been removed from the article on page 99. Read the article (but not the paragraphs which have been removed).

- Summarise in a few words what each paragraph in the article is about.
- Underline any words and phrases that link the text together, particularly where the writer is clearly referring to something they have previously mentioned. This will help you to place the missing paragraphs when you read them.

A welcome/unwelcome visit

It's a Wednesday afternoon. I open an email from my journalism tutor. I blink, slowly, as I realise I'm staring at an exhaustive list of all my bank details, passwords, usernames, everything. Someone, somehow, has managed to get past my supposedly bullet-proof internet security system and hacked their way into all of my accounts. Then, an instant message pops up on my screen: £10,000 or I lock you out of everything you own – forever. I'm almost shaking with fury. What sort of person would do such a thing?

1 ☐

'Don't panic, it was only me,' my friend Lucia declares breezily, inviting herself into my apartment. 'Your accounts took about thirty seconds to hack into, and I sent you the email via your tutor's account to make sure you opened it when you logged on,' she explains. My brain stops screaming at itself and I start to calm down. 'Just – please – update your passwords more often, like I keep telling you. Shall I make coffee?'

2 ☐

For many people, the term is an oxymoron: one word associated with admirable morality, the other with shameful activity. But be in no doubt, these ingenious people are the cybertroops we will increasingly be relying on to protect us in our ever more connected world. Lucia will be paid to hack into the vast computer networks of businesses and governments and identify those systems' vulnerabilities so they can have greater protection should they receive a visit from hackers with far less honourable intentions.

3 ☐

While some of them might recognise elements of their past selves in the stereotype of a hoodie-wearing teenager, tapping away at a laptop in the dark of their parents' basement, full of fury at the injustices of the world, Lucia most certainly does not. Nor would she identify with the Hollywood cliché of hackers as fresh-faced, wonderfully stylish, but utterly dishonourable characters who take under thirty seconds to crack entire national defence systems just for fun.

4 ☐

She even seems a little embarrassed to confess that, with the '£10,000 ransom' stunt, part of her just wanted to show off her ever-expanding skill set to her friend. This reluctance to boast about her considerable talent is entirely typical. Generally speaking, ethical hackers refer to themselves as such purely and simply because it's the accepted, industry-wide job title – not because it sounds mysterious or cool.

5 ☐

Perhaps, given the ordinariness of their working environment, you'd be forgiven for being surprised at the eye-watering sums they earn. But the cost of all this illegal activity to the worldwide economy is startling. Some estimates suggest the figure could be as high as $10 trillion in the past year alone.

6 ☐

So, we should all pay far more attention to our online security than we currently do, as we scroll through the pages of our favourite sites, unthinkingly signing in to one account after the other with our automatic logins, never shutting down our devices properly. We may be able to filter out annoying pop-up ads, but without people like Lucia, we'd be helpless against the cyber-attackers, threatening our lives and livelihoods.

3 **Choose from the paragraphs A–G the one which fits each gap (1–6). There is one extra paragraph which you do not need to use.**

A

There are thousands of these cybercriminals at work, and the world is facing a severe shortage of technicians with the skills needed to mount an effective defence against them. People like her – brilliantly clever, studious and principled, dedicated to doing the right thing – are filling those gaps.

B

Fluent in dozens of programming languages, Lucia can already negotiate her way past vastly complex security systems. Within a few short years, she'll be commanding huge fees by helping organisations protect themselves from hostile cyber-attacks, when she begins her career as an ethical hacker.

C

Data hacks like these, on home Wi-Fi systems, are just one cause for concern, and the number of cyber-attacks on the digital infrastructure within utilities or telecommunications companies, even governments, is growing. Thankfully, so is the number of good guys who come to protect us: hackers known as 'white hats'.

D

I asked her once if there was a more suitable alternative that she'd prefer. 'Offensive security professional', apparently, is the best title for anyone operating in this role. It summarises what they do: on the front foot, battling the bad guys from anonymous offices, rather than clandestine basements.

E

I feel privileged to be able to call Lucia my friend. What might that amount have been, were it not for the intervention of her, and of people like her? Ten, fifty, a hundred times higher? It doesn't bear thinking about.

F

When paying top dollar to keep your data safe and constantly backing up your files isn't enough to stop these attacks happening, being consumed with anger is a perfectly logical reaction. I curse the unexpected knocking at my front door, distracting me from figuring out what to do next.

G

As Lucia and I sit down with our coffee, chatting to one another about this and that, I can't help but be reminded that, while she might be young, any other similarities to such self-assured, glamorous characters do not apply.

4 **Work in pairs.**

1 Would you like to work as an ethical hacker? Why? / Why not?

2 Should learning these types of skills be given more importance in schools and colleges?

9

Grammar

Objects, reflexives and reciprocals

The COMPLETE grammar reference
▶ Scan the QR code, watch the video, then turn to page 176

1 **Look at these extracts from Reading and Use of English Part 7 and write one word from the box in each gap. Then check your answers in the text on page 99.**

another	from	herself	itself	you	selves	themselves

1 I open an email .... my journalism tutor.
2 'Don't panic, it was only me,' my friend Lucia declares breezily, inviting .... into my apartment.
3 I sent .... the email via your tutor's account to make sure you opened it when you logged on.
4 My brain stops screaming at .... and I start to calm down.
5 While some of them might recognise elements of their past .... in the stereotype of a hoodie-wearing teenager, …
6 … ethical hackers refer to .... as such purely and simply because it's the accepted, industry-wide job title – not because it sounds mysterious or cool.
7 As Lucia and I sit down with our coffee, chatting to one .... about this and that …

2 **Correct the sentences by either adding or taking away one word.**

1 I'm sure my programming and coding skills would improve if I had an online tutor to teach.
2 Thank goodness my computer's operating system updates – I'd never remember to do it otherwise.
3 My dad is one of those people who have almost no technical know-how, yet never blame when they have problems with their devices.
4 I'd love it if someone bought for me a new VR headset for my birthday.
5 My friends and I will always support each one other unquestioningly, whatever the circumstances.
6 The only way you can guarantee something will be done right it is by doing it.

3 **For questions 1–4, complete the second sentence so that it has a similar meaning to the first sentence, using the word given. Do not change the word given. You must use between three and six words, including the word given.**

1 Mia was bought a smartphone by her mother as a graduation present.
FOR
Mia's .... as a graduation present.

2 I'm proud of the fact that we built our home recording studio without any help.
BY
The fact we built our home recording studio .... feel proud.

3 The constant arguments between Martyn and Fayed led to them falling out.
ONE
Because Martyn and Fayed were .... they eventually fell out.

4 Last night, I foolishly left my apartment without a key and couldn't get back in.
LOCK
Last night, I was foolish enough .... my apartment.

Vocabulary

Multi-word verbs

1 **In each of these extracts from Reading Part 7, correct the multi-word verbs in bold. Then check your answers in the text on page 99.**

1 Someone, somehow, has managed to get past my supposedly bullet-proof internet security system and **hacked** their way **around** all of my accounts.
2 Then, an instant message **pops down** on my screen: £10,000 or I **lock** you **away** of everything you own – forever!
3 I sent you the email via your tutor's account to make sure you opened it when you **logged down**.
4 … as we **scroll on** the pages of our favourite sites, unthinkingly **signing along** to one account after the other, never **shutting out** our devices properly.
5 We may be able to **filter off** annoying pop-up ads, but without people like Lucia, we'd be helpless against the cyber-attackers, threatening our lives and livelihoods.

2 **Use the correct form of the multi-word verbs in the box to complete the sentences describing technology-related problems.**

hack into lock out log on/in pop up
run out scroll through shut down

a Having your social media or bank account .... and your details stolen.
b Not .... your phone or laptop properly and .... of battery at an important moment.
c Seeing an angry message .... on your screen from someone you thought you'd blocked.
d Forgetting your password and getting .... of your accounts when you try to ....
e .... the pages of pointless websites to avoid doing the work you're supposed to be doing.

3 **Tell a partner which of the situations in Exercise 2 you have experienced. Then rank them in order of which would cause the most/least concern.**

action, *activity*, *event* and *programme*

1 **Complete these sentences with *action*, *activity*, *event* or *programme* in the correct form.**

1 There was a period of intense .... in which the programmers worked tirelessly to ensure they released their latest video game on time.
2 I've just spilt a glass of water on my keyboard so now my laptop is completely out of ....
3 Will people lose interest in Olympic .... when athletes no longer break records?
4 The government claims to be introducing a comprehensive .... of economic reform.

2 **For questions 1–8, use one verb in the correct form and one adjective from the box to complete each statement (these verbs and adjectives form strong collocations with the nouns in bold).**

verbs	adjectives
attend	criminal
commemorate	decisive
involve	glamorous
offer	historic
participate	legal
present	outdoor
take	popular
threaten	varied

1 Every single college or university has a responsibility to .... **programmes** of study to cater for all students' educational needs.
2 The best bit about being a movie star must be .... **events** when your new film is released.
3 Most people in my family are the type who prefer to sit back and wait for something to happen, rather than .... **action** themselves.
4 There are nowhere near enough children .... in .... **activities** these days, and I blame technology for that.
5 It is becoming increasingly common for people to be .... with .... **action** for a comment they posted on the internet.
6 In my country, we should have more public holidays and festivals to .... important .... **events**.
7 You need to have a particular type of personality to be good at .... **programmes** on TV.
8 I have a very strong sense of moral duty and would never .... myself in .... **activity**.

3 **Discuss your ideas on each statement in Exercise 2 with a partner.**

Speaking Part 2

▶ **Page 207 Speaking bank**
Speaking Part 2

1 **Work in pairs. Look at the photos and the examiner's instructions. Which of these phrases might you use with each photo?**

blank everything out | bring a subject to life | breakthrough technology | conventional study aid | display the study materials | focus on something intently | gain a detailed understanding | provided by the teacher | stream a few songs | see something up close | take traditional notes | work without distraction

'Here are your pictures. They show people using technology while studying. I'd like you to compare two of the pictures and say why they might be using that type of technology, and how difficult it would be to study without it.'

1

2

2 **Now take turns to do the task in Exercise 1.**

3 **Listen to Anna and Daniel doing the same speaking task. Which of these does Anna do? Write *Yes* or *No*.** 37

1 Although she's not sure, she guesses what the children's devices are called.

2 She explains what the devices are and what they can be used for.

3 She suggests just one way in which the children might be using the device.

4 She corrects herself when she realises she hasn't used the right word for something.

5 She tries to use phrases she's not sure about in order to express herself more clearly and show a greater range of vocabulary.

6 She deals with all parts of the task.

4 **Complete each of these phrases by writing three words in each space. Then check your answers by listening again.** 37

1 … they're each wearing a virtual reality .... – glasses? Or would you call them headsets?

2 … presumably they've been provided by the teacher to bring a subject to life in .... another …

3 … the students might be using them for something .... of visiting an interesting landmark …

4 The second picture is .... as the first one …

5 … in that it also shows someone wearing a headset .... …

6 … but in this case it's a pair of wi-fi headphones, ... 'wireless' headphones …

7 … listening to music helps him to – .... – blank everything out …

8 He's also using his – it's not .... clear whether it's a tablet or a laptop.

5 **In which sentence(s) in Exercise 4 does Anna**

a correct herself?

b say she's guessing what something is, or is for?

c say she's not sure what the correct word is?

d make a comparison?

3

6 Work in pairs. Look at the six photos. Which of these phrases would you associate with each photo?

assembly line | calmness under pressure | closely monitoring | deep underground | heat and humidity | high-pressure environment | intense concentration | the heat and noise | lack of oxygen | lose yourself in the moment | pottery wheel | skilled craftsmanship | tracking growth | strict safety precautions | welcome distraction

7 Work in pairs.

38 **Student A:** Look at photos 1–3 in Set A, listen to the examiner's instructions and do the task.

Set A

- Why might this technology be important to these people?
- How might they be feeling as they use this technology?

1

2
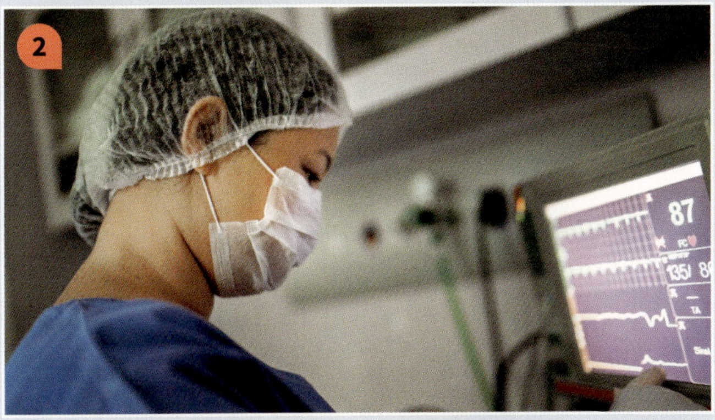

3

Exam advice

- Be ready to speculate or guess about what the photos show.
- If you notice you've made a mistake, correct it – don't pretend it hasn't happened!
- If you don't know a word, don't avoid the problem. Explain the idea using other words.

39 **Student B:** When Student A has finished, look at photos 4–6 in Set B, listen to the examiner's instructions and do the task.

Set B

- How are the machines helping these people in their work?
- How rewarding might this work be?

4

5

6

Reading and Use of English Part 4

1 Correct the mistakes in these Part 4 answers.

1 The judge was shocked when the defendant unexpectedly denied being responsible for the accident.

OF

The judge was shocked by the defendant's denial of a responsibility for the accident.

2 After rain was forecast, they decided to postpone their party for a week.

PUT

After rain was forecast, the decision was taken to put back their party for a week.

3 Because we were so far from home, our only option was to take a taxi.

BUT

We were so far from home that we could've walked but we chose to take a taxi.

2 For questions 1–6, complete the second sentence so that it has a similar meaning to the first sentence, using the word given. Do not change the word given. You must use between three and six words, including the word given.

1 Paula and Maria are so similar that I'm not always sure who is who.

TELL

I can rarely .... Paula and Maria.

2 The school dress code should be comprehensively reviewed.

REVIEW

There needs .... the school dress code.

3 'I'm sorry to have disappointed the team with my behaviour,' said Adrian.

APOLOGISED

Adrian .... down with his behaviour.

4 I was always convinced that our business would be a success.

MIND

There was never .... that our business would be a success.

5 If you hadn't phoned, it's highly likely I wouldn't have woken up.

WELL

Had .... have stayed asleep.

6 The way we view the world has been hugely affected by technology.

IMPACT

Technology has had a .... which we view the world.

Exam advice

- Read the original sentence, the word given and the sentence with the gap. Think about:
  - whether you need an expression, e.g. *it's not worth it.*
  - whether you need a multi-word verb, e.g. *turn out*
  - what grammar you will need, e.g. do you need to change a verb from active to passive, put something into reported speech, use a verb + *-ing*?

Writing Part 1: An essay

Page 193 Writing bank
An essay

1 Read the writing task and underline the key points.

Your class has attended a discussion on the factors which teenagers should consider to ensure their online safety. You have made the notes below:

Factors which teenagers should consider to ensure their online safety
- not sharing personal information
- raising concerns with parents or teachers
- updating security details

Some opinions expressed during the discussion:

'Giving your real name or address is extremely risky.'

'Always tell someone if you're worried about something that happened online.'

'It's so important to update your passwords regularly.'

Write an **essay** discussing **two** of the factors above. You should **explain which factor is more important** for young people to consider, **giving reasons** in support of your answer.

You may, if you wish, make use of the opinions expressed during the discussion, but you should use your own words as far as possible.

2 Work in small groups. Discuss these questions and note down your opinions and ideas.

1 What might happen if someone fails to consider each of the three factors in the essay task? Think of examples.

2 Which of the three factors can cause the most problems if it is ignored?

3 **Work in pairs and answer these questions.**

1 Read the essay below without paying attention to the gaps. Which ideas and examples were also mentioned during your discussion in Exercise 2?

2 Which opinion(s) from the essay task did the writer use? Did she express them using the same words or her own words?

3 Do you agree with the writer's conclusions? Why? / Why not?

While young people undoubtedly benefit from the internet as a valuable social and educational resource, they also need to feel confident in dealing with any threats to their online safety.

(1) .... , teenagers today are acutely aware of the potential dangers that come with having an active online presence and, **(2)** .... , should be trusted by their parents and teachers to exist in their digital world without adult interference. **(3)** .... , understanding how cybercriminals operate does not necessarily prevent someone from becoming a target, and no one of any age should attempt to deal with the consequences if that does happen. I would argue that it is imperative for young people to inform someone they trust, whether friend, family member or teacher, **(4)** .... they have concerns about their online safety.

Another area of concern comes with failing to update personal security details regularly enough, which leads to the risk of being hacked. While under-18s rarely own a bank account, and are less likely than adults to suffer any financial loss at the hands of cybercriminals, there are still a host of other dangers. These might include having their private photos stolen, or someone threatening to blackmail them or damage their online reputation after gaining access to their social media accounts. **(5)** .... it would be heartbreaking to have to delete all personal accounts purely **(6)** .... being careless with their login details.

Any threat to a teenager's online security, whether digital or emotional, will eventually arrive at the need to inform a parent or another relative, or a teacher. **(7)** .... , I would argue that this should be prioritised above anything else.

4 **Complete the essay in Exercise 3 by writing a phrase from the box in each of the gaps, 1–7.**

all things considered | as a consequence of | as and when | as such | it goes without saying that | on the whole | that said

5 **Choose an alternative phrase from the box for each of the gaps 1–7 in Exercise 3.**

accordingly | at any given point when | by and large | as a result of | having said that | needless to say | ultimately

Exam advice

- Use a formal, academic style when you write an essay.
- Write a structured argument and link your ideas with phrases such as *for example, in contrast, in conclusion*.
- Show that you are aware of counter-arguments.
- Make sure that your opinion on the subject is clearly expressed.

6 **Work in pairs. Which paragraph in the essay**

1 explains why online security is important?

2 explains why any worries should be taken to parents/teachers?

3 summarises the writer's argument?

4 introduces the focus of the essay?

7 **Read this writing task. Note down your ideas and opinions.**

Your class has attended a talk about the areas of modern life which greatly benefit from developments in technology. You have made the notes below:

<u>Areas of modern life which greatly benefit from developments in technology</u>

- interpersonal communication
- health and wellbeing
- education

Some opinions expressed during the discussion

'People are far happier when they know they can contact anyone at any time.'

'The care and treatment people receive if they become ill is unbelievably advanced.'

'There are so many apps and websites that help people to learn without needing a teacher.'

Write an **essay** discussing **two** of the factors above. You should **explain which area benefits most** from technology, **giving reasons** in support of your answer.

You may, if you wish, make use of the opinions expressed during the discussion, but you should use your own words as far as possible.

8 **Write an essay plan with a similar structure to the sample essay in Exercise 3. Note down the ideas and opinions you will express in each paragraph.**

9 **Write your essay. Try to use some of the linking phrases from Exercises 4 and 5.**

10 Learning for life

Starting off

1 Work in pairs. Use the context to clarify the meaning of each underlined word. Then discuss the questions with your partner.

1. Look at the photos of different educational contexts. How many of these have you attended or participated in? Which did you enjoy most? Why?
2. Tell each other about your education to date. What do/did you most like and dislike about the process?
3. What do you think is the optimum number of students in a class at primary, secondary and higher education levels?
4. Which do you think produces more effective results, online or in-person lessons?
5. How might technology influence the manner in which people study and learn in the future?

2 How far do you agree or disagree with these opinions about education? Use the context to clarify the meaning of each underlined word. Then tick the boxes (1 = strongly agree; 5 = strongly disagree).

	1	2	3	4	5
a Parents should have the choice of sending children to school or educating them at home themselves.					
b An education system which does not teach young people how to think for themselves is a catastrophic failure.					
c My country's education systems encourage conformity and discourage originality and creativity.					
d A teacher's main job is to facilitate learning so that pupils or students can pass examinations.					
e The main purpose of education is to teach young people how to be pragmatic and to equip them with the practical skills they need for work.					
f The purpose of a university education is to produce future generations of leaders.					

3 Compare ideas with your partner and discuss any points of disagreement.

Listening Part 2

Exam advice

- Read the gapped sentences before you listen. This will show you how the recording is organised and give you an idea of the topic. The gaps in the sentences should provide a clear idea of what information you are listening for.
- Fill in the gaps with the actual words you hear, without changing them in any way.
- Check that your completed sentences are grammatically correct.
- Answer every question even if you are not sure.

1 **Work in pairs. Discuss the questions.**

1 How are the skills and qualities people need in life and work today different from the past?

2 What difficulties do young people experience after they finish their education?

3 What can schools, colleges and universities do to ensure that students are prepared for a successful future in the 21st century?

2 **You will hear a British high school student called Samia giving a presentation in class about her research into the essential skills and qualities needed in the 21st century. Work with a partner and brainstorm ideas in answer to the question below. (there is an example to help get you started).**
What vocabulary might you expect to hear when someone talks about this topic?

21st-century skills and qualities

- *technological know-how*

3 40 **Listen to the recording to find out if any of your ideas are mentioned.**

4 **Now read the sentences below. Can you guess what word or phrase is missing from each sentence?**

Developing 21st-century skills

Samia says her group has made available a **(1)** .... of the research they used.

Samia says she finds current and future changes in **(2)** .... particularly concerning.

Samia mentions how research concludes that **(3)** .... will increasingly become an essential skill.

Samia reports the agreement of education experts highlighting the ongoing benefits that **(4)** .... provides.

Samia reinforces the need to access **(5)** .... in order to make use of prior learning.

Samia uses the word **(6)** .... to capture her sense of how best to view places of study.

Samia is critical of how **(7)** .... is prioritised as the main academic goal.

Samia encourages educational establishments not to neglect the **(8)** .... of their students.

5 40 **Listen to the recording again. For questions 1–8 in Exercise 4, complete the sentences with a word or short phrase.**

6 **Work in pairs.**

1 Look at the completed sentences in questions 1–8 in Exercise 4 again.
   - Which of Samia's conclusions do you agree with? Why?
   - Do you share any of Samia's concerns? Why? / Why not?

2 How can lessons and lectures be adapted to ensure that young people are given the relevant preparation they need for the future?

Reading and Use of English Part 1

1 **How much do you remember about Use of English Part 1? Circle the correct alternative in each sentence in the Exam round-up box.**

> **Exam round-up**
>
> In Use of English Part 1:
>
> 1 there is a text with *eight* / *ten* gaps.
>
> 2 For each gap you are given a choice of *three* / *four* possible answers.
>
> 3 You should read the text *before* / *after* reading the options.

2 **Match the definitions (a–d) with the different types of thinking skills in the box.**

critical thinking	lateral thinking
logical thinking	wishful thinking

a a way of solving a problem by thinking about it in a different and original way and not using traditional or expected methods

b imagining or discussing a very unlikely future event or situation as if it were possible and might one day happen

c solving a problem by thinking about it in a direct and straightforward way, following reason to establish each step

d the process of thinking carefully about a subject or idea without allowing feelings or opinions to affect you

3 **Think of the different situations where people might use these thinking skills. Discuss your suggestions with a partner.**

4 **Look at the picture, read the instructions below, and discuss how you would solve the problem with a partner.**

You have a small candle, a box of drawing pins and a book of matches.

Your task is to attach the candle to the wall so that, when lit, it does not drip wax on to the floor below it.

5 **Read the article. Which types of thinking skills do people use when trying to solve the Candle Problem?**

6 **Read the article again. For questions 1–8, decide which answer (A, B, C or D) best fits each gap. There is an example at the beginning (0).**

The Candle Problem

German psychologist Karl Duncker's 'Candle Problem' experiment **(0)** .... out one way in which our minds approach tasks differently. Duncker's proposition was that, by **(1)** .... the power of creative thought, we can look at a familiar object and consider how it might otherwise be used in order to serve a new purpose. This test is **(2)** .... used by psychologists to measure the personality trait of 'functional fixedness', a type of thinking that prevents people from using their creativity to **(3)** .... problems.

Those who fail to provide the correct answer to the Candle Problem usually **(4)** .... this trait, and they are not alone. In fact, the vast majority of people see an object purely for its **(5)** .... use, and rarely stop to consider an alternative, even a purpose for which it might **(6)** .... highly suitable. However, those who do succeed have the **(7)** .... to be creative and flexible thinkers who are capable of avoiding functional fixedness, and do not naturally conform to **(8)** ...., particularly when a problem requires them to think 'outside-of-the-box'.

0	**A** turns	**B** gives	**C** puts	**D** sets
1	**A** employing	**B** affirming	**C** fulfilling	**D** appointing
2	**A** authentically	**B** commonly	**C** naturally	**D** entirely
3	**A** determine	**B** address	**C** reach	**D** contend
4	**A** disclose	**B** expose	**C** display	**D** present
5	**A** decided	**B** shown	**C** provided	**D** given
6	**A** verify	**B** confirm	**C** prove	**D** demonstrate
7	**A** privilege	**B** reliability	**C** principle	**D** tendency
8	**A** convention	**B** assumption	**C** opinion	**D** prediction

Speaking Part 4

Page 213 Speaking bank
Speaking Part 4

Exam advice

- Listen very carefully to the question you are asked, but also to your partner because you may be asked to respond to something they say.
- Express your opinions clearly and be prepared to justify or explain what you say, or to suggest a range of possible ideas to answer the question.
- Remember that fluency is important, so make sure you give full answers.

1 **Work in pairs. Discuss these written prompts for a Speaking Part 3 task.**

For what purposes are these approaches to learning suited?

- self-study
- group work without a teacher
- a lecture to many people
- one-to-one: a teacher with a student
- a class of 20–30 with a teacher

2 **Questions 1–6 below are some possible Part 4 questions which might follow on from the written prompts you have been discussing. Which questions**

a ask you to choose between two options?
b ask for an explanation of an established fact?
c ask whether you agree with something or not?
d ask for a number of different ideas?

1 Why do you think lectures are more common as a form of teaching in universities than in schools?
2 Are there more advantages than disadvantages of one-to-one teaching from a student's point of view?
3 Some people think that individual study is the least effective way of learning. Do you share this view? Why? / Why not?
4 Do you think project work is an approach more suited to older or younger students? Why?
5 Which do you think is more important from a student's point of view: a good teacher or a small class? Why?
6 Do you think that exams are the best means of assessing students? Why? / Why not?

3 **How would you answer questions 1–6 in Exercise 2? Make brief notes.**

4 (41) **Listen to two exam candidates discussing two of the questions in Exercise 2. Which questions do they discuss? Do they express any ideas that are similar to yours?**

5 **Look at the following words and phrases from the recording. Which ones could you use to answer questions 1–6 in Exercise 2?**

academic study   class teaching
individual student   learning style
pair or group work   primary school
programme of study   range of abilities
secondary school   give clear instructions
manage one's own learning
work independently   effective   motivated

6 **Work in pairs. Answer the questions in Exercise 2, taking turns to start the discussion. Use some of the language from Exercise 5 in your discussion.**

Reading and Use of English Part 8

Exam advice

- The questions or statements precede the text(s) in this part of the exam. Study these carefully before you read the text(s).
- Read the text(s), looking for the information referred to in the ten questions or statements.
- Many of the sections may say similar things, so you will have to read carefully to decide which section answers the question exactly.

1 Look at the photos and discuss the following questions.

1. What are the people doing?
2. Why might they have chosen to do these activities?
3. Have you ever done any of these activities?
4. Which do/would you most enjoy?

1

2

3

2 Number the following activities according to which you would most (1) and least (10) like to try. Compare lists with a partner and explain your choices.

- ☐ yoga
- ☐ writing a novel
- ☐ volunteer work
- ☐ surfing or windsurfing
- ☐ magic tricks
- ☐ knitting
- ☐ tightrope-walking
- ☐ meditation
- ☐ cooking the food of another nation
- ☐ an online course on something you know little or nothing about (your choice)

3 You are going to read comments from five people talking about learning something new. First read questions 1–10 and underline the key ideas.

Which person:

aimed to differentiate themselves from their peers?	1
gained a sense of determination from an existing interest?	2
found amusement in a subsequent outcome of their efforts?	3
understood the importance of adopting a set routine?	4
experienced a gain in proficiency after a chance meeting?	5
took advantage of a sudden change in self-belief?	6
felt relief after a change in their physical appearance?	7
paid frequent close attention to constructive remarks?	8
allowed concerns about their ability to delay the pursuit of their ambition?	9
was convinced of the widespread appeal of what they had learnt?	10

4 Now read the texts. For questions 1–10, choose from the texts (A–E). The texts may be chosen more than once.

5 Work in small groups.

1. Discuss what measures could be taken to improve education in your country. Think about all levels, from nursery school to university.
2. Make a list of five suggestions to present to the rest of the class.

A First Time for Everything

A SARA

While playing on a beach at the age of four, I was suddenly hit by a huge wave. It left me terrified of the sea for such a long time. Ten years later, splashing around nervously on another beach, I got distracted by the sight of a surfer, gracefully riding a breaker in the distance. Along came another wave, slamming me into the sand once again. But this time I wasn't terrified; I'd accidentally caught myself being fearless, and immediately understood that I couldn't let this moment turn into a missed opportunity. I signed up for surfing lessons that day, a complete novice desperate to learn everything about the sport. My friends and I thought it was hilarious that, despite constantly being bottom of my science class, I suddenly became obsessively interested in tide tables and wave hydrodynamics.

B KAZUMI

For the course I want to study at university – Business Management – competition for places is fierce. I realised that, to set myself apart from the rest when I apply later this year, I needed to do something interesting to add to my CV, so taking an online course seemed like a solid idea. Although I couldn't choose one initially (the possibilities really were endless), I ultimately opted for something just outside my comfort zone, but still somewhat relevant to my application: Fashion Management. I've little interest in clothes, but felt confident this would demonstrate how I thrive off challenge. I showed up to every class on time, put aside two hours each weekend for homework, and revised each night. I couldn't have finished the course without that degree of discipline.

C ESME

While, to everyone in college, I'm known as captain of the athletics team, I've always secretly dreamt of becoming a performance poet. Each time I visualised myself doing it on stage in real life, though, I'd always imagine someone in the audience whispering, 'her poems are awful, is she going to stop soon?'. One day, I realised that, with my athletics, even if I didn't feel motivated or energetic enough to train, I'd still just get out there and push through a session. Similarly, I shouldn't have to wait for the moment I'd magically feel brave enough to go on stage: I should just do it. I forced myself into the writing habit, drafting poems whenever I could, and booked my first gig. There was a real sense of occasion that night, and it turned out I needn't have worried – everyone loved it.

D AQIL

Whenever people learn something new, they often try to get through the beginner stage as quickly as possible in their rush to improve. As my grandfather insisted, after beginning to teach me chess, this is invariably a mistake. During those first lessons, I fixated on every instruction he gave, considering every possibility in the moves he demonstrated, determined to absorb everything I had to know in order to avoid getting beaten within five moves, as I did every game for eight years. Finally, when I was twenty, I managed to beat him – an enormous personal victory. Plus, I was delighted to realise, having spent all that time burning my eyes into sixty-four squares on a board, I'd been able to replace my smartphone addiction with a far healthier alternative – one I had little doubt anyone would grow to love, given the chance.

E TYRONE

For many years, I was the tallest in my group of friends, and always got picked last for games or sports. My legs were unnaturally long, and I'd often trip over my own feet while running. Despite this, I never saw myself as being any more or less clumsy than the other children in the playground. In time, the rest of my body caught up, and I could finally, gratefully, take up the sport I'd wanted to try for ever – parkour. Initially, I was hopeless, and spent more time injured than practising. Then I happened to bump into an old school friend who was now a fellow parkour runner and got some invaluable advice. At that moment, everything clicked, and my technique and ability rapidly caught up with the faith I'd had in my own potential. Now, it almost seems like everyone I know has followed me into the world of parkour. We could happily do it forever.

Grammar

Expressing ability, possibility and obligation

The COMPLETE grammar reference
▶ Scan the QR code, watch the video, then turn to page 177

1 **Read the sentences. Which sentences express ability, which possibility and which obligation, and do they refer to the past, the present or the future?**

1. Knowing little about them meant I couldn't choose which one to have.
2. I couldn't just turn up whenever I liked.
3. She had to decide, there and then, what course to take.
4. He could design something amazing that we all want to use.
5. I needn't have sent him a letter. He knew already.
6. After failing his exams, he didn't have to choose which course to take.
7. I'll be able to teach as soon as I'm qualified.
8. You mustn't enter that room under any circumstances.

2 **Read these pairs of sentences and decide if both in each pair are correct. If both are correct, discuss the difference in meaning between them.**

1 **a** I have to finish this essay, so I can't go out.
b I must finish this essay. I really want to do well.

2 **a** I didn't need to catch a taxi home from the airport. My brother picked me up.
b I needn't have caught a taxi home from the airport. My brother would have picked me up.

3 **a** You don't have to go to the lecture this afternoon. It's optional.
b You mustn't go to the lecture this afternoon. It's only for first-year students.

4 **a** After a lot of effort, I could finally start the car engine.
b After a lot of effort, I finally managed to start the car engine.

5 **a** He can stay for up to 90 days with this kind of visa if he wants to.
b He could stay for up to 90 days with this kind of visa if he wanted to.

6 **a** In the future, we might not study in classrooms with other students.
b In the future, we could not study in classrooms with other students.

3 **Exam candidates often make mistakes with modal verbs. Find and correct the mistakes in the sentences below.**

1. He must have correct his work before he gave it to the teacher.
2. The students at the back of the lecture hall became frustrated because they can't hear very well.
3. I think they might lie to you when you bought the TV last week.
4. I'm happy to tell you that we could offer you a place on the degree course.
5. Could you tell me the name of the manager, so I would be able to contact him in the future?
6. If we afford the fees, our daughter will apply to this college.

4 **Work in pairs (Student A and Student B). Tell your partner about something …**

A
- you'd really like to be able to do
- you were worried about, but realised you needn't have been
- you couldn't do for a long time but eventually managed to.

B
- you can't understand but you would like to
- you couldn't have done without the help of a friend
- you really must do over the course of the next year.

5 **Swap topics (A to B and vice versa) and repeat Exercise 4.**

Vocabulary

chance, occasion, opportunity and *possibility*

1 **These sentences are taken from Reading and Use of English Part 8. Try to remember what words you need for the gaps. Then look back at the text on page 111 to check your answers.**

1 I couldn't let this moment turn into a missed ....
2 There was a real sense of .... on the night.
3 During those first lessons, I fixated on every instruction he gave, considering every .... in the moves he demonstrated …
4 [It's a game] I had little doubt anyone would grow to love, given the ....

2 **Read these definitions. Then circle the correct alternatives in *italics* in the sentences below.**

occasion

a particular time when something happens

My sister's wedding was a very special ***occasion****.*

Collocations
Adjectives *formal, historic, memorable, rare, solemn, special, unique*
Verbs ***mark*** *the occasion,* ***rise*** *to the occasion*
Use ***on*** *one occasion, the occasion* ***when*** + clause

opportunity

a situation in which it is possible to do something you want to do

I'm going to work in Hong Kong for a year. It's a great ***opportunity****.*

Collocations
Adjectives *equal, excellent, golden, perfect, tremendous, welcome*
Verbs *have, lose, miss, seize, take + the opportunity, opportunity + arise/occur*
Use *the opportunity* ***to do*** *something, the opportunity* ***for*** + noun

possibility

a situation where something may or may not happen

There's a definite ***possibility*** *of a strike by train drivers next week.*

Collocations
Adjectives *definite, distinct, real, remote, serious, slight, strong*
Verbs *face, accept, rule out, recognise, ignore + the possibility*
Use *the possibility* ***of doing*** *something [not ~~possibility to do~~], the possibility* ***that*** + clause

1 Schools try to ensure that all students have an equal *opportunity* / *possibility* to succeed.
2 On several *occasions* / *opportunities* recently the university has made changes to the syllabus without consulting students.
3 If you study abroad, you should take every *occasion* / *opportunity* to learn the language.
4 There's a strong *opportunity* / *possibility* that you will win one of the three available scholarships.
5 Our graduation ceremony next week will be a very special *opportunity* / *occasion*.
6 According to the weather forecast, there's a distinct *possibility* / *occasion* of rain tomorrow.

3 ***Chance*** **can mean** ***possibility*** **or** ***opportunity*****, but is generally used less formally. Read these definitions and complete the sentences below with** ***chance, occasion, opportunity*** **or** ***possibility*****. Sometimes two answers are possible.**

chance

1 an occasion which allows something to be done; an opportunity

I'm afraid I didn't get the ***chance*** *to tell him the good news.*

Collocations
Adjectives *good, ideal, last, second, unexpected*
Verbs *get, have, deserve, welcome, give someone, take, turn down + the chance*
Use *the chance* ***to do*** *something*

2 likelihood; the level of possibility that something will happen

There's an outside ***chance*** *that I'll have to go to Japan next week.*

Collocations
Adjectives *fair, outside, realistic, reasonable, slim*
Verbs *be in with a chance / stand a chance of + -ing*
Use *the chance* ***of doing*** *something, there's a chance* ***that*** + *clause, by any chance, on the off chance, No chance!*

1 If you don't do well in your exams, you'll have the .... to retake them next summer.
2 Our education system is based on the principle of equal ....
3 Have you ever considered the .... of training to be a teacher?
4 If you go on working hard, you stand a good .... of getting into Harvard.
5 Your exams start on Monday, so this weekend is the last .... you'll have to revise.
6 I think there's a real .... that I'll get the grades I need.
7 We're having a party to celebrate the end of our exams – it'll be a great ....
8 Is there any .... that you could help me with my homework?

4 **Complete these sentences with your own words, then compare ideas with a partner.**

1 I hope one day I'll have the opportunity …
2 Next year there's a possibility that I'll …
3 Unfortunately, I have very little chance of ever …
4 I hope the occasion never arises when I …

Writing Part 2: A report

▶ **Page 200 Writing bank**
A report

Exam advice

- Read the instructions carefully to identify who will read the report and what its purpose is.
- Deal with all the information in the input material.
- Give factual information and, if required, make recommendations.

1 **Consider the facilities in a school or college that you know. How would you rate them, from your point of view as a student? Think about the following areas and give each one a star rating (★★★ = excellent, ★★ = adequate, ★ = inadequate).**

- classrooms
- technology
- leisure or sports facilities
- study areas
- food and drink

2 **Work in pairs. Explain why you have given these ratings and, where the facilities are not adequate, how they could be improved in order to achieve ★★★.**

3 **Read this writing task question and the sample answer without paying attention to the missing headings. Does the writer make any points that are similar to ones you and your partner made?**

The college you attend is considering whether or not to make improvements to the student canteen. The principal has asked you to conduct a student survey to gain feedback about the canteen and how any problems might be addressed.

Write a report in which you describe how you conducted the survey, explain what you discovered and recommend what you think the college should provide.

Write your **report** in 220–260 words.

Report on improving the student canteen

1 ....

The purpose of this report is to explain how we conducted a survey on improving a student canteen, to present our findings and to suggest ways in which the canteen could be improved for students.

2 ....

We contacted all the pupils in the school via email, inviting them to take part in an online survey. The survey consisted of 20 questions and used a variety of different question types. The survey was open for two weeks. During that fortnight, a total of 240 responses were received.

3 ....

4 ....

Lack of choice was the main issue. Vegetarians feel that their needs are only 'adequately' satisfied with the range on offer, while vegans report that they are only 'occasionally' catered for. Dissatisfaction was also conveyed regarding the limited provision of snacks available. This point was raised by two-thirds of respondents.

Additionally, we put forward a suggestion of themed lunches (e.g. varying the menus to represent different national cuisines). This was supported by 88% of respondents.

5 ....

There were hardly any complaints from students regarding the cost of canteen meals. In fact, 76% suggested they would be willing to pay more if improvements were made to the menu.

6 ....

Many respondents considered the state of the furniture in the canteen to be an issue. Many feel a lot of it is in an unacceptable state of repair – it is not uncommon to find broken seating or tables.

7 ....

To successfully address these complaints, we would recommend improving the range of non-meat and plant-based options, providing more snacks and offering themed lunches. We would also recommend repairing, or replacing, the canteen furniture. To fund these improvements, we suggest implementing price increases. We would be grateful if the school were to follow these recommendations and implement changes as soon as possible.

4 **Choose the correct alternative in each of these statements about headings in a report.**

a Headings *need* / *don't need* to be brief.

b They *are* / *are not* usually in the form of a full sentence.

c They should cover *all the ideas* / *the main topic* in the paragraph that follows.

5 **Now think of suitable headings for the sample report (1–7).**

6 **Discuss these questions.**

1 Apart from the title, how can you tell that the sample text is a report?

2 What structures are used with the verbs *recommend* and *suggest*?

3 What reporting verbs are used instead of *said*?

4 What verbs and phrases are used to mean *would like*?

7 **Read the writing task below.**

1 Who will read the report you write?

2 How many sections will you include in your report?

3 What headings will you give these sections?

> The number of foreign students attending a language school in your town has been falling recently and a governors' committee has been established to increase future numbers.
>
> The school principal has asked you to write a report for this committee on the current situation and to recommend how more students could be attracted to the school. Your report should address the following:
>
> - what attracts foreigners to your town
> - new teaching methods and facilities that could be offered
> - how leisure facilities and opportunities for socialising could be improved.
>
> Write your **report** in 220–260 words.

8 **Look at these phrases and think of more formal equivalents, which you might want to use in your report.**

1 families students stay with

2 learning with the help of a computer

3 mix with people

4 more chance to speak

5 pick up (a language)

6 teachers who know what they're doing

7 the number of students in a class

8 things to do in your free time

9 ways of teaching

10 working on your own

9 **Write your report for the task in Exercise 7, making use of the following:**

- the verbs *suggest* and *recommend*
- a variety of reporting verbs
- a variety of words and phrases meaning the same as *would like*.

9 Vocabulary and grammar review

Vocabulary

1 Complete the sentences below by writing the correct form of the words *action*, *activity*, *event* or *programme*.

1 Can you look on the .... to see which stage *The Bends* are playing on?
2 The school canteen was a hive of .... , with final-year students busily comparing their exam results with each other.
3 I was really looking forward to seeing our new striker in .... , but she wasn't quite fit enough to play today.
4 In an astonishing turn of .... , it was today revealed that tourist flights into space would be offered free to the first ten customers.
5 Thanks to prompt .... by the fire service, the blaze was prevented from spreading to the neighbouring houses.
6 After eight years, the panda breeding .... at the zoo has finally welcomed its first cub.
7 The final .... of this weekend's festival of Irish culture will be a traditional folk dance.
8 It's generally pretty quiet on my street but there's always a burst of .... when the school day ends.

2 Choose the correct word in *italics* to complete the sentences.

1 Sorry. I saw your message pop *in* / *up* on my phone, but I was too busy to read it.
2 Thieves stole money from my friend by hacking *into* / *out* his email account.
3 I've forgotten my password and I've been locked out *from* / *of* my laptop.
4 Sorry, we'll have to talk later. I'm running out *of* / *from* power and forgot my spare battery.
5 I have set up my email so that it filters *in* / *out* all of the junk I get sent.
6 For security purposes, I have to sign *in* / *on* whenever I want to access my work computer.
7 I found some really interesting stuff while scrolling *around* / *through* my social media channels.
8 It is so annoying! As soon as I log on *to* / *in* social media, she sends me a message.

Grammar

3 Use the verbs in the box in the correct future forms to complete the sentences.

be	charge	get	launch	offer	renew	teach	wait

1 After the theft of our personal data, we absolutely .... our subscription to your online security system this year.
2 My brother .... for three years soon, and he's already Head of the Technology & Computing Department.
3 In October, my sister and her partner .... together for ten years.
4 TVYOU is .... a new streaming service aimed at 15- to 18-year-olds in the autumn.
5 I'd love to go to the cinema with you later, but I .... home from the gym by the time you want to leave.
6 A man arrested this morning is .... with hacking, phishing and a range of other online scams.
7 If they don't arrive in the next ten minutes, we .... for them for over an hour!
8 During the summer, we .... a 20% discount to any customer with a valid student card.

4 Complete the sentences with a suitable word in each gap.

1 I hate watching scary movies by .... It's far better when other people are there.
2 We don't know our neighbours at all. They very much keep to ....
3 We rented our flat out after we bought it. Within five years, it had paid for .... and we were mortgage free.
4 Talk to each .... before coming to a decision or you may really come to regret it.
5 Jake and Sandra are sat over there, talking to .... another about all sorts of things.
6 Whenever I've gone online, David is always there. I like playing with .... but I do hope he sleeps sometimes.

Vocabulary and grammar review 10

Vocabulary

1 Circle the correct alternative in *italics* in each of these sentences.

1. The system aims to give everyone *an equal* / *a same* opportunity at the beginning of their lives.
2. Friday is the *last* / *late* chance we'll have to enter the competition.
3. The swearing-in of the first woman president was a *historic* / *historical* occasion.
4. There's a *slight* / *little* possibility that I won't be back in time for tomorrow's meeting.
5. Don't *lose* / *miss* this *gold* / *golden* opportunity to win a two-week holiday in the south of France.
6. There seems to be a *factual* / *real* possibility that the party will lose at the next election.
7. The funeral of the firefighters who died in the blaze was a very *depressed* / *solemn* occasion.
8. In my opinion, everyone deserves a *next* / *second* chance in life.
9. The chances of something bad happening are very *slim* / *few* so you really shouldn't worry.
10. This course will give you the *possibility* / *opportunity* to learn an in-demand skill.

Grammar

2 Complete these sentences with the correct form of *must*, *need* or *have to*. In some cases more than one answer is possible.

1. My new job starts next Monday. Hopefully, I .... work such long hours as I do now.
2. I .... make sure I wake up in time for my first lecture. Yesterday, I didn't have any lectures, so I .... get up at all.
3. Our lecturers have told us that we .... send them our assignments by email, otherwise they won't mark them. This means we .... have our own email.
4. Take it easy! Today's lecture's been cancelled, so you .... hurry.
5. You .... run in the corridors. Didn't you see the sign? If you want a run around, you .... go outside.
6. I .... get some cash out before the weekend – otherwise I'm going to run out.
7. They .... have bought tickets before the game. They were still selling them on the door.
8. The party starts at 7, but I .... get there so early, so I could meet you for a coffee beforehand.

3 Five of these sentences have mistakes with modal verbs. Correct the mistakes.

1. It's a complicated route – I hope I could find my way back.
2. You can find all the information you'll ever need on Wikipedia.
3. We're delighted to inform you that we could offer you the post of manager.
4. At the fourth attempt I could pass my driving test. The first three times, I failed spectacularly.
5. If you were a fast reader, you could be able to finish that novel in one evening.
6. I couldn't have worried because everything turned out fine in the end.

11 Globetrotters

Starting off

1 **Work in pairs and discuss the questions. What's the most memorable journey you've ever taken? What's the most ambitious trip you'd like to take in the future?**

2 **Work in the same pairs. Complete the table with the words and expressions about travel in the box. Are there any that fit into more than one category?**

adventurous cautious challenging cosmopolitan cramped delayed enthusiastic environmentally friendly exotic harsh hassle-free hostile inconvenient inhospitable isolated luxurious off the beaten track open-minded remote respectful resourceful scenic stressful uncompromising urban well-organised

Means of transport	Types of destination	Types of traveller

3 **Use words and phrases from Exercise 2 to discuss the following questions.**

1 Why might people want to travel to the places shown in the photographs?

2 How often do you fly long distance? Are there any downsides to travelling in this way? Would you ever consider using a more environmentally friendly alternative for long-distance travel?

3 What kinds of places are you hoping to travel to in the future?

4 Do you prefer travelling alone, or with a companion? What kind of traveller are you?

5 What problems do people tend to face when they're travelling?

Listening Part 1

1 **Read the Exam round-up and choose the correct options in *italics* in sentences 1–5.**

In Listening Part 1:

1 you hear *three / five* different extracts

2 the extracts are on *the same theme / different themes*

3 you must choose *A, B* or *C / A, B, C* or *D* and you hear each piece *once / twice*

4 before you listen, you should *read the questions / read the questions and underline the key ideas*

5 you should *listen to the whole extract before making your choices / make your choices as you listen.*

Exam round-up

2 **You will hear three different extracts. Before you listen, underline the key idea in each question.**

Extract One

You hear two friends discussing long-distance air travel.

1 How does the woman feel about travelling by air?
- **A** concerned about the possibility of losing her belongings
- **B** irritated by the restrictive nature of it
- **C** unhappy about the inevitable high costs involved

2 What do they agree about air travel?
- **A** The inconveniences can ultimately be worth it.
- **B** There are few practical alternatives on offer.
- **C** It needs to be approached with a positive attitude.

Extract Two

You hear two friends discussing the man's round-the-world trip.

3 What is the man trying to do regarding travel advice?
- **A** play down his perceived expertise in the field
- **B** encourage people to be more adventurous in their plans
- **C** explain why he believes his chosen route would suit others

4 He admits one regret about the trip was that
- **A** his experience may have been limited by his over-cautiousness.
- **B** he hadn't found a suitable companion to accompany him.
- **C** he was too unwilling to compromise on certain things.

Extract Three

You hear two friends discussing difficulties they've faced when travelling.

5 When describing something that happened to him, the man
- **A** states that a lack of information was to blame for the event.
- **B** recognises that he made an error of judgement.
- **C** insists he felt little sense of panic as a result.

6 When relating her own experience, the woman
- **A** is keen to stress it wasn't as serious as the man's.
- **B** suggests that she learnt a vital lesson from it.
- **C** reveals her pride in the skills that got her out of trouble.

3 42 **Listen and for questions 1–6, choose the answer (A, B or C) which fits best according to what you hear.**

4 **Work in pairs. Discuss the questions.**

1 Have you ever had something go wrong when you've been travelling?

2 Did you agree with any of the speakers you heard? Did any story particularly impress you?

Vocabulary
Fixed phrases

1 **These fixed phrases all come from the recordings in Listening Part 1. Match each one with its meaning.**

1 get sick and tired of
2 spend a fortune on
3 rough it
4 without a trace
5 keep your cool
6 the whole point of
7 out in the open
8 be kept waiting

a do something without any comforts
b pay a lot for
c the main reason
d in the fresh air
e with no sign of
f be delayed by something or someone
g stay calm
h become extremely uncomfortable with an ongoing situation

2 **Complete these sentences by writing one of the fixed phrases from Exercise 1 in the correct form in each gap. There is one phrase you don't need to use. Then discuss your answers to the questions in pairs.**

1 Do you usually manage to .... when things go wrong during a journey?
2 Is the .... travelling widely to broaden the mind? And is it effective?
3 If your passport disappears ...., is that one of the worst experiences possible when you're abroad?
4 Would you prefer to .... a luxury holiday, or .... a bit and save your money?
5 What kind of things do you .... when you're travelling? What makes you irritated?
6 Would you rather sleep .... underneath the stars or in a bed in a hotel?

Grammar
Conditionals

The COMPLETE grammar reference
▶ Scan the QR code, watch the video, then turn to page 179

1 **Work in pairs. Look at the five sentences (a–e). Which sentences refer to**

1 past time?
2 past and present time?
3 just present time?
4 future time?
5 any time because the speaker is making a general point?

a If you leave yourself open to whatever comes up, it can be very rewarding.
b Even if we'd stayed at home it would have been better, because I'd be relaxing in front of the TV rather than being miserable.
c So what'll you do if you get itchy feet again?
d If I'd known what would happen, I definitely wouldn't have got off!
e If only I could adopt your mindset, it'd make this trip easier.

2 **Read this sentence and answer the questions.**

If I hadn't done the trip, I wouldn't even be talking to you now!

1 Why is the underlined verb in the continuous?
2 Do the verbs in this sentence refer to present or past time?

3 **Complete the sentences with the correct form of the verbs in brackets. You will need to decide on the correct conditional form and whether the verb should be simple or continuous.**

1 If you .... (not leave) the map at home, we .... (not wander) around this forest right now, looking for somewhere to spend the night.
2 Innsbruck is a lovely city and if I .... (not rush) to catch a train just now, I .... (be) happy to show you around a bit.
3 Kamal always thinks he knows best, and if he .... (not be) such an obstinate man, we .... (probably reach) the hotel by now instead of being stuck in this traffic jam.
4 If I .... (be) you, I .... (carry) my money in a money belt.
5 It was your own fault. The accident .... (not happen) if you .... (concentrate) properly at the time.
6 If you .... (like) to come with me, I .... (show) you to your room.

4 **These sentences each contain one mistake made by exam candidates. Correct the mistakes.**

1 If you eat so much chocolate, you wouldn't enjoy the delicious cake I've made.
2 I would be grateful if you send me a reply at your earliest convenience.
3 If you do not give me a refund, I am obliged to write to the local council.
4 In my country few people smoke, so if I were you, I won't smoke at all.
5 If I was able to travel back in history and I had the chance to choose where exactly to go, I would have travelled four centuries into the past.
6 If we had followed all my instructions, we would now stand in front of the cathedral.

5 **For questions 1–6, complete the second sentence so that it has a similar meaning to the first sentence, using the word given. Do not change the word given. You must use between three and six words, including the word given.**

1 As long as I know you'll support me, I won't worry about money.
COUNT
Provided I .... support me, I won't worry about money.

2 I don't think we'll miss the train if we leave home on time.
LONG
We should manage to catch the train .... off from home on time.

3 Martin is only working late tonight because he has to finish an urgent job.
UNLESS
Martin would not .... he had to finish an urgent job.

4 Nisha was given a trophy by her school because she had worked so hard.
PRESENTED
Nisha's school .... a trophy if she had not worked so hard.

5 Could you please cancel my appointment?
GRATEFUL
I .... cancel my appointment.

6 If it had not been for some unexpected difficulties, we would not be feeling so stressed.
COME
If some unexpected difficulties ...., we would not be feeling so stressed.

wish and *If only*

The COMPLETE grammar reference
▶ Scan the QR code, watch the video, then turn to page 181

1 **Complete the gaps in the second sentence so that it has a similar meaning to the first one.**

1 We can't go out because it's still raining.
I wish .... stop raining, so that we .... go out.
2 I wrote a lot of postcards to friends while I was away, but it cost a fortune to send them, which I regret!
If only .... postcards to friends while I was away.
3 I'm not happy about travelling home by plane tomorrow.
I wish .... home by plane tomorrow.
4 It's really not easy to call home from here.
If only .... easier to call home from here.
5 Why don't you get up a bit earlier in the morning? Not doing so means we can't do as much sightseeing!
I wish .... get up a bit earlier! Then we .... sightseeing!
6 Oh no! I didn't bring the picnic! Now we can't have anything to eat!
If only .... Then we .... to eat!

Reading and Use of English Part 5

1 **Read the Exam round-up box and decide if the statements (1–4) are true (T) or false (F).**

> **Exam round-up**
>
> In Reading and Use of English Part 5:
>
> 1 there are six questions and you have to choose the best option: A, B, C or D
>
> 2 you should read the questions before reading the text
>
> 3 the questions are answered in random order in the text
>
> 4 you should read the options after reading the section of text that is relevant to each question.

2 **Work in pairs. You will read an article about a journey across the Sahara Desert. Before you start reading, think about what aspects of the journey the writer might mention.**

3 **Now read the text quickly. Were your predictions correct?**

4 **For questions 1–6, choose the answer (A, B, C or D) which you think fits best according to the text.**

1 When talking about describing deserts in his work, the writer
- **A** claims it's a challenge that he enjoys taking on.
- **B** suggests it may always lie beyond his capabilities.
- **C** is confident he can convey the uniqueness of certain visual aspects.
- **D** finds it difficult to separate his emotions about them from his descriptions.

2 What does he say about his first trip to the Sahara Desert?
- **A** His feelings were often in contrast with what he was witnessing.
- **B** He realised that the scenery was not exactly how he'd imagined it.
- **C** His reaction to it took him completely by surprise.
- **D** He wondered to what extent his life would be changed by it.

3 After meeting the group's guide, the writer found himself
- **A** regretting his own lack of intuitive knowledge of the desert environment.
- **B** being swept along by the guide's infectious enthusiasm.
- **C** envying the guide for the sheer beauty of the landscape he lived in.
- **D** wishing he had more extensive background information about local culture.

4 At the oasis, the writer was especially impressed by
- **A** the respite it provided from harsh conditions.
- **B** the welcoming nature of the people who live there.
- **C** the ready availability of essential supplies.
- **D** the contrast between everyday life and the nearby desert.

5 In the fifth paragraph the writer
- **A** reveals his fascination with the ever-changing nature of the landscape.
- **B** identifies with a moment that made the unique appeal of the Sahara apparent.
- **C** begins to feel a connection between the urban and desert habitats.
- **D** admits a reluctance to move on from the comfort of the camp.

6 A theme that recurs in the article is the writer's
- **A** initial hesitancy towards people he meets.
- **B** varying attitude to conditions in the desert.
- **C** sense of awe when faced with evidence of the desert's power.
- **D** underlying doubts at not being up to the challenges ahead.

5 **Work in small groups. Discuss the questions.**

1 Would you be keen to travel across a desert, like the writer?

2 What might be the benefits/drawbacks of a journey like this?

Into the desert

by John Walters

A writer describes his journeys to the Sahara Desert

I've spent a lot of time in the many deserts that there are in the world, all equally striking in their wildness, and written articles about my experiences to the best of my ability. Yet the question I almost fear the most following my return is 'What was it like?' Doing these places justice in words has proved to be something of a sticking point, and could well turn out to be something that forever escapes me, even though on the face of it, it doesn't appear that difficult. After all, it's quite straightforward to describe how they look, as that's relatively well known thanks to the big screen: the waves of unending golden sand, the dry landscape, the decreasing signs of life as you approach the dunes. Yet conveying the feelings it inspires is quite another matter. There's the potentially intimidating prospect of mile upon mile of nothingness, and the thought that your very survival depends on you and your companions alone. However, for me, that doesn't really detract from the appeal of one of the most spectacular environments on earth.

Probably my most memorable trip was my first one to the Sahara in Africa where, far from missing the lively comings and goings of everyday life at home, as I'd anticipated, I actually welcomed the vast, enveloping silence, and the strange sense that the surrounding landscape was somehow deeply asleep. The only signs of movement were the rippling waves of heat rising up from the ground. The overall effect became extraordinarily calming, rather than threatening. And as the journey wore on, I could see I'd inevitably be fundamentally transformed by the experience, and arrive home desperate to return. As expected, it was the first of many adventures there.

On my most recent trip to the Sahara, I travelled with a group in a minibus, driven by a guide. On the first night of our journey towards the desert, we'd made camp in a valley that was flooded with light at sunrise, against a backdrop of mountain peaks. It was the first view so far that I'd found truly breathtaking, but I knew there'd be plenty more to come. Our very experienced and knowledgeable guide was descended from nomads. He was completely at home in the area and knew all its traditions. Like many others we met, he seemed instinctively tuned in to our precise location and even the time of day from his observations of the sky – skills I realised I ought to acquire for myself. He had a contagious self-assurance with other people we met along the way, and became increasingly animated the closer we got to the desert. As we drove along, he played traditional music from the area – music I was familiar with, but that was given a new and moving significance for me by actually being in the landscape where it originated.

Our final stop before entering the Sahara was at an oasis, common in those parts. It's a place where the extreme climate releases its grip and provides water, trees, and even a place for people to settle and thrive. The local population has managed to set up comfortable homes, and make a living from tourism and cultivating dates – all on the edge of a very hostile environment. In fact, while at a shop selling headscarves, we were forced to take shelter, as a sudden sandstorm swept in and blew the scarves violently in the wind. It was a timely and rather alarming reminder of the sheer unpredictability of the desert we were heading for, and that we'd underestimate at our peril.

Then, before leaving the oasis, it was time to meet our camel master, a man who would prove himself totally at ease in the extreme surroundings. As we set off into the Sahara on our camels, and the animals padded across the soft sand, the landscape slowly opened up. To my mind, nothing has ever really compared to the sheer size of the Sahara. Its infinite sea of sand was mesmerising; dunes rolled into the distance, constantly transforming and combining with each other, as the wind blew across them. The camels' shadows lengthened in the setting sun, matching the yellow sand gradually passing through its daily mutations. Finally we reached our camp for the evening, a welcoming group of tents. After dinner and music in the cosy atmosphere of a campfire, I fell asleep under the stars in the silence of the desert thinking of the noisy, busy streets in the city I call home, a place which now seemed further than just a few thousand miles away.

Vocabulary

at, *in* and *on* to express location

1 **Complete the sentences below with *at*, *in* or *on*. Then check your answers by looking again at the text in Reading and Use of English Part 5.**

1 I've spent a lot of time in the many deserts that there are .... the world.
2 ... one of the most spectacular environments .... earth.
3 ... my most memorable trip was my first one to the Sahara .... Africa ...
4 .... the first night of our journey towards the desert, we'd made camp .... a valley that was flooded with light .... sunrise ...
5 [The music] was given a new and moving significance for me by actually being .... the landscape where it originated.
6 Our final stop before entering the Sahara was .... an oasis, common .... those parts.
7 ... our camel master, a man who would prove himself totally at ease .... the extreme surroundings.
8 ... . the cosy atmosphere of a campfire, I fell asleep under the stars .... the silence of the desert ...

2 **Each of these sentences contains a mistake with prepositions made by exam candidates. Correct the mistakes.**

1 I come from Mendoza, a town of Argentina.
2 I'd like to introduce you to my boss, whose office is at the 5th floor.
3 Portugal is one of the most beautiful countries of the world.
4 Public phones are available at almost every large square.
5 She spends far too long talking at her mobile phone.
6 There's a garage at the left and I live just two doors along from it.
7 We waited at a queue for more than twenty minutes.
8 You will find a youth hostel in almost every island.
9 You'll find a large shopping centre at the outskirts of the city.
10 She decided to go and live for a year to Italy.

Reading and Use of English Part 2

1 **Work in pairs. Read the Exam round-up box and answer the questions 1–5.**

Exam round-up

In Reading and Use of English Part 2:

1 How many questions are there?
2 What should you do before you start filling the gaps?
3 If you can't think of a word for a gap, what should you do?
4 How important is correct spelling?
5 What should you do when you have finished?

2 **Work in pairs. Discuss the questions.**

1 Where might your dream job be located? Would you be happy to work on a desert island, for example?
2 What would be the downside of living in a remote place?

3 **You will read a short article about jobs available on remote islands. Read the article quickly, without paying attention to the gaps. What kind of places are the jobs available in? What are the possible advantages of the jobs?**

4 **For questions 1–8, read the article and think of the word which best fits each gap. Use only one word in each gap. There is an example at the beginning (0).**

Caretakers wanted!

Are you the kind of person who'd prefer to live as far removed as possible **(0)** ....from.......... the hustle and bustle of city life? **(1)** .... indeed you feel you fit that description and want to get **(2)** .... from it all, then look no further than the many adverts in the media for a highly unusual job opportunity. There are plenty **(3)** .... seek caretakers to look after remote islands.

The jobs can cover a huge range of possibilities – anything from the most luxurious living conditions to a more back-to-basics situation, with very **(4)** .... of the facilities we might nowadays **(5)** .... for granted, such as mains electricity.

However, the upsides can **(6)** .... than make up for these. There could be free accommodation and food, **(7)** .... to mention the spectacular views from wherever you're located. Indeed, some of those who've undertaken these jobs may wish their stay had been extended well **(8)** .... the end of their contract, and often describe them as a once-in-a-lifetime experience on their return.

5 Work in pairs. Would you be interested in living in a remote castle? Why? / Why not?

6 Read the text below and think of the word which best fits each gap. Use only one word in each gap. There is an example (0) at the beginning.

Living in a castle

What would your dream home be? How about moving to a remote ancient castle – complete **(0)** ....with........... tales of resident ghosts?

A castle home may appear to outsiders to be the height of luxury. Yet according to those who've been **(1)** .... up in a castle as children, the chances are it's **(2)** .... nearly as glamorous as it may seem. For **(3)** .... thing, imagine the distance from your bedroom to the kitchen, if you required a late-night snack. Or you might have to run along endless corridors to the front door to collect a parcel delivery, **(4)** .... to find you're too late, and the driver has already pulled **(5)** .... Life in a castle might indeed appear idyllic, with endless numbers of rooms entirely **(6)** .... your disposal. That's **(7)** .... you discover, for example, that the heating is **(8)** .... than adequate and you're freezing for the majority of the winter months.

However, the upside for many is the pride in maintaining a historic building for the future – and the pleasure of looking out over the surrounding scenic countryside.

Speaking Part 1

▶ **Page 205 Speaking bank**
Speaking Part 1

Exam advice

- Before going to the Speaking test, make sure you can speak about your work, your studies, your family, the area where you live and your free-time interests.
- Expand your answers with reasons, examples and extra information.

1 **Work in pairs. Which of the questions below could you answer using conditional verb forms?**

1. If you could travel anywhere in the world, where would you choose to go? Why?
2. If some friends from abroad were visiting your region, which places would you take them to see? Why?
3. What things do you most enjoy doing when travelling on holiday? Why?
4. Do you find it's useful that you can speak English when you travel? Why?
5. What's the best time of year for people to visit your country? Why?
6. Would you enjoy going on an adventurous, possibly dangerous journey? Why? / Why not?
7. What is the most interesting place you have ever travelled to? Why?
8. If you could choose something completely different from your usual type of holiday, what would you choose? Why?
9. Would you enjoy working with tourists? Why? / Why not?
10. Would you prefer to spend a year travelling or to spend a year working? Why?

2 43 **Listen to three people, Laura (Student A), Daniel (Student B) and Marta (Student C), answering the questions in Exercise 1. Answer the questions 1–5.**

1. Which question is each of them answering?
2. Which speakers use conditional forms in their answers?
3. Do they use conditional verb forms all the time? Why? / Why not?
4. Who sounds most enthusiastic in their answer? What words do they use which show enthusiasm? What other way do they have of showing enthusiasm?
5. Do the speakers repeat the words of the questions, or do they express the ideas using their own vocabulary? Why is this a good idea in the exam?

3 **Take turns to ask each other the questions in Exercise 1.**

Student A: Ask your partner questions 1, 3, 5, 7 and 9.
Student B: Ask your partner questions 2, 4, 6, 8 and 10.

Writing Part 2: A review

▶ **Page 198 Writing bank**
A review

Exam advice

- You will often have to compare two things in your review.
- Think about your target readers and what information they need.
- Write a plan thinking about each of the things you want to describe and in what order.
- Decide what recommendation(s) you are going to make and include them in your answer.

1 Read this writing task and underline the points you must deal with in your answer.

You see the announcement below on a website called travelsfortravellers.com.

> HOTELS NEAR ME
>
> We'd like to know what local people think of different hotels in their area, so we're opening a section written by local people to help visitors choose the hotel which suits them best.
>
> Send us a review recommending two hotels in your area for two different types of visitor, explaining what type of visitor each hotel would suit and why.

Write your **review** in 220–260 words.

2 Work in pairs. Make notes on the following points.

- the two types of visitor you could write for
- what things each type of visitor would want to know about when reading a review

3 Which of these do you think would be the best plan for the review?

Plan A:

Para 1:
Introduction: why different types of hotel suit different visitors
Paras 2 and 3: Features of hotel 1
Paras 4 and 5: Features of hotel 2
Para 6:
Conclusion: the type of visitor each hotel would suit and why

Plan B:

Para 1:
Introduction: the range of hotels available in your area, which two you have chosen to review and why
Para 2: Comparison of rooms and prices in each hotel
Paras 3 and 4: Comparison of other features in each hotel, e.g. business facilities, restaurant, gym
Para 5:
Conclusion: the type of visitor each hotel would suit and why

Plan C:

If you don't like either Plan A or Plan B, discuss and write your own plan for the review.

4 Read this review without paying attention to the gaps. Which plan, A, B or C, does it follow? If the answer is C, write the plan.

Two hotels in Shanghai

Shanghai is an important business as well as tourist destination. [1] ...., businesspeople often don't like sharing their hotels with tour groups and require different facilities. [2] ...., holidaymakers want a break from the serious atmosphere of a business hotel. Each of the hotels I recommend caters for a different type of visitor.

Situated on Nanjing Road not far from the Bund, the International Hostel is a compact, moderately priced hotel which would suit backpackers and tourists on a tight budget. The rooms are clean and airy, [3] .... quite basic, with twin beds and en-suite bathrooms.

Nanjing Road is a busy shopping street, so the hostel wouldn't suit light sleepers [4] .... you should expect some noise [5] .... from the constant traffic and perhaps from other boisterous guests. Unfortunately, the hotel lacks a restaurant, so you'll have to find your own breakfast in one of the many cafés nearby. However, the staff are friendly and helpful. [6] .... the hotel has bicycles available for its guests to explore this beautiful city at their leisure.

The Sun Hotel is an elegant, moderately sized business hotel situated in a new building with fabulous views across the Huang Pu River. [7] .... its five stars indicate, the hotel offers luxurious, spacious rooms at a price. It contains a range of well-equipped conference rooms [8] .... a gourmet restaurant allowing businesspeople to entertain clients in style. The management and staff are competent and professional, as you'd expect, and will organise trips and events to make your stay [9] .... productive but pleasurable too.

Whichever hotel you stay at, Shanghai won't fail to delight you.

5 **Complete the review in Exercise 4 by writing one of these linking words/phrases in each gap.**

an added attraction is that   as (x2)   both   equally   however   not only   though   together with

6 **Read the review again and note down adjectives used to describe**

1 the hotels in general
2 the rooms
3 the staff.

7 **Work in pairs. Discuss the questions.**

1 How would you describe the style of the review? Choose a, b or c and give reasons for your choice.
   a very colloquial and informal
   b informative, but with some informal features; it addresses the reader personally
   c formal and academic
2 The style in which the exam task is written often indicates the style in which the answer can be written. Which two style features of the task in Exercise 1 are also used in the sample review?

8 **Prepare to write your own review.**

- Choose a plan from Exercise 3 and amend it for your review.
- Consider whether you want to use any of the adjectives you noted down in Exercise 6.
- Underline any other words and phrases you would like to use from Exercises 4 and 5.

9 **Write your review.**

12 Our planet

Starting off

1 **Work in pairs. Look at the photos and discuss these questions.**

1 Where might the photos have been taken?
2 Why might people have decided to live and work there?
3 What challenges might those people face on a daily basis?

Listening Part 2

1 **Listen to the brief introduction to McMurdo station. What information does the speaker give about the questions you discussed in Starting off, Exercise 1?** 44

2 **You are going to listen to a podcast about living and working at McMurdo. First, look at the photo on page 129 and discuss these questions.**

1 How would you describe McMurdo's appearance?
2 Which types of job are the residents there likely to have?
3 When might be the best time of year to live there? Why?

3 Read the Exam round-up box and decide if the statements (1–5) are true (T) or false (F).

In Listening Part 2:

1 you have to complete six sentences

2 no more than two words will be missing from each sentence

3 the sentences are not identical to sentences on the recording

4 you should read the gapped sentences after you have listened

5 if you are not sure of an answer, leave it blank.

Exam round-up

4 45 Now listen to part of a podcast in which a woman called Kirsty Steele talks about her experiences working in Antarctica . For questions 1–8, complete the sentences with a short word or phrase.

Kirsty says that she was given a placement at a research station that operated on a **(1)** .... basis.

Kirsty uses the term **(2)** .... to describe her initial impression of McMurdo research station.

Kirsty highlights the sense of **(3)** .... that was apparent in everyone she worked with.

Kirsty suggests that there is regular demand for **(4)** .... staff in Antarctica.

Kirsty mentions potential issues resulting from the lack of **(5)** .... found in the area.

Kirsty recommends being at McMurdo when **(6)** .... come from overseas and spend time there.

Kirsty says that the inhabitants of McMurdo frequently suffer from **(7)** .... during the winter months.

According to Kirsty, poor **(8)** .... is to blame when pilots are unable to land at McMurdo.

5 Discuss these questions.

1 Would you like to experience living at McMurdo? What job would you apply for if you decided to go?
2 What drives some people to explore, or work and live in, extreme environments?

Vocabulary

Prepositions following verbs

1 Choose the correct prepositions in *italics* in these sentences from the two listening exercises.

1 Each year it serves *as / for* an important laboratory and logistical hub for hundreds of scientists from around the world …
2 … In the winter, McMurdo depends *on / of* the remaining people – around 200 civilian support personnel and a few scientists – to keep it going.
3 Over the years, this has contributed *to / for* our global understanding of the causes of climate change …
4 [Scientists] incorporate their daily findings on McMurdo *into / with* their research.
5 Those who do choose to live and work there must adapt quickly *at / to* the cold climate.
6 … there's no shortage of positions you can apply *to / for*.
7 There are … an additional 50 facilities that run seasonal operations, one of which I was attached *with / to*.
8 … we worked extremely well together, bonding *with / to* each other through our shared circumstances …

2 Exam candidates sometimes use the wrong prepositions after verbs. Correct the mistakes in these sentences.

1 Many people firmly believe to the traditional wisdom of their ancestors.
2 It is difficult to concentrate in your work if there is loud music playing.
3 I recently participated on a charity event at my college.
4 The company is insisting in the use of low-energy light bulbs in their offices.
5 The government will double the amount it spends in the environment.
6 Every flight you take contributes with global warming.
7 Many TV documentaries are now focusing in environmental issues.
8 The new energy-saving laws apply for all factories and offices.

▶ Page 188 Dependent prepositions

Reading and Use of English Part 7

1 Read the Exam round-up box and circle the correct alternative in *italics* for the statements 1–4.

In Reading and Use of English Part 7:

1 the text has *six* / *seven* gaps where missing paragraphs belong

2 there *is one* / *are two* extra paragraph(s) that you do not need to use

3 you should start this task by reading the *gapped text* / *missing paragraphs*

4 you should focus on identifying *the writer's views* / *words, phrases and logical development* to establish the correct answers.

Exam round-up

2 **You are going to read an article about a young naturalist and environmentalist. Before you read, discuss these questions.**

a Why might Mya-Rose Craig have become known as the 'Birdgirl'?

b What can people do to connect with nature more often?

c How might young people generally become involved in environmental activism?

3 **Read the article quickly (but not the missing paragraphs A–G) to gain an overall understanding of the text. Summarise Mya's achievements with a partner.**

4 **Which two of the following sentences do not follow on logically from the first paragraph and why?**

1 In 2020, at the age of 17 – three months before her final high school exams – she received an honorary Doctor of Science degree from the University of Bristol.

2 The additional realisation that this was hardly a rare occurrence, prompted her to investigate further.

3 'I used to think of it as a very competitive treasure hunt,' she explains.

4 This idea is explored in her book, *We Have A Dream*.

5 **Read the remaining paragraphs in Exercise 4 again. Discuss with a partner which one you think fits best in gap number 1.**

6 **Choose from the paragraphs A–G the one which fits each gap (1–6). There is one extra paragraph which you do not need to use.**

The Dramatic Life – so far – of *Birdgirl*

Mya-Rose Craig was nine days old when her parents first took her on a birdwatching trip (not that she remembers it, of course). From an early age, her fascination with ornithology – the study of birds – grew to such a point that she would never be content with merely leafing through the pages of an ornithological encyclopaedia. In August 2019, after seventeen years' travelling the globe, Mya became the youngest person in the world to have seen, in the flesh, half of the entire world's known bird species – 5,369 birds – the pursuit of which she documented in her blog, *Birdgirl*.

1

Yet, while this life of tranquillity undoubtedly has its appeal – as does seeing her name in the record books – Mya's achievements elsewhere make her even more impressive. A defining moment came during a birdwatching trip at the age of 13, when she noticed that not only was she the youngest birder by far, but she was also the only person of colour in the group.

2

Opportunity plays its part, certainly – young people from these backgrounds are much less likely to live in rural areas, or have access to urban green spaces. In 2016, inspired by her British-Bangladeshi roots, Mya set up *Black2Nature*, a camp for less privileged, city-dwelling, Visible Minority Ethnic (VME) teenagers, her aim being to encourage them to become more engaged with the natural environment. She followed this with several other camps welcoming children from all ethnicities and backgrounds, all with the same goal in mind.

3

Thus, her journey – from record-breaker to equality champion and activist – was complete. She credits those early years of extensive travel for allowing her to see first-hand the impacts of climate change, deforestation, and discrimination; these experiences formed the basis of her mission to campaign for global climate justice, which, according to Mya, is 'basically making sure that everyone's voices are heard in the climate change conversation.'

4

Almost everyone interviewed was dealing with adverse effects of the climate crisis in their day-to-day routines, whether that meant having increasingly limited access to clean water, or fighting to protect their land from exploitation by super-rich companies. For Mya, this was the most affecting aspect of collecting their stories together and she readily admits that, coming from a country like the UK, because 'we're not immediately impacted by climate change, it can be more abstract.'

5

What better honour could there have been for someone who has taken their fascination with ornithology and the natural world and channelled that into working with such energy and passion, constantly pushing themselves to try to raise awareness about inequality for a more tolerant, more inclusive world?

6

But what about those without a garden or park within easy reach? Mya says that, even in the middle of a concrete jungle, you can 'listen to the dawn chorus, watch the clouds, watch the sunset or the night sky, put a birdfeeder and some water somewhere you can see them outside, or just watch any wildlife you can see in trees or bushes.' I say, listen to Mya. She talks a lot of sense.

A This sums Mya up perfectly. She has always seemed like 'an old head on young shoulders', going about her business with a maturity and focus far beyond her years. It's an impression that is only reinforced by the calmness with which she speaks.

B Their success strengthened within her the firm belief that 'an unequal world is not a sustainable one. We need to encourage everybody from every community to tackle the environmental crisis we find ourselves in.' Mya began campaigning forcefully for environmental organisations to become more diverse.

C She has never strayed from the belief that forming a strong connection with nature is a crucial aspect of a rewarding life. Ideally, everyone should find time each day to relax in outdoor green spaces, to 'cope with anxiety and stay mentally and emotionally well.'

D In 2020, at the age of 17 – three months before her final high school exams – she received an honorary Doctor of Science degree from the University of Bristol. In doing so, she broke another record and became the youngest UK-born person to be given such an award.

E The additional realisation that this was hardly a rare occurrence, prompted her to investigate further. She began to wonder why, of all the people working in the UK as environmental professionals, less than 1% were from minority-ethnic families.

F 'I used to think of it as a very competitive treasure hunt,' she explains; 'a mission to track down as many as possible.' Since then, her determination has softened, and she has learnt to appreciate the 'simple pleasure of being outdoors, surrounded by birds and by nature.'

G It's an idea she explores in her book, *We Have A Dream*. In it, Mya profiles 30 young environmental activists, all indigenous people or people of colour, giving accounts of the impact of environmental damage on their lives.

Grammar
Countable and uncountable nouns

The COMPLETE grammar reference
▶ Scan the QR code, watch the video, then turn to page 181

1 **Work in pairs. Find the following in the text below.**

1 two singular countable nouns
2 three plural countable nouns
3 three uncountable nouns
4 two of these three uncountable nouns that could be countable in other contexts
5 two proper nouns (names), apart from *Baobab*

Baobab trees, which are found in Africa, are frequently compared with elephants because their bark resembles the skin of an elephant. They consist of the most bulky, twisted tissue of any plant on Earth. The most ancient are believed to be 1,000 years old.

2 **Many words have different meanings depending on whether they are countable or uncountable. What is the difference in meaning between these pairs of sentences?**

1 a I like *coffee*.
  b I'd like a *coffee*.

2 a I can't see – my *hair* is in my eyes.
  b I've got a *hair* in my eye.

3 a Most English *cheese* is hard.
  b There are more than 1,000 British *cheeses*.

4 a Anna lost a lot of *weight* when she was ill.
  b Lifting *weights* strengthens your muscles.

5 a Car windscreens are made from toughened *glass*.
  b I only wear *glasses* for reading.

6 a He has no *experience* of living in a cold climate.
  b But he has read about the *experiences* of other people.

7 a *Exercise* is good for you.
  b We've got four *exercises* to do for homework.

Grammar
Articles

The COMPLETE grammar reference
▶ Scan the QR code, watch the video, then turn to page 182

3 **Choose the correct articles in these extracts from Reading and Use of English Part 7 (Ø = no article). Then check your answers by looking back at the text on pages 130 and 131.**

1 Mya-Rose Craig was nine days old when her parents first took her on *a* / *the* birdwatching trip …
2 Mya began campaigning forcefully for *the* / Ø environmental organisations to become more diverse.
3 What better honour could there have been for someone who has taken their fascination with *the* / Ø ornithology and *the* / Ø natural world …
4 She has never strayed from *the* / *a* belief that forming a strong connection with nature is *a* / *the* crucial aspect of *a* / Ø rewarding life.
5 … of all *the* / Ø people working in *the* / Ø UK as *the* / Ø environmental professionals, less than 1% were from *the* / Ø minority-ethnic families.

4 **Complete this text with the correct article: *a*/*an*, *the* or no article (Ø).**

(1) .... South China tiger population was estimated to number 4,000 individuals in **(2)** .... early 1950s, but over **(3)** .... following 30 years, approximately 3,000 tigers were killed as the subspecies was officially hunted as **(4)** .... pest. Although **(5)** .... Chinese government banned **(6)** .... hunting in 1979, and declared the tiger's survival **(7)** .... conservation priority, by 1996 **(8)** .... surviving population was estimated to be less than **(9)** .... hundred individuals. And, as no tiger has been sighted in **(10)** .... wild for more than 25 years, **(11)** .... scientists believe that it is 'functionally extinct'. It is thought that even if **(12)** .... few individuals remain, the existing protected areas or **(13)** .... habitat are not sufficiently large or undisturbed to sustain **(14)** .... viable tiger population.

5 The following sentences contain mistakes with articles made by exam candidates. There may be more than one mistake in each sentence. Find and correct the mistakes.

1 Make sure you wear suit and tie if it's formal occasion.
2 You should get job even though you haven't got high-level qualifications.
3 This report aims to describe advantages and disadvantages of green taxes.
4 Students can access internet in their classrooms.
5 Society needs to provide affordable accommodation for homeless.
6 A most important thing is to get people talking about the issues.
7 Tokyo is a capital of Japan.
8 Nowadays the technology is everywhere.
9 I have basic knowledge of French, German and Spanish.
10 Even though he hasn't got the degree, he should find the work in the IT.

6 Work in pairs. First discuss why the words in bold are used in the following sentences, and then discuss the topics with your partner.

- **The** first thing you remember
- **The** most frightening or **the** most exciting thing that has happened to you
- **A** job you'd like to do
- **The** advantages and disadvantages of being single (or married)

Vocabulary

Word formation

1 What are the noun forms for each of these verbs from the article in Reading and Use of English Part 7?

appreciate	encourage	explain	inspire	investigate	receive

2 What are the verb forms for each of these nouns from the article?

access	belief	conversation	determination	equality	pursuit

3 What are the adjectives from each of these nouns from the article?

access	activist	account	community	damage	honour

4 Complete the sentences from the article in Reading and Use of English Part 7 with compound nouns, verbs, adverbs and adjectives. The first letter of each word is given (in brackets). Then look back at the article on page 131 and check your answers.

0 A defining moment came during a ......birdwatching...... (*bw*) trip at the age of 13 …
1 She credits those early years of extensive travel for allowing her to see .... (*f-h*) the impacts of climate change, deforestation, and discrimination …
2 Mya set up *Black2Nature*, a camp for less privileged, ... (*c-d*) teenagers …
3 Her journey – from .... (*r-b*) to equality champion and activist – was complete.
4 … everyone should find time each day to relax in .... (*od*) green spaces, to 'cope with anxiety and stay mentally and emotionally well.'
5 … put a .... (*bf*) and some water somewhere you can see them .... (*os*), or just watch any .... (*wl*) you can see in trees or bushes.

5 Word stress for compound words is usually on the first word. In which two of the compound words in Exercise 4 is the second word stressed?

6 Complete the sentences using the words in the box. Then discuss your answers to the questions with a partner.

eco	eye	forward	high	narrow	play	rip	time	work	world

1 Which three songs would you put on your perfect ....list?
2 People often say that cheap, disposable gadgets are always a complete ....-off. Would you agree?
3 What is the most ....-consuming thing you've done in the past year?
4 If you were an ....-witness to environmental crime – like someone dumping waste in a river – what would you do?
5 What might make you consider someone to be ....-minded?
6 Have there been times recently when your ....load has got too heavy?
7 In terms of being ....-friendly, who is the most ....-thinking person you know?
8 How important are ....-profile, ...-renowned environmental campaigners like Mya-Rose Craig and Greta Thunberg for solving our problems?

Speaking Part 3

▶ **Page 211 Speaking bank**
Speaking Part 3

1 **Read the Exam round-up box and circle the correct alternatives in *italics*.**

> In Speaking Part 3:
>
> 1 you speak to your *partner* / *the examiner*
>
> 2 you will be given a set of *pictures* / *written prompts* to talk about
>
> 3 you and your partner will be expected to talk for *three* / *four* minutes
>
> 4 communication skills are *more* / *less* important than expressing correct opinions
>
> 5 you *must* / *need not* agree with your partner.
>
> **Exam round-up**

2 **Look at the photos and match them with the environmental problem. Then answer the questions.**

air pollution deforestation drought
forest fires oil spills overfishing

1 What other phrases related to environmental problems can you think of?

2 To what extent are humans to blame for each of these problems?

3 **Read these Speaking Part 3 written prompts and spend a few moments thinking about possible answers.**

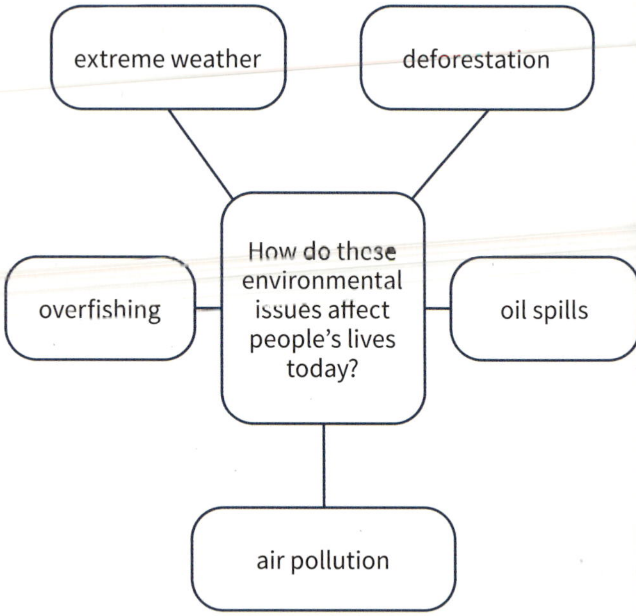

4 (46) **Listen to two candidates discussing the prompts in Exercise 3.**

1 How well do they describe the way in which the environmental issues can affect people's lives?

2 How could their discussion be improved?

3 What solutions could you suggest that might make Anna and Lukas feel more optimistic?

5 (47) **Now listen to the examiner's final instruction in Part 3 and the discussion that follows. Do the candidates reach agreement?**

6 **Work in pairs. Discuss the prompts in Exercise 3.**

- Try to describe clearly how the threats can affect people's lives.
- Include some of the compound nouns in the box in your discussions.

fire risk	fire damage	insurance costs
desert region	water shortage	crop failure
rainforest	farmland	cash crops
oil rig	fuel consumption	fuel shortage(s)
exhaust fumes	vehicle emissions	
factory chimneys	breathing difficulties	
flood water(s)	flood defences	river banks

- Finally, try to reach an agreement about which environmental problem poses the greatest threat.

Reading and Use of English Part 3

1 **Make as many words as you can from the root words in the box.**

able	friend	help	know	live
move	nation	sense		

able: ability, inability, disability, enable, disable, unable, disabled, ably

2 **Each of these sentences contains at least one word in the incorrect form. Correct the mistakes.**

1. Arthropods (the group that includes insects, arachnids, and crustaceans) number mammals by a ratio of about 312 to 1.
2. Her humour blog documents the six months she spent in McMurdo, Antarctica.
3. Many predators hunt under cover of darkness and sleep during day hours.
4. I know a little about geology, but haven't studied it in a huge amount of deep.
5. Politicians of all parties are working hard to be seen as the 'green' candidate in the come election.
6. On our hiking trip to the mountains, Kenji wore these utterly practice, slip-on canvas trainers.
7. The National Weather Service has published some useful advice information on what to do if the hurricane passes over coastal areas and hits the land.
8. In the town where we went on holiday this summer, the nightlife was exist – everything closed at 9.30!

3 **Read the text '*What drives an eco-warrior?*'. For questions 1–8, use the word given in capitals at the end of some of the lines to form a word that fits in the gap in the same line. There is an example at the beginning (0).**

What drives an eco-warrior?

The term 'eco-warrior' is a **(0)** ......relative...... **RELATE**
newcomer to the English language. It describes
someone who campaigns **(1)** .... **TIRE**
for environmental causes, highlighting instances of ecological damage, and confronting those responsible for it. This might entail using court
action, even when the **(2)** .... of **LIKELY**
success in the face of huge corporate wealth is
low. Some eco-warriors **(3)** .... **PRIDE**
turn their backs on their 'normal' lives and commit wholeheartedly to their cause as if it were a full-time job.

Whichever route a person takes into this type of
activism, a **(4)** .... awareness of **HEIGHT**
environmental issues is what lays the
(5) .... of their cause. Some **FOUND**
are inspired to become eco-warriors after seeing something deeply
(6) .... to **AGREE**
them on the news; a forest fire, perhaps, or a sea bird covered in thick, black oil after a devastating spillage. Many are driven by feelings of anger about what they see as the
(7) .... **JUST**
of our world, and see direct action as the only possible way to
(8) .... **COME**
the imbalance between humans and nature.

Exam advice

- Remember that changing the word given could mean using a prefix or a suffix or both. You may have to make a word with a negative meaning.
- Check the spelling of the words you form.
- Finally, read through the complete text to make sure that it makes sense and is grammatically correct.

4 **Discuss these questions in pairs or groups.**

1. What can individuals do to convince governments and businesses to pay more attention to the climate crisis?
2. Why do some people feel less personal responsibility than others for protecting the environment?

Writing Part 2: A proposal

▶ Page 202 Writing bank
A proposal

1 **Read the Exam round-up box and decide if the statements (1–5) are true (T) or false (F). If false, rewrite it to make it true.**

In Writing Part 2:

1 proposals are normally written for personal friends

2 proposals should include suggestions or recommendations

3 factual information need not be included

4 you may use headings in a proposal

5 you should always write a proposal using formal language.

Exam round-up

2 **Work in pairs. Read this Part 2 writing task and then follow the instructions below.**

You see this announcement from an environmental agency on a local news website.

> We are running a campaign in our town to persuade organisations (e.g. schools/colleges, companies, shops, sports centres, etc.) to use resources (e.g. electricity, water, fuel, etc.) more carefully and to reduce waste. The agency invites you to submit a proposal outlining the current situation in an organisation that you know well and to suggest ways in which this situation could be improved. We will provide financial support for approved proposals.

Write your **proposal** in 220–260 words.

1 Think about an organisation you know well. What kind of resources is this organisation currently wasting?

2 Make a list of things that individual members of this organisation could do to reduce waste. Start with simple things that everyone can do, like turning lights off at night, and then go on to actions that require greater cooperation, like agreeing to work from home on a set number of days each week.

3 **Read the sample proposal and discuss these questions.**

1 Has the writer dealt fully with all parts of the task? Is there factual information as well as suggestions?

2 Is the proposal clearly organised?

Introduction

The purpose of this proposal is to suggest ways in which my college could use resources more carefully and reduce wastage. A range of measures will be suggested that should help to achieve this.

Paper

Excessive use of paper affects the environment in two ways: firstly by using valuable resources, and secondly by causing unnecessary waste. The college currently uses twice as much printing paper as it did two years ago. This is despite the fact that all information and study material could be moved to a cloud-based storage system. I suggest that in future no documents should be printed unless there is a good reason for doing so, and students should be required to submit each of their assignments electronically.

Electricity

Currently, very few lights and heaters are ever turned off when the building is unoccupied, while computers and other electrical devices are commonly left on stand-by overnight. This contributes greatly to the college's energy consumption. Students and staff should be reminded to turn off all such equipment when it is not needed.

Fuel

It is widely acknowledged that excessive vehicle usage leads to unnecessarily high levels of fuel consumption. In order to encourage both staff and students alike to minimise their use of motor vehicles, I would recommend that the number of spaces in the car park be reduced by at least two-thirds, and that these be replaced with bicycle racks. Public transport and bicycles would be more likely to be used if this happens.

Conclusion

I believe that if all the suggested measures were implemented, the college would be able to reduce wastage by at least 20% every year.

4 **What do the words and phrases in *italics* refer to in these extracts from the sample proposal? Why are reference words like these used?**

1. The college currently uses twice as much printing paper as *it* did two years ago.
2. *This* is despite the fact that all information and study material could be moved to a cloud-based storage system.
3. I suggest that in future no documents should be printed unless there is a good reason for *doing so*.
4. Students and staff should be reminded to turn off all *such* equipment when it is not needed.
5. *This* contributes greatly to the college's energy consumption.
6. I would recommend that the number of spaces in the car park be reduced by at least two-thirds, and that *these* be replaced with bicycle racks.
7. Public transport and bicycles would be more likely to be used if *this* happens.

5 **Work in pairs.**

1. Identify all the passive verbs in the sample proposal.
2. Discuss why the passive has been used in preference to the active.
3. Which of the following sentences could be rewritten using passive verbs?
   - **a** We need to encourage people to use the recycling bins.
   - **b** If they replaced the air conditioning system, they would waste less electricity.
   - **c** The problem has become worse over the past year.
   - **d** The builders should have insulated the roof when they constructed the building.
   - **e** I believe all residents will agree with this proposal.
   - **f** At present no one is taking the problem seriously enough.
   - **g** Engineers have been developing more efficient forms of solar heating.
4. Rewrite the sentences you have identified and say why the others cannot be changed.

6 **Read this writing task and follow the steps below.**

> You see this announcement on the notice board of your local council.
>
> The Environmental Planning Committee is organising a campaign to make our town more ecologically sustainable. You are invited to submit a proposal related to your neighbourhood. Present some factual information about the area, pointing out any relevant environmental issues, and suggest practical measures which individuals and families could take to make the neighbourhood more green.
>
> Write your **proposal** in 220–260 words.

1. Underline the key ideas in the task.
2. Write brief notes under these headings:
   - Facts about the current situation
   - Suggestions for improvements (number these in order of priority)
3. Make a paragraph plan and think of suitable headings.
4. Write your proposal, using passive verbs where appropriate and any phrases from the following list that may be useful.

buy local produce
dispose of rubbish responsibly
recycle waste   save energy
share car journeys   switch to natural energy
use public transport

11 Vocabulary and grammar review

Vocabulary

1 **Complete each of the sentences below with a phrase or expression from the box**

keep your cool kept waiting out in the open
rough it sick and tired of spend a fortune
the whole point of without a trace

1 You can .... on travelling if you don't take time to seek out the bargains.
2 If you want to travel cheaply, you should be prepared to .... occasionally, for example by camping rather than staying in a hotel.
3 I'm a busy man and I hate being .... by people who are late.
4 I'm .... people phoning me to sell me things and interrupting my work.
5 If you travel with a group, you miss .... travelling, which is to have completely new experiences and meet completely new people.
6 He disappeared .... somewhere in the Pacific, some weeks after setting off in a small boat to sail round the world.
7 It's important to be able to .... if you have a problem when you're travelling.
8 When I'm on holiday, I much prefer being ...., on beaches or in the mountains, to being inside.

2 **Complete these sentences by writing *at*, *in* or *on* in each of the gaps.**

1 I'll be waiting .... the news stand when you arrive.
2 Did you see Ferenc .... the conference?
3 Samya is .... her third year .... university.
4 Don't interrupt me while I'm .... the phone!
5 We do all our shopping .... that big new shopping centre .... the outskirts of town.
6 I'd love to spend my holidays .... a Pacific island!
7 I've just moved to a new flat .... the heart of the city.
8 We waited ages .... the station for our train to arrive.

Grammar

3 **Complete the second sentence so that it has a similar meaning to the first, using the word given. Do not change the word given. You must use between three and six words, including the word given.**

1 Dieter missed the plane because he overslept.
WOULD
If Dieter had .... missed the plane.

2 Nelson didn't get the job because when he came to his job interview, he arrived late.
TIME
If Nelson .... his job interview, he would have got the job.

3 Eva couldn't apply for the job in IT because she knows that her computer skills aren't good enough.
BETTER
Eva knows that if her computer skills .... for the job in IT.

4 Could you please refund my money as soon as possible?
GRATEFUL
I .... would refund my money as soon as possible.

5 We would have gone swimming if Bruno hadn't advised us not to.
FOR
If it ...., we would have gone swimming.

6 I am only participating in this activity because my teacher asked me to.
PART
I .... this activity if my teacher had not asked me to.

7 I really want not to be scared of flying anywhere in a plane.
AFRAID
I wish I .... travelling by air.

8 You should have sent me a message saying you'd arrived as I would have picked you up.
CONTACT
If only you .... with me, I would have given you a lift.

Vocabulary and grammar review 12

Vocabulary

1 Use the word given in CAPITALS to form a word that fits in the gap in each of these sentences.

1. People working on Antarctica can combat .... by forming strong friendship bonds with their co-workers. LONELY
2. In the 1980s, CFC chemicals were .... acknowledged by scientists as being responsible for much of the damage caused to the Earth's ozone layer. WIDTH
3. I'd be a famous pop star by now if it weren't for my complete .... to sing a single note in tune. ABLE
4. The TV documentary grossly .... the complex science behind the climate change debate. SIMPLE
5. .... , due to the minimal amount of precipitation it gets, Antarctica technically qualifies as a desert. APPEAR
6. To raise money for charity, I'm selling this beautiful, ... jewellery that I also designed myself. MAKE
7. We hope that the statement on our website will .... our reasons for continuing to use recycled plastic in our packaging. CLEAR
8. My mum says she often misses the days when she was young and .... , without a single worry in the world. CARE

2 Two of these sentences are correct, but the others contain mistakes with prepositions. Correct the mistakes.

1. Over a hundred thousand people participated with yesterday's marathon.
2. Whether we go skiing or not depends to the weather and the state of the snow.
3. Do you have anything useful to contribute in our discussion?
4. This morning's lecture will focus on Picasso's early work.
5. You needn't fill in that section of the form – it doesn't apply for you.
6. If the phone doesn't work properly, I'd take it back to the shop and insist for a refund.
7. Can you turn the TV down? I can't concentrate to what you're saying.
8. Do you believe in supernatural phenomena?

Grammar

3 Complete this text with *a/an*, *the* or Ø (no article).

For some years, **(1)** .... global warming, which is the gradual heating of **(2)** .... Earth, was **(3)** .... topic of heated debate in **(4)** .... scientific community, but today the consensus among **(5)** .... researchers is that **(6)** .... phenomenon is real and is caused by **(7)** .... human activity, primarily **(8)** .... burning of fossil fuels that pump **(9)** .... carbon dioxide and **(10)** .... other greenhouse gases into **(11)**.................... atmosphere. Scientists have found that the number and severity of **(12)** .... extreme weather events, which include high or low temperatures and intense storms, are **(13)** .... effective measure of **(14)** .... climate change and global warming. Indeed, it is now agreed that global warming will have **(15)** .... far-reaching and, in many cases, devastating consequences for **(16)** .... planet.

4 Complete the text with the correct form of the nouns below.

fuel human hydrocarbon matter organism product reaction requirement setting year

'A biofuel is a **(1)** .... that is made by or from a living organism that **(2)** .... can use to power something.' This definition of a biofuel is rather formal. In practice, any hydrocarbon fuel that is produced from organic **(3)** .... in a short period of time is considered a biofuel. This contrasts with fossil **(4)** .... , which take millions of years to form, and with other types of fuel which are not based on hydrocarbons – nuclear fission, for instance.

What makes biofuels tricky to understand is that they need not be made by a living **(5)** .... Biofuels can also be made through chemical **(6)** .... , carried out in a laboratory or industrial **(7)** .... that uses organic matter to make fuel. The only real **(8)** .... for a biofuel are that the starting material must be CO^2 that was fixed by a living organism and the final fuel **(9)** .... must be produced quickly rather than over millions of **(10)** ....

13 A healthy lifestyle

Starting off

1 **Work in pairs. Use words from the box to describe the health advantages and disadvantages of the following.**

ache allergy asthma blister bruise contagious disease early riser fracture fresh fruit and vegetables immunity infection insomnia muscles pollution sleep patterns sprain sting vitamins

1 using apps to monitor your health
2 sleeping seven or more hours each night
3 living in a rural area
4 living in a city
5 eating healthily
6 childhood vaccinations
7 doing sport
8 gardening

2 **Discuss these questions.**

- Which do you think has a greater influence on someone's health, their lifestyle or their genes?
- What do you do to make sure you stay fit and healthy?

Listening Part 3

1 **Read the Exam round-up box and circle the correct option in *italics* in statements 1–6.**

In Listening Part 3:

1 you will hear a *monologue / conversation*

2 the recording lasts approximately *two / four* minutes

3 you have to answer *six / eight* multiple-choice questions

4 there are *three / four* alternative answers for each question

5 the correct alternative will *express the same ideas / use the same words* as the recording

6 you should read the questions *before / after* you listen for the first time.

Exam round-up

2 **Work in pairs. You are going to hear a radio interview on the subject of sleep. Before you listen, discuss questions 1–3.**

1 Do you think more people suffer from sleep problems now than in the past? What might be the reasons for this?

2 What do you think the term 'split nights' might mean?

3 Are you an 'early riser' (you prefer to get up early in the morning) or a 'night owl' (you prefer to stay up late)? Does your preference cause you any problems?

3 48 **You will hear an interview with two authors called Karen Nash and Paul Crosby, who are talking about their research into sleep for a book they're writing. For questions 1–6, choose the answer (A, B, C or D) which fits best according to what you hear.**

1 Which discovery about dreams intrigued Karen most during her research?
- **A** They could indicate the quality of sleep that individuals were getting.
- **B** They were an essential way of sorting out problems tackled during the day.
- **C** They could prepare people for situations they hadn't encountered before.
- **D** They were an inevitable part of sleep, whether remembered or not.

2 When Karen found an author who wrote about sleep problems, she
- **A** was unsure whether he could make a difference to her own sleep issues.
- **B** was relieved to learn about his theories on the nature of sleep.
- **C** sought advice on increasing her physical activity in order to sleep better.
- **D** wondered whether she would have the discipline to apply his sleep recommendations.

3 What has Paul observed about the sleep patterns of some individuals?
- **A** They may not fit in with conventional working hours.
- **B** They can take a lot of effort to change.
- **C** They attract too little attention from researchers.
- **D** They mean some people may lose valuable hours of sleep.

4 How did Paul feel about the 'split-night' sleep pattern he adopted?
- **A** concerned about any possible future consequences of it
- **B** pleased that it seemed to fit his lifestyle so easily
- **C** anxious that he's become over-reliant on it
- **D** reassured to discover there was historical evidence for its benefits

5 What has been the effect on Karen of adopting Paul's sleep pattern?
- **A** She's been far more productive in her work than ever before.
- **B** She feels more in tune with her natural sleep rhythms.
- **C** She regrets the loss of some activities she enjoyed.
- **D** She frequently can't return to sleep after a period of wakefulness.

6 What do they agree is the most important thing they've discovered about sleep?
- **A** It's easy to become persuaded by sleep experts to adopt unsuitable cures for sleeplessness.
- **B** There are a lot of myths surrounding sleep and how it should be done.
- **C** Over-focusing on sleep can be counter-productive.
- **D** The benefits of sleep are hugely underestimated by many people.

4 **Work in pairs.**

1 What is meant by the 'sleep business' that Karen refers to, do you think? What examples of it can you think of?

2 Do you agree that our modern culture is becoming too obsessed with the state of our health?

Vocabulary
Prepositions following adjectives

▶ Page 188 Dependent Prepositions

1 **Complete these extracts from Listening Part 3 with the correct prepositions.**

1 … schools aren't very tolerant .... late arrivals.

2 … getting enough sleep is critical .... maintaining good health.

3 That inevitably meant having early nights – which though damaging .... my social life, removed any worries I had …

4 … this sleep pattern would have been familiar .... people centuries ago.

5 … I got tired .... lying awake, and frustrated .... feeling I was wasting valuable time …

6 [Sleep is] something we've all got in common .... each other …

7 The more obsessed you are .... getting enough sleep, the harder it is to achieve.

8 … the moment you're aware .... it, it gets more difficult to do.

2 **Exam candidates often make mistakes with prepositions after adjectives. Seven of the following sentences contain mistakes and one is correct. Correct the mistakes.**

1 We sincerely apologise and hope this 10% discount will be acceptable by you.

2 Drivers exceeding the speed limit are responsible for 90% of accidents in the city.

3 I am delighted for your invitation and look forward to seeing you at the event.

4 Living on the outskirts of the city is very convenient to the motorway system.

5 Teachers should try to be sensitive for the needs of their students.

6 That part of the stadium is closed for visitors – it's for athletes only.

7 She is someone who isn't aware with what is going on in the news.

8 I hope you will be capable to putting your plans into practice.

3 **Complete the sentences using a word from the box.**

about	against	by	for	in	of	to	with

1 We decided to move to this side of town because it's convenient .... the airport, so it's useful when we need to fly home.

2 After five years here, I'm more than capable .... holding a business meeting in the local language.

3 Sorry, I was just surprised .... the news that you're on the move again.

4 Since an early age, I've been obsessed .... Manga and that's why we came to Japan.

5 The thing I can't get over is just how prejudiced .... others some people are.

6 She's really quite anxious .... going home. What if her family don't recognise her after all these years?

7 After 20 years with us, it's quite clear he's devoted .... the company.

8 The easiest way to meet people is to become involved .... lots of different clubs and organisations.

4 **Read the text below and think of the preposition which best fits each gap.**

I used to be really proud **(1)** .... my work ethic. I've always been capable **(2)** .... working harder than many of my peers and I liked nothing more than to be totally devoted **(3)** .... a task. I was a complete workaholic.

Last year I started a new job as an account manager. It was a role I was perfectly suited **(4)** ...., what with the long hours and competitive culture of the company.

At first things went well. I was quickly promoted and my boss said that he was pleased **(5)** .... the progress I was making. But then things went wrong. I lost a big account and everyone was disappointed **(6)** .... me. My performance got worse after that and I lost the job.

Without any money coming in, I was anxious **(7)** .... losing my flat. The stress pushed me to the edge, and I didn't know what to do. I turned to my family, who were shocked **(8)** .... the state I was in. They made me get the help I needed.

I pay a lot more attention to my mental and physical health. I realise that working long hours can lead to burnout and that when things go wrong, I need to be kind **(9)** .... myself. I've learned some important lessons and I'm confident **(10)** .... not making the same mistakes again.

Grammar

Ways of contrasting ideas

The COMPLETE grammar reference
▶ Scan the QR code, watch the video, then turn to page 183

1 **In these extracts from Listening Part 3, underline the words and phrases used to point out a contrast between two facts or ideas.**

1. However, despite the author arguing there was neuroscientific evidence to support [his theory], the jury's still out, sadly.
2. Coincidentally, though, I also took on more daily exercise …
3. … you should get up and do something calming, whereas I'd just stay in bed.
4. While people clearly need different amounts of sleep, it seems they fall into two distinct groups …
5. … even though sleep was a perfectly normal thing for our bodies, sometimes we just had to relearn how to do it.

2 **Work in pairs. Discuss these questions about the words/phrases you underlined in Exercise 1.**

1. Which words or phrases contrast facts or ideas in a single sentence?
2. Of these, which words or phrases must be placed between the two clauses?
3. Which word is an adverb which contrasts facts or ideas in separate sentences?
4. What other contrasting words and phrases do you know?
5. Which words or phrases could replace *whereas* and *even though* in sentences 3 and 5 ?

3 **Complete the following sentences using words from the box.**

although   but   even though   however   whereas

1. I recognised you as soon as I saw you, ………………………… we'd never met before.
2. Some people seem to enjoy cold, rainy weather, ………………………… I'm not one of them.
3. Adults can be slow to learn new skills, ………………………… children pick things up very quickly.
4. We thought the case was over. ………………………… , new evidence has just come to light.
5. ………………………… I'd been there twice before, I forgot where the post office was.

4 **We can also use *despite* / *in spite of* (*the fact that*) to express contrast. Which two sentences in Exercise 3 can you change to use one of these, and what other changes would you have to make?**

5 **Exam candidates sometimes make mistakes in their use of linking words for contrast. Find and correct the mistakes in each of these sentences. (There are several possible ways of correcting them.)**

1. Despite you are not a mechanic, you should learn to understand how cars work.
2. There are several kinds of snacks you can have between 9:00 am and 6:00 pm, however hot meals are limited to lunchtime.
3. However he was usually a very efficient teacher, he wasn't available when I needed this information.
4. I appreciate being asked to give this talk again. Though I would like to suggest ways of improving this year's event.
5. My parents used to have very few ways of contacting family and friends, where nowadays we have many more choices.
6. While he left school at the age of sixteen, he went on to become one of the most famous politicians of his generation.

6 **Complete these sentences with your own endings.**

1. I don't mind going to the dentist, but …
2. I realise that it's very important to keep fit. However, …
3. Whereas most people I know go to the gym at least twice a week, I …
4. Even though many people eat better food than they did a hundred years ago, …

Reading and Use of English Part 8

1 Read the Exam round-up box and choose the correct options in *italics* for the statements 1–5.

> **Exam round-up**
>
> In Reading and Use of English Part 8:
>
> 1 there are *ten* / *fifteen* questions or statements
>
> 2 the questions or statements come *before* / *after* the texts
>
> 3 you should read the *text(s)* / *questions or statements* first
>
> 4 you have to match *all* / *some* of the questions and statements with the texts
>
> 5 the texts are *likely* / *unlikely* to contain similar information.

2 Look at the photos of sports and discuss these questions in pairs.

1 What are the most popular sports in your country? Who plays them? Are they mainly amateur or professional?

2 What kinds of sports are they? For teams or individuals? For men, women or both? Where are they played?

3 You are going to read an article about different people's experiences of playing sport. Read questions 1–10 below and underline the key idea in each one.

When talking about their chosen sport, which person

found their determination increased when things weren't going well during a game?	1
was surprised to discover how demanding it was?	2
has applied lessons learnt from it to aspects of everyday life?	3
found it could compensate for disappointments outside of sport?	4
has had to learn to adopt a different attitude when playing it?	5
suggests it helped them get over previous negative sporting experiences?	6
mentions they felt liberated by being introduced to a fresh perspective on it?	7
regrets the absence of certain aspects of other sports?	8
accepted that their relative lack of talent meant compromising on their dreams of success?	9
expresses doubts as to the suitability of it for their character?	10

4 Read quickly through the texts. Which sports have the four people been involved in?

5 Read the texts again. For questions 1–10 above, choose the correct person (A–D). Each person may be chosen more than once.

6 Work in pairs. Which of the sports mentioned have you played? Do you prefer individual or team sports? Do you share any of the experiences that the four people mentioned?

Sports and me!

Four people describe their experiences with different sports

A

Marta

Every member of my sport-obsessed family seems to excel at no fewer than three sports each! As a result, I held the childhood belief that I would be a star at any sport I liked. Nevertheless, I was a reluctant sportsperson by the time I started college – more of a couch potato, really, having tried football and hockey without much enthusiasm. But it soon sank in that I really had no option but to get involved if I wanted a social life – and the basketball team was by far the most sociable. And actually, basketball provided consolation on those occasions when I was facing poor grades and my self-esteem was plummeting to rock-bottom, as it was instantly restored whenever I scored on court. I'd be the first to admit, though, that I wasn't a naturally brilliant player, so had to come to terms with the fact that I was unlikely do sufficiently well at this sport to get the glowing results I'd imagined. And I'm also far from convinced that basketball instilled a desire to persevere, no matter what, which other players mentioned. But it did add a sense of balance to my life – a welcome respite from studying when I needed it.

B

Tom

My sports teacher at school always tried to impress on us all the benefits of sport – interacting with others, being part of a team and so on. To be honest, I wasn't convinced – and anyway, I'd already told myself I was no good at anything physical, borne out by the fact that when it came to captains picking teams, I was conspicuously left till last. As a result, I became more and more desperate to avoid signing up for any sports at all when I started at university. However, when I was finally persuaded by friends to get involved in rugby – together with the tough training – it actually triggered a kind of recovery from all the discouragement I'd felt. What's more, I actually became far more resilient on the pitch when a match seemed to be heading toward defeat. And I was soon keeping my cool under unbearable pressure, like having to score to win the match. I'd say those learning situations aren't encountered as frequently away from the pitch as when you're playing, really.

C

Levi

Looking back, I have to admit that my general self-confidence was low when I started playing cricket, but I soon threw that off and started taking the game a bit less seriously, like when an umpire's decision didn't go our way, for example. And I was lucky – our coach had really innovative methods and never made us feel the only thing worth pursuing was to win at all costs, and that anything else was abject failure. As a result, I was free to hone my technique without fear of criticism, and I began doing stuff to the best of my ability even when it didn't matter, really helping me enjoy the game rather than worry about it. The other thing about cricket, of course, is that, in comparison with football, say, it requires much more patience. I knew that wasn't my strong point when I started, and I still haven't mastered it even now, so whether cricket is really the sport for me is debatable. But I'm still hanging in there!

D

Sophie

Before I took up tennis, I don't think I'd fully appreciated to what extent sheer endurance was involved. Matches can last for what seems like hours, and your reactions have to be quick, so there aren't nearly as many opportunities to switch off as in other sports. I've had to develop my ability to focus and the mental training that's required has stood me in good stead when the going's got tough with my studies, for example. Most surprisingly for me, though, I missed the camaraderie I'd get from football or hockey – not to mention that shared sense of joy when we actually scored. And you were kind of required to put the team's collective needs above your own, passing the ball to a better-placed teammate rather than attempting to score the winning goal and cover yourself in glory – and then failing. That didn't come as naturally to me as to some others. But even so it's taken a while to adjust to operating without the support of a team, I must say. At least if I win at tennis, though, the victory's all mine!

Grammar

The language of comparison

The **COMPLETE** grammar reference

▶ Scan the QR code, watch the video, then turn to page 184

1 Complete these extracts from Reading and Use of English Part 8. Then check your answers in the texts on page 145.

as … as (x2) a bit less by far far more fewer more and more more of most surprisingly much more nearly as many … as well

1 Every other member of my sport-obsessed family seems to excel at no .... than three sports each.
2 I was .... a couch potato, really.
3 The basketball team was .... the most sociable.
4 I was unlikely to do sufficiently .... at this sport to get the glowing results I'd imagined.
5 I became .... desperate to avoid signing up for any sports at all.
6 I actually became .... resilient on the pitch when a match seemed to be heading toward defeat.
7 I'd say those learning situations aren't encountered .... frequently away from the pitch .... when you're playing.
8 I started taking the game .... seriously.
9 In comparison with football, it requires .... patience.
10 There aren't .... opportunities to switch off .... in other sports.
11 .... for me, though, I missed the camaraderie …
12 That didn't come .... naturally to me .... to some others.

2 Answer these questions about the language of comparison used in the extracts above.

1 What kinds of words can follow *more* and *most*?
2 *More* has two opposites: *less* and *fewer*. How are these words used differently? What kinds of words can follow each?
3 What does the phrase *by far* add to the meaning of a superlative adjective? Compare these sentences:
He's the brightest student in the class.
He's by far the brightest student in the class.
4 What is the opposite of *much* in this sentence?
I'm feeling much better now.

3 Rewrite these sentences, using the words in brackets.

1 Many people don't earn as much money as they did five years ago. (*less*)
2 Finding a new job was easier than I expected it to be. (*difficult*)
3 I've never seen a funnier film than that. (*funniest*)
4 There aren't as many unemployed people today as there were ten years ago. (*fewer*)
5 Working conditions are worse than they used to be. (*good*)
6 Petrol is become increasingly expensive. (*more and*)

4 Exam candidates sometimes make mistakes in their use of comparative words. Find and correct the mistakes in these sentences.

1 I think watching football is far much interesting than playing it.
2 Actually, eating junk food is even worst for your health than smoking.
3 The other actor wasn't as handsome like James.
4 I noticed that there were less angry people than there had been a year ago.
5 Easily the harder thing about football for me is the training I have to do.
6 If you travel at night, you'll find there is fewer traffic on the roads.
7 This will make the problem of obesity difficult even more.
8 If you learn English, you will have much fewer problems when you travel abroad.

5 Compare the food in these photos in different ways, using words from the box.

Nouns:	a balanced diet calories cholesterol fat fibre minerals protein seafood vitamins
Adjectives:	appetising fattening greasy (un)healthy low-fat oily tasty
Verbs:	diet lose weight

Speaking Part 2

Page 207 Speaking bank
Speaking Part 2

1 **Read the Exam round-up box and decide if the statements (1–6) are true (T) or false (F). If a statement is false, rewrite it to make it true.**

In Speaking Part 2:

1 you have to speak about three photos

2 you have to answer three questions about the photos

3 each candidate has to speak for one minute

4 you should not try to describe the photos in detail

5 you have to answer a question on your partner's photos

6 if you notice that you've made a mistake, don't correct it.

Exam round-up

2 **Work in pairs. Look at the six photos and discuss these questions.**

1 What do all six photos have in common?

2 Which of these activities are popular with people in your country? How would you explain their popularity?

3 **Read the examiner's instruction for the photos in Set A. Write some notes on how you would answer these questions.**

'Here are your pictures. They show people involved in physical activities. I'd like you to compare two of the activities, and say how effective the activities are as a means of keeping fit, and why they might be so popular.

Student A: talk about two photos for one minute, with Student B listening.

Student B: you then answer this question: Which groups of people get the most benefit from activities like these?'

Set A

4 **Now read this instruction for the photos in Set B. Write some notes on how you would answer these questions.**

'Here are your pictures. They show people involved in demanding physical activities. I'd like you to compare two of the activities, and say what qualities a person needs to succeed in them, and why people want to participate in them.

Student B: talk about two photos for one minute, with Student A listening.

Student A: you then answer this question: How are activities like these different from sports like football or basketball?'

Set B

5 **Listen to two candidates doing the tasks.**

49

1 Which candidate does the task more successfully?

2 What advice would you give each candidate to help them do better next time?

6 **Work in pairs. Using your notes, practise the tasks in Exercises 3 and 4.**

Reading and Use of English Part 3

1 Read the Exam round-up box and answer the questions 1–6.

In Reading and Use of English Part 3:

1 How many gaps are there in the text?
2 How many words can you write for each gap?
3 Should you use a different form of the given word in capitals?
4 If you need a negative form of the given word, how can you change it?
5 How important is spelling?
6 What should you do when you have completed the gaps?

Exam round-up

2 Some of the given words in Part 3 tasks are root words to which you have to add a prefix or a suffix or both, For example: *appear* → *appearance*, *disappear* → *disappearance*. But you have to make more complex changes to other root words, e.g. *destroy* → *destruction*, *destructive*, *indestructible*.
Complete this table with words related to the root verbs 1–9. Often more than one word is possible.

verb	noun	adjective	adverb
1 destroy	destruction destroyer	destructive indestructible	destructively
2 intend			
3 apply			
4 explode			
5 advise			
6 know			
7 repeat			
8 include			
9 describe			

3 For questions 1–8, read the text below. Use the word given in capitals at the end of some of the lines to form a word that fits the gap in the same line. There is an example at the beginning.

THE JOY OF A WARM BATH

Do you find hot baths a very	
(0) ......enjoyable...... way to unwind?	**ENJOY**
Then you might be interested in some recent research that suggests having a hot bath can be just as	
(1) .... as doing	**BENEFIT**
exercise. Researchers found that hot baths have **(2)** .... with	**SIMILAR**
aerobic exercise in terms of the health advantages they bring. Time spent in a hot tub won't help you lose weight, but it can raise core temperature and result in **(3)** .... in blood	**IMPROVE**
flow, for example. This in turn can **(4)** .... blood pressure,	**LOW**
control blood sugar and calm down **(5)**	**INFLAME**
This is obviously appealing for those with the **(6)** .... to	**ABLE**
commit to periods of regular exercise. For the effects to be achieved, though, the water needs to remain hot for a sustained period, without the heat **(7)** .... of domestic	**LOSE**
bathtubs. However, studies show that saunas might achieve broadly the same effects, and that people using them regularly could experience a significant **(8)** .... in	**REDUCE**
their risk of cardiovascular disease, for instance.	

4 Discuss these questions in pairs or groups.

1 How much exercise do you do a day or a week? What kind of exercise do you do?
2 What is your main reason for exercising? Do you enjoy it? Why? / Why not?
3 If you were told you needed to do more regular exercise, what would you do?

Writing Part 2: A letter

▶ **Page 196 Writing bank**
A letter

1 **How much do you remember about Writing Part 2? Read the Exam round-up box and complete the sentences (1–6) by writing a word or a number.**

In Writing Part 2:

1 You have a choice of .... tasks.

2 The task may be an email or letter, a .... , a report or a proposal.

3 In order to write in the correct style, it is important to remember who the .... is.

4 You should write 220–.................................. words for this part.

5 When you are writing a report or a proposal you can divide what you write into .... and put a .... above each one.

6 When you are writing a proposal, you are trying to .... someone to act on your ideas or suggestions.

Exam round-up

2 **Read this writing task and then read Marek's letter, without paying attention to the alternatives in *italics*. Does he cover all parts of the task?**

You belong to a small sports club and have been asked by other members to write a letter of complaint to the club manager. Your letter should include the following:

- why club members are not satisfied with the club and the way it is organised
- how the club could be improved
- what may happen if improvements are not made

Write your **letter**.

3 **Work in pairs. Look at the structure of the letter. What is the topic of each paragraph?**

4 **Find phrases that are used in Marek's letter to introduce**

- explanations for the decline in membership
- suggestions for solving the problem.

5 **A letter like this should be written in a style which is not too informal. Circle the appropriate words and phrases in *italics*.**

Dear Sir,

I am writing on behalf of a number of members of the sports club who are [1]*concerned about / fed up with* the club and [2]*the way it is being run / how you run it*.

It has been clear to us for [3]*quite a while / some time* that we have a membership problem. The club, which I visit regularly, has been [4]*noticeably less busy / pretty empty* in recent months. In the view of members, there are two possible explanations for this decline. [5]*For a start, / Firstly,* we believe that some members are joining other clubs with more state-of-the-art facilities. Secondly, the cost of membership at the club appears to be high compared with other clubs [6]*in the area / round here*.

As to what action can be taken, our main suggestions are for all the club's gym equipment to be replaced and for management to [7]*change / adjust* the cost of membership. While the charge for adult members could remain the same, reduced fees could be [8]*brought in / introduced* for [9]*old people / retired people*. There could also be a new family rate to encourage parents to come with their children. We also believe that the tennis courts should be resurfaced, because they have been neglected for several years. They are now not fit for purpose.

We believe that if these improvements are not made soon, more members will vote with their feet and move to other clubs on a permanent basis. We trust that you will [10]*think about / consider* our ideas and we would be grateful if you could look into making the improvements we have suggested [11]*as soon as possible / very soon*.

Yours faithfully,

Marek Novák

6 **What is the meaning of the expressions in bold in these extracts?**

1 I am writing **on behalf of** a number of members …
2 … clubs with more **state-of-the-art** facilities.
3 The tennis courts are now **not fit for purpose**.
4 … more members will **vote with their feet** …

7 **Read the following writing task. What facilities are currently missing for this age group in your area? Make a list of the top three that you think would make a difference to your area.**

It has been announced that your area will receive funding for new sports and fitness facilities for young people. Your local council is inviting residents to write letters suggesting how funds should best be spent. Your letter should explain:

- why this funding is to be welcomed
- what facilities should be provided
- how the new facilities will make a difference to young people in the area.

Write your **letter**.

8 **Make a paragraph plan. Then write your letter using appropriate language for explanations and suggestions.**

14 A new land

Starting off

1 **Work in pairs. Discuss the questions.**

1. Why do people migrate? Think of as many reasons as you can.
2. Would you like to migrate? If so, why and where? If not, why not?

2 **You are going to hear six people who have migrated talking about their experiences. Listen and match each person with the aspect of migration (A–H) that they focus on. (There are two aspects you do not need.)** 50

Speaker 1 ....
Speaker 2 ....
Speaker 3 ....
Speaker 4 ....
Speaker 5 ....
Speaker 6 ....

A I migrated to fulfil my ambitions.
B I had little choice in the matter.
C I've felt homesick since I left.
D I find it difficult to stay in one place for long.
E I moved because of a relationship.
F I wanted a better environment for my children.
G I was fed up with the weather.
H I'm surprised how well my life has turned out.

3 **Work in small groups. Discuss the questions.**

1. Do you know anyone whose reasons for emigrating or experiences of emigrating are similar to the ones you've just heard?
2. How can emigration benefit
   - the country people emigrate from?
   - the country people immigrate to?

Vocabulary

Comment adverbials and intensifying adverbs

Page 185 Comment adverbials and intensifying adverbs

1 **Look at this extract from Starting off, Exercise 2. Which word or phrase in each sentence shows the speaker's attitude or opinion about what he says?**

You see, unfortunately I'm one of those typical expatriates who spends two years working in this country and three years working in that. I don't think I could ever go back to my home country because, quite honestly, I just wouldn't fit in.

2 **Rewrite each sentence below, replacing the underlined words with a comment adverbial from the box in each gap.**

apparently	fortunately	generally speaking	generously	obviously	personally	to be honest	undoubtedly

1 It's lucky that she has a very supportive family.
...., she has a very supportive family.

2 I'm absolutely certain that he's the best player.
He's .... the best player.

3 Most of the time the weather here is pleasant.
...., the weather here is pleasant.

4 I'm telling you the truth when I say that I found the journey very uncomfortable.
...., I found the journey very uncomfortable.

5 From what I've heard, Bill is thinking of emigrating to Canada.
...., Bill is thinking of emigrating to Canada.

6 Anaya's parents have invited me to stay with them, which is very kind of them.
Anaya's parents have .... invited me to stay with them.

7 It's clear that he wasn't happy with the way he was treated.
...., he wasn't happy with the way he was treated.

8 To give you my opinion, I wouldn't buy that car.
...., I wouldn't buy that car.

3 50 **Listen again to the speakers in Starting off, Exercise 2. Follow the steps a–c.**

absolutely	completely	incredibly	totally	utterly

a Complete the sentences below by writing an intensifying adverb from the box in each gap. One intensifying adverb isn't needed.

b Say which other adverbs in the box could also be used for each gap.

c Decide how adding an intensifying adverb affects each sentence.

1 We were .... fed up with the crime and feeling of insecurity that surrounded us.

2 I just found the short grey days and the continual rain .... depressing.

3 I'd be .... out of touch.

4 I've been .... lucky, though.

4 **Complete these texts by choosing the alternatives in *italics* which form a collocation. There may be one or two correct answers to each question.**

The Japanese drummers' performance was **(1)** *extremely / utterly / absolutely* amazing. We'd never seen anything like it. The audience was **(2)** *absolutely / completely / totally* delighted and applauded for about ten minutes.

For migrants, finding somewhere to live and work is **(3)** *totally / incredibly / perfectly* simple and presents no problem. The difficulty is integrating into the community because local people are **(4)** *absolutely / utterly / completely* indifferent to foreigners, so many of them end up feeling **(5)** *extremely / incredibly / perfectly* depressed.

Temperatures often rise above 40° C in the summer, so this heat is **(6)** *perfectly / incredibly / absolutely* normal. Many newcomers to this part of the world feel **(7)** *totally / extremely / utterly* exhausted by the end of the day unless they have air conditioning.

You'll need to work hard to learn the language because it's **(8)** *utterly / incredibly / totally* hard. However, if you persist, you'll find it isn't **(9)** *extremely / absolutely / incredibly* impossible and you will make progress.

Reading and Use of English Part 6

1 **Read the Exam round-up box and answer the questions 1–3 about Reading and Use of English Part 6.**

In Reading and Use of English Part 6:

1 How many texts does it contain and how many questions must you answer?

2 Should you read the questions before or after you read the texts for the first time? Why?

3 What does this part test your ability to do?

Exam round-up

2 **Work in small groups. You will read four extracts by psychologists discussing emigration. Before you read, discuss these questions.**

1 What effects do the following have on someone's ability to relocate successfully to another country?
- personality
- openness to self-reflection
- prior experience of travel
- communication skills

2 Which other areas do you think are important?

3 **Academic texts may contain ideas expressed in complex ways. Decide what each of these sentences means. Choose either *a* or *b*.**

1 Moving to an entirely new country, where interpersonal support networks are suddenly lacking or even non-existent, can easily turn life upside down.

a Emigration can often be an isolating and confusing process.

b Successful emigration is unlikely to occur when undertaken alone.

2 Anyone assuming that emigration will pose challenges as straightforward as those faced while visiting a region or country, purely and simply for leisure purposes, is greatly mistaken.

a The demands of moving overseas to take on work are equal to those experienced when travelling.

b The demands of emigration are entirely distinct from those that arise from travelling/tourism.

3 Often, people mistakenly believe that the knowledge gained from a particular lived experience is transferable to all other seemingly comparable situations.

a Having lived experience of a given situation is not necessarily a guarantee that it will prove useful in another context.

b The knowledge or experience gained in a situation is only ever useful for that one particular context.

4 At home, people are often unwilling to question whether their beliefs are truly their own, or are in fact a product of their surroundings.

a Few people consider how extensively they are affected by outside influences while in their own domestic environments.

b In their land of birth, it is to natural for people to base their opinions on those that are dictated to them by family members.

5 Studies have long investigated the decision-making processes that drive a person to emigrate, and there is sufficient data available to anticipate confidently the psychological challenges that it will bring.

a It would be extremely helpful for people emigrating to refer to academic research to inform their decision to relocate.

b It has become increasingly possible to predict the ways in which people are likely to react after a move overseas.

6 Generally, those naturally inclined to embrace the opportunity to bond with unfamiliar people in new situations are likely to find relocation far less challenging than those without such qualities.

a Successfully relocating overseas tends to be less stressful for people with a particular personality type.

b Successfully relocating overseas is entirely dependent on the ability to make new friends.

7 After any permanent relocation, there is an initial settling-in period, during which time the novelty of the situation inspires them to deal efficiently with any barriers put in front of them.

a When people first move overseas, they realise that they need to take a fresh approach to solving any problems that may arise.

b When people first move overseas, the newness of their environment stimulates within them a greater capacity for problem-solving.

8 At some point, conversations with the locals will seem to change, the result of a growing tendency in the migrant to read between the lines of what is being said, questioning whether they themselves have, and have been, truly understood.

a There is a moment when a recent migrant becomes self-conscious about being able to communicate entirely effectively in their adopted language.

b There is a moment when a recent migrant gains a deeper knowledge of the subtle complexities of communication in their adopted language.

The psychology of emigration

A Typically, when someone begins their new life overseas, it soon becomes clear how they had taken for granted the ease with which they moved through their previous day-to-day existence. Moving to an entirely new country, where interpersonal support networks are suddenly lacking or even non-existent, can easily turn life upside down, hence the perfectly reasonable urge to form immediate relationships with local people and establish that support in the surrounding area. The person will then experience a period of constructive growth, through exposure to new customs and conventions, questioning their own, homegrown values, which are either rejected or strengthened. Given this, those who find socialising with strangers a chore – or even a source of anxiety – may find integration particularly challenging, and they should reflect seriously on whether moving abroad is truly right for them. Similarly, someone assuming that emigration will pose challenges as straightforward as those faced while visiting a region or country, purely and simply for leisure purposes, is greatly mistaken.

B Often, people mistakenly believe that the knowledge gained from a particular lived experience is transferable to all other seemingly comparable situations. A prime example is found in the case of moving overseas: those relying solely on their extensive familiarity with international tourism are regularly shocked by the difficulties that a permanent move brings. Such a reliance is naïve at best, and ignores the exhaustive wealth of information and opportunity available online to prepare oneself for a major life change. Contact with local residents can be made through message boards or social media sites, creating a ready-made safety net on arrival. With this in place, the worry about making new acquaintances vanishes, allowing new contexts to encourage self-reflection instead. At home, people are often unwilling to question whether their beliefs are truly their own, or are in fact a product of their surroundings. Living overseas makes avoiding this question impossible; it must be tackled head-on.

C Studies have long investigated the decision-making processes that drive a person to emigrate, and there is sufficient data available to anticipate confidently the psychological challenges that it will bring. Without question, someone moving overseas is bound to undergo a re-evaluation of whether they truly are who they believe themselves to be, or merely a product of their upbringing, and this is fundamental to the successful transition into a new life. There are other generalisations we might choose to make, of course. Generally, those naturally inclined to embrace the opportunity to bond with unfamiliar people in new situations are likely to find relocation far less challenging than those without such qualities. Interestingly, the former are commonly individuals who have spent prolonged periods of time touring through other nations, since doing so establishes the foundations that ensure a comfortable adjustment to a permanent move.

D Many of those who move abroad assume that any earlier, frequent passages through passport control in miscellaneous countries will somehow magically guarantee a flawless transition from home to adopted nation. Undoubtedly, after any permanent relocation, there is an initial settling-in period, during which time the novelty of the situation inspires them to deal efficiently with any barriers put in front of them. These could be social or linguistic, and affect everyone, regardless of their character. However, at some point, conversations with the locals will seem to change, the result of a growing tendency in the migrant to read between the lines of what is being said, questioning whether they themselves have, and have been, truly understood. While reflecting on such matters is necessary, and key to improving interpersonal communication, problems inevitably arise if doing so prompts a complete internal re-evaluation of their sense of identity.

4 **Now do the Exam task. For questions 1–4, choose from the extracts A–D. The extracts may be chosen more than once.**

Which person

expresses a similar view to C on how someone's personality can increase the likelihood of a successful relocation?	1
has a different opinion to the others regarding the benefit of self-analysis while living in a new culture?	2
expresses a different view to the others about how useful prior experience of travel is likely to be?	3
makes a similar point to B about taking advantage of opportunities for social interaction?	4

Listening Part 4

1 **You will hear five short extracts in which people are talking about moving abroad. Before you listen, read the Exam round-up box and decide if the statements 1–4 are true (T) or false (F). If a statement is false, rewrite it to make it true.**

> In Listening Part 4:
>
> 1 you have to do two tasks
>
> 2 you hear five different speakers and you have to choose from seven options
>
> 3 you hear the piece twice; you should do the first task the first time you listen and the second task the second time you listen
>
> 4 you may hear the answer to Task Two before the answer to Task One.
>
> **Exam round-up**

2 **With a partner, discuss which option might be correct in questions 1–4 below. Give reasons for your answers.**

1 In the year 2020, there were an estimated .... international migrants worldwide.

- **a** 272 million
- **b** 180 million
- **c** 412 million

2 What percentage of the world's population does the figure in question 1 represent?

- **a** 8.4%
- **b** 3.5%
- **c** 11.2%

3 The primary destination for all migrants was .... ; the highest number of international migrants came from ....

- **a** Germany, Mexico
- **b** Saudi Arabia, China
- **c** The United States, India

4 In a survey of 15,000 people worldwide, the following were given as the main reasons for moving abroad. Rank them from most to least common, and suggest why you have chosen that order.

- ☐ sent by their employer
- ☐ to improve language skills
- ☐ to go to school or university
- ☐ found a job independently
- ☐ to simply enjoy living abroad
- ☐ to find a better quality of life
- ☐ to look for adventure / personal challenge
- ☐ to live in their partner's home country / for love

3 **Look at the options A–H given in each exam task below. Discuss with a partner which would most likely be your reason for moving abroad (Task One), and what you would most likely find challenging about your move (Task Two).**

4 **Listen and complete the two tasks.** 51

TASK ONE

For questions 1–5, choose from the list (A–H) the motivation each speaker gives for moving abroad.

- **A** to seek out a preferable climate
- **B** to find a better standard of living
- **C** to improve employment prospects
- **D** to become more independent
- **E** to experience a different culture
- **F** to be closer to a family member
- **G** to expand on their education
- **H** to achieve a long-term aim

Speaker 1	**1**
Speaker 2	**2**
Speaker 3	**3**
Speaker 4	**4**
Speaker 5	**5**

TASK TWO

For questions 6–10, choose from the list (A–H) what each speaker found challenging about moving abroad.

- **A** getting a steady job
- **B** losing touch with friends
- **C** adjusting to a faster pace of life
- **D** dealing with domestic tasks
- **E** finding like-minded people
- **F** adapting to their accommodation
- **G** accepting social norms
- **H** setting aside time to relax

Speaker 1	**6**
Speaker 2	**7**
Speaker 3	**8**
Speaker 4	**9**
Speaker 5	**10**

5 **Work in small groups. Discuss the questions below. Try to use some of the comment adverbials from Vocabulary Exercise 2 on page 151 when you speak.**

- At which point in your life would you be most likely to move permanently abroad? Why?
- How important would it be for you to speak the language of your adopted nation fluently?

Grammar
Emphasis

The COMPLETE grammar reference
▶ Scan the QR code, watch the video, then turn to page 186

1 In Listening Part 4, the speakers say the following sentences in a different way to give them more emphasis. With a partner, discuss how you could make the sentences more emphatic.

1. Being able to shape a new persona for myself has made it all worthwhile.
2. The apartment block where I'm living is this huge, modern building right in the centre of town, but my studio is so cramped.
3. … hopefully we'll become good friends, but you never know. I know I haven't got a great set of qualifications …
4. No one in my family could imagine why I wanted to come here.
5. … my mood would always take a turn for the worse. That, more than anything, drove my decision to go.
6. The days of being stuck inside, feeling low, are gone.
7. That conversation completely changed my life.

2 Listen and compare what the speakers say with your suggestions for Exercise 1. Then, match the sentences to the techniques for emphasis (a–e) listed below. 51

a Auxiliary verb ....
b *It-* cleft sentence ....
c Fronting ...., ..., ..., ...
d Reflexive pronoun ....
e *Wh-* cleft sentence ....

3 Complete these sentences so that they are true for you. Then write three more sentences or questions using emphasis, and discuss them all with a partner.

What I really enjoy about .... is ....

It is .... that I find so enjoyable about ....

Why I always ...., I will never know.

Your friends, do they always .... ?

Vocabulary
learn, *find out* and *know*; *provide*, *offer* and *give*

1 Exam candidates often confuse *learn*, *find out* and *know*. Match the words (1–3) with their definitions (a–c) from the *Cambridge Dictionary Online*.

1 know 2 find out 3 learn

a to get information about something because you want to know more about it, or to learn a fact or piece of information for the first time
b to get knowledge or skill in a new subject or activity
c to have information in your mind

2 *Provide*, *offer* and *give* often have very similar meanings. However, sometimes their meanings are slightly different. When their meanings are different, which word, *provide* or *offer* or *give*, means

1. to supply someone with a service they need?
2. to ask someone if they would like to have something or if they would like you to do something?
3. to supply someone with something?

3 Complete each of these sentences written by exam candidates with *learn*, *find out*, *know*, *provide*, *offer* or *give* in the correct form.

1. I've just texted Yoriko to .... if we should bring anything to the party.
2. We will .... overnight accommodation if you miss the last train.
3. You should go to the information desk to .... where to pick up your luggage.
4. While studying English, you also .... about their customs and traditions.
5. Do you .... what time the next train to Łódź leaves?
6. The government should make an effort to .... more facilities in rural areas.
7. During the lecture, we .... how Turkish people lived in the past.
8. Comfy Catering Services aims to .... good food for students at low cost.
9. We feel that the authorities should be prepared to .... a solution to those parents who require one.
10. Studying at the Ace School in London will .... you the opportunity to make new friends and meet people.
11. I'm writing to complain about the service you .... during our stay in your hotel last weekend.
12. This watch is important to me because my parents .... it to me for my 18th birthday.

Speaking Part 4

▶ **Page 213 Speaking bank**
Speaking Part 4

1 **Read the Exam round-up box and circle the correct alternative in *italics* in the sentences 1–4.**

> **Exam round-up**
>
> In Speaking Part 4:
>
> 1 The task lasts for about *three / five* minutes.
>
> 2 You are asked to give your opinions on *subjects connected with the theme in Speaking Part 3 / a new theme.*
>
> 3 You and your partner *are each asked different questions / are expected to discuss your ideas about the same questions.*
>
> 4 You should give *brief answers / quite long answers.*

2 **Work in pairs. Which of the phrases in the box could you use when answering each of the questions below? (You can use some of the phrases with more than one answer.)**

aptitude for language learning broaden your experience of life a change in your mindset   climate change encourage tolerance   grow as a person long-term effects of pandemics open to new possibilities   political instability relative cost of international travel stand on your own two feet

1 How might someone benefit from moving to another country?
2 Why do some people find the idea of moving to another country more attractive than others do?
3 What do you think are the main factors influencing international migration today?

3 (52) **Now check your answers by listening to two candidates, Laura and Daniel.**

4 (53) **With a partner, complete these extracts from Laura and Daniel's answers, suggesting modal verbs (*can, may, should*, etc.) for each gap. Then listen and check your answers.**

1 Living in another country .... broaden your experience of life.
2 Even a short period of time living away – five or six months, say – .... bring about a complete change in your mindset …
3 [It] allows someone to appreciate another culture in a way that they .... not or, more likely, ... not do otherwise.
4 I .... imagine it .... make someone of my age mature more quickly …
5 … the relative cost of international travel is perhaps higher than it was a few years ago, so that .... well put people off the idea.

5 (54) **Listen to the extracts and complete the phrases that the speakers use to express a firm opinion.**

1 … the benefits definitely outweigh any disadvantages, ...
2 .... that it encourages tolerance …
3 … I'm not sure it's .... the case that you need have an outgoing personality to move away.
4 .... that the logistics of moving overseas would become more complex with more than one person to consider …

6 **Work in pairs. Discuss your answers to the three questions in Exercise 2. Try to use some of the words and phrases from Exercises 2, 4 and 5 when you speak.**

7 **Work in pairs and discuss these questions.**

1 Would you say that moving to and setting up a new life in another country is generally easier today than it was in the past? Why? / Why not?
2 Many companies expect their employees to be ready to move to different places and countries to work. Do you think everyone should be ready to move for their job? Why? / Why not?
3 Some people argue that anyone who moves to a new country should be completely fluent in the language of the country they go to. Do you agree?

Reading and Use of English Part 4

1 **Read the Exam round-up box and complete the gaps 1–8 with words from the box.**

In Reading and Use of English Part 4:

change contractions given number
same six three word

There are (1) .... questions.

You have to write between (2) .... and six words in each space, using the (3) .... given.

(4) .... count as two words.

You must not (5) .... the word given.

Read the question and decide what grammar and vocabulary you need. When you have finished, read your answer and check that:

- it means the (6) .... as the original sentence
- you have used the correct (7) .... of words
- you haven't changed the word (8) ....

Exam round-up

2 **For the Part 4 question below, which is the correct answer: a, b, c or d? Why are the other answers incorrect?**

Tom should have contacted us the moment he arrived.

TOUCH

Tom was supposed .... as soon as he arrived.

a getting in touch with us
b to get in touch with us
c to have got in touch with us
d to have made contact with us

3 **For questions 1–4, complete the second sentence so that it has a similar meaning to the first sentence, using the word given. Do not change the word given. You must use between three and six words, including the word given.**

1 Could you remind me to phone Charlie on Friday?

GRATEFUL

I'd .... me to phone Charlie on Friday.

Clue: There are two parts to this answer: a request and an indirect question.

2 Joe managed to complete the project without help.

ALL

Joe succeeded .... himself.

Clue: Use an expression which means 'alone'.

3 Fatima can't decide whether or not she wants to study Engineering next year.

MINDS

Fatima is ....
Engineering next year.

Clue: Which expression with 'minds' means 'unable to decide'?

4 Kristof is spending December in Porto, aiming for a permanent relocation next year.

VIEW

Kristof is spending December in Porto
.... next year.

Clue: As well as using a phrase that means 'aiming to do something', you also need to change the form of two words.

4 **Now do this Part 4 task without clues. Use between three and six words in each gap.**

1 It's possible that the heavy traffic is delaying Katya.

HOLDING

What may .... the heavy traffic.

2 Franz didn't get to the office until lunchtime.

NOT

It .... Franz got to the office.

3 While my little brother is often naughty, he is even more badly behaved when he's tired.

DOES

My little brother is often naughty, but he
.... when he's tired.

4 No one would ever question whether or not Pat possesses an astonishing intelligence.

INTELLIGENT

That ...., is something that no one would ever question.

5 Tim has taken up landscape photography, mainly because he loves to be outdoors so much.

LOVE

It .... that has inspired Tim to take up landscape photography.

6 A cheap power supply left on overnight might have been to blame for the fire.

CAUSED

What .... a cheap power supply left on overnight.

Writing Part 1: An essay

▶ **Page 193 Writing bank**
An essay

1 **Read the Exam round-up box and put the advice in the correct order (1–7).**

> How much do you remember about how to approach Writing Part 1?
>
> ☐ Check what you have written, looking for specific mistakes you know you make.
>
> ☐ Organise your notes into a paragraph-by- paragraph plan, including some of the vocabulary you'd like to use.
>
> ☐ Brainstorm ideas and make rough notes.
>
> ☐ Identify the reader, decide what would be a suitable style and what effect you want to produce on the reader.
>
> [1] Analyse the question, underline the things you must deal with and identify your objectives in writing.
>
> ☐ Write your answer (220–260 words) following your plan.
>
> [7] Take about 45 minutes to do the whole task.
>
> **Exam round-up**

2 **Read the essay task below and underline the key points.**

Your class has watched a television documentary about the help which can be provided to support immigrants after their arrival in a new country. You have made the notes below.

Areas covered
• language • culture • work

Some opinions expressed in the documentary:
'Newly arrived immigrants would benefit from being offered language classes.'
'Local people can help immigrants to become familiar with cultural norms and expectations.'
'Businesses could set up schemes to provide immigrants with a route into employment.'

Write an **essay** discussing **two** of the ways in which immigrants can be supported and **provide reasons** in support of your answer, and explain which of the ways would provide the most benefit to migrant communities.

You may, if you wish, make use of the opinions expressed in the documentary, but you should use your own words as far as possible.

3 **Work in small groups. Expand the opinions expressed during the documentary by**

- adding reasons and examples
- saying whether you agree or disagree with each opinion and giving your reasons
- expressing a counter-argument (which you may or may not agree with).

4 **Read this sample essay without paying attention to the gaps. Which ideas expressed in the essay did you mention in Exercise 3?**

The world we live in is more globalised than ever before, [1] .... large numbers of people move abroad in search of a better life. [2] .... , it seems logical to provide assistance for anyone arriving from overseas, enabling them to adapt more successfully to a new life in a new community.

[3] .... people should aim to acquire the necessary language skills before being allowed to settle permanently in a country. I am broadly in agreement with this point of view [4] .... learning the language of the country is the key to integrating with the local culture. However, generally speaking it is difficult to reach a level of language proficiency until you have spent some time in the country itself, [5] .... immigrants should be provided with language lessons, particularly during the early years of their relocation.

[6] .... local businesses, organisations and enterprises can play their part by providing jobs or training programmes. [7] .... , in my city, there are a number of companies that have established workplace schemes to provide employment, whether part-time or permanent, for those who have decided to make it their home. Undoubtedly, [8] .... immigrants have been able to establish themselves in the community, build new friendships, and become self-reliant, [9] .... undoubtedly enrich their lives.

[10] .... it is providing opportunities to find both the reassurance of a daily working routine and the chance to communicate socially with the residents of a town or city that makes integration most successful.

5 **The phrases below link ideas together in the sample essay and also refer to the documentary mentioned in the task. Complete the essay by writing each of the phrases in the correct gap.**

all of which consequently
during the documentary it was suggested that
for this reason, I personally believe that
it is through these experiences that
on the grounds that to offer some examples
so what I would suggest is that with the result that
I entirely agree with the point made during the documentary that

6 **In groups, discuss the following questions. Do not take notes yet. What effect might growing migration from the countryside to cities worldwide have on:**

- *overcrowding* – what happens when there are increasing numbers of people in a limited amount of space?
- *access to resources and utilities* – what happens to demand for schools, public transport, etc?
- *employment* – what happens to the number of available jobs? Do wages go up or down?

7 **Decide which two of the three areas in exercise 6 you were able to come up with the most ideas for. Then choose two main ideas from each area.**

8 **Read the following question and write your essay.**

Your class has watched a television documentary about the problems that arise from ongoing, large-scale migration from the countryside to cities around the world. You have made the notes below.

Areas covered
- overcrowding
- access to resources and utilities
- employment

Some opinions expressed in the documentary:
'When too many people live in too little space, they are more likely to feel stressed and be unhealthy.'
'Schools and transport systems might eventually be unable to cope with the increase in demand.'
'When there is an ever-growing level of demand for work, there are not enough jobs for everyone.'

Write an **essay** discussing **two** of the areas in your notes. You should **explain what effects the issues in these areas might have on cities and their residents** and **provide reasons** in support of your answer.

You may, if you wish, make use of the opinions expressed in the documentary, but you should use your own words as far as possible.

13 Vocabulary and grammar review

Vocabulary

1 Complete these sentences with the correct prepositions.

1. Be careful what you say. He's very sensitive .... criticism.
2. As the manager of the department, you are responsible .... recruiting new staff.
3. There are more and more viruses which are resistant .... traditional antibiotics.
4. Are you familiar .... the music of Jan Gabarek?
5. If you want to be better .... playing the guitar, you'll have to practise more.
6. I can't eat omelettes because I'm allergic .... eggs.
7. I like the house itself, but it isn't very convenient .... the supermarket or the station.
8. Please let us know if our offer is acceptable .... you.

Grammar

2 Correct the errors in the use of words or phrases to express contrast.

1. He thought he had some terrible disease, however it was just a bad case of flu.
2. My sister seems to catch every cold going, although I am rarely ill.
3. Despite he didn't feel well, he went to work as usual.
4. But I exercise every day, I'm still overweight.
5. He refused to see his doctor. Although everyone he knew advised him to.

3 Complete the second sentence so that it has a similar meaning to the first sentence, using the word given. Do not change the word given. You must use three to six words, including the word given.

1. The public health service is worse than it was ten years ago.
   GOOD
   The public health service is .... ten years ago.
2. We don't have as many qualified nurses as we need.
   FEWER
   We .... we need.
3. My new job is not as easy as I expected.
   DIFFICULT
   My new job .... I expected.
4. I'm really tired. I'll be very glad when we get home.
   SOONER
   I'm really tired. The .... better.
5. I earned less money than I thought I would last week.
   MUCH
   I .... as I thought I would last week.
6. Your diet is just as bad as mine.
   BETTER
   Your diet .... mine.

Vocabulary and grammar review 14

Vocabulary

1 **Complete the sentences below by writing *learn*, *find out*, *know*, *provide*, *offer* or *give* in the correct form in the gaps. You can use any verb more than once.**

1 How old were you when you .... your multiplication tables?
2 I've been trying to .... what I need to do to get a working visa for New Zealand.
3 I think it's the government's duty to .... free education for all young people up to the age of 21.
4 Now where are my keys? I .... they're in my bag somewhere!
5 Rebecca has been .... the chance to improve her Spanish by studying in Argentina for a year.
6 My sister has been .... a job in the company and she's considering it at the moment.
7 I don't think the police will ever manage to .... who stole the money.
8 You'll never .... to drive properly unless you go to a proper driving school.

2 **Complete the letter below with adverbs or adverbial phrases from the box. Use each adverb / adverbial phrase once only. In some cases more than one answer is possible.**

actually almost certainly apparently hopefully obviously quite surprisingly thoughtfully to be honest

Dear Odile,

Thank you for so **(1)** .... inviting me to stay with you and your family for a few months later this year. I will **(2)** .... take you up on your offer as I've been thinking for some time of doing a gap year before I go to university. **(3)** ...., I need a break from studying and I think a spell of living abroad would suit me perfectly.

(4) ...., because I'm rather tired of school life, I haven't been working particularly hard this term, but **(5)** ...., I've managed to pass all my exams with quite good grades. **(6)** ...., when I go to university next year I'll have to work quite a lot harder. I already know several people on the course I want to do and **(7)** .... it's very demanding. So **(8)** .... a few months abroad will refresh me enough to really get down to work when I get back.

I'll be in touch when I've got my plans a little clearer.

Very best wishes,

Candice

Grammar

3 **Complete the second sentence so that it has a similar meaning to the first sentence, using the word given. Do not change the word given. You must use between three and six words, including the word given.**

1 We didn't have as much time as we wanted to understand all this information.
TAKE
What we wanted .... in all this information.

2 Everybody agreed that the music at Lenka's presentation was very annoying.
OBJECTED
It was the music .... at Lenka's presentation.

3 First, you complete this form and then you post it to the embassy.
FILL
What you have .... this form and then send it to the embassy.

4 Audrey is not prepared to leave her current job.
LAST
'Getting a new job is .... do!' cried Audrey.

5 Alfredo wanted nothing more than to relax when he got home.
TAKE
All Alfredo wanted to .... easy when he got home.

6 I spend most of my time doing paperwork.
TAKES
It .... most of my time.

1

VERB FORMS TO TALK ABOUT THE PAST

Past simple

The past simple tense is used for completed past actions. We use it to describe:

- an action that happened or a state that existed at a specific time in the past:
  *Yesterday **I felt** so tired that I **didn't go** to work.*
- an action that lasted for a period of time in the past, but is now finished:
  *I **studied** in Paris for four years from 2005 to 2009.*
- a habitual action over a specific period in the past:
  *While he was away, he **rang** his girlfriend every day.*

Past continuous

The past continuous tense is used to describe:

- an activity in progress at a point in the past:
  *She **was driving** home when the police stopped her.*
  (The activity of driving was interrupted by the police's action.)
  *I **was cooking** lunch when I heard the news.*
  (And I continued to cook lunch afterwards.)
- a situation which was temporary at a time in the past:
  *I remember that summer well. I **was staying** with my aunt at the time, while my parents were away.*
- something that frequently happened, with *always* or *forever*, often to express amusement or irritation:
  *My dad **was always dressing up** in funny hats.*

We generally don't use the continuous form with verbs which describe states or emotions (e.g. *know*, *hate*, *understand*, *want*).

would and *used to*

Would + infinitive and *used to* + infinitive are used to talk about things which happened repeatedly in the past but don't happen now.

*When I was small, my mother **would** read to me in bed and she'd sing me a song to help me to sleep. While she sang, my father **used to** play guitar.*

- Use *used to*, not *would*, to talk about past states which no longer exist:
  *There **used to** be a grocer's opposite the bus station.*

The present perfect tenses

The present perfect tense is used:

- to describe an action that happened at an unspecified time in the past up to now:
  *They**'ve recorded** a lot of albums.*
- to describe a past action when the emphasis is on the result in the present:
  *Someone**'s stolen** my phone!* (It's not here now.)
- typically with time adverbs that connect the past to the present, e.g. *just*, *already*, *lately*, etc.:
  ***Have** you **seen** any good films **lately**?*

  Note:
  In American English, the past simple may be used: ***Did** you **see** any good films **lately**?*
- with *for* or *since* to describe an activity or state that started in the past and is still continuing in the present:
  *She**'s lived** in Spain for nearly ten years.*

The present perfect simple and continuous are sometimes interchangeable, although we only use the simple form with state verbs. However, note the differences in the table below.

present perfect simple	present perfect continuous
• emphasises the result: *They've studied hard so they deserve to pass the exam.*	• emphasises the action: *They've been studying so hard. They must be exhausted.*
• often focuses on an activity being complete: *I've done all the homework, so I'm going to see my friends.*	• often emphasises that the action is incomplete: *I've been doing homework all night but still haven't finished.*
• may give the idea that something is permanent: *He's been a police officer all his life.*	• may give the idea that something is temporary: *We have both been doing part-time jobs over the holiday period, but we go back to university next week.*
• is used for repeated actions if we want to say how many times an action has been repeated: *I've listened to that new album every day this week.*	• is used for repeated actions without a specific duration: *I've been listening to that album every day.*

The past perfect tenses

The past perfect simple tense is used:

- to indicate that we are talking about an action which took place, or a state which existed, before another activity or situation in the past, which is described in the past simple: *When Maria got home, they* ***had eaten*** *dinner.*
- typically with time expressions like *when*, *as soon as*, *after*, *before*, *it was the first time*, etc.: *He went home* ***as soon as*** *he****'d finished*** *his work.*

The past perfect continuous tense is used:

- to focus on the length of time: *My eyes were really tired because* ***I'd been reading*** *for two or three hours in bad light.*
- to say how long something happened up to a point in the past: *It was two months before any of the teachers noticed that Mike* ***hadn't been coming*** *to school.*

PRACTICE

1 Choose the correct past tense forms in *italics*.

1 Larissa can't play tennis this weekend because she *has injured / had injured* her wrist. She *fell over / was falling over* while she *ran / was running* for a train yesterday.

2 Could you get me a bandage, please? *I'd cut / I've cut* my finger.

3 While I *had / was having* lunch, my phone *rang / was ringing* six or seven times.

4 It wasn't the first time Jess *had broken / has broken* the law. When she *was / was being* a child, she *would often steal / was often stealing* sweets in shops.

5 What time *did you get / have you got* home last night?

6 Ben *had been playing / has been playing* computer games all morning. He must be hungry by now.

2 Choose the correct past tense forms to complete the conversation.

Anna: You look pretty rough. [1]*Did you have / Have you had* any breakfast yet?

Sofia: No – I'm not hungry.

Anna: What's the matter? Are you OK?

Sofia: No, I feel terrible. [2]*I didn't sleep / I haven't slept* a wink last night.

Anna: What's the problem?

Sofia: I should be getting my exam results any day now. It's Thursday already. [3]*I looked / I've looked* online every morning this week. I must get them soon.

Anna: Calm down! You'll just have to be patient.

Sofia: But it's nearly three months since [4]*I took / I've taken* the exams. [5]*I never had / I've never had* to wait as long as this before. It's absolute torture.

Anna: I'm sure you'll be OK. [6]*You revised / You've been revising* for months.

Sofia: I know, but geography and music aren't my strongest subjects. [7]*I'd failed / I've failed* every geography exam [8]*I ever took / I've ever taken.*

Anna: What was that noise?

Sofia: An email arriving. It could be the message [9]*I've waited / I've been waiting* for. Can you check it for me, Anna?

Anna: Sure! Brilliant! [10]*You'd passed! / You've passed!* Congratulations!

Sofia: That's amazing – [11]*I really thought / I've really thought* that [12]*I've failed / I'd failed.*

3 Complete the gaps with verbs in the present or past perfect simple. Where a continuous version fits, use it instead of the simple form.

1 She .... (copy) her friend's work for over a year, before one of her teachers found out.

2 The tsunami completely destroyed the bungalow where they .... (stay) just two days before.

3 It was only after she had arrived that she realised she .... (forget) to bring her phone charger.

4 You are looking very sweaty. .... (you exercise) this morning?

5 I .... (repair) the gears on my mountain bike, so I can't come with you until I've had a shower.

6 They .... (drive) for most of the morning, when they decided to stop off and have a picnic lunch.

7 They .... (go) backpacking to India twice this year. Each visit was a disaster because of the foul weather.

2

EXPRESSING PURPOSE, REASON AND RESULT

Expresses	Phrase(s)	Followed by	Position	Example(s)
purpose	*so (that)*	a clause	between clauses	*He always dresses smartly* ***so (that)*** *people will notice him.*
	for the purpose of / with the intention of	verb + *-ing*	after the main clause	*Teresa got up early* ***with the intention of studying*** *before going in to university.*
	so as to / in order to	infinitive		*Carla came home early* ***so as not to have*** *an argument with her parents.*
	to	infinitive		*Dieter goes to the gym every day* ***to keep*** *fit.*
reason	*because/since/as*	a clause	between clauses or at the beginning of the sentence (more emphatic)	*We'd better postpone the meeting* ***because/since/as*** *Eva has been delayed.* ***Because/As/Since*** *he was feeling ill, he spent the day in bed.*
	in case		after the main clause	*Take your mobile with you* ***in case*** *you need to call me.*
	otherwise			*Candice always writes things down,* ***otherwise*** (= because if she doesn't) *she forgets them.*
	because of / due to / owing to	noun or verb + *-ing*	at the beginning of the sentence or after the main clause	*All flights have been cancelled* ***because of / due to / owing to*** *the bad weather.*
	For this/that reason	a sentence	at the beginning of a sentence and referring to the previous one	*Someone called me unexpectedly.* ***For this reason****, I was late for the meeting.*
result	*so / with the result that / hence / thus* (*Hence* and *thus* are likely to be used in formal contexts.)	a clause	between clauses	*The bridge was damaged,* ***so*** *we couldn't get across the river.* *Children are no longer learning their tribal language,* ***with the result that*** *fewer and fewer people speak it.*
	Consequently / Therefore / As a consequence / As a result	a sentence	at the beginning of a sentence or clause, referring to the previous sentence or clause. *As a consequence* and *as a result* can also be used at the end of the sentence.	*Ranjit injured himself in training yesterday.* ***As a consequence****, he won't be taking part in the match today.* *Keiko didn't write a very good letter of application. She was rejected* ***as a result****.*
	Conditionals (see page 179) *If children start learning foreign languages when they're young, they learn them effortlessly.* (*If* clause = possible action, *they learn them effortlessly* = the result)			

PRACTICE

1 Choose the correct option to complete the sentences. If both are possible, put a tick (✓).

1 Many people are prepared to buy expensive branded goods *because / so* they think they enhance their social status amongst their peers.

2 *Since / So that* I don't want to increase my carbon footprint, I've decided to become a vegetarian.

3 *Because of / Because* the popularity of gaming, many people are spending a disproportionate amount of time on their tablets and iPhones.

4 I'm going to start a programmed fitness course *due to / so that* I can reduce fat and build up muscle.

5 *Due to / As a consequence* the speed of technological change, people need to retrain more frequently throughout their careers than they used to.

6 They are going to enrol in an online English course *in order to / thus* prepare themselves for a recognised certificate of proficiency.

7 I am leaving at 8am, *so / so that* if you want a lift to work, you need to get to my house by five to eight.

8 Liverpool won the Champions League Final two years in a row, *thus* / *therefore* becoming the only English team to defend their European title.

9 You'll need to return my suitcase *as* / *due to* I am going on holiday next week and don't have another I can take.

10 I was caught driving over the speed limit yesterday by the police and *as a result* / *as a consequence* was given an on-the-spot fine.

2 Correct the following sentences.

1 I'm not going to save all my money just that I can buy an overpriced flat.

2 I left the house this morning with the intention of buy a coffee.

3 Very few people turned up to the meeting owing the 7am start time

4 David didn't speak very good English. As a consequently, he couldn't really communicate with his partner's parents.

5 I missed my train. This reason, I'm late for work.

6 Fewer people are learning the language, with the result ancient traditions are slowly being lost.

7 I left work early so not to get stuck in traffic.

8 Everyone is moving away because the closure of the coal mines.

3 Complete the sentences using the words in the box.

as	consequently	due	in	of	order	result	with

1 Many people are breaking with tradition. .... a result we're seeing more and more modern ceremonies.

2 I came to this country .... the full intention of learning the language, but it's just so difficult.

3 Because .... the bad weather, we'll have to postpone tonight's concert until next week.

4 Download this dictionary app .... case you need to know what a word means while you're out.

5 Our planned speaker is unable to join us tonight .... to the rail strike.

6 The passenger started to become loud and unruly. .... she was removed from the plane.

7 My mother stopped speaking to her family many years ago with the .... that we have now lost touch with our aunts and uncles.

8 We're trying to save some money at the moment in .... to have enough to start a family.

3

NO, NONE, NOT

no

- *No* means *not any* or *not even one* and can be used with countable or uncountable nouns:
  *I have **no idea** what you're talking about.*
  *There were **no cars** on the road at that time of night.*
  *There's **no salt** on the table.*
- It can also be used with comparative adjectives or adverbs and with the word *different*:
  *The traffic is **no worse** today than it was yesterday.*
  *I had to work late every evening last week, and so far this week has been **no different**.*

none

- *None* is a pronoun which means *not one* or *not any*. It is usually followed by *of* + a plural or uncountable noun or a pronoun:
  ***None of my friends** know/knows it's my birthday today.*
  ***None of the milk** in the fridge is fresh.*
- It can also be used on its own:
  'How much coffee do we have?' 'None (at all). We finished it yesterday.'
  *We need to buy some more eggs – there are **none** left.*
- In formal written English *none* is considered to be a singular word and is followed by a singular verb:
  *None of my colleagues **speaks** Japanese.*
  However, in everyday speech a plural verb is more commonly used:
  *None of this morning's flights **have been delayed**.*

not

- *Not* is mainly used to make verbs negative and is often contracted to *n't*:
  *You **have not** / **haven't answered** my question.*
  *That **isn't** / That**'s not** the correct answer.*
  *She told me **not to phone** her after ten o'clock at night.*
  *He was silent, **not knowing** what to say.*
- It can also make other words or phrases negative:
  *I ordered tea, **not coffee**.*
  ***Not many** people voted in yesterday's election.*
  ***Not everyone** can win the lottery.*
  ***Not all** Canadians speak French.*
  ***Not surprisingly**, he failed his driving test.*
  *'Can you come out?' 'No, **I'm afraid not**.'*

Note:
No, *none* and *not* are not used with negative verbs or adverbs with a negative meaning such as *hardly*:

~~*There's **hardly no** food left.*~~ → *There's **hardly any** food left.*

PRACTICE

1 Correct the sentences.

1. No one of my teammates could offer me a lift to the next game as they all lived on the other side of town.
2. I can find anybody to take this chest of drawers away to be recycled.
3. We need to go to the supermarket and buy some milk. There is not in the fridge.
4. I went to the bookshop on Friday, but I couldn't find no books that I wanted to buy.
5. My family were no very pleased when I arrived home without the shopping.
6. The restaurant was awful. We sat down at our table but there were none waiters available to take our order.
7. Many classmates of mine were no pleased to have to do homework on a Friday night.
8. The train company had hardly no information available about the journey.
9. As far as I'm aware, there's none difference between the two paintings. They're identical.
10. Even though I went to the party, none my so-called friends turned up and I had a terrible time.

THE PASSIVE

The goods	**are** **were** **are being** **were being** **are going to be** **have been** **had been** **will be** **can be** **have to be** **might have been** **must have been**	**imported**	from Italy.

- The passive is formed with the verb *be* + past participle.
- Intransitive verbs (verbs with no object, e.g. *appear*, *come*, *go*) cannot be used in the passive form.
- There is no passive form for the present or past perfect continuous tense or the future continuous tenses. (We do not say ~~*The goods have/had been being imported*~~ or ~~*will be being imported*~~.)

We use the passive to focus attention on the person or thing that is affected by the action of the verb:

- when the identity of the person/thing doing the action (= the agent) is unknown or unimportant:
  My office ***was broken into*** *last night.*
  Tonight's football match ***has been cancelled****.*
- when it is obvious who/what the agent is:
  He ***was arrested*** *and* ***charged*** *with theft.* (Only the police can arrest and charge people.)

If we want to mention the agent in a passive sentence, we use the preposition *by*:
The goods are imported ***by*** *a chain of supermarkets.*

The passive is often used when writing in an official or formal style, for example, scientific language:
The outbreak of the disease has been controlled by imposing a quarantine on the area.

The passive is also used to describe technical or scientific processes:
Water ***was added*** *and the mixture* ***was heated*** *to 85°C.*

With verbs like *know*, *believe*, *think*, *consider*, *expect*, *report* we can use the passive + infinitive. We can also use an impersonal construction with *It* + passive + *that* + clause:
Jeff Bezos ***is known to be*** *one of the world's richest people.*
Twenty people ***are reported to have been*** *injured in the fire.*
It is believed that *the accident was caused by a gas leak.*
It has been estimated that *average house prices will rise by 5% this year.*

Structures like these are often used:

- to express an opinion that is widely accepted as true
- when you can't or don't want to identify a source of information.

We also use the passive to create a 'flow' in text:

- to put 'known information' at the beginning of a sentence:
  The police have started to take a tougher line with petty criminals. Many of them ***are*** *now* ***being given*** *prison sentences.*
- to avoid the awkwardness of a very long subject:
  The player who has won 'footballer of the year' most times addressed the club management. → *The club management* ***was addressed*** *by the player who has won 'footballer of the year' most times.*

In informal English we can sometimes use *get* instead of *be* to form the passive, especially when we want to say that something bad happened to someone or something:
Some of our more fragile ornaments ***got smashed*** *when our neighbour came round for tea with her hyperactive toddler.*

PRACTICE

1 **Rewrite these sentences using appropriate passive verbs. Only one passive sentence needs to include the agent.**

1 They'll hold interviews for the other top jobs next week.
2 You have to see this form to believe it. The applicant has written it in pencil.
3 They have appointed no one to replace Ms Kirkby since they promoted her last year.
4 They asked applicants to send in hand-written letters to accompany their CVs.
5 You must send your application as a PDF.
6 The company will require successful applicants to start work on Monday.
7 Jeffrey Bowman will announce the name of the new CEO at the next board meeting.
8 You couldn't expect someone with experience to work for that salary.

2 **Rewrite this newspaper story about a damaged building, making the active verbs passive.**

> Illegal squatters have finally abandoned a city centre mansion worth £5 million after a week of destruction. They had covered three of the bedroom walls with graffiti and had ripped cupboards apart. They had chopped up most of the furniture and used it as firewood. They had torn up the carpets and smashed the mirrors and windows. Builders have estimated the damage at more than £1 million.

3 **Rewrite these short texts about 'memory', replacing the <u>underlined</u> active verbs with passive verbs. You do not always need to include the agent in your answer.**

1 We <u>use</u> the term 'amnesia' to refer to a partial or complete loss of memory. It is usually a temporary condition which only affects a certain part of a person's experience. Specific medical conditions <u>can cause</u> amnesia.

2 We all know that our real experiences <u>form</u> our memory. But could someone <u>put</u> a false memory into our heads? Could they <u>persuade</u> us that we had experienced something that never actually took place?

3 We <u>use</u> our semantic memory to store our knowledge of the world. Everyone has this knowledge base, and normally we <u>can access</u> it quickly and easily.

4 We <u>can think</u> of our working memory as the ability to remember and use a limited amount of information. However, this information is erratic. If someone <u>distracts</u> you, you <u>can lose</u> the information and you <u>have to start</u> the task again.

4 EXPRESSING POSSIBILITY, PROBABILITY AND CERTAINTY

Possibility: modal verbs *may, might, could*

- Use *may* (*not*), *might* (*not*) or *could* (but not *could not*) to say it's possible that something is true, happens or will happen, but we don't know:
  *The photocopier isn't working – there **may** be some paper stuck inside.* (not ~~*there can be some paper*~~)

  Note: *can* is used to say that something is a general possibility but not with reference to any particular occasion or event:
  *It **can** rain heavily in this region in autumn.*
  But *It **might** rain this evening.*
  *Children **can** be very irritating.*
  But *You **may** find my children annoying when they make a lot of noise.*
- Use *may, might, could* + *well/easily* to say something is a strong possibility:
  *The weather **may well** improve by the weekend.*
  *I'd better write it down, otherwise I **could easily** forget.*
- Use *may, might, could* + *possibly/conceivably* or *just might* to say something is a remote possibility:
  *My boss **could conceivably** change her mind and decide to give me a pay increase.*
  *I **just might** have time to finish that report this week.*

Other words and phrases

- *It's* (*just/quite/very/entirely*) *possible that* + clause:
  *It's **just possible that** we'll finish the project by March.*
- *There's* (*a/some / a slight / every / a good/strong/real*) *possibility/chance that* + *clause* or *of* + *-ing* verb:
  *There's **every possibility that** the business will succeed.*
  *There's **some chance that** the weather will improve tomorrow.*
  *Is there **any chance of seeing** you this weekend?*

Possibility: modal verbs *should, shouldn't*

- Use *should* and *shouldn't* to say that you expect something is or will be true:
  *You're extremely well qualified – you **should** have no difficulty landing the job.*

Other words and phrases

- *be* (*quite/very/highly*) *likely/unlikely* + infinitive or *It's* (*quite/very/highly*) *likely/unlikely that* + clause:
  *He**'s unlikely to make** the same mistake again.*
  *It**'s quite likely that** they'll be on the 8:30 train.*
- *There's little / some / every / a strong likelihood of* + *-ing* verb or *that* + clause:
  *I'd say **there's a strong likelihood of** him **getting** a first class degree.*
  ***There's little likelihood that** we'll manage to meet our deadline.*

Certainty: modal verbs *must*, *can't*, *couldn't*

- Use *must* (affirmative) and *can't/couldn't* (negative) to express things you feel certain about because you have evidence:
  With so many customers, they ***must*** *be making a lot of money.*
  He didn't know what we were talking about, so he ***can't/ couldn't*** *have read our letter.*

  Note: *mustn't* is not used to express certainty (see Expressing ability, possibility and obligation on page 177).

Other words and phrases

- *be bound* + *to* infinitive:
  This machine is badly designed. It's ***bound to break down*** *before long.*

Notes on modal verbs

- To talk about actions in progress now or arranged for the future, use the continuous form, i.e. modal verb + *be* + *-ing*:
  You all ***must be wondering*** *why I have called this meeting.*
- To talk about actions in the past, use modal + *have* + past participle:
  Martin is abroad at the moment, so you ***can't/couldn't have seen*** *him yesterday.*
- To talk about actions which took place over a period of time in the past, use the past continuous form, i.e. modal + *have been* + *-ing*:
  Ulrike wasn't in when I called – she ***may have been doing*** *the shopping, I suppose.*

PRACTICE

1 Choose the correct word to complete the sentence.

1. With so few customers here, you *can't / mustn't* be making much money.
2. The heavy rain this region experiences *could / can* regularly lead to the river bursting its bank.
3. She just *must / might* have time to get to the shops before they close.
4. Your qualifications are excellent and you're really interested in the topic so you *should / could* have no difficulty on this course.
5. I tried to call him but it went straight to answerphone. He *can't / may* have been talking to someone else at that time.
6. No, sir. I've never been to Budapest. You *must / could* have made a mistake.
7. There's *just / every* possibility that this year will see economic conditions worsen.
8. I better make a note of that. Otherwise I *can / could* easily forget it.
9. There's *real / every* possibility that the team can get a good result in Milan this evening.
10. Regarding your car. I need to look at it a bit more but it *might not / could not* be possible to repair it.

2 Complete the second sentence so that it has a similar meaning to the first sentence using the word given. You must use between three and six words including the word given.

1. I can't see the business being a success.
   CHANCE
   There's .... business will fail.
2. David said that he won't give me a promotion, but I think he might.
   CONCEIVABLY
   David could .... a promotion.
3. The car is going to break down on this journey. I'm certain of it.
   BOUND
   The car .... during this drive.
4. I can't believe that the building is still standing.
   FALLEN
   That building .... by now.
5. Do you think it might rain later tonight?
   CHANCE
   Is there .... raining later tonight?
6. We're going to win tonight. I'm certain of it.
   HIGHLY
   It's .... we will lose tonight's match.

5 VERBS FOLLOWED BY *TO* + INFINITIVE OR THE *-ING* FORM

Verbs followed by the infinitive

The infinitive without *to* is used after:

- modal verbs:
  We ***must hurry*** *or we'll be late.*
- *let* (*sb*) *do* (*sth*):
  They ***let*** *the animals* ***escape*** *into the wild.*

The *to* infinitive is used after:

- some verbs which are modal in meaning:
  I ***have to go*** *to work tomorrow.*
  You ***ought to get*** *more sleep.*
  You ***need to think*** *again. You* ***don't need to worry.***

  Note: The verb *need* has an alternative negative form, *needn't*, which is followed by the infinitive without *to*:
  You ***needn't worry.***
- certain verbs, e.g. *afford, agree, arrange, appear, attempt, choose, decide, expect, hope, intend, learn, manage, offer, pretend, promise, refuse, seem*:
  We can't ***afford to go*** *on holiday this year.*

- certain verbs + object, e.g. *advise, allow, ask, convince, enable, encourage, forbid, force, get, instruct, invite, order, persuade, remind, require, teach, tell, train, want, warn, wish*:
  You can't ***force people to believe*** *something.*
  My father ***taught me to swim****.*

  Note: After the verb *help*, the *to* can be omitted before the infinitive:
  She helped me (to) revise for my exam.

Verbs followed by the *-ing* form

The *-ing* form of the verb is used after:

- some verbs which express likes and dislikes, e.g. *dislike, enjoy, loathe, (don't) mind, (can't) stand*:
  She ***can't stand getting*** *stuck in a traffic jam.*

  But note the following exceptions:
  – *hate/like/love/prefer* are usually followed by the *-ing* form but are sometimes followed by the *to* infinitive (see below).
  – *would + hate/like/love/prefer* is always followed by the *to* infinitive:

  I'd ***hate to get up*** *early every morning.*
- certain verbs, e.g. *admit, appreciate, avoid, can't help, consider, delay, deny, finish, give up, imagine, involve, keep, miss, postpone, prevent, put off, recommend, report, resent, resist, risk, suggest*:
  The prime minister has just ***finished speaking****.*

Verbs followed by *to* infinitive or *-ing*

A small number of verbs can be followed either by the infinitive or by the *-ing* form.

With no difference in meaning

begin, can't bear, cease, commence, continue, hate, intend, like, love, propose, start:
I've just ***started to learn*** */* ***learning*** *to ski.*
He had ***intended to leave*** */* ***leaving*** *before midnight.*

Note: With the verbs *like, love, hate* there can be this slight difference in meaning:
I like ***to clean*** *my car every week.* (The focus is on the result of the activity.)
I like ***cleaning*** *my car every week.* (The focus is on the activity itself, i.e. I enjoy cleaning it.)

With different meanings

- verbs expressing perception
  I ***saw*** *the plane* ***land****.* (= I saw the whole action.)
  I ***saw*** *the plane* ***landing****.* (= I saw part of the action.)
- *forget*
  I ***forgot to phone*** *my brother.* (= I didn't phone him.)
  I'll never ***forget phoning*** *my sister that night.* (= I phoned her and I recall it well.)
- *remember*
  Tom ***remembered to close*** *the windows before he left.* (= He did something he had to do; he didn't forget.)
  Tom ***remembered closing*** *the windows before he left.* (= He recalled doing it.)
- *go on*
  She won her first race when she was seven and ***went on to break*** *the world record.* (= Breaking the world record was something she did later.)
  He ***went on walking*** *even though he was exhausted.* (= He didn't stop walking.)
- *mean*
  I'm sorry, I didn't ***mean to be*** *rude.* (= intend)
  If we want to catch the early train, it'll ***mean getting*** *up at 5:00.* (= involve)
- *regret*
  I ***regret to inform*** *you that you have not passed the test.* (= I'm sorry about something unwelcome I'm about to say.)
  He now ***regrets taking*** *the day off work.* (= He wishes he hadn't taken the day off work.)
- *stop*
  We'd better ***stop to look*** *at the map.* (= stop what we are doing in order to do something else)
  There's nothing you can do about it, so ***stop worrying****.* (= finish worrying)
- *try*
  I've been ***trying to repair*** *my computer all morning.* (= attempt something difficult)
  Have you ***tried kicking*** *it?* (= do something which might solve a problem)

Other uses of *to* + infinitive and *-ing*

After adjectives

- Some adjectives, when used without a preposition can be followed by the *to* infinitive:
  afraid, anxious, certain, difficult, happy, impossible, pleased, ready, right, shocked, stupid, surprised, welcome
  Everyone was really ***surprised to see*** *me at the party.*
  I'm ***pleased to tell*** *you that you've passed your driving test.*

After prepositions

- When a verb follows a preposition (after, before, by, etc.) it is always in the *-ing* form.
  Instead of catching *the bus, I walked home.*
  We found our way there ***without looking*** *at a map.*
- This applies to verbs following adjective + preposition and verb + preposition
  Are you ***interested in joining*** *our squash club?*
  I'm quite ***capable of finding*** *my own way home.*

  Note: We use the *-ing* form after *to* when *to* is a preposition:
  I look forward ***to hearing*** *from you soon.*

  → **See also page 188:** Dependent prepositions

As nouns

- *-ing* forms can also be used like nouns, as the subject or object of a sentence or as the complement of the verb *be*.
  Flying *is much less expensive than it used to be.*
  My favourite method of relaxation ***is reading*** *a good novel.*

PRACTICE

1 Choose the correct form of the verb: – infinitive or *-ing* form.

I'd always refused [1]*to buy / buying* lottery tickets because I thought they were a waste of money. But last week, for the first time in my life, I decided [2]*to get / getting* just one. It was just a bit of fun and I didn't really expect [3]*to win / winning*, but despite this I couldn't help [4]*to think / thinking* about how I'd spend the money if I actually won. My brother had won £1000 the year before, and I had really enjoyed [5]*to see / seeing* the expression on his face when he realised. All week I looked forward to [6]*watch / watching* the TV programme when the winning numbers were announced, but that evening I was so busy that I forgot [7]*to put / putting* the TV on. I checked my numbers on the website the next day – and of course I hadn't won. At that moment I promised myself never [8]*to buy / buying* another lottery ticket. I couldn't risk [9]*to be / being* so disappointed again.

2 Correct any mistakes in the sentences. Two are correct.

1. I suggest to take the overnight train to Vienna.
2. Part of my job is helping maintaining the machinery in good working order.
3. I would strongly recommend going by plane.
4. If I were you, I'd consider to spend less time at work.
5. I found it impossible sleeping because of the noise.
6. I nodded and smiled and pretended understanding what she was saying.
7. I remember to see that show in New York. It was incredible.
8. I didn't mean to break the TV. It was an accident.

6 AVOIDING REPETITION

Using pronouns

- Instead of repeating a noun or noun phrase, use a pronoun:
  ***Derek Foster** worked in advertising after the war. **He** became a professional painter in the early '60s.*
- Use *they/them/their* to refer to plural nouns and to a person in the singular when you cannot state whether the person is male or female:
  *If you ask **an artist** how **they** started painting, **they**'ll often say that one of **their** parents taught **them**.*
- Use *himself, herself, themselves*, etc. when the object is the same as the subject:
  ***He** poured **himself** a glass of water.*
  (Compare: *He poured **him** a glass of water,* where *him* refers to a different person.)
- *It, this, that, these, those* may refer to a noun / noun phrase, or to the whole of the previous clause or sentence:
  ***Artists now have a vast range of materials at their disposal. This** means that they can be much more versatile than in the past.*

  That is often used when giving reasons:
  ***The artist is my cousin** and **that's** why I'm here.*

one/ones, another, the other(s), both, either, neither, all, none

- Use *one* to refer to a singular countable noun in a group, and *ones* to refer to plural countable nouns in a group.
  *I've made some **sandwiches** – would you like **one**?*
  *There are some excellent exhibitions on. I strongly recommend **the one** at the National Gallery.*
  ***Our neighbours** are generally nice, but the **ones** in flat 4 aren't very sociable.*
- Use *a(n)/the … one* or *(the) … ones* with an adjective:
  *I've bought a lot of new **shirts** recently, but for gardening I prefer to wear **an old one**.*
  *I enjoy **romantic films**, especially **sad ones**.*
- Use *another* to refer to a second/third (etc.) singular countable noun in a group:
  ***One picture** showed a girl combing her hair. **Another** was of the same girl dancing.*
- Use *the other* when referring to the second of two things/people already mentioned, and *the others* when referring to the rest of a number of things/people:
  *Pablo has **two houses**. One is in São Paulo and **the other** is in Singapore.*
  ***Most of the actors** went to a party. **The others** went home.*
- Use *both, either* and *neither* to refer to two things/people:
  *He's written **two novels** and **both** have won prizes.*
  ***Neither** is autobiographical.*
- Use *all* and *none* to refer to more than two things/people:
  *He's written **twenty novels** and I've read **all of them**.*
  *Mariella invited **her friends** but **none of them** came.*

who, which, whose

See pages 171–172: Relative clauses.

Using auxiliary and modal verbs

- Instead of repeating a whole verb or verb phrase, we can often use an auxiliary or modal verb:
  *Not many people **have read 'The Dungeon'** and I'm one of the few that **have**.*
  *A year ago I **couldn't drive a car**, but now I **can**.*
- Use a form of *do* to replace a verb in the present or past simple:
  *I really **enjoy good comedy films**, but then I think everyone **does**.*
  *Most people **liked the film**, but I **didn't**.*

Using *so*

- *So* refers back to something mentioned previously:
  I experienced difficulty keeping focused on all the rules and conventions when I first joined the debating club, and ***so*** *did my friends.* (= my friends also experienced difficulty)
- With verbs like *think*, *suppose*, *believe*, *hope*, etc., use *so* to avoid repeating a clause or sentence:
  'Do you think Real Madrid will win the championship?'
  'I guess ***so****.'* (= I guess they will win the championship.)
- Use *do so* to avoid repeating a verb or verb phrase:
  I told my students to hand in the essay on Monday and all of them ***did so****.* (= handed in the essay on Monday)

Omitting words

- With a verb or adjective that is followed by the *to* infinitive, it is sometimes possible to use *to* on its own, instead of repeating a whole phrase.
  Kim suggested ***going to the ballet****, but I didn't want* ***to****.*
  Give me a call later *if you're able* ***to****.*
  I'd like to ***solve your problems*** *but I just don't know if I'd be allowed* ***to****.*

PRACTICE

1 Correct the mistake in each of these sentences.

1 There are only a few slices of cake left. Take it while you've got the chance.

2 Because of the snow, all the trains were cancelled. I would have been really angry but I realised that when things like these happen, it's better to just relax.

3 She exhibited some wonderful photos, the best of these was taken in the townships of South Africa.

4 The best candidates are these that show that they have done their homework prior to interview.

5 The fans were chanting for Simons, the man in who ability the crowd always put their faith.

6 She is a baker who knows how to produce some excellent cakes. And those are what matters.

7 Having broken mine while climbing a mountain, I really needed a new camera, so I was delighted when my partner gave me it as a present.

2 Replace the <u>underlined</u> parts of these sentences. You may have to change the word order.

1 It was clearly a dangerous journey, and everyone had told her <u>it would be a dangerous journey</u>.

2 We used to go to the cinema every weekend, but we haven't <u>been to the cinema</u> recently.

3 Most of the class are walking to college now. <u>You should walk to college</u>.

4 **A:** Is Sophie meeting us there?
B: I think <u>Sophie is meeting us there</u>.

5 Hundreds of people want to travel to Mars but only a small number <u>of these people</u> will be accepted.

6 My children won't eat green apples. Do you have any red <u>apples</u>?

7 **A:** We only have vanilla or chocolate ice-cream left.
B: That's fine. <u>Vanilla or chocolate ice-cream</u> will be OK.

7 LINKING IDEAS: RELATIVE AND PARTICIPLE CLAUSES; APPOSITION

Relative clauses

She's the woman	**who** **that**	bought our car.
	whose	son bought our car.
	from whom	we bought our car.
They've got a car	**which** **that**	runs on electricity.
This is the town	**where**	I grew up.
Sunday is a day	**when**	many people relax.
There's no reason	**why**	you should be worried.

- To introduce a relative clause, use *who*, *that*, *whose* and *whom* to refer to people.
  Note: *whom* is formal and is used mainly with prepositions:
  The person ***to whom*** *this letter is addressed lives in Athens.*
- Use *that* and *which* to refer to things.
- Use *where*, meaning 'at which', 'in which' or 'to which', to refer to places:
  The village ***where*** (= in which) *they live is in the middle of nowhere.*
  This is a restaurant ***where*** (= to which) *we often go.*
- Use *when* to refer to times:
  I'm not sure of the date ***when*** *they're leaving.*
- Use *why* to refer to reasons:
  The reason ***why*** *I'm late is that my flight was cancelled.*
- A relative clause can be at the end of a sentence or it can be embedded in another clause:
  Madrid is the city ***where I grew up****.*
  The city ***where I grew up*** *is Madrid.*
  Madrid, ***where I grew up****, is the capital of Spain.*
- *Who*, *that* and *which* can be the subject or the object of the verb in the relative clause:
  Subject: *The people* ***who know*** *me best are my friends.*
  Object: *The people* ***who I know*** *best are my friends.* (The subject is *I*.)

- *Where*, *when* and *why* are always the object of the verb:
  We're going back to the hotel ***where we stayed*** *last summer.*
  (The subject is *we*.)

Defining relative clauses

- A defining relative clause defines the noun which immediately precedes it, and is therefore essential to the meaning of the sentence:
  The couple ***who brought me up*** *were not my real parents.*
  (The relative clause tells us which couple.)
- *Who*, *that* and *which* can be left out when they are the object of a defining relative clause:
  The people (who) I know best are my close friends.
  The DVD (that) you gave me for my birthday is fantastic.
- *When* and *why* can also be left out:
  2009 was the year (when) she left university.
  That's the reason (why) I'm so disappointed.

Non-defining relative clauses

- Non-defining relative clauses give additional information, but are not essential to the meaning of the sentence:
  The hotel, ***which has a hundred bedrooms****, is on the outskirts of the city.*
- Another type of non-defining clause is a comment clause, using *which* to introduce a comment on a previous clause:
  It had been raining nonstop for 24 hours, ***which is why I didn't go out****.*
  We were stuck in the traffic jam for ages, ***which I found really frustrating****.*
- The pronoun *that* cannot be used to introduce a non-defining relative clause.
- In writing, a non-defining relative clause is separated from the main clause by commas:
  My car, which is seven years old, has already done 200,000 kilometres.

Participle clauses

Linking actions

With a present participle:
Concentrating *on my work, I didn't realise how late it was.*

With a perfect participle:
Having finished *his speech, he left the room.*

With a past participle:
Seen *from a distance, the Pyramids look quite small.*

- Use a present participle clause to describe something happening at the same time as the main action or immediately after it:
  Opening the door*, I saw a parcel on the doorstep.*
- Present participle clauses can also be used with some conjunctions and prepositions:
  After watching that film*, I was too scared to go to bed.*
  In this case, the participle clause can follow the main clause:
  She became interested in art ***while travelling in Italy****.*
  You can take the train ***instead of catching the bus****.*
- Use a perfect participle clause to describe something that happened before the main action. It may provide a reason for that action:
  Having left our map at home*, we got lost.* (= Because we had left our map at home …)
- Use a past participle clause when the meaning is passive:
  Eaten in small quantities*, chocolate is good for you.*
  Built in 1889*, the Eiffel Tower is now a symbol of Paris.*
- Note that in all these cases the subject of the participle clause is the same as the subject of the main clause.

Used instead of relative clauses

Participle clauses can also be used instead of relative clauses. They are sometimes called reduced relative clauses.

- Use the present participle when the meaning is active:
  There are three pictures ***hanging on the wall****.* (= that/which are hanging …)
  I noticed a man ***wearing a suit*** *and* ***carrying a large box****.*
  (= who was wearing …, who was carrying …)
- Use the past participle when the meaning is passive:
  Anyone ***caught shoplifting*** *will be prosecuted.* (= who is caught …)
  I've brought you a jar of plum jam, ***made by my mother****.*
  (= which was made …)

Linking ideas: apposition

A common, economical way of linking two or more facts about the same person, thing or place is to put them next to each other in a sentence.

As with relative clauses, the second noun / noun phrase can be defining or non-defining.

- If it tells us who or what, no commas are used:
  Her friend Klaus *is a computer engineer.*
- If it provides additional descriptive information, commas are used:
  I'm going to see ***Bev Jackson, my maths tutor,*** *this afternoon.*

PRACTICE

1 Choose the correct participles in these sentences.

1 We came out of the theatre *wondered* / *wondering* what the play had been about.

2 We'd seen a play *based* / *having based* on a contemporary novel.

3 *Reading* / *Having read* the novel, I'm now interested to see how they would make it into a play.

4 It was the first play *written* / *having been written* by this young director.

5 I'd read a review of the play in a magazine *specialising* / *specialised* in modern drama.

2 **Combine the sentences into a single sentence using relative or participle clauses.**

1 We walked along the path by the canal. We watched children. They were opening and closing the lock gates to allow boats to pass through.

2 The police officer referred to written notes and described how she had heard someone. This person was screaming at the top of their voice.

3 Before Jeff moved to Barcelona, he lived near Houston in Texas. He worked in a school there. He taught English to students from other countries.

4 The Eiffel Tower was built in 1889. It has dominated the Paris skyline for over a century. During this period it has been repainted 19 times.

5 Bob Marley was a Jamaican singer. He recorded the best-selling reggae album of all time. His full name was Robert Nesta Marley.

3 **Finish the sentence beginnings A–D with two endings from the box. Add a relative pronoun where necessary.**

has the best weather	said he couldn't come to the meeting
I'd buy if I had enough money	most tourists come here
Mike recommended	Ariana's going on holiday with
we celebrated your birthday	
~~won an award for outstanding design~~	

A That's the house …

1 *That's the house that/which won an award for outstanding design.*

2 ……………

B What's the name of that hotel …?

3 ……………

4 ……………

C Which is the season … ?

5 ……………

6 ……………

D Is it Pete or Jayden …?

7 ……………

8 ……………

8

REPORTED SPEECH

Verb tense changes

When we report what someone said, the tense of the verb is often 'further back' in time:

'I'm feeling ill.' → *He said he **was feeling** ill.*
'You can borrow my phone.' → *She said I **could borrow** her phone.*
'The rain has stopped.' → *He said the rain **had stopped**.*
'We drove all night.' → *They said they **had driven** all night.*
'We'll try to help.' → *They said they **would try** to help.*

The past perfect tenses and the modal verbs *would*, *could* and *should* cannot move 'further back', so they remain unchanged:

*'I'**d** never spoken to her before.'* → *He said he'**d** never **spoken** to her before.*
*'I **wouldn't go** skiing again.'* → *She said she **wouldn't go** skiing again.*

The tense of the reported speech does not need to change:

- if we want to make it clear that what the speaker said is still true now or remains relevant:
  *'I **love** black coffee.'* → *He said he **loves** black coffee.*
  *'Picasso **was born** in Spain.'* → *She told us that Picasso **was born** in Spain.*
- if the reporting verb is in the present:
  *'I'm **looking** forward to my holiday.'* → *She **says** she'**s looking** forward to her holiday.*

Pronoun, possessive adjective and adverb changes

- Pronouns and possessive adjectives often need to change in reported speech, especially when the reporter is different from the original speaker:
  *'I love **you**,' Dan said.* → *Dan said **he** loved **me**.*
  *'**You** didn't give **me your** address,' said Jane.* → *Jane said **we** hadn't given **her our** address.*
- Time and place adverbs change if the time or place is no longer the same as in the direct speech:
  *'I'll see you **tomorrow**.'* → *Jackie said she would see me **the next/following day**.*
  *'We've lived **here** for six years.'* → *They said they had lived **there** for six years.*
- The adverb does not change if the time/place remains the same:
  *'I came **here** yesterday.'* → (reported the same day) *He says he came **here** yesterday.*

- These are some of the time reference changes:

Direct speech	Reported speech
(ten minutes) ago	(ten minutes) before/earlier
last week/month/year	the previous week/month/year the week/month/year before
next week/month/ year	the following week/month/year the week/month/year after
now	at that time / immediately / then
this week	last/that week
today	that day / yesterday on Monday/Tuesday, etc.
tomorrow	the next/following day the day after
yesterday	the previous day the day before

Reporting questions

- When we report a question, we change it into the form of a statement. This means that we change the word order and do not use the auxiliary *do*, *does* or *did* in the present and past simple:
  'What are you doing?' → *He asked us* ***what we were doing***.
  'Where do you live?' → *She asked me* ***where I lived/live***.
- When we report *Yes/No* questions, we add *if* or *whether*:
  'Do you speak Italian?' → *He asked me* ***if/whether*** *I spoke/speak Italian.*

Reporting verbs

There are many verbs which we can use to convey someone's action when speaking. Most of them can be followed by more than one grammatical pattern.

verb + *to* infinitive

- agree: *They agreed* ***to broadcast*** *the programme.*
- offer: *He offered* ***to buy*** *me lunch.*
- promise: *The mayor has promised* ***to give*** *us an interview.*

verb + object + *to* infinitive

- advise: *The newspaper advises* ***people to be*** *careful about using social media.*
- ask: *She asked* ***the reporter to repeat*** *his question.*
- invite: *They've invited* ***us to attend*** *the show.*
- order/tell: *Mum ordered/told* ***the children to wait*** *outside.*
- persuade: *I persuaded* ***the magazine to print*** *my story.*
- remind: *Can you remind* ***me to update*** *my blog?*
- warn: *She warned* ***him not to be*** *late for the interview.*

verb + preposition + noun / verb + *-ing*

- complain about: *The actress has complained* ***about the paparazzi*** *outside her house.*
- apologise for: *The organisation has apologised* ***for publishing*** *misleading information on its website.*
- accuse (somebody) of: *The president accused the press* ***of distorting*** *the truth.*

verb + noun / verb + *-ing*

- deny: *The minister has denied* ***the accusation***.
- admit: *He admitted* ***inventing*** *some details in his report*
- recommend: *She recommended* ***doing*** *more research.*
- suggest: *The directors have suggested* ***paying*** *for online content with advertising.*

verb + clause

- These verbs can also be followed by (*that*) + clause:
  admit, agree, complain, deny, promise, recommend, suggest:
  She suggested ***that*** *they should interview local people.*
- These verbs must be followed by an object before (*that*) + clause:
  persuade, remind, tell, warn:
  We warned ***our audience*** *that they might find some of the photos distressing.*

→ **See also pages 168–169:** Verbs + *to* infinitive or *-ing*

PRACTICE

1 Choose the correct option.

1 James denied *to steal / stealing* the money.
2 Mandy insisted *to come / on coming* to every meeting.
3 Pierre's father agreed *to help / on helping* him with his assignment.
4 The doctor warned Alex *not to take / not taking* the pills without water.
5 Eva suggested *to have / having* the party at her place.
6 Can I persuade you *to give / on giving* me a hand?

2 Rewrite the reported speech in direct speech.

1 They said they were looking for someone with my qualifications.
2 The manager said I had the right experience for the job.
3 He said I wouldn't have to work at weekends.
4 He said they'd provide me with a company car.
5 They said employees were allowed to work from home occasionally.
6 He said I could start the following Monday.

3 **Change the direct speech to reported speech. Use *say* and change all time and place references.**

1 'I'll see you tomorrow morning.' (Rob)
2 'I didn't do anything wrong.' (Irina)
3 'We can meet at my office.' (Steve)
4 'I'd never expected to be here today.' (Ahmet)
5 'Megan and I were here yesterday. We waited for you until 7 o'clock.' (Polly)
6 'Pedro's looking forward to starting his new job next week.' (Sacha)
7 'You can come on holiday with us.' (Zoë)
8 'It's been raining here all night.' (Luisa)

TRANSITIVE AND INTRANSITIVE VERBS

English verbs are classified as transitive or intransitive.

Dictionaries identify them with the letters *T* and *I*.

- A transitive verb must be followed by an object:
  She ***found the information*** *on the internet.* (*the information* is the object of the transitive verb *found*.)
- An intransitive verb has no object:
  At five past seven our train ***arrived****.*
- Because transitive verbs have an object, they can be used in the passive form:
  Active: *Someone* ***stole our car*** *from outside the house.*
  Passive: ***Our car was stolen*** *from outside the house.*

Intransitive verbs cannot be used in the passive form.

- Some transitive verbs can have two objects, a direct object and an indirect object:
  They will send ***you an email*** *to confirm your booking.*
  (*an email* is the direct object of *will send*; *you* is the indirect object.)
- Either of these objects may become the subject of a passive sentence.
  You *will be sent an email to confirm your booking.*
  An email *will be sent to you to confirm your booking.*
- Many verbs can be used transitively and intransitively, sometimes with different meanings:
  Could you help me ***move this table****?* (transitive)
  We're ***moving*** *tomorrow.* (intransitive)

  I think I ***left my books*** *at college.* (transitive)
  They ***left*** *at three o'clock.* (intransitive)

  She ***runs her business*** *from home.* (transitive)
  A river ***runs*** *through our village.* (intransitive)

PRACTICE

1 **Choose the correct word to complete the sentence.**

1 Despite it being closing time, the man *refused* / *allowed* to leave the store.
2 I spoke to my grandmother and she *talked* / *told* to us about what it was like growing up in this town 50 years ago.
3 Having no bike for the race, my father *borrowed* / *lent* my brother a bicycle that once belonged to a professional cyclist.
4 I have to say that I was disappointed when Mahmood *mentioned* / *informed* me that he was looking for another job. He's an excellent employee.
5 My friend Jake *admitted* / *reminded* me of the time he took my laptop and I got really angry.
6 Thanks for meeting with me today. I'd like to *talk* / *discuss* your plans for the new music venue you'd like to build in the old cinema.
7 I'd like to give you the opportunity to *see* / *look* for yourselves the issues we've discovered over the last six months.

2 **Correct the mistakes in these sentences.**

1 I spoke to someone at the tourist information office and he told that there is a bus we can take to get to the castle.
2 We went into the private room, but the security guard instructed to leave the room immediately.
3 My friend Jason runs himself around the park every day.
4 Your car is blocking the exit and I can't get out – can you move please?
5 Our train is at 3pm. We need to leave it in 30 minutes.
6 Look, I don't care what he said, you can't call that name. It's rude and disrespectful.
7 I found it difficult to make friends at college until my roommate introduced to her friends from the football team.

9

FUTURE PERFECT AND CONTINUOUS; *BE* + *TO* INFINITIVE

Future continuous

We use the **future continuous** to talk about actions and events that will be in progress at a particular time in the future. We also use the future continuous to talk about something that we think is happening at the time of speaking:
He ***will be attending*** *his graduation ceremony this time next month.*
I imagine ***he'll*** *be* ***getting*** *ready to board his train right now.*

We also use the **future continuous** to ask about and describe a definite intention. As a question, it can be quite a polite form.
Will you be participating *in next term's fundraising event?*

Future perfect

We use both the **future perfect simple** and the **future perfect continuous** to project ourselves forward in time and 'look back'. The future perfect simple tense refers to a completed action in the future and the future perfect continuous refers to events or actions that are currently unfinished, but will be finished at some future time. Both tenses are usually used with time expressions.

Future perfect simple	Future perfect continuous
• refers to a completed action in the future. *Get a move on, or the match* ***will have started*** *by the time we make it to the ground.* *They* ***will have emptied*** *their water bottles by the time they are half way round the course.* *Hopefully they* ***will have completed*** *all the road works before the tourist season starts.* • is used with state verbs (e.g. *know, own*) *I can't believe that this time next week we* ***will have known each other*** *for five years.*	• used when we're looking back to the past from a point in the future and we want to emphasise the length or duration of an activity or event. *At midnight, we* ***will have been waiting*** *in the queue for concert tickets for three hours.* *They* ***will have been working*** *on that Roman wall for over a year by the time it's fully restored.*

be + *to* infinitive

We often use the structure *be* + *to* infinitive to talk about formal or official arrangements, instructions and orders in the future. It is common to see this structure in the passive form.
The Prime Minister ***is to announce*** *his resignation this evening due to the corruption scandal.*
Bags and suitcases ***are not to be left*** *unattended at any time or they will be removed.* (passive form)
This jumper ***is only to be washed*** *at 30°C.* (passive form)

We do not use it for situations beyond human control:
The forecast says that the weather ~~is to~~ ***will*** *be pretty good tomorrow.*

We often see this structure in conditionals in the *if* clause to express an idea that is dependent on the result clause happening:
We must act now to reduce emissions ***if we are to protect*** *the planet for future generations.*
If she is to pass *her driving test this time, she will have to practise her reversing and parking skills.*

PRACTICE

1 Choose the correct option to complete the sentences.

1 This time next year, we will *be sipping / have sipped* mocktails on the terrace of our holiday villa in the Algarve.

2 Will you *be attending / have attended* my graduation ceremony in October?

3 It's no good trying to Skype them now as they will *be relaxing / have relaxed* in their hot tub.

4 I really hope I will *be having / have had* the opportunity to go on a world cruise in a luxury liner before I reach thirty.

5 I promise I will *be finishing / have finished* my essay in time for the seminar next Friday.

6 I'm confident that when I'm 55 years old, I *will have retired / will be retiring*.

7 I hope I won't *have gained / be gaining* any more weight by the end of the holiday.

8 You are *not to turn over / won't be turning over* your exam paper until I give you permission to do so.

9 The election result is *to announce / to be announced* at 11am tomorrow morning.

10 If we *are to get / will have got* there by 6pm, then we need to be on the road by midday.

2 Complete this text with the verbs in the box in the future continuous or future perfect form.

become choose demand eat increase reduce

In the near future vegetable proteins like Quark [1] .... an established alternative to meat and other animal products. Around 20% of the population [2] .... only vegetarian food, and the rest of us [3] .... the amount of meat we consume. Awareness of the dangers of pesticides, artificial fertilizers and intensive farming [4] .... and we [5] .... chemical-free fruit and vegetables. We [6] .... diets both to keep fit and to counter disease.

OBJECTS, REFLEXIVES AND RECIPROCALS

Position of direct and indirect objects

When there is a direct and an indirect object in a sentence, the indirect object comes first:
My friend gave ***the homeless person*** (indirect object) ***twenty pounds*** (direct object).
She gave ***him*** (indirect object) ***twenty pounds*** (direct object).

The exception to this rule is when we can rephrase these sentences with a prepositional phrase + the recipient. The direct object goes first.

Verbs that often take an indirect object + direct object or prepositional phrase with *to*:
bring, give, lend, offer, owe, show, teach, tell, write
Our line manager ***offered the company credit card to us all.***

Verbs that often take an indirect object + direct object or prepositional phrase with *for*:
buy, find, get, make, order, save
I bought ***a new bike for my son.***

Reflexive pronouns

We use reflexive pronouns when 1) the subject and object of a verb refer to the same person or thing, and 2) for emphasis. They refer back to the subject forms of personal pronouns. They end in *-self* in the singular, and in *-selves* in the plural.

Personal subject pronouns	Reflexive pronouns
I	myself
you (singular)	yourself
he	himself
she	herself
it	itself
we	ourselves
you (plural)	yourselves
they	themselves

*He severely injured **himself** when rock climbing without a safety harness in the Italian Alps.*

*Her parents blamed **themselves** when, contrary to all expectations, she suddenly dropped out of university.*

Reciprocal pronouns

A reciprocal pronoun is a pronoun which is used when two people or groups each do the same thing to the other person or group. Any time an action or feeling is exchanged, reciprocal pronouns are used.

There are only two reciprocal pronouns:
each other
one another

The two reciprocal pronouns are often used interchangeably but *each other* is more common.
*Max and Kyra gave **each other** platinum gold rings when they got married.*
*The new members of parliament congratulated **one another** after successfully making their maiden speeches.*

Note:
Reflexive and reciprocal pronouns convey different meanings. Look at the following examples:
Andres and Pedro blamed themselves for losing the match.
(They both thought they were both to blame)
Andres and Pedro blamed each other for losing the match.
(They each thought/said that the other one was to blame.)

PRACTICE

1 Complete the sentences with a reflexive or a reciprocal pronoun.

1 My friend Maria likes to 'think out loud' and she can often be heard talking to ....

2 Please help .... to more vegetable pie – there's another one languishing in the oven.

3 'Do you need any help with the decorating?' 'No, we're fine, thanks. We can do it by ....'

4 We talk to .... on the phone every day.

5 The kids spent the afternoon wildly kicking a ball to ....

6 The advantages and disadvantages of working from home even .... out over the year.

2 Rewrite the sentences using *to* or *for*.

1 I've just bought my gran a top-of-the-range iPhone.

....

2 I lent my tennis partner my new fibreglass racquet and she accidently smashed it!

....

3 They offered us all a massive increase in salary, in recognition of our contribution to the company.

....

4 I ordered my children the up-market presentation set of 'Horrible History'.

....

5 He got his wife a 'genuine' fake designer handbag on her birthday.

....

10 EXPRESSING ABILITY, POSSIBILITY AND OBLIGATION

Ability: *can, could, be able to*

- Use *can/can't* for abilities in the present:
  *Cats **can** see in the dark.*
  *I **can't** drive.*
- Use *could/couldn't* for general abilities in the past:
  *When I was younger, I **could** run very fast.*
  *I **couldn't** walk until I was nearly two years old.*
- For ability to do something in a specific past situation, we use the negative *couldn't*, but we don't often use the affirmative *could*. Instead of *could*, it is usually better to use *be able to, manage to* or *succeed in -ing*:
  *We **couldn't** open the door with the key. Eventually we **managed to** break a window and **were able to** get in.*
- For future abilities, use *will be able to*:
  *My little sister **will** soon **be able to** read and write.*
- Use *be able to* for other forms where there is no option with *can* or *could*:
  *I'd like to **be able to** see better.*

Possibility: *can* and *could*

- Use *can/could* to describe what it is possible to do. Use *can/can't* for the present and future, and *could/couldn't* for the past. We also use *be able to*, especially for the past and future:
  Passengers ***can*** *get to London from here in 35 minutes.*
  Where we used to live, we ***couldn't*** *get there by train.*
  We ***can*** */ We'****ll be able to*** *discuss this at tomorrow's meeting.*
- Use *could* (but not *can* and not *couldn't*) for uncertain future possibilities:
  I think it ***could*** *rain later.* (not ~~*can rain*~~)
  But *It may/might not rain tomorrow.* (not ~~*couldn't rain*~~)
- Use *could have* (not ~~*can have*~~) + past participle for uncertain past possibilities:
  I don't know where she went. I suppose she ***could have gone*** *to the supermarket.*
- Use *can't/couldn't* + *be* for logical impossibility in the present, and *can't/couldn't have* + past participle for the past:
  It ***can't/couldn't be*** *Paul at the door. He's in Japan.*
  He ***can't/couldn't have had*** *lunch yet. It's only 11:15.*

→ **See also page 167:** Expressing possibility, probability and certainty, for other modals and structures to express possibility.

Rules and obligations: *must* and *have to*

Use *must* and *mustn't / must not*:

- to state rules and laws, often in a formal context:
  Meat packaging ***must*** *comply with the new regulation.*
  Motorists ***must not*** *exceed 120 kph on the motorway.*
  You ***mustn't*** *ride your bike without a helmet.*
- to express a personal feeling of obligation or a personal belief that something is important:
  I ***must*** *phone my sister today. I* ***mustn't*** *forget.*
  You ***must*** *see this film – it's great!*

Use *have to*:

- to describe a duty or obligation, often coming from an external source:
  She ***has to*** *be at a meeting at 8:30 tomorrow morning.*

  Compare these sentences:
  I ***have to*** *finish this report by tomorrow.* (= This is something that someone else is insisting on.)
  I ***must*** *finish this report by tomorrow.* (= I myself feel that this is essential.)
  He ***has to*** *go to the police station.* (= The police have given this order.)
  He ***must*** *go to the police station.* (= I believe it's essential for him to go.)

Use *don't have to*:

- to describe a lack of obligation or necessity:
  You ***don't have to go*** *to the party if you don't want to.*

Compare these sentences:
We ***don't have to*** *use this machine.* (= We can use it if we want to, but it isn't essential.)
We ***mustn't*** *use this machine.* (= We're not allowed to use it – it's prohibited.)

Necessity

- For necessity, use *need to* or *have to*:
  *To get to the airport in time, we'****ll need to*** */* ***have to*** *catch the 4:30 train.*
- There are two negative forms of *need*:
  We have plenty of time, so we ***needn't hurry*** */* ***don't need to hurry****.*

  In the past, these two forms have different meanings:
  We ***didn't need to hurry****.* (= We didn't hurry because there was no need.)
  We ***needn't have hurried****.* (= We hurried but it wasn't necessary.)

PRACTICE

1 Choose the correct verbs.

1 Sorry, I can't come out with you this evening. My teacher said I *must* / *have to* finish this essay.

2 I *don't need to* / *can't* catch a train home. My brother's picking me up.

3 He *can* / *must* stay for 90 days with this type of visa if he wants to.

4 You *mustn't* / *don't have to* go to the lecture this afternoon. It's optional.

5 In Britain, you *can't* / *needn't* leave education until you're 18.

6 These tablets will make you feel better, but you *mustn't* / *don't have to* take more than two at a time.

7 The meeting will be quite informal, so you *mustn't* / *needn't* wear a suit.

2 Complete conversations 1–2 with verbs from those listed for each conversation.

1 couldn't / can't / could have

A: Jo? Thank goodness it's you. I [1]............................... tell you how good it is to hear your voice.

B: You [2]............................... called me.

A: I tried, but I [3]............................... get through. Either your phone was switched off or you just didn't answer.

2 managed / being able / couldn't

A: Are you OK?

B: I'm OK now, but it was a very strange feeling not [4]............................... to get out of my own car.

A: What happened exactly?

B: I fell asleep with the radio and the heater on. When I woke up, I was very hot and I [5] .... hear the radio. The battery was flat.

A: So, what did you do?

B: I climbed into the back and [6] .... to open the boot from the inside.

3 Complete the second sentence so that it has a similar meaning to the first. You must use the word given. Write between two and five words.

1 Although I'd bought a ticket before getting on the bus, there was no requirement to do so.

HAVE

I .... a ticket before my bus journey.

2 The law states that drivers on this road are not allowed to exceed 100 mph.

GO

You .... 100 mph while driving on this road.

3 We were able to open the window enough with a crowbar that we could sneak in.

MANAGED

Using a crowbar, my friends and I .... enough to sneak in.

4 I believe that in the near future, it will be possible for people to live on other planets.

ABLE

It is my belief that soon humanity .... live on other planets.

5 You are under no obligation to buy a timeshare, I should stress that now.

PURCHASE

I would like to stress that you don't .... timeshare.

6 I heard a knock at the door and thought it was Chris, but that isn't possible as he's in China.

BEEN

Despite what I first thought, the knock at the door .... Chris as he's in China.

11

CONDITIONALS

First conditional		
Form	**Use**	**Examples**
If/Unless + present simple/continuous – *will/may/must*, etc. + infinitive	To talk about very possible or probable situations/events in the present or future	*If you**'re** hungry, I**'ll start** getting the lunch ready.* *We **should get** there by midday if the trains **are running** on time.*
Second conditional		
If/Unless + past simple/continuous – *would/could/might* + infinitive	To talk about improbable or imaginary situations/events in the present or future	*I **might miss** the city if we **moved** away from here.* (but we probably won't move) *If I **was driving** the car, we**'d be arriving** by now.* (but I'm not driving, so we aren't arriving yet)
Third conditional		
If + past perfect simple or continuous – *would have / could have / might have* + past participle	To talk about imaginary situations/events in the past	*I **could have got** better results if I**'d taken** the photos earlier.* (but I didn't take them early enough.) *If it **hadn't been snowing**, we **wouldn't have got** lost.* (but it was snowing, so we got lost)

- *Unless* is sometimes used instead of *if … not*, especially in first conditional sentences:
  *We'll have to eat indoors **unless** the weather improves.*
  (= if the weather doesn't improve)
- The following can also be used instead of *if* in first conditional sentences:
  when, as long as, as soon as, provided (*that*), *even though, even if, in case, on condition that, in the event that, assuming* (*that*), *given that*
- The following are alternatives, which can be used instead of *if* in second and third conditional sentences and questions:
  supposing, assuming, even if/though

- Note that *would* and *could* can be used with a conditional meaning in sentences without *if* or *unless*. The idea that we are talking about an unreal situation is understood without being explicitly stated:
  *'How **would** you communicate with someone whose language you **couldn't** speak?' 'I'd use sign language.'*
- *Otherwise* may be used with *would* or *could* to introduce a conditional idea:
  Arsenal played well in the last 20 minutes. ***Otherwise*** (= If the situation had been different) *they **would have lost** the match.*

Mixed conditionals

If one part of the sentence speaks about the present/future and the other part about the past, second and third conditionals can be 'mixed':

- *If I **hadn't met** Julia in Bulgaria last year* (past – 3rd conditional), *we **wouldn't be** married now* (present – 2nd conditional).
- *If Anastasia **didn't need** this book for her PhD* (present – 2nd conditional), *she **would** never **have bought** it* (past – 3rd conditional).
- *If you **weren't leaving** tomorrow* (future – 2nd conditional), *we could have had more time together* (past – 3rd conditional).

Other uses of conditionals

You can:

- give advice using *if I were you* + *I would* + infinitive:
  ***If I were you, I'd take** that laptop as hand luggage.*
- make criticisms or strong requests using *If you would* + infinitive; *would* + infinitive:
  ***If you'd stop** making so much noise, perhaps we**'d all be able** to enjoy the programme.*
- make polite formal requests using *I'd appreciate it / I'd be grateful if you would/could*:
  ***I'd appreciate it if you could** hand in the report by Thursday.*

PRACTICE

1 Choose the correct words to complete the sentences.

1. The current is extremely strong today, so if you don't stay close to the coast, you *could get/ could have got* carried out to sea.
2. You can dehydrate and die if you *didn't drink / don't drink* water for three or four days.
3. If you *would stop / had stopped* moaning for a while, we might start to enjoy the holiday.
4. If you *will take / can take* a seat in the waiting room, the dentist will call you in a few minutes.
5. If we *weren't visiting / hadn't been visiting* the forest, Jake would never have met you.
6. Even if I *do have / did have* some spare cash at the moment, I can assure you that I wouldn't be interested in booking one of those low-budget package holidays.
7. Provided you *train / trained* in a committed way, you should attain the level of fitness you aspire to.
8. If you *were concentrating / had been concentrating* during your lesson yesterday, you would know what the square root of 144 is.

2 Correct the mistakes in these sentences.

1. If you haven't taken these photographs, I wouldn't have remembered our holiday.
2. I'd tell you if I see anything unusual.
3. If I felt tired, I usually go to bed early.
4. If we don't reduce our dependence on fossil fuels in the near future, global warming would have become a more serious problem.
5. If the petrol engine hadn't been invented, there will still be plenty of oil left.

3 Complete the sentences with an appropriate conditional form using the verb in brackets.

1. Female bears .... (not usually attack) humans unless they .... (have) their cubs with them.
2. If you .... (keep on) working hard, I think you .... (promote) next year.
3. If you .... (not insist) on leaving the house so early, we .... (not walk) around the airport right now with nothing to do.
4. It was obvious that you .... (not get) the job unless you .... (apply) for it.
5. She .... (run) the marathon next week if she .... (keep) to her training plan over the last few months.
6. If the weather .... (not improve) on the second day, last weeks' holiday .... (ruin).
7. If you .... (pay) the man on the door when we arrived, we .... (allow) to watch the rest of the film.

CONDITIONALS: *WISH* AND *IF ONLY*

wish

We use *wish* with various verb forms to express the following ideas:

- We use *wish* + past simple or past continuous to express unhappiness about a present or future situation which is impossible to change.
  I was so carefree when I was younger. ***I wish I were/was*** *a teenager again.*
  I wish I wasn't *an only child. I'd love to have a brother or sister.*
  I wish I didn't *have to go to school today.*
  Jan wishes the wedding ***was taking place*** *in the spring.*
- We use *wish* + past perfect to express regret for something in the past which is impossible to change.
  She wish *her brother* ***had told*** *the truth.*
  I wish we hadn't spent *so much money on that holiday.*
  Don't you wish we hadn't arranged *to go away at the weekend?*
  Peter ***wished he hadn't arranged*** *to go out that evening.*
- We use *wish* + *could* + infinitive to express frustration about a situation which is possible, but difficult, to change.
  I wish I could speak *English more fluently.*
  My friend wishes he could get *a job in the film industry, but it's very hard to get in to.*
- We use *wish* + *would/wouldn't* + infinitive to express irritation at another person's behaviour or at an annoying situation. We use it in the hope that the person or the situation will change.
  I wish you'd listen *to what I'm saying for once.*
  I wish my parents wouldn't treat *me like a child.*
  We all wish the weather would improve.

Note: We cannot say ~~*I wish I would*~~ *do something.*

if only

We use *if only* to express strong wishes or regrets. It can be used instead of *I wish* to add strength to the wish or regret followed by the same verb forms:
If only I were/was *a teenager again.*
If only we hadn't spent *so much money on that holiday.*
If only I could speak *English more fluently.*
If only you'd listen *to what I'm saying for once.*
If only it would stop *raining.*

PRACTICE

1 Complete the sentences with the correct form of the verb in brackets. You may need to add an auxiliary verb.

1 Katie wishes she .... (work) harder when she was at school.

2 I wish I .... (find) the present I bought for my mum's birthday. It must be here somewhere.

3 I wish my sister .... (be) so untidy. Her bedroom is always a mess.

4 If only you .... (tell) me when you were going to arrive. I'd have come to meet you.

5 I wish I .... (not eat) so much chocolate. I'm starting to feel sick.

6 I wish you .... (not keep) interrupting me.

7 I wish people .... (stop) criticising our football team.

8 If only I .... (not turn down) that job offer. I'd be working in Milan now.

12

COUNTABLE AND UNCOUNTABLE NOUNS

Countable nouns

- Countable nouns can be singular or plural and are used for individual things which we can count.
  In our family we have ***a cat*** *and* ***two dogs.***
- In the singular form they can be preceded by *a/an* or *one*, or determiners such as *this/that*, *each*, *every*:
  A human being has two hands. Each hand has ***a*** *thumb and four fingers.*
- In the plural form they can be preceded by numbers or determiners such as *some*, *any*, *many*, (*a*) *few*, *no*, *these/those*:
  There are ***a few*** *teenagers in the room but* ***no*** *children.*

Uncountable nouns

- Uncountable nouns are neither singular nor plural and are used for things that are not normally divided into separate items:
  We use ***gas*** *for cooking and* ***electricity*** *for heating.*
- They are used with singular verbs and can be preceded by determiners such as *some*, *any*, *no*, *much*, *this/that*:
  'Is there ***any*** *coffee left?' 'No, but there's* ***some*** *tea.'*

  Note: *a/an*, *one*, *each* and *every* cannot be used with uncountable nouns.
- To refer to particular quantities of an uncountable noun, use a phrase which includes a countable noun + *of*:
  a jug of water, two cups of tea, a loaf of bread, three slices of toast, twenty litres of oil

  Note: Some nouns which are uncountable in English may be countable in other languages, e.g. *accommodation, advice, applause, bread, damage, equipment, fruit, furniture, homework, housework, information, knowledge, luggage, money, news, rubbish, shopping, toast, traffic, travel.*

Nouns that can be countable or uncountable

Many nouns can be countable or uncountable, depending on how they are used.

- *Would you like some chocolate?* (= the food substance in general)
  There are only two chocolates left in the box. (= individual items)
- *French people love wine and cheese.* (= these substances in general)
  France has many different wines and cheeses. (= individual products)
- *I don't eat lamb or chicken.* (= general types of meat)
  I'm going to roast a chicken tonight. (= a whole bird)
  I love lambs and chickens. (= animals)
- *Coffee is expensive here.* (= the type of drink)
  Can I have two coffees, please? (= cups of coffee)
- *People are crazy about sport.* (= the general field of activity)
  Football is a great sport. (= one of many individual sporting activities)

PRACTICE

1 Tick the correct sentences. Correct the sentences with mistakes.

1 The behaviours of the tourists was disrespectful of the local culture.
2 She had some memorable experience during her gap year in USA.
3 There wasn't a room in the tiny removal van for all his furnitures.
4 He did not choose to accept the advices from his tutor.
5 BBC News have a worldwide reputation for unbiased reporting.
6 When his dessert arrived at the table, he realised he had ordered an enormous portion of cheesecake.

ARTICLES

The indefinite article *a/an*

A/an is used for something general or non-specific, or when we refer to something for the first time:
*Have you got **a** bicycle?* (= any kind of bicycle)
*He's **a** good gymnast.* (= one of many)
Other uses:

- to refer to someone's job or function:
  *She used to be **a** hotel receptionist.*
- to mean one:
  *I have **a** sister and two brothers.*

The definite article *the*

The is used with any type of noun when it is clear which thing/ person we are referring to. It may be specifically identified in the sentence, it may have been mentioned before, or there may be only one of these things:
*Where's **the** furniture we ordered last week?* (I'm identifying the furniture I mean)
*We ordered a table and six chairs. **The** chairs have arrived but **the** table hasn't.* (= the one(s) I've just mentioned)
*She's at **the** station.* (= the local station, the only one)
*We're meeting at **the** café later.* (= you know the one I mean – the one we always go to)

Other uses:

- to refer generally to some geographical locations, e.g. *the beach, the coast, the mountains, the sea, the road*:
  *We're spending a fortnight in **the mountains**, but I'd prefer to be somewhere on **the coast**.*
- to refer to a type of musical instrument:
  *He's learning to play **the trumpet**.*
- to refer generally to public transport and other services:
  *You can take **the train** to Edinburgh.*
  *Have they contacted **the police**?*
- with adjectives used as nouns for groups of people, e.g. *the rich, the poor, the living, the dead, the blind, the deaf, the unemployed*:
  *There's a growing gap between **the rich** and **the poor**.*

No article

No article is used:

- with plural and uncountable nouns with a general meaning:
  ***Cats** chase **mice**.*
  ***Pollution** is ruining our towns and cities.*
- in certain phrases which relate to a type of place or institution, but not a specific one:
  *Did you go to **university**?*
  *What did you do in **class** today?*

  Other similar phrases:
  be in / go to church, court, hospital, prison, bed
  be at / go to sea, school, university, college, work,
  be at / go home

PRACTICE

1 Complete the gaps with the correct article or Ø if no article is required.

1 Can you buy .... bread and .... milk from .... shop next to .... station?
2 I think we should all try to save .... planet and make .... life better for .... future generations.
3 I spend a lot of .... time looking at .... sea from .... balcony of .... hotel where I'm staying.

4 He really likes .... apples but today he chose .... orange for lunch.

5 .... cheapest ferry trip in .... world is from .... Staten Island to .... Manhattan. It's free!

6 She has .... brother who goes to .... different school on .... other side of town.

13

WAYS OF CONTRASTING IDEAS

Conjunctions: *but*, (*and*) *yet*, *whereas*, *while*, *although*, (*even*) *though*

- ***But*** can contrast words, phrases and clauses, normally within the same sentence:
  *The work was tiring **but** worthwhile.*
  *The work was tiring **but** it produced worthwhile results.*

  However, in informal writing it may be used to start a sentence:
  *We were half dead by the end of the day! **But** at least the job turned out well.*
- ***Yet*** can also be used to show contrast. It often occurs after *and*:
  *So many questions **and yet** so few answers.*
  *It felt strange **and yet** so wonderful to swim in the sea in winter!*
- ***Whereas*** and ***while*** are used to contrast different, but not contradictory, ideas:
  *He can eat anything he likes without putting on weight, **whereas** most people have to be more careful.*
  ***While** I know she can be difficult at times, I'm very fond of her.*

  The *while* clause usually comes before the main clause.
- ***Though*** / ***although*** / ***even though*** introduce an idea that contrasts with the one in the main clause:
  *He failed his driving test **although** / **even though** he had practised every day for the previous two weeks.*
  Even though is more emphatic than *though/although*.
- ***Even if*** is similar to ***even though***, but adds a conditional meaning:
  *I'm going to New Zealand for my holiday next year **even if** I have to save all year.*

Prepositions: *despite*, *in spite of*

- ***Despite*** and ***in spite of*** are prepositions and therefore they are followed by a noun or an *-ing* form:
  *The journey was very quick **despite** / **in spite of** the heavy traffic.*
  ***Despite** / **In spite of** feeling ill, / the fact that I felt ill, I enjoyed the party.*

Adverbs: *however*, *nevertheless*, *still*, *even so*

- ***However*** is used to contrast a new sentence with the previous one(s). It normally goes at the beginning of the sentence, but may be placed within it or at the end:
  *This is one possible solution to the problem. **However**, there are others. / There are others, **however**. / There are, **however**, others.*

  Note: Unlike *but*, *however* cannot be used to link two contrasting clauses in the same sentence.
- We can also use ***still*** at the beginning of the sentence with the same function:
  *I don't really like parties. **Still**, I'll have to go or they'll be upset.*
- ***Nevertheless*** has the same function but is more formal. It normally goes at the beginning of the sentence:
  *This is an extremely difficult decision. **Nevertheless**, it is one that we have to make.*
- ***Even so*** introduces something surprising that contrasts with what was said before:
  *The weather was terrible, but **even so**, we enjoyed the beach.*

Other phrases for showing contrast

- ***On the other hand*** is used to introduce the second of two contrasting points:
  *The outside skin of this exotic fruit is a dirty brown colour and bitter; the heart, **on the other hand**, is creamy white and sweet.*
- ***On the one hand*** / ***on the other hand*** are used to compare two different facts or two opposite ways of thinking about a situation:
  ***On the one hand**, I know I really ought to stop playing online strategy games, but **on the other hand**, I simply don't have the willpower to do it.*
- ***All the same*** is used to mean 'despite what has just been said'. It can go at the beginning of the sentence, within it or at the end:
  *Our hotel was terrible – but we had a good holiday **all the same**.*
  *I know he's very capable, but **all the same**, I wish he'd ask for help sometimes.*
  *The flight is extremely early in the morning. **All the same**, I think we should book it.*

PRACTICE

1 Choose the correct option to complete sentences.

1 Even *but* / *though* I'm mainly vegetarian, I occasionally 'treat myself' to a chicken soup.

2 There was a lot disagreement over the venue for the college reunion; *nevertheless* / *whereas* they did finally manage to reach a consensus.

3 I really like being active, *though* / *whereas* most of my friends from college are extremely lazy.

4 The inside of the igloo was very shiny and incredibly smooth; the outside, *on one hand* / *on the other hand*, was rough and uneven.

2 **Tick the correct sentences. Correct the sentences with mistakes.**

1 On the other hand, I really ought to cut down on the amount of carbohydrates I eat, but on the one hand, I simply can't resist potatoes, rice and pasta.

2 Even although it was a roasting hot day, we decided to stay indoors and finish the decorating.

3 In the nineteenth century some famous scientists and mathematicians managed to do some incredible work despite not having computers.

4 In spite the high temperature, she felt extremely cold and shivery because of a bout of flu.

5 I couldn't fall asleep even though the noisy celebrations in the street had long ceased.

6 That author has created some highly imaginative short stories despite that he is homeless.

THE LANGUAGE OF COMPARISON

Comparative adjectives and adverbs

Use comparative adjectives or adverbs to compare two things or actions:
*This camera is **smaller** and **more compact** than mine.*
*Glíma is **less violent** than other forms of wrestling.*
*She works **more efficiently** than most of her colleagues.*

- *no* + comparative adjective:
  *Running is **no better** for you than walking fast.*
- *as* + adjective/adverb + *as* to show similarity or equality:
  *My younger brother is **as tall as** me.*
  *She doesn't play the piano **as well as** she used to.*
- *the* + comparative adjective/adverb + *the* to show a process in which one thing/action depends on another:
  ***The higher** he climbed, **the narrower** the path became.*
  ***The faster** we walk, **the sooner** we'll get there.*
  ***The more** I read, **the less** I understand.*

  Note: With adjectives we often leave out the verb *be*:
  ***The stronger the material** (is), the longer it lasts.*
  *The sooner we leave, **the better** (it will be).*
- repetition of a comparative adjective/adverb to express an increasing rate of change:
  *He walked **faster and faster** until he was out of breath.*
  *Food is getting **more and more expensive**.*

Superlative adjectives and adverbs

Use superlative adjectives or adverbs to put one thing or action above all others in the same category:
*Glíma is the **oldest** form of wrestling in Iceland.*
*That was the **least interesting** film I've ever seen.*
*She works **most efficiently** in the morning.*

- *the* + superlative adjective + *of* + plural noun:
  *It was **the simplest of** ideas.*
  *He was **the most inspiring of** teachers.*
- *the* + superlative adjective + noun + *imaginable/possible/available*:
  *We had **the worst** weather **imaginable**.*

more, most, less, fewer + noun

Use *more/most* + noun to express a greater / the greatest number or amount:

- *more/most* + plural noun or uncountable noun:
  *There were **more people** here than there were last year.*
  *I wish I could spend **more time** with my friends.*
  ***Most sharks** are quite harmless.*
  ***Most cheese** is made from cow's milk.*
- *most of* + noun/pronoun when referring to part of a specific thing or group:
  *The pizza was awful. I threw **most of it** away.*
  ***Most of our relatives** live in Canada.*
  ***Most of the oil** in the tanker leaked out into the sea.*

Use *less/fewer* + noun to express a smaller number/amount.

- *less* + uncountable noun:
  *I'm getting **less money** now than in my last job.*
- *fewer* + plural noun:
  *There were **fewer people** than usual at today's match.*

Qualifying comparatives

To intensify or qualify comparative adjectives/adverbs use:

- *a lot / a great deal / far / much / considerably / substantially*
- *slightly / a bit / a little*
- *even*

*My sister is **a lot more intelligent** than me, but my younger brother is **even cleverer** than her.*
*We've had **far less** snow this year than last year.*
*We are **much happier** now we finally have our dance outfits.*
*Could you drive **a bit more carefully**, please?*

Qualifying superlatives

To intensify or qualify superlative adjectives, use: *by far, easily, nearly, one of:*
*Your English accent is **by far the most authentic**.*
*He is **easily the most athletic** member of the cross country club.*
*Ben is **nearly the oldest** person working here.*
*He's **one of the best** singers I've ever heard.*
*She's **definitely** the **greatest** runner of her generation.*

PRACTICE

1 Complete the sentences with appropriate comparative words or phrases.

1 They are as involved .... us in the preparations for the street art festival.

2 I was surprised to discover that squirrels are a lot more aggressive .... most other rodents.

3 He was .... more upset about the breakup with his girlfriend than I expected.

4 The time we were in Japan when the tsunami struck was the .... frightening experience I have ever had.

5 The more I study the complexities of English grammar, ... I enjoy learning the language.

6 She was .... the most successful player in the ten-minute chess matches.

2 Correct the mistakes in these sentences.

1 I'd say that this laptop is by far the better one we've looked at.

2 The thing about Julie is that she is not as athletic than she thinks she is.

3 The long I live in this city, the more I love it.

4 If you need advice about diet, Ignacio is probably best person to speak to.

5 The neighbour's dog seems quite aggressive at first, but he is much friendly than he first appears.

14 COMMENT ADVERBIALS AND INTENSIFYING ADVERBS

Comment adverbials

Comment adverbs and adverbial phrases:

- express how certain the speaker is about something. Some common adverbs: *certainly, possibly, probably, undoubtedly*
  *She's **certainly** happier now than she used to be.*

  Some common phrases: *without a doubt, in theory, in all likelihood/probability*
  ***In all likelihood**, the meeting will have to be postponed.*
- express the speaker's attitude or opinion about what they are saying. Some common adverbs: *frankly, personally, (un)fortunately, obviously, surprisingly, strangely*
  ***Strangely**, I haven't heard from her since she moved.*
  (= I think her failure to communicate is strange.)
  ***Personally**, I'd prefer to live abroad.*

  Some common phrases: *to be honest, generally speaking, to my surprise*
  ***To be honest**, I don't think you should have given him money.*

Comment adverbials expressing opinions often go at the beginning of a sentence. However, they can also be placed:

- in a middle position in the sentence (often after the subject or after the verb):
  *Martina, **unfortunately**, didn't arrive until midday.*
  *She was, **unfortunately**, too late for her appointment.*
- at the end of the sentence:
  *Luca is thinking of going to Australia, **apparently**.*

These comment adverbials are usually separated from the rest of the sentence by commas.

Intensifying adverbs

There are a number of intensifying adverbs in English which we use to give emphasis and strengthen the meaning of adjectives. Different adverbs apply to different adjective forms:

- **Adverbs that intensify gradable adjectives:**
  We use the following adverbs to intensify gradable adjectives: *really, very, extremely, incredibly, perfectly*
  *She is **incredibly** passionate about politics.*
  *The car crash was **very** serious and we were **extremely** lucky that no one was injured.*
  *I was **perfectly** happy to go to the cinema alone.*

  Note: *Perfectly* forms collocations with specific adjectives (for example, *honest, normal, good, clear*), so these need to be learnt separately.
- **Adverbs that intensify extreme adjectives:**
  We use the following adverbs to intensify ungradable adjectives:
  absolutely, totally, completely, utterly
  *Even the elite runners were **utterly** exhausted at the finishing line of the marathon.*
  *Her juggling skills are **absolutely** amazing.*

→ **See also:** *qualifying comparatives* and *qualifying superlatives* on pages 184–185

PRACTICE

1 Choose the comment adverbial which fits best. For some sentences, both options are possible.

1 *Frankly / Fortunately*, the corporation's idea of customer service is very poor.

2 *Personally / In theory*, I was surprised to hear Sandra's news.

3 They're *obviously / certainly* not going to give us a tip after we dropped soup on their laps.

4 This will surprise you, but my brother is *probably / incredibly* tall.

5 Following today's sell-off, many shareholders will *undoubtedly / strangely* find themselves much poorer than they were yesterday.

6 I don't envisage you having a career here in the long term, *unfortunately / sadly*.

7 He is *apparently / certainly* the best performer I have ever seen in my life.

8 *To be honest / Honestly*, there is nothing you can do now that would change my mind.

2 Choose an appropriate adverb in the box to intensify the adjectives. There may be more than one possible answer.

easily	far	completely	really	totally	much

1 I think she is unsuitable for that job in the tourist information office because of her personality.

2 He is more considerate than the rest of his family.

3 They are better off than the other students from the UAE, because they are fully funded by government grants.

4 He is the most impolite person I have met so far on my travels round the UK.

5 She is depressed after getting the results of her exam.

6 I was amazed by the fact that she was a successful vlogger on YouTube.

EMPHASIS

Emphasis involves showing that something is particularly important or worth giving attention to. There are a number of techniques to give prominence to information in a sentence:

Cleft sentences

The term 'cleft sentence' refers to sentence structures which are used to emphasise certain information. These two examples compare the structure of 'normal' sentences with cleft sentences. The emphasised information is in bold.

Normal sentences: *They bought things online.*
Pete paid for our flights.

Cleft sentences: *What they did was* ***buy things online****.*
It was Pete *who paid for our flights.*

Common cleft sentence structures start with *What*, *All* and *It*.

What

- *My brother wanted a new car for his birthday.*
  What *my brother* ***wanted*** *for his birthday* ***was*** *a new car.*
- *You should arrange a dental appointment if you have toothache.*
  What *you* ***should*** *do if you have toothache* ***is arrange*** *a dental appointment.*
- *I decided to write a letter of complaint.*
  What *I* ***decided*** *to do* ***was to write*** *a letter of complaint.*
- *All* can often be used instead of *what*.
  All *I really wanted was to sleep all day.*

We use *to* + infinitive if the verb in the first part of the sentence is followed by *to* + infinitive (e.g. *intend*, *want*).

We use the infinitive without *to* if the verb in the first part of the sentence is followed by the infinitive without *to* (e.g. *should*).

- *Why* can be used to start a cleft sentence but normally a phrase is used instead.

  I asked the question to find out what's going on.
  Why *I asked the question* ***was to find out*** *what's going on.*
  The reason why *I asked the question* ***was to find out*** *what's going on.*

It

- In cleft sentences which start with *It*, we can choose which information to emphasise. For example, from this 'normal sentence' we can make the three cleft sentences below.
  Pete had his bike repaired last weekend.
  It was Pete *who had his bike repaired last weekend.* (It was Pete not Ben.)
  It was last weekend *that Pete had his bike repaired.* (It was last weekend not yesterday.)
  It was his bike *that Pete had repaired last weekend.* (It was his bike not his car.)

Cleft sentences beginning with a noun phrase

Instead of *what*, these noun phrases may be used: *the only*, *the last thing*, *something*, *all*, (*the*) *one* …

- ***The only thing*** *I didn't find in the shop was toothpaste.*
- ***The last thing*** *I was expecting was to lose my job.*
- ***Something*** *you should know about me is that I'm terrible with money.*
- ***The one thing*** *you should remember is to always tell the truth.*
- ***One person*** *you should thank is your father. He has been very supportive.*

Fronting

Another way to add emphasis to a sentence is *fronting*. This means starting a sentence with information you wish to emphasise. Some of these structures may involve the inversion of subject and verb. Here are some common examples. (Where appropriate, more 'normal' word order is given in brackets.)

- Starting with an adverb
  Carefully, *he dragged himself out of the treacherous quicksand.*
  (He dragged himself out of the treacherous quicksand carefully.)
- Starting with an adverbial phrase of time or place
  Next to me *sat an elderly man reading a newspaper.* OR
  Next to me *an elderly man sat reading a newspaper.*
  (An elderly man reading a newspaper sat next to me.)
- Starting with a comparative structure
  More important than anything else *is the need to look after the children.*
  (The need to look after the children is more important than anything else.)
  Faster than all the other runners *was my brother, who won the race in 10.5 seconds.*
  (My brother was faster than all the other runners and won the race in 10.5 seconds.)
- Starting with *So* + adjective
  So preoccupie*d was he that he forgot to leave the motorway soon enough.*
  (He was so preoccupied that he forgot to leave the motorway soon enough.)
- Starting with a superlative adjective
  Best of all *was the sweet creamy dessert.*
  (The sweet creamy dessert was best of all.)
  Most challenging of all *was the last 10 km of the race.*
  (The last 10 km of the race was the most challenging of all.)

do, does or *did*

You can add *do*, *does* or *did* to emphasise, disagree or argue a point. The auxiliary verb is stressed when speaking:

A: *The problem is the students nowadays don't study enough.*
B: *They* ***do*** *study enough, but the tests are too hard!*

A: *You didn't get me a birthday present!*
B: *I* ***did*** *get you one! I bought you that toolbox that you were asking for.*

A: *If you don't want to stay for the rehearsal, you can go now. If you* ***do*** *want to stay, take a short break and be back in ten minutes.*

Reflexive pronouns

Reflexive pronouns can also be used for emphasis:
The manager of the restaurant wrote to us ***herself*** *to apologise for the awful service.* OR
The manager of the restaurant ***herself*** *wrote to us to apologise for the awful service.*

Reflexive pronouns aren't used on their own as the subject of a clause, but they can be used with a noun or pronoun to emphasise the subject:
Parents and caregivers always pass on to children what ***they themselves*** *were taught.*

PRACTICE

1 Rewrite these sentences starting with *It* or *What*.

1 I'd really like to write stories for children.
2 The doctor advised me to reduce the amount of sugar I eat.
3 My best friend suggested I should apply for a postgraduate degree course.
4 My father, not my brother, lost his job when the office closed down.
5 I'm to blame, not you.
6 I don't understand why so many people voted for her.

2 Rewrite the sentences by moving the phrases in *italics* to the front of the sentence and making any changes that are necessary.

1 A few students stood chatting *at the back of the hall.*
2 The steak tartar was delicious. But the cheese board was *even more delicious*.
3 He ordered a bottle of juice and a glass of sparkling water. He gulped down *the sparkling water* in one go.
4 It was self-evident *that she had been jogging.*
5 He *meticulously* repaired the stitching on his shirt.
6 A rabid dog *ready to attack* crouched *in front of me.*

3 Rewrite the sentences to make them more emphatic. Use the word in CAPITALS.

1 I find her constant sarcasm most annoying. WHAT
2 I hope that she passes her driving test this time. DO
3 We first met on a beach in Thailand. IT
4 He left the party because he had an argument with his girlfriend. WHY
5 I received a letter from the Prime Minister promising to take up our cause. HIMSELF

DEPENDENT PREPOSITIONS

Many verbs, nouns and adjectives are followed by a particular preposition before a noun, noun phrase, pronoun or verb + *-ing*:
The film reminded me ***of*** *my childhood.*
He apologised to them ***for*** *damaging their car.*

There are no clear rules to help you decide which preposition to use: the best strategy is to learn the preposition with the word. Examples given in a dictionary will show how they are used.

Here are some common words + prepositions: sb = somebody; sth = something).

Verb + preposition

account for
accuse sb of
accustom sb to
agree with sb/sth about
amount to
apologise (to sb) for
appeal to
apply to
approve of
attach sth to
attribute sth to
base sth on
believe in
blame sb/sth for
charge sb for
charge sb with
comment on
compare sb/sth to/with
compete with
concentrate on
connect sb/sth with
consider sb/sth as
consist of
contrast sb/sth with
cope with
dedicate sth to
depend on
devote sth to
differ from
disapprove of
discourage sb from
distinguish sb/sth from
distract sb from
divide sth into/between
dream of
exclude sb/sth from
experiment on
focus on
help (sb) with
hope for
impress sb with
include sb/sth in
insure (sth) against
interfere with/in
invest (sth) in
involve sb in
link sb/sth to/with
listen to
object to
operate on
participate in
persist in
prepare (sb/sth) for
prevent sb/sth from
prohibit sb/sth from
protest against
provide sb with
react to/against
recognise sb/sth as
recover from
refer sb/sth to
regard sb/sth as
relate sb/sth to
rely on
remind sb of
resort to
result in
search for
separate sb/sth from
spend sth on
suffer from
think about/of
warn sb about/against

Adjective + preposition

acceptable to
afraid of
angry with/about
anxious about
available to/for
aware of
capable of
closed to
confident of/in
convenient for
critical of
damaging for
delighted with/by/at
dependent on
devoted to
different from/to
disappointed with
familiar with/to
good/bad/clever at
in common with
independent of
interested in
involved in
kind to
obsessed with
open to
pleased with/about
prejudiced against
proud of
relevant to
responsible to/for
sensitive to
shocked at/by
sorry about/for
suitable for
suited to
surprised at/by
tired of
tolerant of
upset about

Noun + preposition

attention to
belief in
capacity for
confidence in
criticism of
difficulty in/with
discussion about
experience of/in
information on/about
problem of/with
reputation for
trust in

Multi-word verb builder

Multi-word verbs are verbs that consist of a verb and one or two particles (prepositions or adverbs e.g. *up*, *over*, *in*, *down*, etc.) The meaning of a multi-word verb is often different from its separate parts. The following are all multi-word verbs.

multi-word verb	definition
to back up sth	to make a copy of information that is stored separately
to bail sb/sth out	to help someone or something such as a company, esp. by giving or lending money
to bounce back	to start to be successful again after a difficult period
to bring sb together	to cause people to be friendly with each other
to brush up (on) sth	to improve your knowledge of something already learned but partly forgotten
to build sth up	to increase or develop
to bump into sb	to meet someone you know when you have not planned to meet them
to bump sth up	to increase in price
to burn through sth	to spend money quickly
to call sth off	to decide to stop an activity
to call on sb to do sth	to ask someone in a formal way to do something
to catch on	to become popular
to catch up (with sb/sth)	to reach the same level or quality as someone or something else
to cater for sb/sth	to provide what is wanted or needed by a particular group of people
to cater to sb/sth	to give people exactly what they want, often something unusual or something that people think is wrong
to check (up) on sth	to try to discover how something is progressing or whether someone is doing what they should be doing
to check sth out	to examine something or get more information about it in order to be certain that it is true, safe, or suitable / to go to a place in order to see what it is like
to clean sb/sth up	to make a person or place clean and tidy
to clear sth away	to make a place tidy by removing things from it, or putting them where they should be
to close sth off	to put something across the entrance to a place in order to stop people entering it
to come across	to seem to be a particular type of person or thing
to come at sb	to move towards someone in order to attack them
to come between sb	to cause problems between two people or interrupt two people
to come in for	to receive blame or criticism
to come into	to receive something (often money) not as a result of your own actions
to come off	to happen successfully
to come on	to start to happen or work
to come round	to become conscious again after an accident or medical operation
to come under sth	to be in a particular part of a book, list, etc.
to come up	If a job or opportunity comes up, it becomes available

multi-word verb	definition
to come up against sth	to have to deal with a problem or difficulty
to come up with sth	to suggest or think of an idea or plan
to cover sth up	to put something over something else, in order to protect or hide it
to creep up	to slowly increase or appear without being noticed
to curl up	to sit or lie in a position with your arms and legs close to your body
to cut across sth	If a problem or subject cuts across different groups of people, all of those groups are affected by it or interested in it
to cut sth out	to remove something or form a shape by cutting, usually something made of paper or cloth / to stop eating or drinking something, usually to improve your health
to depend on sb (for sth)	to need something, or need the help and support of someone or something, in order to live or continue as before
to derive sth from sth	to come from or be developed from something
to devote yourself to sth	to spend all your time or energy doing something that you think is important
to dispose of sth	to get rid of something, especially by throwing it away
to do away with sth	to get rid of something or stop using something
to double up	to laugh a lot
to draw on sth	to use information or your knowledge or experience of something to help you do something
to draw sth up	to prepare something, usually a plan, list, or an official agreement, by writing it
to drop down	to appear underneath in a list form
to dry (sth) out	to make something dry, or to become dry
to dwell on/upon sth	to keep thinking or talking about something, especially something bad or unpleasant
to eat away at	to gradually damage or destroy something
to fall off	If the amount, rate, or quality of something falls off, it becomes smaller or lower
to feel up to sth	to have the energy to do something
to fend for oneself	to take care of and provide for yourself without depending on anyone else
to filter sth out	to select or remove a type of information from something
to finish sth off	to complete the last part of something that you are doing
to fit in	to feel that you belong to a particular group and are accepted by them
to fit in with sth	If something fits in with a situation, idea, method, etc. it is suitable and works successfully as part of it

multi-word verb	definition
to fit sb/sth in	to find time to do or deal with something/ someone
to fix sth up	to arrange a meeting, date, event, etc.
to free up sth	to make something available to be used
to freeze over	to become covered with ice
to get at sth	to suggest or express something in a way that is not clear
to get back to sb	to talk to someone, usually on the telephone, to give them some information they have asked for or because you were not able to speak to them before
to get (sb/sth) out	to escape from or leave a place, or to help someone do this
to get out	to go out to different places and meet people in order to enjoy yourself
to get into sth	to become interested in an activity or subject, or start being involved in an activity
to get off	to leave work, often at a scheduled time
to get on	to be getting late
to get (sth) through to sb	to succeed in making someone understand or believe something
to go down	if a machine (especially a computer) goes down it stops working
to go into sth	to start to do a particular type of work
to go into sth	to discuss, describe, or explain something, especially in a detailed or careful way
to go off	if a bomb or a gun goes off, it explodes or fires
to go out	if the tide goes out, it moves back and covers less of the beach
to grapple with sth	to try to deal with or understand a difficult problem or subject
to hack into sth	to access someone else's computer system without permission
to hand sth in	to give something to an authority or responsible person
to hear from sb	to get a letter, a telephone call, or message from someone
to hold sth back	to not tell everything you know about something
to hold on	something you say when you are confused or surprised by something that you have just heard and want to understand it
to hold sb/sth back	to prevent someone or something from moving forward
to huddle together	to come close together in a group, for example because it is cold
to insist on sth	to keep doing something, even if it annoys other people or people think it is not good for you
to keep sb/sth from doing sth	to prevent someone or something from doing something
to kick in	to start to be effective or to happen
to kick off	When a football match or other event kicks off, it starts
to kick sb out	to force someone to leave a place or organisation
to knuckle down	to start working or studying hard
to lay sb off	to stop employing someone, usually because there is no work for them to do

multi-word verb	definition
to lay sth out	to explain something clearly, usually in writing
to level off	to stop rising or falling and to stay at the same level
to lie ahead	if an event/situation that will cause problems lies ahead, it will happen in the future
to line sb/sth up	to plan for something to happen
to lock sb out	to prevent somebody from taking part in an activity
to log on (to)	to connect to a computer or system
to look on/upon sb/sth as sth	to consider someone or something in a particular way
to look up	to become better
to mess about/ around	to spend time playing and doing things with no particular purpose, to waste time
to move on	to start doing a new activity, to start speaking about a new topic
to occur to sb	to come into someone's mind
to opt in	to choose to be part of an activity or arrangement
to pass sb by	if an event or opportunity passes you by, you do not notice it or get pleasure or an advantage from it
to pass over sb/sth	to ignore or to not give attention to someone or something
to piece sth together	to put the parts of something into place; to collect and study in order to understand
to pop up	to appear or happen suddenly, often without warning
to prey on/upon sb/sth	to hurt or deceive a group of people, especially people who are vulnerable
to pride oneself on sth	to value a special quality/ability that you have
to print sth out	to produce writing or images on paper or other material with a machine
to push on	to continue doing something challenging
to put down sth	to make an initial payment
to put sth forward	to state an idea or opinion, or to suggest a plan, so that it can be considered or discussed
to put on sth	to add to someone's weight or height
to put sth together	to prepare a piece of work by collecting several ideas and suggestions and organising them
to put sth in	to install a device and make it ready to operate
to read up on sth	to read a lot about a particular subject in order to learn about it
to refer to sb/sth	to mention or talk about someone or something
to relate to sb	to understand how someone feels
to rent sth out	to receive money from someone for their use of your property
to run sb/sth down	to criticise someone or something, often unfairly
to run on sth	if a machine runs on a supply of power, it uses that power to work
to rush into sth	to start doing something without thinking about it enough first
to scare sb/sth away/off	to make someone or an animal so frightened that they go away or decide not to do something

multi-word verb	definition
to screw up sth	to twist a part of the body, often the face
to scroll up / down	to move text or picture on a computer screen to view different parts of a page
to see sth through	to continue until something is finished
to set sb/sth back	to make something happen more slowly or later than it should
to settle down	to start living in a place where you intend to stay for a long time, often with a partner
to settle in	to begin to feel relaxed and happy in a new home or job
to shake sb up	to make someone feel disturbed or frightened
to shake sth up	to cause large changes in something
to sign in	to enter your details into a website in order to use it
to sink in	to slowly become understood or known
to slip away	to pass quietly
to slow (sb/sth) down	to go or happen more slowly, or to make someone or something slower
to speed (sth) up	to go or happen faster, or to cause something to happen faster
to stand up to sb/sth	to defend yourself against a powerful person or organisation when they treat you unfairly
to start out	to begin your life, or a certain part of it, in a particular way
to stay away from sb/sth	to avoid someone or something
to stay on	to continue to be in a place, job or school after other people have left
to stem from sth	to develop as the result of something
to store sth up	to remember something, usually so that you can make use of it later
to strike sth up (with sb)	to create or establish a relationship or conversation with someone
to suck up to sb	to try to make someone in authority approve of you by doing and saying things that will please them
to switch sth on/off	to stop or start a device powered by electricity
to take sth on	to accept a particular job or responsibility
to take to sb/sth	to start to like someone or something
to take over sth	to get control of something, or to do something instead of someone else
to tear sth up	to tear paper into a lot of small pieces
to tense up	to become nervous and unable to relax
to think sth up	to produce a new idea or plan
to thrash sth out	to discuss a problem in detail until you reach an agreement or find a solution
to throw yourself into sth	to start doing something with a lot of enthusiasm and energy
to toughen sb up	to make somebody stronger
to waste away	to gradually get thinner and weaker, in a way that is unhealthy
to work sth off	to work in order to pay back a debt

MULTI-WORD VERBS USED IN THEMES

Relationships

1 Choose the correct option in *italics* to complete the sentences.

1 We've been best friends for years. Nothing will ever come *up* / *between* / *over* us.

2 He's really sucking up *with* / *on* / *to* the boss. He wants a promotion.

3 I struck *on* / *off* / *up* a conversation with someone at the bus stop and we learned we had lots in common.

4 We got stuck in a lift and that really brought us *up* / *down* / *together*.

5 I haven't heard *of* / *from* / *between* my sister in ages. I'll give her a call.

6 My aunt's ill. She really depends *on* / *with* / *from* her husband for help and support.

Personality

2 Complete the sentences with a particle or preposition.

1 Dave is still upset after Sarah shouted at him. He really needs to toughen ....

2 She's always come .... as a cheerful person.

3 This company prides itself .... producing the best widgets in the country.

4 I was struggling to hold .... the tears at the end of that film. It was so sad!

5 The accident has really shaken her .... She swears she will never drive again.

6 No, I just don't feel .... to it at the moment. I haven't got over my cold yet.

Work

3 Complete the sentences with the words in the box below.

hand in	take over	get off
be passed over	knuckle down	see through

1 What I'm most upset about isn't her getting the job but my .... for promotion once again.

2 Having won the lottery, I've decided to .... my notice and take a year off.

3 There's nothing wrong with hard work. You should .... for a few years and try to build your career.

4 I'm determined to .... this job .... through right till the end.

5 My boss is hoping to retire next year so his son will .... the business.

6 With a bit of luck, I can .... work early tomorrow and meet you for a coffee.

Multi-word verbs with *come*

4 Choose the correct option in *italics* to complete the sentences.

1 Your tennis skills have come *on / up / through* enormously in the last few years. You're a really good player these days.

2 My friend's uncle died last year and he came *onto / into / in for* a lot of money.

3 During the argument, my friend came *through / across / down* badly. She seemed rude and insensitive to others feelings.

4 The President has come *down / in / over* for a lot of criticism in recent years due to his handling of the crisis.

5 My uncle comes *up / out / over* with some amazing inventions. He's so clever.

6 Suddenly, the wild boar came *on / to / at* us, snarling and showing its teeth. We were so scared!

The natural word

5 Complete the sentences with the words in the box below.

on	out	for	over	away	up

1 The Gulf of Finland often freezes ...., making sea travel difficult.

2 The cliffs are being eaten .... by the sea, meaning landslides are common.

3 The owls prey .... small rodents that haven't found shelter by nightfall.

4 The drought has resulted in the lakes and rivers drying .... and water becoming scarce.

5 Once the tide has gone .... we can go to the beach and look for shellfish.

6 The mother leaves her cubs, which now have to fend .... themselves.

Time

6 Complete the sentences with a particle or preposition.

1 I am going to free................................ some time next week so we can have a catch up.

2 While I was away, a lot of news just passed me .... What's happened?

3 I need to fit .... some time to train next week, but I'm so busy!

4 Let's do this tomorrow. It's getting .... a bit now and we should really go home.

5 Is it summertime already? Time has really slipped .... this year.

6 The holiday seasons creeps .... on me every year. I'm never prepared for it.

Multi-word verbs with *on, off, up or down*

7 Choose the correct option in *italics* to complete the sentences.

1 Trevor put *on / off / up* 5kg during the winter.

2 Retailers are bumping *on / down / up* the price of goods once again.

3 I want you all to push *off / up / on* this season and aim for promotion.

4 I used to love that restaurant, but recently the quality of the food has really fallen *down / off / in*.

5 It seems the market has reached the bottom and prices are levelling *down / off / up*.

Thinking activities

8 Complete the sentences with the correct form of the verb.

piece	grapple	think	thrash	occur

1 I've been .... with what you were saying in the lecture and I still don't understand it.

2 He's trying to .... up a plan for your birthday.

3 Let's try to .... out a few ideas in this workshop.

4 While I was driving home, it .... to me that I'd forgotten to email my colleague in Japan.

5 With all these clues, the detective was determined to .... everything together and solve the crime.

Money

9 Choose the correct option in *italics* to complete the sentences.

1 It turned out that his company was burning *through / off / away* money without realising it.

2 I'll have to get a job and work *off / on / away* my debts.

3 This car will set you *to / back / over* a cool $100,000.

4 I had run up such a large credit card bill that I had to ask my dad to bail me *away / off / out*.

5 We're looking to relocate, so we'll rent *off / away / out* our flat while we stay with friends.

The body

10 Complete the sentences with a particle or preposition.

1 As the disgusting smell of the bag hit her, she screwed .... her face in disgust.

2 I've been ill and lost a lot of weight. It looks like I'm wasting ....

3 The cat enjoyed nothing more than curling .... on the rug in front of the fire.

4 The crowd of people huddled .... in an attempt to stay warm.

5 My uncle doubled .... with laughter because the joke was so funny.

WRITING PART 1: AN ESSAY

1 Study the Part 1 exam task and answer the questions.

1 How many of the points in the notes do you have to discuss?

2 What do you have to explain about the point(s)?

3 Why are the three opinions given?

4 Do you have to refer to these opinions in your essay?

2 Study the model answer. Which two of the ways in the notes are discussed? Does the writer make use of any of the opinions?

Your class has listened to a discussion about ways that individuals can help the environment. You have made the notes below:

How individuals can help the environment

- shopping
- food
- travel

Some opinions expressed in the discussion:

'Supermarkets use too much plastic.'

'We should eat less meat.'

'Public transport is better than private cars.'

Write **an essay** discussing **two** of the ways in your notes that individuals can help the environment. You should **explain which way you think is more effective, giving reasons** to support your answer. You may, if you wish, make use of the opinions expressed in the discussion, but you should use your own words as far as possible.

MODEL ANSWER

[1]Many people feel that it is only governments and large corporations that can make a difference to the environment. However, I believe that each individual can contribute by changing their habits in small ways. [2]I will explain two ways of doing this and indicate which of them I think would be more effective.

One way we can help the environment is by choosing goods with less packaging. [3]For example, in the supermarket, we should buy fruit and vegetables loose rather than pre-packed. Hopefully businesses will gradually realise that customers do not want unnecessary packaging. Similarly, we could ask the government to change the law so that all packaging must be recyclable. [4]Doing these two things could save millions of trees and reduce pollution in our oceans.

[5]The most effective way of helping our planet would be to switch to plant-based agriculture. Farm animals, especially cows, produce a lot of greenhouse gases and many forests are cut down to provide animals with land for grazing, increasing greenhouse gas levels. Growing food plants instead would actually help to reduce these levels in the atmosphere. It is so easy to cook excellent vegetarian and vegan dishes these days that we no longer need to eat so much meat, and anyone can do it. [4]Moreover, it would be cheaper for shoppers.

[6]In conclusion, as consumers, our choices matter and can be effective in protecting the planet. Using less packaging and consuming less meat would both make a big difference, with [5]the second of the two points being, [7]in my opinion, the more impactful.

[1] Start by introducing the topic.

[2] Clearly state which two options you will talk about.

[3] Give specific examples to support your points.

[4] Give reasons for your ideas/arguments.

[5] Clearly indicate which of the two ideas you think is more effective/beneficial, etc.

[6] Conclude by summarising your points/arguments/ideas.

[7] Use phrases to express your opinion.

3 **Read the Part 1 task and choose the best introduction and conclusion for the essay, A or B.**

Your class has listened to a discussion about how funding should be spent to improve a local park. You have made the notes below:

Ways funding can be spent to improve the local park

- landscaping and design
- an outdoor gym
- a café

Some opinions expressed in the discussion:

'Everyone appreciates a beautiful place to relax.'

'People want to use the park for free exercise.'

'We want to attract more families.'

Write **an essay** discussing **two** of the ways the funding might be spent to improve the local park in your notes. You should **explain which way would be most beneficial to the community, giving reasons** to support your opinion. You may, if you wish, make use of the opinions expressed in the discussion, but you should use your own words as far as possible.

Introductions

A St Charlotte's Park is a place where all members of the community go to relax, exercise and enjoy themselves. In my essay, I would like to discuss two ways of spending money on improvements – landscaping the area and an outdoor gym.

B The park already has a lot of plants, trees and flowers, and it is well-designed. We don't really need to spend any more money on them. That is why the options I choose to discuss are the outdoor gym and the café.

Conclusions

A To sum up, all three of these ways of spending money are good. I suggest we divide the money between all three of them so that everyone is happy and visits the park more often.

B In conclusion, while an outdoor gym would be great for the local community, I prefer the option of spending money on landscaping and planting more trees and flowers as they can be enjoyed by everyone, while also benefiting the environment.

4 **Which two body paragraphs below (A–D) use the structure: topic sentence + one main idea + supporting examples/ arguments/evidence/reasons?**

A It is nice to have a drink or snack when you go to the park. On the other hand, not everyone will use the café every time they visit the park. For that reason, I think it would be better to spend the money on landscaping the area, because the main reason people go to parks is to enjoy nature.

B The next suggestion I wish to discuss is an outdoor gym. In my view, this is the most beneficial of the three options. Firstly, it will last a long time so will be a good investment for the park. Secondly, it will benefit less well-off people who can't afford a gym membership. Thirdly, outdoor gyms, unlike most indoor gyms, can be used by children as well as adults, so it is a healthy activity for the whole family.

C My view is that having a café in the park would be the best idea. It would be enjoyable for friends to meet up and share a coffee while enjoying a natural environment rather than just sitting in a café in town. Although it would cost money to set up, the money could soon be earned back through the sale of drinks and snacks. This money could be used to benefit the park in one of the other ways.

D If you want to have a tea or coffee in the park, you can bring your own from home, which is more economical and environmentally-friendly anyway. Where else can you go to enjoy a beautiful, natural landscape if you live in the city? Not many people have gardens so parks are their only chance to experience nature. Children, in particular, really need to see and learn about trees, plants and flowers.

5 **Study the words and expressions in the *Key language* box.**

KEY LANGUAGE FOR ESSAYS

Expressing your opinion:
in my opinion, in my view, I would say that, personally speaking

Giving reasons for opinions:
this is because, the main reason for this is, due to, because (of)

Giving examples:
one example of this is, for instance, take for example

Sequencing:
first of all, to begin with, secondly, next/then, finally, last but not least

Referring back:
as mentioned earlier, as previously discussed, the former/latter

Referring forward:
This essay will …, in the following paragraphs I will …, the purpose of this essay is to …

6 **Complete the extract by deciding what the function of each gap is and then choosing an appropriate expression from the *Key language* box. Not all the options fit logically or grammatically.**

All of us need to make an effort to stop our planet becoming more damaged. **(1)** .... discuss two ways people might protect the environment. **(2)** .... , I'd like to discuss the possibility of taking fewer flights **(3)** .... , I'll go on to discuss consider the option of reducing meat consumption.

(4) .... , restricting the number of flights people take won't work. **(5)** .... they see that leaders and celebrities are still flying frequently. **(6)** .... is that international political conferences still involve each country's representatives travelling thousands of miles by air.

(7) .... , ordinary citizens will not agree to limit their flights if their leaders will not.
(8) .... , I'd focus on developing fuels for aircraft that are less harmful to the environment.

7 **Use the table to plan your response to the exam task below.**

Your class has watched a documentary on ways to improve road safety in the town where you are studying. You have made the notes below:

How to improve road safety

- speed limits
- car-free zones
- road safety education

Some opinions expressed in the discussion:

'Drivers need to keep to the speed limit.'

'Cars should be banned from shopping areas.'

'Children should learn about road safety at school.'

Write **an essay** discussing **two** of the ways to improve road safety in your notes. You should **explain which way would be most effective, giving reasons** to support your opinion. You may, if you wish, make use of the opinions expressed in the discussion, but you should use your own words as far as possible.

	IDEAS	USEFUL PHRASES
Introduction		
Paragraph 1		
Paragraph 2		
(Paragraph 3 - optional)		
Conclusion		

8 **Write your essay. Write between 220 and 260 words.**

9 **Check your essay and make changes if necessary.**

- Is your essay clearly divided into paragraphs?
- Does your essay start by introducing the topic?
- Does your introduction state which points you're going to discuss?
- Have you discussed two out of the three points in the notes?
- Have you clearly stated which of the two points discussed is more effective?
- Have you given reasons/explanations/examples to justify your ideas?
- Have you written between 220 and 260 words?

WRITING PART 2: AN EMAIL/LETTER

1 Study the Part 2 exam task and answer the questions.

1 Who should you address your letter to?

2 Should you use a formal or informal style?

3 What should you include in your letter?

Due to lack of funding, your local council must spend less money on its regular arts and culture programme next summer. It has asked the public for their views on whether to cancel its music events for teenagers or exhibitions of works by local artists. Write a letter to the council giving your view and suggesting which activity should be saved, and why.

Write your **letter** in reply. You do not need to include postal addresses.

2 Study the model answer. What cultural activity does the writer want to keep and why?

MODEL ANSWER

[1]Dear Sir or Madam,

I was extremely disappointed to hear about the reduction in spending on your arts and culture programme. I personally feel that all the events the council runs are beneficial for members of our community, and ideally, we should save them all. Nevertheless, it is clear that one of the activities you have mentioned will need to be cut and [2]I'm writing to express my opinion on this.

[3]I feel very strongly that the exhibitions by local artists should be preserved. [4]There are several reasons for this. [5]Firstly, the exhibitions are always well attended by people of all ages. School groups usually visit them as well as families with children and the elderly. [5]Secondly, many local artists have launched their careers through these exhibitions and brought fame to our area. [5]Thirdly, the council receives income from the sale of artwork, which partially covers the cost of running the exhibitions.

Although I do not support any loss of cultural activities, I suggest that music events for teenagers are a less valuable use of resources than art exhibitions. [4]That is because they are aimed at a limited group of people. Many older teenagers have already left for college or university, so the events only benefit the 13–17 age group. Moreover, there are a large number of concerts and festivals in neighbouring towns that young people can attend quite easily.

[6]Therefore, I would like to request that you continue to promote local artists by maintaining the art exhibitions.

[7]Yours faithfully,

[1] Begin with a formal salutation.
[2] Make the purpose of your letter clear in the first paragraph.
[3] Clearly state your opinion as required by the task.
[4] Give reasons for your opinion(s).
[5] Use sequencing language when you want to list your points.
[6] End by stating what you want the recipient to do.
[7] Close your letter in a formal way.

3 Read the task. Then choose the five most suitable sentences to include in an answer.

You see this …

Your local library is due to close next year as it is expensive to run. You think the library should remain open. Write an email to your local council in which you give your reasons for wanting to save the library, explaining its importance to the community and suggesting two ways in which it could remain open in the future.

Write your **letter** in reply. You do not need to include postal addresses.

1 I've got to say that the library is absolutely brilliant, with some really cool books.

2 Not only is the library of importance to students, it is also essential for those who do not have computers at home.

3 I am writing with regard to the proposal to close Bexhampton Library.

4 The library shouldn't close because my grandma likes it there very much and uses it all the time.

5 One idea for keeping the library open would be to use volunteers to man the reception.

6 We must keep the library open because everyone agrees that the decision to close the library is completely stupid.

7 In conclusion, the library provides a range of valuable services to the community and should remain open.

8 Another suggestion is to hold regular fund-raising events to cover the cost of new resources.

9 Let's have a bake sale to get some money for books, because everyone loves cakes, right?

4 Match the unsuitable sentences in Exercise 3 to the reasons they are not appropriate.

A The language is too informal for the target audience.

B The statement is too vague and the tone is impolite.

C The reasons given should refer to benefits to the community, not just individuals.

5 **Match the five suitable sentences from Exercise 3 with the paragraphs in the exam task plan.**

Paragraph 1: The purpose of your letter [3]

Paragraph 2: Reasons for saving the library [ ]

Paragraph 3: Ways it could remain open [ ] [ ]

Paragraph 4: Summary [ ]

6 **Are the sentences below more suitable for a formal (F) or informal (I) email/letter?**

1 I think it'd be a brilliant chance for you.
2 Don't forget to let me know how you get on.
3 I would be grateful for the opportunity to be involved with the project.
4 I've been to that park a couple of times.
5 I have travelled widely, which has given me a broader perspective on life.
6 We appreciate the effort you have made on our behalf.
7 Well, actually, I'm pretty good at working with others.
8 Could you provide me with further information on this?

7 **Study the words and expressions in the *Key language* box.**

KEY LANGUAGE FOR INFORMAL EMAILS AND LETTERS

	Formal letters/emails	Informal letters/ emails
Greeting	*Dear Sir/Madam*, (name not known) *Dear Mr/Mrs/Ms* (surname), *To whom it may concern*, (name not known)	*Dear Jilly,* *Hi Brenda,* *Hello Tommy,* *Hey Joe*
Opening	*I am writing to respond to / apply for / complain about / apologise for*	*Thanks for your email.* *How's it going?*
Closing	*I look forward to hearing (back) from you (at your earliest convenience).*	*I'd better end there.* *Write soon / See you soon.*
Goodbye	*Yours faithfully, (after Dear Sir/Madam)* *Yours sincerely*	*All the best,* *Best wishes,* *Love (from),*

8 **Decide if the words/phrases below are more suitable for a formal or informal letter/email and which part of the letter/email you would find it in (opening, closing or goodbye).**

1 Sorry for not writing sooner. informal, opening
2 Please do not hesitate to contact me if there is any other information you require.
3 I've been meaning to write for a while.
4 Let me know as soon as you can.
5 The purpose of this email is to …
6 Regards,
7 Glad to hear that you're enjoying your new job.
8 Hope you are well.
9 Take care of yourself,
10 I hope I have provided you with the information you requested.

9 **Read the exam task and use the table to plan your letter.**

You have received the email below from a friend.

> I'm thinking about doing a short course in photography this summer. I know you did one last year. Would you recommend it for a beginner like me? What features of the course did you find most useful and do you think it was value for money?
>
> Thanks for your help!
>
> Jacob

Write your **email** in reply.

	IDEAS	USEFUL PHRASES
Introduction		
Paragraph 1		
Paragraph 2		
(Paragraph 3 - optional)		
Conclusion		

10 **Write your email. Write between 220 and 260 words.**

11 **Check your email and make changes if necessary.**

- Have you started with an informal salutation?
- Have you referred to Jacob's email?
- Have you clearly stated whether you recommend the course for a beginner?
- Have you described the features that were useful?
- Have you explained whether you think the course was good value for money?
- Have you used appropriately informal language throughout?
- Have you ended the email appropriately?
- Have you used between 220 and 260 words?

WRITING PART 2: A REVIEW

1 Read the exam task. What three points should you include in your review?

A new shopping mall opened in your town recently. You have been asked to write a review of it for a local newspaper, describing what kind of shops and facilities are available. Explain one or two of the features that make the shopping mall special, and suggest any improvements that would make it provide better for the needs of the local community.

Write your **review**.

2 Study the model answer and answer the questions.

1 Does the review cover all the points in the task?

2 How many of the mall's positive aspects does the writer describe?

3 Is the language in the review appropriate for its target audience?

3 Read the exam task and complete the paragraph with the words in the box.

A gaming magazine is asking for reviews of a newly released computer game. You should say how the game compares with similar games you have played, what you liked most about it and how you think it could be improved.

Write your **review**.

as more most much prefer rather unlike wide

In Other Waters is different from any other science-fiction game I have played. **(1)** .... most games, which take place on Earth or in space, this game is played under the ocean. It is a **(2)** .... gentler game than others, allowing you to explore and learn **(3)** .... than simply fight an enemy. Even though it is **(4)** .... educational than many games, *In Other Waters* is just **(5)** .... engaging as others I have played, because you are responsible for the well-being of the main character, Ellery. I feel the game will appeal to a **(6)** .... variety of people because it includes scientific knowledge as well as the usual excitement of gaming. Generally, I **(7)** .... slightly faster-paced games, but this is still one of the **(8)** .... fascinating games I've played.

MODEL ANSWER

[1]Like many other people in Newtown, I was delighted to hear the long-awaited mall would finally be opening. I went along a few weeks after it opened with a group of friends, and we were not disappointed.

Unlike many other shopping centres, the new mall offers more than just shops. The children's play area, cinema, bowling alley and food court make it a place that will appeal particularly to families and teenagers. [2]What makes the mall stand out is its [3]marvellous atmosphere. The music being played is [3]upbeat and the water fountains and plants give it a [3]more natural and calming feel than you might expect. [2]Another special feature is that the food court has an emphasis on healthy eating, with salad and juice bars in addition to the usual fast food outlets. [4]For me, this was a major plus point.

On the flip side, I would like to see a wider variety of shops. At present, the mall only has the typical high street stores selling clothes and shoes. In my view, this is too limited, making it less attractive for shoppers. [2]Currently there are no designer or independent shops selling something a little different. However, there are some vacant shops, so hopefully this will change.

[5]Overall, the Central Mall is a great addition to Newtown, offering entertainment, dining and shopping facilities for the whole family in a relaxing atmosphere. There is some room for improvement in terms of the current lack of variety in shops, but nevertheless, [6]I strongly recommend visiting it.

[1] Start with a general comment on how you know about the product or service.

[2] Make sure your review focuses on the specific aspects outlined in the task.

[3] Use complex descriptive adjectives and phrases.

[4] Make it clear which aspect(s) you liked most.

[5] Finish with a summary of your overall view and recap any main points briefly.

[6] Include a recommendation.

4 **Make the sentences more emphatic by using cleft sentences. Begin each sentence with the word in brackets.**

1 The storyline impressed me most. (It)
It was the storyline that impressed me most.

2 I liked the sound effects best. (What)

3 I was disappointed because I couldn't get to the highest level. (What)

4 The quality of the animation really stands out. (It)

5 The designers went wrong by making the higher levels too difficult. (Where)

5 **Replace the underlined descriptive language in the sentences with the synonyms in the box. The number of possible answers is given in brackets. The synonyms can be used more than once.**

absolutely atrocious, absolutely breathtaking, absolutely extortionate, absolutely riveting, beautifully designed, excessive to say the least, extremely user-friendly, not of a high standard, not up to scratch, totally awesome, shockingly bad, well thought out, utterly gripping

1 The film was very interesting. (2)

2 The photography was really beautiful. (2)

3 The game play was not so good. (2)

4 The website was very easy to navigate. (3)

5 Her portrayal of the heroine, Selena, was very good. (4)

6 The service at the restaurant was really awful. (2)

7 For what you receive, I think the price you pay is extremely high. (2)

6 **Study the words and expressions in the *Key language* box.**

KEY LANGUAGE FOR REVIEWS

Comparing and contrasting:
(not) as + adj + as, although, however, in spite of, on the one/other hand, whereas, unlike

Praising:
what I impressed me most was, it was the (noun) that most stood out for me, one/another of the plus points/benefits/ advantages of this is

Criticising:
one of the main drawbacks is, one area/thing that could be improved is, on the negative side, it is probably not suitable/ appropriate/ideal for, I was a little/extremely disappointed with

Suggesting and recommending:
One area/improvement that could be made is, I would suggest that, I wholeheartedly/highly/strongly recommend, I (strongly) advise against, If I were you, I would avoid/steer clear of this …

7 **Correct the mistakes in the sentences.**

1 Although I enjoyed the film, it was not as good than the other films in the series.

2 What did impress me most was the band's performance in a live context.

3 In spite of the restaurant was crowded, the staff were always very attentive and helpful.

4 It was the scenery that stood out the more.

5 Personally, I strongly advise to not buy the app.

6 If I were you, I avoid this film like the plague.

8 **Read the exam task and use the table to plan your review.**

A travel magazine has asked for reviews from people who have made interesting journeys on public transport in their country. You decide to write about a journey you have made, briefly describing where you went and your reason for choosing public transport. Your review should explain what was interesting about the journey and encourage other people to consider going on journeys by public transport themselves.

Write your **review**.

PARAGRAPHS	IDEAS	USEFUL PHRASES
Introduction (Why you decided to use public transport)		
Where you went and type(s) of transport used		
What was interesting about the journey		
Conclusion (encourage others to use public transport)		

9 **Write your review. Write between 220 and 260 words.**

10 **Check your review and make changes if necessary.**

- Have you explained why you decided to use public transport?
- Have you written about where you went?
- Have you highlighted some interesting aspects of the journey?
- Have you encouraged others to use public transport?
- Is your writing clearly divided into paragraphs?
- Have you used language for comparing, praising, criticising, suggesting and recommending?
- Have you written between 220 and 260 words?

WRITING PART 2: A REPORT

1 Read the exam task. What four points do you need to cover in your report?

Your school recently held a one-day international food festival. You have been asked by the Principal to write a report of the event.

Your report should briefly describe the main activities of the event and explain which were the most popular and why. You should also suggest how the event could be improved and whether or not you would recommend holding the festival again in the future.

Write your **report**.

2 Study the model answer. How many areas for improvement does the writer mention?

3 Read the exam task and choose the best heading for each paragraph.

You worked as an activities organiser in a summer camp for children. The camp director has asked you to write a report about the camp.

In your report you should evaluate the camp, saying which activities the children enjoyed most and which were less popular and why. Make recommendations on how the camp could be improved for next year.

Write your **report**.

Paragraph 1: *Report on the camp / Why I went to camp / Introduction*

Paragraph 2: *Overall evaluation / Children's opinions of the camp / The camp was great*

Paragraph 3: *The activities that were most enjoyed / Most popular activities / So what were the best activities?*

Paragraph 4: *What we should do differently next time / Recommendations / My opinion*

4 Correct the mistakes in the sentences. One of the sentences is correct.

1 Many of children enjoyed the arts and crafts activities.
2 Majority of participants preferred the team games.
3 Only few said they did not enjoy the swimming lessons.
4 Only a small minority of participants felt there was not enough activities.
5 Most children felt they had to do too many chores.
6 A big number of children participated in the summer camp.

MODEL ANSWER

[1]**Introduction**

[2]Broadbridge High School held its first international food festival on May 27th in the school grounds. It was organised by the festival committee, which included students, teachers and an advisor from a local restaurant. There were over 70 different food stalls and more than 650 visitors.

[3]**Main activities**

The main activities included cookery demonstrations and classes, food tastings and a 'bake-off' competition, which [4]most people considered the highlight of the day. Inspired by the popular television show, the bake-off was organised in age categories, giving [4]a large number of students and adults the opportunity to show off their skills. [5]Another favourite was the sushi-making masterclass by Chef Yoshi from Café Tokyo. Participants were fascinated to learn the secrets of this highly artistic Japanese dish.

[3]**Areas to improve**

Visitors [6]expressed the opinion that the variety of drinks available did not match the food and drinking water ran out by 2 p.m. Furthermore, [6]several raised concerns about environmental issues, particularly the use of disposable plates and cutlery.

Conclusion and recommendations

[3]I would definitely recommend holding a similar event next year. Based on the aforementioned problems, I would suggest the following:

[7]1. Install more water coolers and washing facilities so cups can be reused or ask people to bring their own water bottles to refill.

2. Invite stallholders to provide soft drinks, typical of their cuisines.

3. Consider hiring plates and cutlery next year.

[1] Divide your report into sections with headings.
[2] Your introduction should contain factual information about the subject of the report to give context.
[3] Make sure you cover what the task asks you to discuss.
[4] Use a range of quantifiers to report on different people's opinions.
[5] Use phrases of addition to add similar points.
[6] Use reporting verbs to give other people's opinions.
[7] You can use bulleted or numbered lists for the recommendations if you have more than one.

5 **Match the three parts of the sentences to make recommendations with justifications.**

1 It is recommended that …
2 I would strongly suggest …
3 One improvement we could try is to …
4 I would advise …

A against having video games available
B allow the children to use Wi-Fi in the evenings for an hour
C more helpers be hired for the busiest months
D increasing the number of team sports

i in order to prevent arguments about losing contact with their friends.
ii because the camp is meant to promote physical exercise and spending time in nature.
iii as these are the most popular activities.
iv due to the number of children who attend at that time.

6 **Complete the report extract with the linking words and phrases in the box. There are four options you do not need.**

also although because due to in addition on the other hand particularly specially therefore the reason is too

Swimming was the possibly the most popular activity for most of the children who attended the camp. **(1)** ...., a large number of them enjoyed arts and crafts, **(2)** .... making jewellery and many of them **(3)** .... had fun sketching the trees and flowers. Pottery was another popular activity.

(4) ...., the nature walks were reportedly not as enjoyable as in previous years. This seems to be **(5)** .... the length of these walks, which the children felt was excessive. Furthermore, **(6)** .... the children are generally interested in nature, they felt there was too much information given, making it 'like school'. **(7)** ...., it might be a good idea to make the nature walks shorter next time.

7 **Study the words and expressions in the *Key language* box.**

KEY LANGUAGE FOR REPORTS

Adding supporting points/arguments/evidence:
in addition, what is more, moreover, furthermore, added to this is the fact that, another aspect/suggestion/ improvement

Making recommendations:
try + -ing, consider + -ing, I would recommend/suggest/ advise, it is recommended/suggested that, I have no hesitation in recommending, it might be a good idea to

Reporting:
report/feel/consider/state/complain/believe/express the opinion + that

Talking about groups of people:
the (vast) majority, most, a few, several, (about/around) half/ a third/a quarter (of), nearly everyone

8 **Report the data in the questionnaire below using the given verb in brackets and an appropriate quantifier.**

Food Festival Questionnaire

1 Did you attend the event on both days? Yes: 51 No: 49 (say)
About half of the people said they had attended the event on both days
2 Was the event well organised? Yes: 93 No: 7 (feel)
3 Was the event good value for money? Yes: 25 No: 75 (believe)
4 Did you enjoy the event? Yes: 97 No: 3 (say)
5 Was it easy to book online? Yes: 53 No: 47 (report)
6 Was there a good variety of food stalls? Yes: 85 No: 15 (think)

9 **Read the exam task and use the table to plan your report.**

You attended a short course related to one of your hobbies. The course organiser has asked you to write a report on the course.

In your report, you should describe the course, say which aspects of it you found most useful, and make recommendations on how the course could be improved to meet the needs of all the participants.

Write your **report**.

SECTION	IDEAS	USEFUL LANGUAGE
Introduction: description of course		
Useful aspects of course		
Aspects that could be improved		
Conclusion – recommendations		

10 **Write your report. Write between 220 and 260 words.**

11 **Check your report and make changes if necessary.**

- Have you divided your report into sections with appropriate headings?
- Does your introduction explain the context for the report?
- Have you covered the three points in the task?
- Have you used language for recommendations?
- Have you used a formal or neutral tone?
- Have you written between 220 and 260 words?

WRITING PART 2: A PROPOSAL

1 Read the statements about proposals and reports. Decide if they are T (True) or F (False).

1 Proposals and reports usually have similar structures.

2 For both, the target audience is always a superior, such as a teacher or a manager at work.

3 Both may require the candidate to evaluate something and make suggestions.

4 A key difference is that a report focuses on a future event/situation whereas a proposal focuses on a past one.

2 Read the exam task. What three points should you include in your proposal?

> Your town has a swimming pool which closed down a few years ago. You would like to see the pool restored for the people of the town.
>
> Write a proposal to the Town Council, saying why you think the swimming pool should be re-opened, explaining how it would benefit the town, and suggesting ways to cover the costs.
>
> Write your **proposal**.

3 Study the model answer. What benefits from restoring the pool does the writer mention in the proposal?

4 Find five examples of the passive in the proposal.

5 Which sentences can be changed into the passive? Rewrite the sentences you choose.

1 We can reduce costs by using local volunteers.
Costs can be reduced by using local volunteers.

2 The pool was a wonderful place to get fresh air.

3 Local people have requested the reopening of the pool.

4 Local businesses will share the profits from the pool.

5 We should give free swimming lessons to children under the age of ten.

6 Older members of the community will benefit from doing more exercise in a safe environment.

7 We can organise a charity event to raise money for the renovations.

MODEL ANSWER

[1]**Background**

The Black Rock Lido was an important outdoor recreational facility for the town of Chester Bridge. [2]The pool was closed down in 2005 and residents who wish to go swimming now need to travel six miles to the nearest pool in Brightsea. However, a recent survey has shown that the majority of local people would like to see the renovation and reopening of our pool.

Benefits

[3]Swimming is a healthy activity for people of all ages. It is also important for all adults and children to have this vital life skill for their own safety. The pool was a wonderful place to get fresh air and spend time with friends and family. Those who don't have cars will find it particularly useful, as public transport to Brightsea is quite infrequent.

The cost of the pool

[4]I suggest that half the cost of the redevelopment of the pool should be paid by the Town Council, with the rest of the money coming from fundraising activities. [4]To oversee this, a committee should be appointed which should include representatives from the Town Council as well as members of the public. [2]Local businesses can be asked for contributions in exchange for a share of the profits that the pool will make in the future, or can be invited to advertise there.

Conclusion

[5]The reopening of the Black Rock Lido will bring enormous benefits to local residents, who would no longer need to travel to Brightsea for a swim. The costs should be met by the Town Council, fundraising with local businesses.

[1] Divide your proposal into sections with appropriate headings that summarise the section content.
[2] Use the passive where appropriate to give a more formal, objective style.
[3] In the 'body' paragraphs, address the three aspects you are asked to discuss in the task.
[4] Use language of suggestion and persuasion.
[5] Don't include new ideas in the conclusion. Use it to sum up the ideas already presented.

6 **Read the task. Then choose the four most suitable sentences to include in the proposal.**

> Your school library has a large number of unused books. You don't want them to go to waste.
>
> Write a proposal to your school principal, suggesting what could be done with the books. Give reasons for your proposed course of action, suggesting how it would benefit the school. Provide practical suggestions as to how it could be achieved.
>
> Write your **proposal**.

1 As we all know, the school library moved to its present location in 2010, because the book collection had grown too large for the original site.

2 The books need to be delivered to the charity's headquarters, which parents and teachers have volunteered to do.

3 The school will gain good publicity from the event, which we will share on our website, social media and the local newspaper.

4 Most of our classes now use e-books, which is much easier for students as they no longer have to carry heavy text books around.

5 The charity we are donating to, Books for Friends, was established in 1989 by Linda Warren, a former politician and government minister who spent a lot of time working with poorer communities.

6 Books which are out of date can still be used by children who may not have access to any books at all.

7 Library staff have identified a total of 364 books which are soon to be removed from circulation.

8 Our school library has spent a similar amount on resources in the last five years, but a higher proportion is now spent on e-books.

7 **Study the words and expressions in the *Key language* box.**

KEY LANGUAGE FOR PROPOSALS

Making suggestions:
I suggest/propose/recommend (that), it would be advisable to, one idea/suggestion/possibility would be to, it's worth considering, one option might be to

Justifying/explaining:
the reason/rationale, justification for this is, for this reason, on the grounds that, with the purpose of, due to

Discussing consequences:
as a result, this would allow us to, the benefit of this would be, this will/would result in, if we do not, the consequences will/could/may be, the problem with this is

Concluding/summarising:
in summary/conclusion, to sum up, overall

8 **Complete the proposal extracts with one word in each space.**

Donation to charity

At present we have a large number of books which are no longer used by pupils. The student's association feels that they are going to waste and we **(1)** .... donating these books to a local charity on the **(2)** .... that they could still be put to good use.

Organising the donation

(3) .... idea would be to ask students and staff for donations of their own to increase the overall total. We **(4)** .... bring them to school and deliver them to the charity all together. What is **(5)** ...., it will benefit the school if we take photos of the event and send them to the local newspapers. This will **(6)** .... in good publicity for the school. We **(7)** .... even feature the event on the school's website for extra publicity.

9 **Read the exam task and use the table to plan your proposal.**

> You belong to a sports club and would like to propose the introduction of more sports and activities.
>
> Write a proposal for the club manager, explaining why you feel change is needed. Suggest which sports and activities should be added, explaining how they will benefit the members and the club in general.
>
> Write your **proposal**.

SECTION	IDEAS	USEFUL LANGUAGE
Introduction –purpose of the proposal		
Why change is needed		
Proposed sports		
Benefits		
Conclusion		

10 **Write your proposal. Write between 220 and 260 words.**

11 **Check your proposal and make changes if necessary.**

- Have you used headings to organise your answer?
- Does your introduction explain the context for the proposal?
- Have you covered the three points in the task?
- Have you used language for recommendations?
- Have you divided your proposal into sections with appropriate headings?
- Have you used a formal or neutral tone?
- Have I written between 220 and 260 words?

WRITING CHECKLISTS

Remember how the writing paper is assessed. Examiners consider the following four things when marking the writing paper:

Content Have you done what the task asked you to do and have you included all the important information?

Communicative achievement Is the writing appropriate for the task? Have you used the right style for what you're trying to communicate? Have you achieved the purpose of the task?

Organisation Is the text put together in a logical and ordered manner and are ideas clearly connected?

Language Is a good range of vocabulary and grammar used, is it used accurately and is it free of any mistakes that would prevent the reader from understanding the text?

PART 1 – ESSAY

- Is your essay clearly divided into paragraphs?
- Does your essay start by introducing the topic?
- Does your introduction state which points you're going to discuss?
- Have you discussed two out of the three points in the notes?
- Have you clearly stated which of the two points discussed is more effective?
- Have you given reasons/explanations/examples to justify your ideas?
- Have you written between 220 and 260 words?

PART 2 – AN EMAIL / LETTER

- Have you started with a suitable salutation?
- If responding to a letter/email, have you referred back to it?
- Have you provided a response to the task?
- Have you used appropriate language throughout?
- Have you used paragraphs to structure your argument?
- Have you ended the letter/email appropriately?
- Have you used between 220 and 260 words?

PART 2 – A REPORT

- Have you divided your report into sections with appropriate headings?
- Does your introduction explain the context for the report?
- Have you covered the three points in the task?
- Have you used language for recommendations?
- Have you used a formal or neutral tone?
- Have you written between 220 and 260 words?

PART 2 – A REVIEW

- Have you covered all the points in the task?
- Have you provided a clear explanation?
- Have you given your own opinion clearly?
- Have you used an appropriate style and register?
- Is your writing clearly divided into paragraphs?
- Have you used language for comparing, praising, criticising, suggesting and recommending?
- Have you written between 220 and 260 words?

PART 2 – A PROPOSAL

- Have you divided your proposal into sections with appropriate headings?
- Does your introduction explain the context for the proposal?
- Have you covered all the required points in the task?
- Have you used language for recommendations?
- Have you used a formal or neutral tone?
- Have you written between 220 and 260 words?

SPEAKING PART 1

1 **Which two of the Speaking Part 1 statements below are false?**

1 The aim of Part 1 is to help you feel comfortable.
2 You will discuss some personal questions with your partner.
3 The first few questions will be about the most familiar topics.
4 Questions may ask about the past, present or future.
5 Topics may include free time, work and study, travel, technology, people in your life and special occasions.
6 All the questions a candidate is asked will be on one topic.

2 **Read and listen to Julia's answers to some Part 1 questions.**
55 **Match the examiner's three questions with the ways Julia responds to them (1–5 below). The questions can be used more than once.**

1 She looks at the question from different perspectives.
2 She gives two answers to the question.
3 She cannot remember a word and uses paraphrase to explain it.
4 She takes her time before answering.
5 She asks for the question to be repeated.

3 **Match the Part 1 questions to the topics.**

1 What do you like most about the place where you live now?
2 Who has been the most important influence on you?
3 What kind of jobs do you think you would be good at?
4 Do you prefer to read or listen to the news?
5 Do you ever wish you lived in a different part of the world?
6 What do you enjoy most about learning English?
7 What was the best trip you have ever taken?
8 How much time do you spend on social media?
9 Do all your friends have the same interests as you?
10 What is the next important event you plan to celebrate?

a future plans and hypothetical situations
b free time
c people and relationships
d travel and holiday experiences
e house and home
f work and studies

MODEL ANSWER

Examiner: What is the next event you plan to celebrate?

Julia: [1]Sorry, I didn't quite catch that.

Examiner: What is the next event you plan to celebrate?

Julia: [2]Well, actually, it's my 18th birthday next week! It is quite a big deal here since you are considered an adult once you're 18. I'm not much of a party person, so it's going to be quite a low-key celebration with my family and a few close friends, but the best thing is my parents are paying for driving lessons! I'll have to borrow their car at first, but I plan to buy my own car when I pass my driving test. [3]I can't wait.

Examiner: What do you enjoy most about learning English?

Julia: [4]Mm, let me see … I haven't really thought about it before. I suppose I like being able to translate things for my family and friends and also help out English-speaking tourists who visit my hometown. Most of them really appreciate finding someone who can explain things to them in their own language. [5]What else? Well, I guess I enjoy it because compared to other subjects, it really challenges me.

Examiner: Do you ever wish you lived in a different part of the world?

Julia: I don't know. I mean, on the one hand, I really like where I come from; there are many positives about living there, but on the other hand I like the idea of living somewhere warmer – [6]say, for example, Latin America maybe, near the beach, somewhere, [7]you know, … what's the word, er …, with less people and technology. I'd want to take my family with me, though, and I'm not sure they'd want to go. And I'd also need to learn Spanish first.

[1] Politely ask the examiner to repeat the question if necessary.
[2] Try to give extended answers in full sentences.
[3] Include your personal feelings and opinions where appropriate.
[4] Use phrases to give yourself time to think of a good answer if necessary.
[5] Extend your answers where possible.
[6] Support ideas with examples.
[7] If you can't think of a word, use paraphrase.

4 Listen to four candidates answering Part 1 questions. Complete the phrases with the words you hear. Which question from Exercise 3 is each candidate answering?

1 Well, **(1)** .... it's my great grandmother. Not many people are lucky enough to know their grandmother's mother. **(2)** .... I admire her is that she's lived through so much, including becoming a widow when she was in her 20s, and still managed to raise and provide for her family, all on her own. She has such strength of character. She's had a hard life but keeps on smiling.

2 Not very much **(3)** .... It's a bit of a waste of time, **(4)** .... , especially when you're very busy like I am. **(5)** .... I actually live really close to most of my friends, so I prefer to meet up with them in person. I do have an Instagram account, though, and I occasionally share photos, but not on a regular basis.

3 I'm sorry **(6)** .... ? I think I'd be good at any kind of work with people and I love travelling, so maybe a tour guide or travel agent, something like that. **(7)** .... , I'd like to use my languages in my job if possible because I've spent many years studying them.

4 Well, **(8)** .... I guess I'd have to say my favourite place was Budapest. You see, I'm an architecture student and there were so many beautiful buildings to see. I went with a group of fellow students and we enjoyed the nightlife too. One night we took a party cruise on the Danube and it was unforgettable.

5 Complete the table with the phrases from Exercise 4.

Asking for repetition	Sorry, I didn't catch that. Could you say that again, please? 1 ....
Buying time	Let me think about that for a second. I've never thought about that before. 2 ....
Adding additional information	What is more … In addition … 3 .... 4 ....
Explaining	This is because … 5 ....
Giving opinions	6 .... 7 .... 8 ....

6 Read and listen to a student's answer to one of the questions in Exercise 3. What words does he use instead of the highlighted ones? Which version would score higher in the exam and why?

Well, yes and no. For example, I **(1)** like reading while they **(2)** like sports a lot, especially team sports. Actually, the only sport we **(3)** all like is swimming. **(4)** It's good because we have **(5)** a big pool in our town, and we often hang out there at the weekend. We do all **(6)** like the same kind of music, though. In fact, some of us play music together. Usually we **(7)** play the songs of our favourite groups. If I am honest, we are not very **(8)** good, but we enjoy it and that's all that matters.

7 Listen to some students using paraphrase. Which word in the box are they describing?

commuters   cruise   great-uncle   horror films
leap year   manual work

1 ....

2 ....

3 ....

4 ....

5 ....

6 ....

8 How could you use paraphrase to express the words below?

1 package tour

2 sister-in-law

3 camel

4 role model

5 groom

6 internet troll

9 Practise answering the Part 1 questions in Exercise 3. Use the tips, strategies and useful language from this section. Record yourself and listen to your answers if possible. How could they be improved?

SPEAKING PART 2

1 **Read the statements about Speaking Part 2 and choose the correct options.**

1 Candidates are given *two* / *three* photos on a connected topic, and have to choose *one* / *two* to talk about.

2 There *is one* / *are two* part(s) to the examiner's question about the photos and candidates have *one minute* / *two minutes* to answer.

3 The focus is on *describing* / *comparing* and speculating about the photos, in relation to the examiner's question.

4 The other candidate will talk about *the same* / *a different* set of photos when they do the task.

5 Each candidate also answers *one* / *two* question(s) about their partner's photos.

2 **Read the tips and tick (✓) the tips that are correct and cross (✗) those which are bad advice?**

1 It's helpful to begin your one-minute turn by indicating which photos you are going to talk about.
2 Make sure you answer both parts of the examiner's question in the time given.
3 If you run out of things to say, talk about the photo that you didn't choose initially.
4 You can also ask your partner's opinions about the photos.
5 When your partner is doing the photo task, listen carefully to their answer to help you prepare to answer a question on it.
6 It's a good idea to practise this task at home with a timer, so that you get comfortable with talking for one minute.

3 59 **Listen to the examiner giving instructions for the one-minute task and answer the questions.**

1 What topic connects the three photos?

2 What two questions do you have to answer?

4 **Read and listen to the model answer. Does Daniel manage to answer both questions in full in one minute?**

MODEL ANSWER

[1]I'd like to talk about the first and third pictures. The first picture shows a potter with his wheel, making a pot from clay. [2]Although it could be his hobby, I think it is more likely that it's his job because [3]he looks like an expert, his pot is pretty professional-looking, and I would guess that he's working in his own studio. [4]In contrast, the child in the third picture looks as if she is making a card with her father. [3]It could be something for her mother's birthday or Mother's Day, something like that, or possibly she just enjoys being creative. [2]As for how they are feeling, both of them seem to be concentrating hard and are totally focused on what they are doing, and I would imagine that, as a result, [4]both are very content, enjoying the way they can express themselves through their work. Whether you are making something as a hobby or a job, [5]it can be a very rewarding experience.

[1] Tell the examiner which pictures you are going to talk about.

[2] Answer both questions in the task.

[3] Speculate about what you see in the photos in relation to the questions.

[4] Draw comparisons and contrasts between the photos where relevant.

[5] Express your opinions where relevant.

5 **Listen to Mariana doing the same task. Complete the gaps with the words you hear.**

I'm going to talk about the first and second photos. Both photos **(1)** .... show people making things as part of their jobs. **(2)** .... the man in the first photo is making something by hand, the men in the other photo **(3)** .... they are making cars in a factory. The potter **(4)** .... self-employed. **(5)** .... he has a workshop at home, but in any case, I would imagine he works independently. The factory workers, **(6)** ...., are part of an automated process. I would speculate that they feel quite differently about their work. The craftsman is **(7)** .... more satisfied as he is making something unique and using his creativity. **(8)** ...., the factory workers have to follow the employer's design and can't use their own ideas. I **(9)** .... they find their work more tiring and less enjoyable, but I might be wrong.

6 **Correct the mistakes in the sentences.**

1 The lady in the photo seems enjoying what she is doing.

2 It looks though they are playing some sort of game.

3 There is possibility that he is doing this as a job.

4 In photo one, they are eating in a restaurant. In photo two, whereas, they are having a picnic outside.

5 The child in the photo looks like very happy.

6 I'm expecting that the people in both photos are feeling excited.

7 The man is making something that looks a boat.

8 I think the lady in this photo is not so happy like the man in that photo.

9 I would say that they both are feeling tired.

10 The activity in this photo is more dangerous that the one in the other photo.

7 **Listen to four students complete the task on the next page. Match each speaker (1–4) with the mistake they make (A–D).**

A answers only one of the questions

B spends too much time on one of the photos

C talks about both photos but doesn't compare and contrast them

D doesn't use language of speculation

- Why might these people have chosen to join a club?
- What might they enjoy about being a member of their club?

8 **Listen to an examiner ask Lola a question about her partner's photos and her response. Does she give a clear answer and provide reasons for her opinion?**

63

9 **Read the task and look at the photographs. Complete the task in pairs and then swap roles. Then listen to the model answer and compare your answers.**

64

Examiner: Student one, here are your pictures. They show people helping others. I'd like you to compare two of the pictures, and say why the people might be helping others in these situations, and how beneficial their help is to those they're helping.

Student two, in which picture do you think the help being given is most important?

SPEAKING PART 3

1 Read the statements about Speaking Part 3 and choose the correct options.

1 First, you and your partner are given a hypothetical situation *orally* / *in print format* with a question related to various options.

2 You have *15* / *30* seconds to read through the task before you begin speaking.

3 After *two* / *three* minutes, the examiner will interrupt and ask another question.

4 You then have a further *minute* / *two minutes* to discuss this second question.

5 This second question usually asks you to negotiate and agree on something which *is unrelated to* / *follows on logically from* the first.

6 Part 3 is an interactive discussion between the *two candidates* / *two candidates and the examiner.*

7 You *will* / *won't* be penalised if you disagree with your partner.

2 Read the Part 3 exam task. What question do you have to discuss? How many prompts are there for you to discuss in relation to the question?

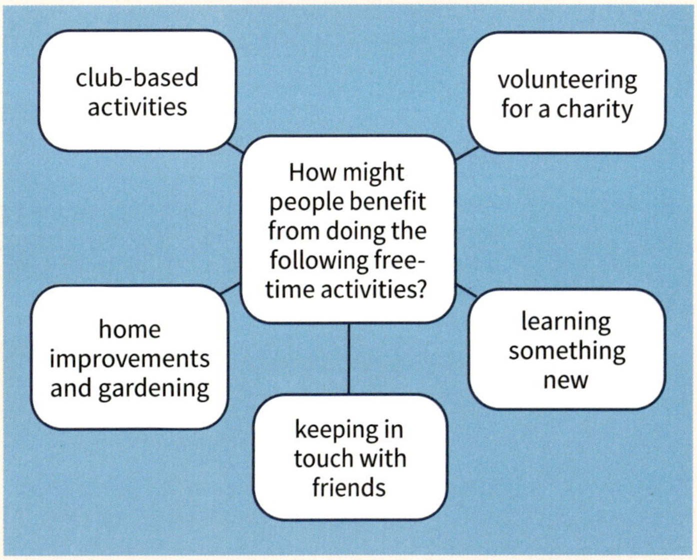

3 Read and listen to the model answer. Do they manage to discuss all the prompts before the examiner interrupts them? 65

MODEL ANSWER

Naomi: OK, where shall we start? What about volunteering for a charity? [1]How might people benefit from doing that, do you think?

Gabriel: Well, I suppose [2]it might make them feel good, you know, to be doing something helpful for the community or a particular cause. What do you reckon, Naomi?

Naomi: [5]Yes, I'd go along with that. In addition, doing volunteer work can also be useful as a way of getting a paid job later on. It looks good on university applications, too. [3]Shall we move on?

Gabriel: Yes, let's talk about learning something new. [1]What do you think about learning something new?

Naomi: Well, it depends what it is, [4]doesn't it? We all benefit in different ways from learning different things.

Gabriel: [5]Of course. I'm learning to drive at the moment and if I pass my test, I won't have to wait for the bus in the rain anymore!

Naomi: Oh, good luck with that! But I was thinking of other benefits. It keeps your brain active, for one thing.

Gabriel: Which is important for everyone. What about club-based activities?

Naomi: Well, again, I'd say it depends on what kind of club but generally, you get to meet like-minded people and share ideas about whatever it is you're all interested in.

Gabriel: Yes, [6]and for younger people, like voluntary work, being a member of a club can look good on your CV, especially if you hold a position of responsibility.

Naomi: [5]Yes, I suppose that's true. [3]Let's talk about home improvements and gardening. Obviously, the main benefit is living in a nice house and looking at a beautiful garden. Would you agree?

Gabriel: [5]Well, only to a limited extent. Where I come from, having a nice garden is more about showing off to the neighbours. Personally, I have never really understood that or why people care so much about their gardens. But I guess it makes them happy, right?

Examiner: Thank you.

[1] Ask your partner's opinion.
[2] Use language of speculation where appropriate.
[3] Move the discussion on and keep it on track.
[4] Use question tags to ask for agreement or to confirm things.
[5] Use a variety of ways to show agreement, disagreement or partial agreement.
[6] Support ideas with examples.

4 **Read the first question of another Part 3 task. Listen to Oliver and Ruby doing the task. Who:**

1 disagrees impolitely?
2 doesn't directly invite their partner to speak?
3 doesn't really give reasons for their opinions?

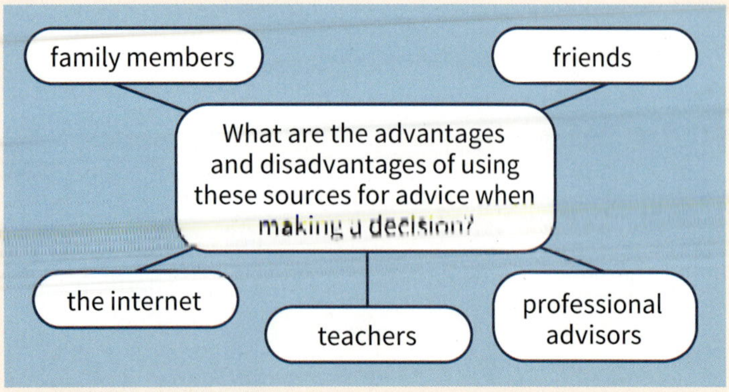

5 **Read the second question for the same task. Listen to two pairs of students (A and B) answer the question. Do they reach an agreement?**

'You now have a minute to decide which two of the sources of advice are likely to be the most useful.'

Pair A: .... **Pair B:** ....

6 **Choose the correct options to complete the sentences. Tick (✓) the sentences if both options are possible.**

1 *I'm not / I don't* agree about that.
2 I agree to *some / a certain* extent.
3 *Let us / Let's* move on to the next option.
4 I think we'll have to *disagree / agree to disagree / agree* on that.
5 *Would / Shall* we move onto the next one?
6 I suggest to *choose / choosing* this one.
7 You're *absolutely / truly* right about that.
8 I don't think that's true *in all / at all*.
9 Would you go *along / in* with that?
10 I don't think that is *necessarily / definitely* the case.

7 **Read the first part of the Part 3 exam task and the conversation. Complete the gaps with a single word.**

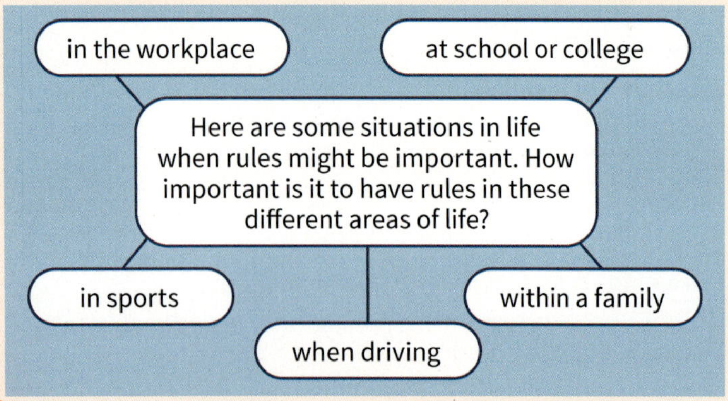

Ella: Right, shall we start with school and college?

Davide: OK, well, I **(1)** .... say rules are essential in school and college even though most students don't like them. **(2)** .... take talking in lessons, for instance. No one will be able to learn if there are no rules about that.

Ella: **(3)** .... , but some rules are quite unnecessary, aren't they? I mean, at my school, our socks had to be white and no other colour. What's the point of that?

Davide: I can see your **(4)** .... , but sometimes at school it is about learning to follow rules so you can avoid trouble in the future.

Ella: I **(5)** .... so, but what about in the family? If there are rules everywhere else, shouldn't we have freedom when we're at home?

Davide: Well, we do have more freedom, but there still have to be some rules, **(6)** .... there? I'm glad that there is a rule in our family that you mustn't borrow something without asking or I'd be losing my stuff all the time.

Ella: Well, possibly but in my **(7)** .... opinion, you should be able to do what you like in your own home. Now, driving, on the other hand, you really need a lot of rules and they need to be enforced.

Davide: Well, that's something we can **(8)** .... on. Without them, people could get hurt. How about sports?

Ella: In sports, it's about fairness, isn't it? But, still, I think professional sport goes **(9)** .... too far. The rules can be so detailed that nobody really understands them. For example, VAR in football is really controversial. Do we need that level of detail in following the rules?

Davide: Mm, I'm in two **(10)** .... about that. I agree that the rules can be complicated, but the stakes are high in professional sport, so maybe the detail is necessary. It can be the difference between being winning and losing …

8 **Read the Part 3 task below and practise doing both sections with a partner. Then listen to the model answer and compare your answers.**

'Here are some decisions people often have to make and a question for you to discuss. Now you have about one minute to say for which of the things it is most important to make the right decisions.'

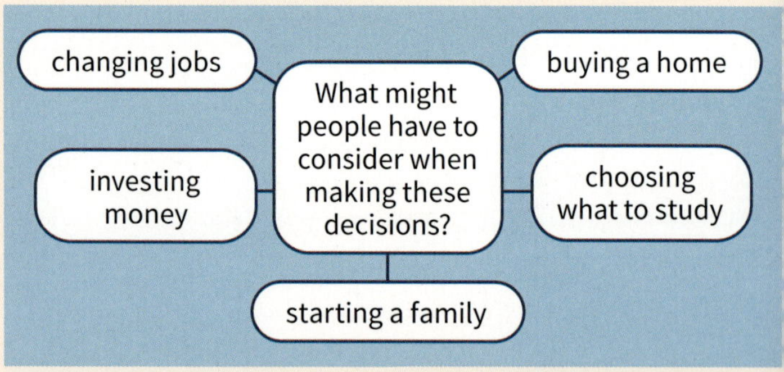

SPEAKING PART 4

1 Read the statements about Speaking Part 4 and choose the correct options.

1 Part 4 lasts for *three* / *five* minutes.

2 Part 4 questions *follow on from* / *are not related to* the Part 3 task.

3 Part 4 gives candidates the opportunity to discuss more *personal* / *abstract* topics.

4 Candidates get the opportunity to explain their ideas in *more* / *less* depth than other parts of the test.

5 Part 4 tests a candidate's ability to exchange information, express and justify opinions and *negotiate* / *speculate*.

6 You are evaluated on your *language and opinions* / *language only*.

2 Complete the tips about Part 4 with the words from the box.

fine interrupt preparation reply topics

Tips for Part 4:

1 Prepare for this part by reading about many .... and getting a friend to ask you questions.

2 It is .... to ask for clarification if you need it.

3 Use expressions to express opinions, agree and disagree and gain .... time.

4 Don't .... your partner. Let the examiner control the discussion.

5 Listen to your partner and .... to his or her points politely.

3 Read and listen to Tom and Maya discussing some Part 4 questions. Do they comment on each other's ideas? (69)

MODEL ANSWER

Examiner: Tom, how important is it for people to have enough leisure time?

Tom: Oh, [3]it's absolutely vital. [1]Why I say that is that people who work too hard can have a lot of problems with their physical and mental health. [2]Not only that, but most people get more enjoyment and happiness from family, friends and activities outside work than from their jobs.

Examiner: What do you think, Maya?

Maya: Well, to be honest, I'm not sure I agree with Tom. I mean, yes, we all need to take time off sometimes, but for some people, their job is what they love doing anyway, so they don't need to spend time on separate hobbies or whatever.

Examiner: Maya, what kind of problems may be caused by people not having enough leisure time?

Maya: Well, I would say health problems, primarily. Both physical problems like high blood pressure and heart issues and mental problems like stress.

Examiner: Do you agree, Tom?

Tom: [3]Definitely. Maya has already mentioned mental and physical problems that can result from overwork and another thing is many jobs involve sitting down all day. If people don't get out in the fresh air and get some exercise, they can have all kinds of difficulties with their health. [2]And also, if they don't spend enough time with their family, it can cause problems with relationships.

Examiner: Maya, what do you think is a good work-life balance?

Maya: Well, I suppose most people would say of the 24 hours in the day, we should spend about eight hours asleep, eight hours working and the remaining eight hours doing other activities, including leisure activities. I would agree that would be the ideal, but it doesn't always work out that way.

Examiner: What do you think, Tom?

Tom: [4]I think it depends on what stage of life you're at. [5]What I mean is when you're young and trying to build up your career, you need to spend more time at work. Then when you start a family, you need to devote time to your partner and children. [6]But as a basic rule, perhaps Maya's suggestion is a good one.

[1] Give reasons and explanations for your answers.
[2] If possible, give more than one reason.
[3] Use a range of phrases to express agreement or disagreement.
[4] Where appropriate answer the question from different perspectives.
[5] Use phrases to clarify your opinions/ideas.
[6] Make generalisations where appropriate.

4 Listen to three other pairs answering Part 4 questions.
70 Match the pairs (1–3) to the bad exam technique mistakes they exemplify.

A not interacting with the other candidate appropriately

B not extending answers sufficiently

C going off topic

5 Listen to Fabio and Leah answering some Part 4 questions.
71 Complete their answers with the expressions you hear.

Examiner: Fabio, some people say you should use your head, not your heart, to make decisions. What do you think?

Fabio: **(1)** ...., I would say it's better to make important decisions with your head. That means you need to think about whether something is practical or not, rather than just considering what you feel like doing. **(2)** ...., I tend to use common sense when I have to decide about something. But, **(3)** .... When it comes to love and getting married, for example, you obviously need to be guided by your heart more than your head.

Examiner: What about you, Leah?

Leah: Well, **(4)** ...., I am a person who tends to go with my heart rather than my head. For example, I'm quite spontaneous and take a lot of risks. **(5)** ...., my heart makes good decisions, which is probably why I continue to do things this way, but **(6)** ....

Examiner: Leah, do you think it is important to get your family's approval when making a decision?

Leah: **(7)** ...., I would say yes. Things will be much easier if you have your family on your side. They'll be more likely to support and help you if they approve of what you're doing. So, yes, it is important but **(8)** .... I don't think you should give up your dreams if others don't agree with them.

Examiner: Do you agree, Fabio?

Fabio: Well, yes, **(9)** ...., I agree with Leah. Most of the time I try to convince my family that what I want to do is a good idea. I do value their support, but **(10)** .... when you need to do something they are not really on board with. Hopefully, they will come around to your way of thinking later.

6 Complete the table with the expressions from Exercise 5.

Generalising	Making exceptions

7 Use the expressions from Exercise 6 to make generalisations on the topics. Then add an exception for each generalisation.

1 People's opinions on climate change

By and large, people would say that banning fossils fuels is vital for protecting the planet, but there are exceptions of course. People who work in the motor industry would say that we still need oil to keep the transport system working . . .

2 Whether video games are good or bad for young people

3 Whether social media has more advantages than disadvantages

4 People's opinions about keeping animals in zoos

5 How interested people are in the lifestyles of celebrities

8 Practise answering these Part 4 questions. Then listen and
72 compare your answers.

1 How important do you think it is for vocational training to be available for young people who need it?

2 Some people say that family matters more than friends. What is your opinion?

3 Do you think parents should limit the amount of time their children spend online?

4 Is it best to make sports compulsory for school students?

Answer key

Unit 1 People like us

Starting off

4

(Suggested answers)

Usually positive: competent, conscientious, considerate, genuine, hilarious, imaginative, open-minded, outgoing, supportive, thoughtful, well-organised

Usually negative: chaotic, insecure, insensitive, naïve, self-centred

Could be either: idealistic, protective, unconventional

Listening Part 4

3/4

1 E 2 C 3 H 4 D 5 F 6 C 7 G 8 D 9 H 10 E

Track 02

1 I can't recall exactly when Bella and I became friends, but once we'd met, we quickly discovered we had more in common than living in the same building. I bumped into her after locking myself out of our apartment block one night. Bella was coming home with a friend, and, seeing my distress, produced a key for the main entrance – until then we'd never seen each other. Things just went from there. Now she's as dear to me as a family member. She's always been quick to forgive when I've let her down, which helped me grasp why you should put up with stuff rather than taking offence and dwelling on it. After all, everyone can make mistakes!

2 I met Caleb on a college course, but we hadn't really talked until we ran into each other at an exhibition. I'd reluctantly promised a friend I'd accompany her – and it turned out Caleb had made a similar promise to someone that he also couldn't get out of. We got chatting – and hit it off! Since then, I've come to realise the strength of our friendship lies in things which we've done together. Having memories like that are a vital part of connecting with someone. We've had our ups and downs, too, over the years, and fallen out. But I've begun to see that disagreements aren't as nearly as significant as the good times we've had.

3 Amara's actually a friend of my cousin, although weirdly, that's not why we became friends. We'd meet occasionally at parties but had different friendship groups, so I never imagined we'd be best friends – for one thing, she didn't seem the kind of person I'd normally hang out with. I couldn't have been more wrong! Since then, I've stopped making such hasty judgements! Anyway, one evening I went to the theatre, to watch a comedian who told some absolutely hilarious stories. During the interval I ran into Amara – it turned out we'd had the same opinion of him. And that's how it all started! After that we met up – and spent the evening giggling over those stories again!

4 I'd known Nigel for years. We'd done the same course at uni, but had never really hung out. Then I happened to attend a conference he was at – and discovered he was just as passionate about nature conservation as I was, so we got chatting! That turned out to be a great foundation for a friendship, and one I've really valued. Our friendship almost fell apart, though, when he bought a jacket for an important occasion, and asked my opinion – so I told him exactly what I thought, expecting he'd be OK if it came from me. How wrong could I be? Anyway, I remembered never to do that again, for the sake of our friendship!

5 I'd always hoped my friendship with Marta would last – and it has. A lot's happened to us individually since we first met, though, and I've come to realise that our friendship wouldn't have survived if we hadn't adjusted to the effects that various life events had on each of us. Anyway, we met when a colleague put on a fancy dress party with a bizarre theme. Nobody was entirely sure who invited Marta, but the costume she was wearing was so astonishing that I simply had to ask her about it – and we took to each other immediately. It turned out we knew several of the same people, too, so we had lots to talk about!

5

1 G 2 F 3 E 4 A 5 C 6 H 7 B 8 D

6

1 fell apart 2 put up with 3 dwell on 4 bumped into 5 hit it off 6 take to

Grammar

Verb forms to talk about the past

1

1 E 2 A 3 D 4 C 5 F 6 B

2

1 has been working, left
2 has been studying, hasn't gone/been
3 came, started, was making/made, continued
4 had, had been working / had worked, hadn't been wearing / wasn't wearing/hadn't worn
5 grew, belonged / had belonged, have sold

3

1 often used to get 2 never used to bring 3 would always ask 4 used to be 5 built 6 used to know 7 have come 8 have gradually been changing 9 used to go 10 were 11 would look

5

1 have had 2 were 3 was 4 hadn't organised 5 didn't take 6 have been invited 7 have only been living, has lived 8 haven't noticed

Reading and Use of English Part 8

3

1 C 2 D 3 A 4 C 5 B 6 A 7 C 8 B 9 D 10 B

4

1 considers me
2 irritate me
3 blocks, interferes with
4 reach the same level as
5 think they are caused by
6 manage without having it
7 left
8 started living comfortably
9 arrive or appear somewhere

Vocabulary

Collocations with *give* and *make*

1

C

2

1 ~~give~~ make 2 correct 3 ~~give~~ make 4 correct 5 ~~made~~ given 6 ~~give~~ make 7 correct 8 ~~made~~ given 9 ~~give~~ make

3

1 give 2 give 3 make 4 give 5 give 6 make 7 make 8 give 9 make 10 give

Reading and Use of English Part 4

1

1 B (A contains seven words where the maximum is six; C does not contain the word given.)
2 A (B is not correct English; C does not contain the word given.)
3 C (A does not mean the same; B contains too many words.)
4 B (A is not correct English; C is both incorrect and contains too many words.)

2

1 not ONLY considerate but
2 had fallen OUT a
3 'm / am not NEARLY as (well) organised
4 LOOKS on/to me as
5 always a good/great etc IDEA to be
6 and I WOULD often

Speaking Part 1

1

a 1, 3, 4   b 2, 5, 6, 7, 8

2

Marta: 2   Lukas: 6

Track 03

Marta: Yes, I was able to give a friend a room once when she had to move out of her house quite quickly. She'd been having problems with one of her flatmates, so she came to stay with us for a while, just for a few months, and I think that helped her quite a lot in her situation, which wasn't easy for her because she was studying at university and it was a long way from her family home.

Lukas: One of the best is from the summer vacations which we always used to spend together as a family at the seaside. I used to do quite a lot of sport with my dad, you know, playing tennis, swimming, that sort of thing, and I remember one time we went water-skiing, which was a great new experience for me. Yes, that's a very good one, because I loved being close to my dad and doing things with him, you know, things I wouldn't have done with my mum.

3

1 F   2 T   3 T   4 T

Track 04

Examiner: Marta, can you tell me, have you ever had the opportunity to really help a friend?

Marta: Yes, I was able to give a friend a room once when she had to move out of her house quite quickly. She'd been having problems with one of her flatmates, so she came to stay with us for a while, just for a few months, and I think that helped her quite a lot in her situation, which wasn't easy for her because she was studying at university and it was a long way from her family home.

Examiner: Thank you. Lukas, a question for you. What's your happiest childhood memory?

Lukas: One of the best is really from the summer vacations which we always used to spend together as a family at the seaside. I used to do quite a lot of sport with my dad, you know, playing tennis, swimming, that sort of thing, and I remember one time we went water-skiing, which was a great new experience for me. Yes, that's a very good one, because I loved being close to my dad and doing things with him, you know, things I wouldn't have done with my mum.

Writing Part 1

An essay

2

(Suggested underlining)

education systems do enough to help young people to find jobs / fit / abilities and interests / courses / work experience / careers advice / two methods / more effective / giving reasons / own words

4

1 F (You must discuss two methods.)
2 T ('explain which method is more effective')
3 F (It's not obligatory – you can use the opinions if you wish.)
4 T (They're written in an informal style, whereas an essay should be fairly formal.)
5 T ('giving reasons in support of your answer')
6 F (You should ensure that everything you write is relevant to the task.)
7 F (You should write in a formal academic style using complete sentences and structured paragraphs.)
8 F (You should aim to complete the task as stated.)

5

Para 1: d   Para 2: c   Para 3: a   Para 4: e   Para 5: b

6

1 To make sure you identify all aspects of the task.
2 You will score higher marks if you write a coherent, structured answer.
3 Not exactly – she also included how students can learn necessary skills while working.
4 Yes.
5 While I understand this viewpoint, I do not entirely share it; I believe; I do not think; I would therefore argue that
6 Students' own answer
7 An academic essay always requires students to develop and express their opinion. If this is not done, the task has not been completed.

7

1 the fact that many young people find it hard to find the sort of job they aspire to
2 employers
3 students
4 students
5 the idea that courses are too theoretical and do not teach students the practical skills they will need in the workplace
6 this viewpoint
7 critical thinking skills
8 developing critical thinking skills
9 work experience
10 students'
11 an excellent general education

Unit 2 More than words

Starting off

1

1 bilingual   2 switch   3 loanwords   4 mother tongue   5 a bit rusty
6 pick up   7 an excellent command   8 highly articulate   9 accurately
10 fluency   11 aims

2

Track 05

1 Where I live people tend to be bilingual – they speak the regional and the national language and they switch between languages with ease. As a result, they seem to find it easier to learn other languages as well. At least I know quite a lot of people who speak several foreign languages.

2 People do worry a bit about how the language is changing. I think, it's due to globalisation but, lots of loanwords are coming into the language, particularly from English, so my mother tongue's not at all the same as it was, say, fifty years ago. Personally, I don't know if that's a bad thing – I mean, if people find it easier to express themselves using loanwords, then perhaps they should.

3 I find it frustrating because I spent years trying to reach an advanced level but now my English has got a bit rusty because I don't use it very often and that's a pity.

4 I spent years at school studying Spanish and never learnt to speak it well. I guess I should have been sent on an exchange to a Spanish or a Mexican school for six months or thereabouts 'cause everyone knows that living in a different country, you just pick up the local language naturally and that may well be the best way to learn it.

5 I'm really dedicated to studying languages. I'm aiming to achieve an excellent command of English, which means becoming highly articulate and being able to use the language accurately and effortlessly.

6 Language is a tool for achieving other things and, frankly, I wouldn't consider accuracy to be as important as fluency when learning a foreign language. I think the main thing is to make oneself understood.

7 We live in a highly competitive world. Countries compete with each other, employers compete with each other and people compete. Consequently, we should be teaching young people to use language for persuasion rather than self-expression. It's all very well being able to say what you think and feel, but you've got to be able to sell yourself, sell your product, achieve your aims.

Listening Part 1

2

They disagree about how the financial benefits of learning a new language motivate people to take language courses.

3

She is learning more about how changes in language both reflect and shape the world.

4

1 B   2 A

Track 06, 07 & 08

Extract One

Examiner: You hear two people talking about a course the woman is doing.

M: Hi, Lois. Have you started your evening classes?

F: Yes. I'm doing a course on the origins of the English language.

M: Good idea. It's interesting to study a language you already speak. I get the impression that people generally prefer to learn a new language, hoping it might help their future earning potential. Or they just want to impress their friends on holiday.

F: Well, it's debatable whether people sign up for courses purely to give their salaries a boost. In any case, I do feel like I'm doing it for the right reasons. And, luckily, the teacher's so engaging, it hardly feels like studying at all.

M: But surely the main thing is less about the lessons being delivered well, and more that you feel you can explore the subject on your own terms.

F: True. And I really get on with the other people on my course, too. It's great fun, all of us singing old English folk songs from centuries ago, which we do together each class. Primarily, though, I'm finding it intriguing to try and make sense of the world through language developments. They're related to historical and political events in ways I hadn't previously recognised.

5

3 A 4 C 5 A 6 C

Track 09

Extract Two

Examiner: You hear two literature students talking about the relevance of their subject.

F: Because great literature is often written in a style that can seem old-fashioned, a lot of people complain that it's completely worthless nowadays. I think that's a bit short-sighted but I do get their argument: That a book was written at a particular time, and although it might bring to life the characters and culture of that age, none of it resembles our society today. But studying literature allows students to look back in time and understand that the anxieties that run through our existence are just as they always have been.

M: Absolutely. And also, if a high school student reads an old novel, there's every chance they'll find a character in it who they identify with, which can be a great source of comfort and reassurance to them. The dominant argument coming from a lot of teachers is that reading more widely leads to improvements in other skills, such as research or writing, which may or may not be the case. What they always ignore is how beneficial it can be for teenagers, who can be so focused on their studies in numerous subjects, to read a work that has stood the test of time.

Extract 3

Examiner: You hear two friends discussing different styles of writing.

F: Did you get that work experience place?

M: No. Apparently, I made an 'unsuitable comment' in my application.

F: What was it?

M: At the end, I wrote, 'hope you give the job to me, not some loser!' It was meant as a joke, but the manager wasn't impressed. I didn't think the email needed to be so formal, it was only for a work experience job. But some people still insist on being traditional, even when the whole world is becoming totally relaxed about it all. Maybe I went too far, but it feels to me like he could have lowered his expectations a little.

F: I know what you mean. Whenever my parents text me, they'll use correct punctuation in every sentence. Capital letters, correct grammar and spelling, no emojis … it seems so formal and harsh to me. Like, if I'm out, my mum'll send a message which she thinks is just letting me know what's for dinner, but in my mind she's ordering me back home at that moment. I feel that texting someone should be the equivalent of having a chat, and it ought to reflect the way you talk to someone face-to-face. Otherwise, it can easily be misread.

Vocabulary

Collocations with *make*, *get* and *do*

1

1 doing 2 makes 3 get 4 get 5 made

2

make: a decision, a mistake, a point, a proposal, a suggestion, an apology, an effort, an improvement, changes, complaints, friends, one's money back, the right choice, use of something

get: a qualification, business, exercise, further information, one's money back, some shopping

do: a job, a qualification, an activity, business, exercise, harm, household chores, one's best, some shopping, sport, the cooking

3

1 ~~make~~ do 2 ~~receive~~ get 3 ~~turn~~ make 4 ~~make~~ do 5 ~~achieve~~ do
6 ~~given~~ made 7 ~~make~~ do 8 ~~practising~~ doing

Reading and Use of English Part 3

1

Speaker 1 southern England, Speaker 2 Scotland, Speaker 3 Wales, Speaker 4 northern England, Speaker 5 Northern Ireland

Track 10

1 My best friend is from another part of the country to me and I absolutely love her accent, it's really different from mine.

2 My best friend is from another part of the country to me and I absolutely love her accent, it's really different from mine.

3 My best friend is from another part of the country to me and I absolutely love her accent, it's really different from mine.

4 My best friend is from another part of the country to me and I absolutely love her accent, it's really different from mine.

5 My best friend is from another part of the country to me and I absolutely love her accent; it's really different from mine.

4

My friend's accent is much softer, so even when she's irritated or having an argument she sounds like she's entirely relaxed. I find it really fascinating that two people who are essentially from the same part of the country can have such dissimilar accents.

6

1 interaction
2 Historically
3 differences
4 unmeasurable
5 assumption
6 ethnicity
7 influential
8 numerous

Reading and Use of English Part 6

3

a 'Script writers today are exceptionally skilled in reproducing genuine discussions'
b Students' own answers
c B: 'learners should avoid the temptation to repeat carefully chosen language of a screenplay with the intention of communicating in an entirely natural way'
C: 'Movie dialogue is perfectly capable of capturing the patterns of everyday speech, so a vocabulary notebook can be filled with examples of useful and authentic dialogue for the learner to adopt as their own.'
D: 'Many people devote hours on end to repeated viewings of the same film in order to build their ability to quote whole sections of dialogue by heart. This is a solid idea, if the only aim is to impress and entertain one's fellow film enthusiasts, rather than being able to converse with somebody else in an authentic way.'
d C

4

1 A 2 C 3 C 4 B

Speaking Part 2

1

Compare two of the photos, say what the speakers might be explaining, say what problems the speakers might have.

2

(Suggested answers)
photo 1: boost morale, decide on / discuss / explain tactics, encourage the team, influence the outcome
photo 2: give a demonstration, take people through the steps
photo 3: argue a case, defend a client, influence the outcome, persuade the judge/jury, reach a verdict

3

1 explain tactics, boost morale, argue a case, defend a client, persuade the jury, reach a verdict 2 He also mentions similarities. 3 Yes

Track 11

Examiner: In this part of the test, I'm going to give each of you three pictures. I'd like you to talk about two of them on your own for about a minute, and also to answer a question briefly about your partner's pictures. Here are your pictures. They show people explaining things. I'd like you to compare two of the pictures and say what the speakers might be explaining and what problems the speakers might have.

Daniel: OK. In this photo there's a team coach who looks as if he's explaining tactics to a team of teenage boys, perhaps at half time. The boys give the impression that they're a bit tired or perhaps disheartened, judging by the expressions on their faces, so perhaps he's trying to boost their morale. In the other photo there's a lawyer, a barrister I think they're called, who seems to be arguing a case to the court. She appears to be defending her client and trying to persuade the jury that he's innocent. In both photos, I imagine the explanation is vital: the coach wants his team to go back on the pitch and win the match while the barrister wants to win her case by persuading the jury to reach a verdict of not guilty. I think both speakers have very similar problems because their success depends entirely on the words they use, although the outcome is something they have no direct control over.

Examiner: Thank you.

4

From the recording script:
1 he's explaining tactics. 2 they're a bit tired or perhaps disheartened … the expressions on their faces. 3 to be arguing a case. 4 to be defending her client. 5 the explanation is vital. 6 his team to go back on the pitch and win the match … to win her case.

6

1*(Suggested answer)* Choose the two you find easiest – the photos are not graded to be easier or more difficult; the examiners will assess you on the quality of your speaking. 2 No, also the adults.

7

(Suggested answers)
1 cheer someone up, give encouragement, put a brave face on things
2 bond with each other, spend quality time together, teach someone basic skills
3 bond with each other, look through an album, remember good times, share family history, spend quality time together

Grammar

Expressing purpose, reason and result

1

1C – Conversely, if the student reads the subtitles in their mother tongue – translated from the original – this minimises any potential for improvement, **as** the viewer relaxes into the role of passive consumer, rather than active learner.
2D – Many people devote hours on end to repeated viewings of the same film **in order to** build their ability to quote whole sections of dialogue by heart.
3A – Learners should avoid the temptation to repeat the carefully chosen language of a screenplay **with the intention of** communicating in an entirely natural way.
4B – First-language subtitles allow the viewer to connect the known language (the one they are reading) to the unknown speech (the one they are hearing), **with the result that** they become more open to learning opportunities.

2

1D – I thought I should pick the language up while I was there, **so** I immersed myself in the life of the local community.
2A – They used to give us dictations in class **to** make sure we knew things like putting a double 'p' in 'approve'.
3B – I always write new vocabulary down in my notebook, **otherwise** there is very little chance I will remember it.
4C – You'll need to use a microphone, **in case** the people at the back can't hear you.

3

1 a in order to, so, to, with the intention of b as, in case, otherwise c with the result that
2 a in order to, to b with the intention of c as, in case, so, with the result that, otherwise

4

1 because 2 For 3 because of 4 so that 5 in order not to

Writing Part 2

1

1 the manager at an education technology company 2 formal
3 methods students use to learn vocabulary, what methods they find are effective, recommendations for a vocab learning app
4 *(Suggested answer)* probably the same order as in the question

2

1 The aim 2 accounting for 3 the effect 4 due to 5 resulted
6 so as 7 as a consequence 8 means

3

1 It has a title and sections with section headings. 2 Yes 3 Yes

1 Vocabulary and grammar review

1

1 gave 2 making 3 give 4 made, giving 5 give 6 gave 7 give
8 making 9 makes 10 give

2

1 found the advice (that) Gustavo gave/found Gustavo's advice to
2 has been living in Berlin 3 had never been/gone skiing before/until/till 4 (Paola gave/by Paola) made a favourable impression 5 has changed in/over/during the last/past 6 I had lost my receipt

3

1 had stopped 2 We'd been standing, were feeling 3 I've driven
4 she's been studying 5 had been eating 6 used to work
7 had been coming, were repairing 8 went

2 Vocabulary and grammar review

1

1 accurately 2 articulate 3 command 4 fluency 5 pick up
6 mother tongue 7 bilingual 8 rusty

2

1 get 2 making 3 doing 4 made 5 make 6 do 7 got 8 do
9 make 10 do

3

1 with the intention of 2 to 3 in case 4 otherwise 5 as
6 with the result that

4

1 intention ~~for~~ **of**
2 **in** case
3 ~~as~~ **with** the result
4 ~~other than~~ **otherwise**
5 ~~as~~ **so** I
6 in order **to** save

Unit 3 Mind, body and soul

Listening Part 2

5

1 biology/science 2 optimistic 3 practical 4 weaknesses
5 luck 6 advertising 7 body language 8 intrigued

Track 12

Examiner: You hear a radio programme in which a journalist called Kate Walsh is talking about doing a personality quiz based on colour preferences.

F: Hi, everyone! I'm Kate Walsh, here to tell you about an online personality quiz I did recently, in preparation for writing a magazine article. You're probably familiar with these personality quizzes – you answer questions, and they'll tell you what kind of person you are. This quiz focused on colour preferences, then analysed my likely personality and best career choices based on my answers. I must admit, I wasn't sure at the beginning. My first degree was in biology, which encourages you to look for concrete proof of theories, so that makes me very critical. However, I subsequently trained in psychology, and my familiarity with this field gave me a more positive attitude to the activity.

I've always considered myself a pretty positive kind of person and expected that if the quiz was accurate, the analysis would tell me I was optimistic – my key characteristic. When that came back, I became a bit more confident about the quiz. Luckily, the results omitted my tendency to be stubborn, and included none of my other more negative characteristics!

However, I was rather taken aback by one of the terms the quiz generated. I'd certainly never consider myself a practical person. Whenever my bike breaks down, I always need to find a mechanic, which points to the fact I'm not a great problem-solver. Still, I was determined not to be put off by that.

The analysis also suggested that colours we don't like have just as much significance as the ones we prefer, as they tell us something about our weaknesses. I'd indicated that yellow was my least favourite colour, but that's because it doesn't suit me. I'd never wear it. More vanity than anything else.

However, I then began to wonder what might be influencing our colour preferences. The colour red, for example, seems to be a universal symbol of considerable power, regardless of culture. But in China, its most popular association is luck, and here in the UK, like many Western countries, it's most often associated with danger or, in complete contrast, with expressions of love.

Anyway, according to the quiz's career suggestions, people who select red as a preferred colour, as I had, are apparently good in unsupervised roles where they can express their creativity – such as acting. I'd imagine the world of advertising would appeal to these people. Admittedly, that wouldn't necessarily suit me, and nor would a role in sales, which was the other job suggested in the quiz.

So how reliable an indicator of personality and career choice is colour preference? Although it may work to an extent, I've also found looking at people's general style of dress can be just as informative. And monitoring someone's body language can tell you more than anything about their character, in my view.

However, despite that, I still wasn't ready to completely abandon the quiz. In fact, having been convinced I'd be extremely sceptical by the end, I was actually intrigued – enough to do more research for my next article!

Vocabulary

Multi-word verbs

1

1 stops working 2 surprised 3 discouraged/dissuaded

2

1 become popular 2 seems 3 become interested in 4 stated an idea or opinion ready for discussion 5 do something in a hurry 6 becomes available 7 got rid of

3

1 put forward 2 rush into 3 got into 4 come across as 5 come up 6 catch on 7 doing away with

Grammar

no, none, not

1

1 not 2 no 3 none

2

1 ~~not~~ no 2 ~~no~~ not 3 ~~no~~ any 4 correct 5 ~~nothing~~ anything (or I know nothing) 6 ~~none~~ no

Grammar

The passive

1

Passive verbs are formed by using the appropriate tense of the verb *be* and adding the past participle of the main verb.

2

a 's (widely) believed b have been found c were omitted

3

1 c by the quiz analysis
2 a, b: people / the general public
3 The identity of the agent is not important or may not be known. The writer wants to focus attention on the action rather than who did it.
4 in an essay, a scientific report, a job application

4

1 This YouTube clip has been watched by over a million people.
2 The film was made over twenty years ago.
3 At the time nothing like it had been seen.
4 Apparently, a new version of the film is being made at the moment.
5 It is going to be released next year.

6

A new study on Albert Einstein (1) has been completed and (2) will be published next month in a journal on neurology. The study suggests that Einstein's extraordinary genius (3) may have been influenced by a uniquely shaped brain. When anthropologist Dean Falk and her team made a comparison with 85 'normal' human brains, (4) it was found that Einstein's brain possessed some remarkable features …
The researchers were using 14 photos of the genius's brain which (5) had only recently been rediscovered. With permission from his family, Einstein's brain (6) was removed and photographed (by scientists) after his death in 1955. The photographs (7) are held by the National Museum of Health and Medicine but (8) (they) had never been fully investigated before.

Reading and Use of English Part 5

2

1 C 2 A 3 D 4 C 5 A 6 B

Vocabulary

Verb collocations

1

make a point of, make ends meet
take things as they come, take your time
catch your eye, catch up with

2

1 caught my eye 2 make a point of 3 take our time 4 make ends meet 5 catch up with 6 ran into 7 takes things as they come

Reading and Use of English Part 2

1

1 background music, influences our reactions to films/advertisements, help you feel calmer, enhance ability in areas such as maths, bring back long-forgotten memories, recover verbal skills
2 Students' own answers
3 1 little (adjective) 2 other (determiner) 3 Even (adverb) 4 far (adverb) 5 what (pronoun) 6 of (preposition) 7 in (preposition) 8 whom (pronoun)

2

1 set 2 not 3 from 4 despite 5 to 6 being 7 In 8 than

Speaking Part 3

2

Students' own answers

Track 13

Laura: I have to admit it's only recently that I started getting stressed about things – I think it coincides with when I started my new job.

Anna: Really? So what makes you feel stressed?

Laura: Oh, all kinds of things. Obviously having too much to do, you know, not having enough time to do everything they want me to do. Then I start thinking: my manager's got it in for me, or that she doesn't like me and is making my life difficult deliberately. Do you know what I mean?

Anna: Yes, I know exactly what you mean. You start by blaming someone else and then you decide it's your fault, that you're inadequate. That's when the stress starts.

Laura: Exactly! Then because you're working so hard and thinking about work even when you're not there, it starts to affect other parts of your life. I lost my temper with my boyfriend last week – for no real reason – just because I'd had a hard day at work. I apologised afterwards of course, but I could tell he was quite upset. That's one of the worst effects of stress, isn't it?

Anna: Yes, it is. Other people are affected if you're stressed, often people you care about. But you know, you're lucky – at least you have a job. I've been really stressed recently because I can't find a job. And I'm running out of money.

Laura: What will you do?

Anna: I don't know. I could borrow some from my parents, but I'd prefer not to. And if I tell them I'm short of money, they'll start to worry and I don't want them worrying because of me. That'll make everything worse and I'll get even more stressed. It's a vicious circle. So, what do you do if you're feeling stressed?

Laura: Well, I thought about going to the doctor and asking for some pills, but then I thought: There must be better ways of dealing with it than drugs. So if I'm feeling particularly stressed after a day at work, I do one of two things: either I phone a friend and suggest we go out for the evening, or I go to the gym. What about you?

Anna: I find talking about my problems is quite helpful. You often find there are lots of people in the same situation or even a worse situation than you – that helps me get things into perspective. And I always try to find reasons to be optimistic. For example, I've got two interviews next week and I'm determined to get one of the jobs. That'll make things easier for me. And I spend time with friends and I try relaxation techniques. Have you tried that?

Laura: No, but perhaps I will.

3

1 mean 2 isn't it 3 do you do 4 about 5 tried

Writing Part 1

An essay

3

(Suggested answers)

1 a Yes, but not explicitly enough. The writer provides examples of how teachers and parents can help students and how time management could help a student organise their time, but doesn't refer back to the points directly (understanding good study habits, having a support network). b Yes c Yes

2 Generally yes. The style used is quite formal.

3 Yes. It's 259 words long, which is one letter under the maximum required for the exam.

4

(Suggested answers)

1 Para 2: One of the factors important for obtaining a good balance between studying and life

Para 3: The second factor that is important

Para 4: Conclusion: the writer's opinion

2 Paragraph 1 shows the writer's general grasp of the topic. Paragraphs 2 and 3 discuss two of the methods listed in the task. Paragraph 2 takes up how others can support students and paragraph 3 looks at how an ability to organise time well is an important factor. Paragraph 4 offers a conclusion and reveals which factor the author feels is more important and why.

3 Opinions are expressed in all four paragraphs.

6

(Suggested answers)

Para 1: 5 and 9 Para 2: 1 and 4 Para 3: 6 and 10

Para 4: 2 and 8

3 and 7 are not appropriate, as they are too informal and personal.

Unit 4 Career paths

Reading and Use of English Part 1

2

1 D 2 B 3 A 4 B 5 D 6 C 7 A 8 A

Reading and Use of English Part 8

3

Question 3. Section A does not address the issue of measuring whether something or someone is suitable for a particular task or use.

Question 5. Although section A singles out two groups of people, one is referred to in negative terms, while the other is praised, but not for their work ethic.

Question 6. Section A does not provide any 'detail' about 'a contemporary interpretation of a traditional process'.

Question 7. There is no obvious prediction of 'the end of a form of communication'.

Question 10. There is a suggestion in section A that 'younger staff could be supported by their superiors' more effectively, but it does not 'specify ways' in which this could happen.

4

Although the question mentions management and 'antiquated, dying industry practice', the writer here is talking about a *belief* of those managers that young people are not tough enough to survive in the world of work, and not a strategy that they use.

5

The question is a direct paraphrase of the text:

'recommend an evaluation of long-term developments?'

'For any business to prosper, [...] a true understanding of the cultural shifts that have taken place in the workplace over the past decade is vital.'

6

1 B 2 A 3 D 4 C 5 B 6 D 7 C 8 D 9 A 10 B

Vocabulary

Dependent prepositions

1

1 from 2 of 3 on 4 on 5 in 6 with 7 for

2

1 focuses ~~of~~ **on** candidates

2 prevents candidates ~~for~~ **from** applying

3 invest money ~~on~~ **in** office perks

Adjective–noun collocations (1)

1

1 major 2 long

2

1 wide 2 extreme 3 big 4 large 5 big 6 severe 7 wide 8 strong 9 high 10 strong

Listening Part 3

1

An 'open salary policy' is put in place when a company or organisation decides to make public the salaries of all employees within the organisation, from top to bottom.

(Suggested answers) Share responsibilities more often, put less emphasis on traditional management structures, promote diversity and equality within the workplace, encourage everyone to become involved in company decisions.

2

1a *Other companies:* In the vast majority of cases, it is rare to discuss your salary with your colleagues.

1b *Staff interaction:* As above, staff rarely discuss matters of their salary with their colleagues.

1c *Consistency in her and Ahmad's company:* Their determination to ensure there were no areas of their business where information remained secret was one of their central, or 'core' values.

1d *Industry research:* Studies suggest that an open salary policy is beneficial because it usually leads employees to recognise that they are paid fairly.

2d, industry research

3

1 B 2 A 3 C 4 B 5 A 6 C

Tracks 14 & 15

Interviewer: I'm with Patricia Freeman and Ahmad Faizan, two business leaders at Oyay game design, to talk about their 'open salary' policy – the unconventional step of publishing the incomes of everyone in their company. Patricia, why did you decide to implement this?

Patricia: Well, it's usually the case in most companies that even discussing what you earn with your co-workers is a taboo subject. But here at Oyay since transparency has always been one of our central core values, we were determined to apply it throughout the business, including this one area where there tends to be such secrecy. We thought that employees would be more likely to think their salary was fair if we published exactly what we'd paid all of our staff. Our instinct told us to go ahead with it, but we've found loads of studies that have supported what we've done.

Interviewer: And can you tell us more about these 'salary charts' that you publish?

Patricia: Well, they provide information about salaries on a number of levels, so, not just about how much other people earn, but why they were given that salary – their knowledge and experience, both in their current position, and potentially in other areas of our business. The availability of this information has been absolutely instrumental in allowing staff to value what their co-workers bring to the table, the sheer range of skills and expertise they have. OK, your working life is laid open for everyone to see, but hopefully it's clear how this information ultimately benefits everyone who works here.

Interviewer: Ahmad, how satisfied were you with the impact of this initiative on the business?

Ahmad: Hugely, but it wasn't just that alone. After the open salary policy, we wanted to make ourselves even more democratic. First, we decided that any profit the company had made by the end of the year should be shared equally among all staff members. This went down pretty well with the staff, as you can imagine, but it was obvious that we could all go further. We started involving everyone in all strategic and financial decisions, including voting on which colleagues should get a salary increase, and by how much. Because of this, I'm proud to say we've managed to deal with a number of issues around fairness, such as the gender pay gap.

Interviewer: Patricia, I understand you refused a pay increase recently, didn't you? Why was that?

Patricia: Well, two years ago, I won an award for my work on a particularly successful game, and accepted a pay increase then without hesitation. But last September, when my colleagues all approved a 7% raise for me, I turned it down outright. We had a lot of new faces in the office, and I suspected they might easily have thought they had to vote it through simply because I'm on the management team. Which is entirely against our values, obviously. Essentially, though, there were several colleagues who'd performed far better than I had during that period who I thought were more entitled to a raise than me.

Interviewer: Given this progressive working culture, how do you ensure new staff are right for Oyay?

Ahmad: Well, any candidate could well come in with a first-class degree, but for us, attitude is everything. For example, it's highly unlikely we'd ever employ someone who wasn't happy to join in with day-to-day discussions about how the business is run. For example, it's vital to value your own input, talents and opinions, so all newcomers suggest a starting salary they think they're worth, and discuss this with existing employees with a similar level of experience, who may or may not agree to that figure. That's a big shift away from the conventional recruitment process, but we want people who can adapt to these sorts of challenging situations.

Interviewer: Overall, you must be delighted with the way things have gone?

Ahmad: On the whole, yes. I mean, we have lost out on potentially valuable clients because they've not been comfortable with the way we operate. Like, recently, I encouraged a 19-year-old intern to call the CEO of a prospective client to talk him through some ideas she'd had. He really wasn't impressed with that, and it ultimately cost us the contract. But success in business involves making mistakes, carefully reviewing your actions, and doing it differently next time.

Patricia: I completely understand where Ahmad is coming from – you probably could argue that we've gone too far with our commitment to workplace democracy sometimes. In situations like that, though, I think you just have to conclude that the client isn't a good fit for us as a company and move on without dwelling on it.

Grammar

Expressing possibility, probability and certainty

1

1 a 2 b 3 a

3

1 ~~probably~~ likely 2 ~~you bound~~ you are bound 3 ~~most~~ more
4 ~~posible~~ possible 5 ~~one of the possibly best~~ possibly one of the best
6 ~~the worst trip I probably have~~ probably the worst trip I have
7 ~~That may be the possible reason~~ That may possibly be the reason

4

1 was bound to be 2 likelihood of Boris winning / that Boris will win
3 may/could/might well have seen 4 must have forgotten to
5 is (quite/very) likely to lose 6 there any chance of (you) helping / you could help

Speaking Part 4

3

a 1, 3, 4 b 2, 5, 6

5

(Suggested answers)

1 a reasonable/heavy/light workload, a work environment, motivate/motivation, recruit, a workplace
2 achieve a good work–life balance, commute, a feeling of isolation, a work environment, a workplace
3 feel valued
4 feel valued, motivate/motivation
5 a job vacancy, recruit, take somebody on, a trainee
6 give praise, a good communicator, motivate/motivation

6

1 commute, workplace, motivation, feel valued, a good communicator, a reasonable workload, give praise

Track 16

Examiner: Daniel, it's now more common than ever to work from home. What do you think are the advantages and disadvantages of working from home?

Daniel: Well, yes, that's certainly the case these days, isn't it? I think I'd say that for most people there are a number of positive features. The most important one, perhaps, is that you don't waste time commuting, which can be quite stressful, especially if your train is late or you can't find a parking space. Also, you don't have to follow a strict dress code if your company has one – you can jump into something vaguely smart if ever you need to be on a video call with your colleagues. That, for me, would be a definite plus. On the down side, I know a lot of people feel concerned that they can't, kind of, disconnect from their jobs. It's so much more difficult to do when your office is at home, you're always checking your messages and emails. Although I suppose that's a problem people have even when they're in the office. If they have their phones with them – which everyone does, of course – they can still be contacted when they're at lunch or leaving for home or wherever.

Examiner: Laura, do you agree with Daniel?

Laura: Yes, although for people with small children, the biggest advantage is that they can combine working life with family life. I mean they don't have to give up work when they start a family.

Examiner: Laura, which do you think is more important in a job: friendly colleagues or a good salary?

Laura: Oh, I think both are essential. Unless there's a good atmosphere in the workplace, people soon lose motivation or lose interest and this affects the quality of their work. Also, employees need to feel valued and in the end this comes down to how much they are paid. If they're not well paid for the job they do, they'll feel that their work is not respected.

Examiner: And Daniel. What do you think?

Daniel: Well, I'm not sure, because I think for me the most important thing is to feel that you're doing something useful, achieving something worthwhile in your job. If people have that impression, then they're not so worried about their pay and they can get their social life in their free time. I'd say it's more important to be efficient than friendly.

Examiner: Daniel, many people complain about their managers. What qualities would you look for in a perfect manager, and why?

Daniel: I think he or she has to be a good communicator, who tells you what's going on, and is also pleasant to work with. They should be someone who gives you a reasonable workload and provides you with the support you need to do your job well and also someone who recognises when you're working hard and gives you praise when you deserve it.

Laura: Oh, I wish my boss was like that!

7

1 T 2 T 3 T 4 F 5 T 6 T

Writing Part 2

1

1 Informal.
2 Yes. Ariel is clearly someone he knows on a personal level.
3 No, he uses more space to answer the second question.
4 No. The first question demands an expanded 'Yes/No' answer, while the second question is far more open and requires Charlie to explain his views and suggest reasons on the topic in question.

2

More formal. The recipient is not a personal friend of acquaintance.

3

b

4

A 1 f 2 d 3 a 4 c 5 e

B

	More formal language (Lola's email)	Less formal language (Charlie's email)
1	a considerable number of	quite a few
2	through choice	because they want to
3	hugely attractive	a big draw
4	not to mention	and let's not forget
5	offer highly competitive salaries	pay really well
6	continue living here	stay put
7	Aside from that,	On the flip side,
8	As such,	So,
9	my interpretation of	my take on

3 Vocabulary and grammar review

1

1 caught 2 took 3 made 4 caught 5 making 6 ran 7 taken

2

1 caught on 2 came across 3 hit it off 4 rushed into
5 putting forward 6 done away with 7 came up 8 getting into

3

1 ~~not~~ no 2 ~~no~~ not / ~~no my sister~~ my sister doesn't 3 ~~none~~ any / ~~didn't get none~~ got none 4 *correct* 5 ~~no~~ none 6 *correct* (*None of Patrick's friends* is also possible.) 7 ~~no~~ not 8 ~~none~~ no

4
(Suggested answers)
1 The term 'amnesia' is used to refer to a partial or complete loss of memory … Amnesia can be caused by specific medical conditions.
2 It is very well known that our memory is formed by our real experiences. But could a false memory be put into our heads? Could we be persuaded (to believe) that we had experienced something that never actually took place?
3 Our semantic memory is used to store our knowledge of the world. Everyone has this knowledge base, and normally it can be accessed quickly and easily. The meanings of words and the names of people and places are included in our semantic memory.
4 … It can be thought of as the ability to remember and use a limited amount of information for a short amount of time … If you are distracted, the information can be lost and the task has to be started again.

4 Vocabulary and grammar review

1
1 of 2 from, of 3 for, for 4 for 5 to 6 on 7 with 8 on
2
1 extensive/huge/specialist/vast 2 huge/powerful 3 constant/huge 4 excellent 5 fierce 6 huge/vast 7 extensive/specialist/vast 8 excellent/specialist
3
1 could 2 might not 3 couldn't have 4 possible 5 highly 6 can't 7 bound

Unit 5 Events to remember

Listening Part 1

1
1 i 2 g 3 d 4 b 5 h 6 e 7 c 8 a 9 j 10 f
3
(Suggested answers)
1 The farmer was probably working on his farm when he lost control of his tractor. Two of the options in question 2 hint at a happy ending.
2 He must have believed that he could tackle the challenge. But because it was such a dangerous thing to do, his feelings before setting off might have been very conflicted.
3 She might have been piloting the other plane, or an incident might have occurred involving the plane that put her at risk.
4
1 B 2 C 3 C 4 A 5 B 6 A

Track 17

Extract One

Examiner: You hear a man telling a friend a story that involves a local farmer and a runaway tractor.

M: Did you hear that story about a local farmer? He'd driven across a field in his tractor, his dog beside him, then got out to fix a fence, only to see his tractor rolling away, out of control – with his dog still in it!

F: Oh, really?

M: Yeah, the dog apparently seemed completely unbothered about being in the tractor, but the vehicle was gathering speed, heading towards a thick hedge, with a main road the other side! So the farmer set off in hot pursuit.

F: What on earth was he intending to do?

M: Well, apparently, to run and catch up with the vehicle, then jump in and pull on the handbrake – but just after he'd started running he tripped and fell, poor guy. In the end, the vehicle rolled down a bank, and came to a stop. Just a few cuts and bruises for both of them.

F: Gosh! It's awful to think that an ordinary day could turn out like that and could've potentially ended disastrously, even if he had managed to climb inside the tractor. What a lucky escape! They got off pretty lightly, didn't they, considering how they might've ended up.

Extract Two

Examiner: You hear an interview with a man who climbed up a very high mountain in order to ski down it.

F: So, what gave you the idea to undertake the trip?

M: Where I grew up skiing's popular, and I quickly became a skilled and confident skier. My uncle introduced me to ski mountaineering – climbing up, then skiing down and I started taking on increasingly difficult climbs and descents, then considered tackling the biggest climb close to home – an absolute monster of a mountain, known to be deadly. Other ski mountaineers had already backed off. But when I finally got a good look at it during a different expedition, I could see it might be feasible.

F: How did you feel before you set off?

M: By then, I was ready to face it – and ignore any negative feelings I was having. Fear can act as a restraint and keep you safe. But in order to undertake something that challenging, I just had to stop being afraid. In fact, I didn't talk much about the trip to family and friends, to avoid seeing how anxious I was making them. Anyway, my psychological preparation paid off because we made it to the top and back successfully – but when we returned to base camp, I just lay in the snow, totally exhausted.

Extract Three

Examiner: You hear a woman talking to a friend about her experiences of flying a light plane.

M: Congratulations on your first solo flight!

F: Thanks! Actually, though, while the Chief Instructor was still flying with me beforehand, checking I was up to it, I completely messed up the take-off, which was down to nerves more than anything. Anyway, we landed again, he pointed out some navigational landmarks, then got out and sent me off alone, first time ever! I flew a couple of circuits – a rectangular route above the airfield – and even I was amazed that I managed OK, and I've done more solo flights since.

M: But what's this story I heard about a disorderly yellow plane? Sounded awful …

F: Well, I was flying the last leg of the airfield circuit, before turning 90 degrees and coming in to land. All approaching aircraft have to join the circuit in exactly the same direction, otherwise it'd be chaos. Anyway, another plane suddenly appeared, completely ignored the rules, and flew straight across in front of me, jumped the queue to land! Totally forbidden – and dangerous – and I'd got hardly any flying experience, remember!

M: Scary!

F: Yeah, I'm still having flashbacks! I somehow managed to keep my head – no idea how – and just went round again. If I'd attempted to land, I would've hit the other plane.

Vocabulary

Idiomatic language

1
1 Flashbacks can be either pleasant or unpleasant; they are often caused by traumatic events.
2 The other mountaineers had changed their minds and withdrawn from the challenge.
3 It means you had a lucky escape – that perhaps the damage caused or injuries sustained could have been a lot more serious.
4 You go in front of other people who are waiting, instead of waiting your turn behind them.
5 You could check they were up to it by, for example, questioning them, observing them, or even checking their qualifications, depending on the thing you were undertaking.
2
1 hope for good luck
2 try hard to persuade me (but without force)
3 betray you or be disloyal to you when you are not expecting it
4 pretend not to notice something
5 joking/teasing

Grammar

Verbs followed by *to* + infinitive or the *-ing* form

1
1 to keep 2 tackling 3 seeing 4 to do 5 to land
2
Verb + *to* infinitive: afford, agree, choose, expect, hope, offer, pretend, promise, refuse
Verb + *-ing*: admit, avoid, can't help, deny, enjoy, finish, involve, keep on, mind, put off, resent, risk, suggest
3
1 a I have a memory of doing this. b Don't forget to do it.
2 a This was an experiment, to see what would happen. b I attempted to do this but failed.
3 a I didn't do something. b I opened it and recall it well.
4 a I wish I hadn't said anything. b I'm sorry to tell you that …
5 a It involves paying attention. b I didn't intend to offend you.

4
1 ~~to take~~ taking 2 ~~maintaining~~ maintain / to maintain
3 ~~to sail~~ sailing 4 ~~to do~~ doing 5 ~~work~~ working 6 ~~going~~ to go

Reading and Use of English Part 4

1
1 Yes 2 Yes 3 No – it doesn't use the key word (until) and it uses more than six words to complete the sentence. 4 n't / not UNTIL the snow had stopped
2/3
Answers to the clues are in brackets.
1 (ever) had any INTENTION of accompanying
(preposition is *of*, and verb takes the *-ing* form after it)
2 nearly as TOUGH as I
(as ... as , (not) nearly)
3 on INCREASINGLY difficult
(take on = tackle)
4 no SOONER had she left than
5 REGRETTED not turning back before
6 MIGHT have been woken (up) by
4
1 f 2 d 3 e 4 a 5 c 6 b

Reading and Use of English Part 7

2
1 G 2 D 3 B 4 A 5 C 6 E (Para F is the distractor)

Speaking Part 2

1
1 three 2 two 3 one minute 4 The other candidate has to answer a question related to what his/her partner was talking about.
4
1 photos 1 and 3
2 The words and phrases express varying degrees of doubt or certainty.
3 Students' own answers
4 Students' own answers

Track 18

Examiner: Here are your pictures. They show people doing dangerous jobs. I'd like you to compare two of the pictures and say what the dangers of the jobs might be and why people choose to do jobs like these.
Lukas: OK, well, in this photo there's a fire fighter putting out a fire and he's almost certainly doing it to save lives and property. It's a pretty dangerous job because obviously he could die in a fire or get seriously burnt. And I suppose he's doing it because someone's got to do it. It must be a worthwhile occupation – you know, very rewarding when you save someone's life. And in this photo there's a diver – he could be a police diver – he seems to be in a lake, or it could be a river. It's probably quite dangerous because the water could be deep or there might be strong currents. There could be glass or other dangerous things in the water. I suppose police divers find their work quite exciting – I'm sure it's never boring and it's very worthwhile – though they must never know what they're going to find in the water. I don't really know why people do jobs like these; perhaps they're people who get excitement from doing dangerous things.

5
(Suggested answers)
Skills and personal qualities: concentration, control, courage, daring, fit, self-confident, stamina, steady nerves, strength
How activities make people feel: adrenaline rush, excitement, exhausted, exhilarated, proud, satisfaction, a sense of achievement, terrified, thrill

Writing Part 2

A proposal
3
1 not well ('not someone I know personally')
2 She rescued a lorry driver from his burning lorry.
3 She could have driven home and left the emergency seervices to deal with the accident.
4 She has shown that you don't need special training to help other people / that anyone can make a difference.
5 She should have an annual award named after her.

4
1 1 in my opinion 2 mother 3 reached 4 suffered burns
5 driven home 6 emergency services 7 make a difference
8 set up a fund 9 an annual prize
2 Yes – including two reasons for choice of hero
5
1 working, relaxing 2 looking, going, leaving
3 writing, driving, coming 4 hesitating, choosing 5 training
6
1 ~~charge~~ charging 2 ~~keep~~ keeping 3 correct 4 ~~hardwork~~ hardworking; ~~interested~~ interesting; ~~for improve~~ for improving / to improve; ~~be offered~~ offered / being offered / that/which is offered
5 ~~To bring~~ By bringing 6 ~~to leave~~ leaving 7 ~~to take~~ from taking
8 ~~visited~~ visiting
7
All the adjectives could be used except cautious, greedy, narrow-minded and self-interested.
8
(Suggested answers)
1 courageously/fearlessly 2 enthusiastically/tirelessly
3 exceptionally/extraordinarily 4 significantly
5 exceptionally/extraordinarily/remarkably 6 passionately
7 kindly 8 creatively 9 enthusiastically

Unit 6 Creative pursuits

Starting off

2
Speaker A: 3 Speaker B: 5 Speaker C: 1
3
1B 2C 3 A 4A 5C 6B

Track 19

A: At first, when the teacher gave us the assignment, I was like – I'm not doing that. I feel pretty self-conscious more often than not, and although I'm perfectly happy to put my selfies up on Instagram or whatever, they're just sort of throwaway pictures that get likes, give me a bit of a confidence boost, and then they're gone. So the idea of creating something permanent that reveals some sort of fundamental truth about myself was pretty scary. Then inspiration hit me – I was born and grew up in London, but my family is from Nigeria, so why not show off my pride in my heritage? I love that I've created a portrait of a strong, young woman of colour, and it's made me feel a little more self-assured in myself and my art.
B: You know, I've done quite a few portraits of friends and classmates over the years and they've always been complimentary about them. This was the first time I'd properly sat down and done one of myself, believe it or not. When they first saw it, they started coming out with things like, 'When do you ever concentrate like that?!', and, 'You seriously need to lighten up in that picture ...', but after the joking about they all said they really liked it, and couldn't believe how realistic it was, even though I only used two pencils. I did it front of a mirror, rather than from a photo on my phone, as a sort of experiment to see if I could do a self-portrait from life like Salvador Dalí or someone. I think it worked out well.
C: Lots of the other students opted for painting something quite abstract and challenging to look at. A fair number of others headed straight for the computer-editing suite practically seconds after they'd taken some photos of themselves that they could fiddle around with. I'm into a more naturalistic approach generally, especially in self-portraiture. I've always loved how the great artists like Rembrandt managed to convey something so personal, almost confessional, in the way they painted themselves, and that was my aim, too. It took me ages to get the right shot, but I think it totally captures how I've never let my disability define me, or constrain me in any way, whatever I want to do in life.

4
1 fiddle around 2 self-assured 3 complimentary 4 throwaway
5 More often than not 6 worked out well

Listening Part 2

2

noun (plural)

3

tips, (extensive) portfolios, studies, competitions, societies, arts events, skills, (fellow) artists. Correct answer: arts events. We can be sure of the answer because Akari mentions 'volunteering', which is a paraphrase of 'helping out at'.

4

1 arts events 2 creative vision 3 openings 4 spectator
5 self-promotion 6 artistic identity 7 commission 8 graphic design

Tracks 20 & 21

My name's Akari and I'm a professional artist, as I'm sure many of you would like to be one day. I'm here to give you some tips on getting to this point after you graduate.

First of all, what should you be doing now? I'm sure you've been building up extensive portfolios over the course of your studies, entering competitions to get your work known, and joining relevant societies available through the student union. Personally, I found volunteering for arts events in the local area the most useful thing to do. It's fantastic to make the arts part of people's lives and a great way to refine skills and get to know some fellow artists.

OK, some tips for getting your art onto the walls of galleries … tip number one: take time to familiarise yourself with all the galleries and find those who exhibit art similar to that which you produce. Curators and owners are looking for artwork that fits their creative vision, so try and find those with whom you'd be a good match.

Once you've identified some galleries that seem like a good fit, the next step is getting yourself known to them – so start networking. Spend a fair amount of time each day on their social media pages. Go to as many openings as you possibly can, it's a great way to build contacts and meet other artists.

You'll benefit greatly if the staff begin to recognise you as a supporter and regular attendee of other artists' exhibitions. A word of warning, though: at someone else's showcase, you are there as a spectator, so never treat these things as public calls for new talent to pitch their own work.

So, how can you get yourself known? Well, although many artists feel quite uncomfortable doing this, self-promotion is one of those invaluable skills you must try and master. At some point, you'll be offered some time with a gallery curator or owner and it's a skill you'll need to display. But, be warned: declaring, 'my work speaks for itself' won't get you far. Be humble and remember who makes the calls here.

If you want to be offered an exhibition, you can improve your chances by communicating how your artistic identity sets you apart from others. All galleries want to put on a memorable and original show, so talk about your work, what inspires you, and the unique themes you're attempting to explore.

Once a gallery sells your first work, their confidence in you will grow, and they'll push to sell more. New artists often complain about the commissions galleries take. Try not to feel too negatively about it. Yes, 40 or 50% may seem unfair, but they're giving you sales that you otherwise wouldn't have had and once you've sold more, you can renegotiate.

Earning a steady income from your art is extremely tough at first. But you can diversify by taking on other work. Teaching can be a great job, as can a move into graphic design. But be wary of taking on too many jobs or those outside of the creative sector. A friend of mine entered sales and the demands of the job meant that art soon took a backseat.

Reading and Use of English Part 5

2

a The writer suggests that very few photos were taken of a family holiday – 'a mere twenty-eight photos of the entire week' – and even fewer were 'genuinely worth keeping'. She expresses some amazement at this situation which is totally different from her own experience of photography.

b Emily describes the stages that people used to go through when they wanted to take and develop their photographs, and suggests that the whole process seems like a long time to her: 'A week later the pictures would eventually arrive through their letterbox'.

c The last line contains a rhetorical question – 'how vastly improved would my family's lives have been, given the chance to retake, edit, and filter their pictures?' – which, coming after a description of the limited options available in the past, signals her appreciation for the technology available today.

d Despite her grandparents' optimism about the quality of the photos they had taken – 'the pictures would eventually arrive through their letterbox, at which point they would excitedly flick through them' – their skills were limited – 'only three or four were worth keeping'. There is a suggestion that Emily might be writing about this in a negative way, but in the final sentence she seems to blame the technology available at that time, rather than anyone in her family.

3

Students' own answers.

4

1 C 2 D 3 A 4 B 5 C 6 D

Grammar

Avoiding repetition

1

1 one, this 2 those 3 so 4 another 5 which, so 6 that

2

1 (said) ~~it~~ so/this 2 ~~it~~ one 3 it one 4 ~~these~~ this 5 ~~all~~ everything / it all / all of it 6 ~~it~~ one/some 7 ~~it~~ that/this 8 ~~yourself~~ you

3

(Suggested answers)

2 Fewer and fewer people listen to classical music these days. This is a shame, as it offers something for everyone.
3 I spend a fair amount of my free time listening to podcasts. The ones / Those I enjoy most are the ones / those about gaming or sports.
4 I'm hoping to get a ticket at some point for a show by my favourite artist/musician. Buying one would make me so happy.
5 Although I enjoy watching my favourite sports team, there are others that are better than the one I support.
6 I don't like spending a lot of money on clothes or trainers so I tend to buy second-hand ones I find in online stores.
7 I've never learnt how to play a musical instrument really well, and I really wish I had / had done / had done so.
8 Whenever I feel strongly about a particular topic or idea, I say so.
9 I don't like staying up late. If I had to, I would, but I prefer to go to bed early if I can.
10 Whenever I meet someone new, I always seem to forget their name when I stop talking to them, even if they have mentioned it to me three times.

Vocabulary

Adjective–noun collocations (2)

1

big

2

1 considerable / huge / large / tremendous
2 amazing / good / great / huge / large / tremendous / wide
3 endless / loud / terrible / tremendous
4 considerable / great / huge / tremendous
5 heavy / terrible
6 amazing / good / great / tremendous / valuable
7 considerable / good / high / large
8 amazing / considerable / good / great / huge / satisfactory / tremendous
9 considerable / huge / wide
10 amazing / considerable / endless / great / huge / tremendous / wide

3

(Suggested answers)

Words like *huge* and *tremendous* have a more extreme meaning than *great*, *considerable* or *large*; they also tend to be used in more colloquial speech. *Amazing* conveys surprise at how much. *Terrible* conveys a negative attitude. *Good*, *valuable*, *satisfactory* and *great* (in most contexts) convey a positive attitude.

Reading and Use of English Part 2

1

1 preposition 2 infinitive verb 3 conjunction 4 noun 5 preposition 6 adverb 7 auxiliary 8 pronoun

2

1 under 2 do 3 but 4 way 5 out 6 far 7 having 8 themselves

8

1 another 2 whether 3 it 4 of 5 which 6 where 7 to 8 but

Speaking Part 3

1

1 Pair A 2 Pair B 3 Pair A 4 Both 5 Pair A

Track 22

Pair A

Examiner: Now I'd like you to talk about something together for about two minutes. Here are some factors which might affect people's enjoyment of a film and a question for you to discuss. First, you have some time to look at the task.

Now, talk to each other about how these factors might affect people's enjoyment of a film and why.

Anna: Do you watch many movies, Lukas?

Lukas: From time to time. I'm hardly what you'd call an obsessive film geek.

Anna: Oh, I love movies. I'm hoping to study film, photography and media at university, so you'll often find me obsessively going over movie-making techniques on videos online … though I do also watch movies in full because they give me pleasure as well.

Lukas: Well, let's look at the task. So, as far as I'm concerned, if I am going to sit down for a couple of hours and see a movie, I want the full, 'in-your-face' experience, watching it on a huge screen at the cinema.

Anna: Oh, yeah, any trip to the cinema is the high point of my week. But, at the same time, I don't think there's anything inherently wrong with watching a film on your phone, sitting there with your earphones in.

Lukas: Hmm, doesn't it entirely depend on the type of movie? Like, I couldn't imagine how anyone could get absorbed in a huge-budget, special-effects blockbuster on a little 15cm screen.

Anna: Perhaps not … yeah, thinking about it, I'll generally only watch a drama or comedy or something on my phone.

Lukas: So, I think we're in agreement that screen size definitely plays a part in your enjoyment.

Anna: Agreed. So, how about being familiar with the actors you're watching?

Lukas: Well, I actually tend to have a slight issue in that regard: if I've seen an actor in some film or other before, particularly if I've enjoyed it, I find it almost impossible to put that to one side and accept them as this new character.

Anna: Really?

Lukas: Yeah, it's a genuine thing I've got. Like, sometimes I'll even get distracted by one of the actors playing a minor part, who's only on screen for a scene or two … 'What's she been in before? What did I see him in again?'

Anna: That must be annoying … and, presumably, something that quite a few people experience, given how much content everyone watches all the time. Having said that, loads of people find they can get more involved in a film if they already feel some sort of connection to an actor. That's certainly true of me, anyway.

Lukas: Lucky you. So, how about being within company or by yourself when you're watching a movie? I'd say that has a huge impact on how much you enjoy it.

Anna: Oh, absolutely. For one thing …

Pair B

Examiner: Now I'd like you to talk about something together for about two minutes. Here are some factors which might affect people's enjoyment of a film and a question for you to discuss. First, you have some time to look at the task.

Now, talk to each other about how these factors might affect people's enjoyment of watching a film and why.

Daniel: Well, I think that being alone or with others will have a huge impact on your enjoyment of a film.

Marta: Yes, especially if it's a comedy. Laughter is really infectious in any situation, so if you're with someone who finds it hilarious, you're probably more likely to find each scene more enjoyable than you might if you were on your own.

Daniel: Yes, I agree – likewise, if you're watching a horror movie with someone who gets scared easily. Now, let's think about the effect of cost. I'd say that everyone expects far more from a film if they're paying however much for a cinema ticket, as opposed to watching a movie for free, or as part of a subscription to a streaming service.

Marta: I wouldn't disagree with you at all. It's pretty expensive going to the cinema, isn't it? Now, time of day … surely that wouldn't have any effect on your appreciation of a film? I'll happily watch movies on my phone whenever.

Daniel: Me too. I have been to a few afternoon showings of films at the cinema, and probably enjoyed it as much as I would have had I gone at night, but it is a bit strange, walking out of a dark theatre and blinking at the daylight.

Marta: Oh, yeah, that is a little weird. OK, next – screen size. I'm not sure that has a massive effect on your enjoyment of a movie, how about you?

Daniel: Umm, probably not.

Marta: OK so, let's move onto familiarity with the actors. If it's an actor I like, then fine, I generally tend to like them in anything.

Daniel: Yeah, that's the same with me …

2

(Suggested answers)

1 Although the pair A speakers don't follow the instructions immediately, they have a much more in-depth, meaningful discussion of a couple of the options and are therefore dealing with the task better. The pair B speakers tend to flit from option to option with little to say.

2 Pair A could get started on the task right away – two minutes is not a lot. Pair B should look at each option they choose to discuss in more depth, without necessarily trying to cover them all.

3

1 I'm hardly what you'd call an obsessive film geek.

2 … you'll often find me obsessively going over movie-making techniques on videos online …

3 … any trip to the cinema is the high point of my week.

4 I don't think there's anything inherently wrong with watching a film on your phone

5 I couldn't imagine how anyone could get absorbed in a huge-budget, special-effects blockbuster on a little 15cm screen.

6 … sometimes I'll even get distracted by one of the actors playing a minor part, who's only on screen for a scene or two

7 … loads of people find they can get more involved in a film if they already feel some sort of connection to an actor.

8 … it's pretty expensive going to the cinema, isn't it?

5

2 Yes. You need to support your opinion and also involve your partner.

3 No. You'll find it hard to keep going for the whole minute.

4 Yes. This builds up the discussion.

5 Yes. This builds up the discussion.

6 No. This is not a way of having a constructive discussion. You don't need to reach agreement in the minute, but you should be reasonable.

6

They use strategies 2 and 5.

Track 23

Examiner: Now you have about a minute to decide which factor has the greatest influence over people's enjoyment of a film.

Lukas: Well, I think for me, already being familiar with the actors on screen can make or break how much someone enjoys a film. As we mentioned earlier, you and I are at opposite ends of the spectrum in terms of the actual effect it has on us, but I think we can probably assume that everyone either gets more distracted or more involved if they recognise the actors on screen. Do you agree?

Anna: I think you're probably right to a certain extent, although I'd suggest that you and I might be more on the extreme ends of that spectrum – I'm not sure everyone feels quite as strongly. In all honesty, I'd be more inclined to say that someone's experience of watching a film can change most dramatically depending on whether they're in company or alone. You know, lost in your own world or in a world you're sharing with friends.

Lukas: Yes, thinking about it again, you may well be right. I mean, there is such a huge difference between an individual's response and a collective response to any sort of art form, isn't there?

Anna: Well, exactly.

Examiner: Thank you.

Writing Part 2

A review

1

(Suggested answers)

a film that they were expecting not to like, only to end up loving it / which film / how the reality differed from your expectations / who you would recommend it to

2

(Suggested answers)

c, d, e, f

3

(Suggested answers)

Para 2: genre of film, setting, outline of story
Para 3: the visual aspect, the characters, the performances of the actors
Para 4: what the writer liked most, recommendations

5

1 resolved 2 cliché-ridden 3 sizeable 4 absorbing 5 vivid 6 dazzling 7 riveting 8 utterly 9 tender 10 snappy 11 undoubtedly

6

1 'Intricate' is mostly used in a positive sense in film reviews to refer to a plot that has many different elements and small details. 'Complex' has a similar meaning, but perhaps with the suggestion that the plot may be difficult to understand in some way. However, to describe a plot as 'complicated' suggests that it is overly difficult to follow, while 'far-fetched' suggests it is difficult to believe.

2 'Juvenile' is used negatively to highlight how simple or childish a reviewer thinks a movie is. 'Mindless' has a similar meaning. 'Hilarious' is entirely positive and means 'extremely funny'. 'Wacky' is also positive, but tends to be reserved for silly, slapstick or slightly crazy comedies.

3 'Light-hearted' means 'not intended to be taken too seriously', and is used positively, as is the case with 'cheery'(short for 'cheerful', meaning 'bright and happy'). 'Nostalgic' can be used in both positive and negative senses, as it suggests looking at the past in a way that creates both happiness and an idealised idea of the way things used to be. 'Sentimental' is generally used negatively, suggesting that the movie is over-emotional.

4 'Charismatic' is positive, describing an actor with great personality who it is extremely difficult to take your eyes away from. Similarly, 'compelling', although with more emphasis on how believable they are in playing the character. 'Charming' is also positive, meaning 'pleasant and attractive', but tends to be used in more light-hearted films (e.g. romantic comedies). 'Implausible', however, is used very negatively and means 'difficult/impossible to believe'.

5 'Bleak' is generally used to describe pessimistic dramas without much to make a viewer feel happy or hopeful but that is not to say that it is used negatively; some films are necessarily 'bleak'. 'Gloomy' has a similar meaning to 'bleak', but with a slightly more negative connotation. 'Depressing', on the other hand, carries a similar idea, but suggests a very negative response from the reviewer. Contrast this with 'uplifting', which is used very positively for films that make people feel happier or more hopeful.

6 'Emotional' can be used in either a positive or negative sense, but generally positive, and refers to a film or scene that makes the viewer feel strong emotions. 'Touching' works similarly, but is specifically related to feeling sadness, sympathy, pity, etc. 'Heart-breaking' recognises how well the film has caused feelings of extreme sadness, and is not used in a critical sense. 'Melodramatic', on the other hand, is usually negative, and suggests unnecessary exaggeration in plot/performance/style.

5 Vocabulary and grammar review

1

1 B 2 C 3 D 4 A 5 C

2

1 looking forward to starting
2 were (very/extremely) lucky to avoid / to have avoided
3 regret making / having made / that I made a/the
4 can't afford to buy
5 denies (ever) seeing / having seen / that he has ever seen
6 we checked out that we settled

3

1 to climb 2 to leave 3 to be rescued 4 waiting 5 phoning 6 to put out 7 realising 8 putting 9 to take 10 getting 11 snowing / to snow 12 climbing 13 to admit 14 to phone 15 to ask 16 to contact 17 regretting 18 to ignore

6 Vocabulary and grammar review

1

1 big 2 wide 3 large 4 deep 5 high 6 heavy 7 big 8 high

2

(Suggested answers)

2 When a child feels unhappy, they will ask for their mother more often than for their father.
3 Gustav bought a large house by the sea about ten years ago, which / This/ It turned out to be a good investment.
4 Leonardo lived in Canada as a child, which is / That's why he speaks such fluent English.
5 Svetlana spent several months trying to decide which car to buy and she finally bought one last week.
6 Matthew likes reading novels, especially romantic ones.
7 Violeta bought some apples in the market. She put some (of them) in the fruit bowl and used the others to make an apple pie.
8 Narayan has had two jobs. Both were in a bank but unfortunately neither was well paid.
9 There are five official languages in Spain and Manolo speaks all of them.
10 Pete had never spoken to Ann, although he'd often wanted to.

3

1 ~~all~~ everything 2 ~~both~~ either 3 ~~these~~ this 4 ~~yourself~~ you 5 ~~it~~ one 6 ~~it~~ so/something 7 ~~me~~ myself 8 ~~likes~~ does

Unit 7 In your free time

Listening Part 4

1

1 disco 2 folk 3 pop 4 classical 5 jazz 6 rap 7 rock 8 Latin 9 dance music

3

The key is C. She says 'I wasn't entirely sure what I was in for', but clearly it was far better than she'd expected – 'I was overwhelmed by the music.'
A is incorrect because she says she'd actually heard good things about it, which were confirmed for her when she listened to it.
B is incorrect because her father is the one who mentions how innovative it was. She doesn't confirm this.
D is incorrect because while she says her expectations of the album weren't completely positive, she also doesn't mention regretting her attitude.

5

1 D 2 C 3 F 4 E 5 H 6 A 7 G 8 E 9 F 10 B

Track 25

1 I guess I didn't have high expectations of the band I went to see, although I'd watched them online, and musically they weren't bad. When they first came on, though, I almost mistook them for the guys doing the sound checks, they seemed so unremarkable in their appearance. However, when they started ripping into their first numbers, I found I was actually able to make out all the words and admire the cleverness of them, which was great. And the event kind of left me wishing I hadn't abandoned my music classes and song-writing efforts quite so readily, but then I think I knew I was never going to really master them.

2 I'd only gone to the gig because of my friend's great obsession with the band – she's a big fan. I didn't know the first thing about them, so didn't know what to expect. However, even though they aren't the best guitarists I've ever seen, the music they played blew me away. Some of the tunes conveyed a sense of love and longing, for example, more effectively than mere words possibly could. I'd never really experienced that before. And I'd always thought, in big venues like the one we were in, that bands can look a bit lost in it all. But this band did their best by addressing us directly to introduce each piece, which helped enormously.

3 The band I saw wasn't well known – far from it, in fact, as they hadn't been playing together long. So maybe that accounted for the amount of effort they put in within minutes of appearing on stage. No sooner had the lead singer introduced them than they started with a number guaranteed to get everyone dancing and having a great time! Quite a lot of stuff they played was what they'd written themselves, and after the gig finished, I felt motivated to try to produce something myself. I've written and recorded a few songs – something I wouldn't have done if I hadn't attended that gig – and I'm pleased with the results.

4 The concert hall was packed, but there was a warm-up band that played first, so the air of excitement had little to do with the band we'd come to see. Still, when they finally appeared in their costumes and started singing, their voices were in total harmony, and they produced some great melodies – a wonderful example of what truly outstanding singers can sound like. What's more, they utilised the entire performance space with a wonderful show that included a beautiful set and an elaborate light show. The audience couldn't take their eyes off them – myself included!

5 Most concerts I'd seen had been well-established acts, so I guess I'd expected the band to come on wearing amazing costumes. But given they were playing a small, inexpensive concert, that wasn't the case. What was striking, though, was the way they just bounced onto the stage with their backing group, ready to go, with not a hint of nerves. And as players, they weren't at all bad, which was a surprise. In fact, one of the songs they played reminded me of a particular far-flung place I once visited. In my mind, I started planning how I could get away from my dreary job and boring hometown and travel there once again.

6
1 gigs 2 musician 3 lively atmosphere 4 lyrics 5 warm-up band
6 blown away 7 backing group 8 master

Vocabulary

Complex prepositions

1
1 in aid of 2 by means of 3 in place of 4 on account of 5 On behalf of
6 with/in regard to 7 in keeping with 8 in exchange for

2
1 d 2 h 3 g 4 a 5 f 6 c 7 b 8 e

3
1 **on** account of 2 in exchange **for** 3 **on** behalf of 4 in place **of**
5 **in** aid of

Reading and Use of English Part 7

2
1 The writer is rather negative, raising questions about whether becoming a young actor is really as good as it may appear.
2 She had a chaperone to look after her, right from her arrival at the airport.
3 She suffered from sleepless nights prior to signing his film contract. / She was very nervous.
4 By the end, the writer sounds more optimistic that young actors will come through the experience well, and be successful as adults.

3
(Suggested answers)
Para B: the possible effects of negative reviews
Para C: a young actor's reflections on her experiences
Para D: One possible reason why there are good young actors in the profession now
Para E: an example of how young actors are supported in their work
Para F: a reaction to watching someone being filmed
Para G: the large amounts of money that young actors can earn

4
1 when they become adults; later in their careers
2 extremely careful searches
3 what negative things might happen to him as a result
4 both positive and negative feelings
5 come through the experience unharmed
6 denied her as many opportunities as it provided
7 losing the opportunity of attending school
8 manage the changes necessary to become an adult actor

5
1 G 2 A 3 E 4 C 5 F 6 B (Para D is not used.)

6
1 *(Suggested answers)* film director, producer, screenwriter, set designer, director of photography, costume designer, props master, make-up artist, casting director, film editor, composer, location manager, lighting technician, researcher

Grammar

Linking ideas: relative and particle clauses

1
1 where 2 which 3 undertaken 4 in which 5 encouraging
6 that/who 7 who/that 8 teaching

2
1 a 1, 2, 4, 6 and 7 b 4, 6 and 7 c 1 and 2 d In sentence 6 *that* can be left out. It introduces a defining relative clause and it is the object of the verb in that clause.
2 a 3, 5, and 8 b present: 5 (encouraging) and 8 (teaching); past: 3 (undertaken) c 3

3
1 which 2 who 3 whose 4 where 5 in which 6 which 7 who/that
8 for whom

5
1 quivering 2 based 3 Having read 4 made 5 specialising

Linking ideas: apposition

6
(Suggested answers)
1 *Tenet*, a science fiction film, was released in 2020.
2 The film follows the story of a secret agent, The Protagonist.
3 The two stars of the film, John David Washington and Robert Pattinson, are both well-known actors. / The two stars of the film are John David Washington and Robert Pattinson, both well-known actors.
4 The title of the film is a palindrome, a word that reads the same forwards or backwards.

Reading and Use of English Part 1

3
1 B 2 D 3 A 4 D 5 C 6 A 7 D 8 B

Vocabulary

Money words and idioms

1
1 renting 2 earn, buying, selling 3 hiring 4 lend, pay 5 borrow

2
1 sell 2 make 3 buy 4 pay 5 afford, costs 6 meet 7 take out
8 burn 9 raise

3
1 mouth 2 trees 3 cash 4 nose 5 way 6 water 7 purse 8 bank

4
1 ~~gaining~~ earning 2 ~~afford~~ cover, ~~spend~~ pay/give 3 ~~pay~~ buy / pay for
4 ~~borrow~~ lend 5 ~~rent~~ borrow 6 ~~buy~~ spend 7 ~~earned~~ raised

Speaking Part 4

3
1 They are answering questions 1 and 4.
2 Extract 1: Her main point is that the activities are worthwhile and people enjoy them. Extract 2: Her main point is that the activities are more useful in large clubs because members find it harder to get to know each other.
3 Extract 1: She partly agrees. Extract 2: She agrees.

Track 26

Extract 1

Laura: No, not at all. I think it's really important for people who are going to be spending time together to get to know each other properly as quickly as possible. I don't have any experience of these activities myself, but I imagine if they're well thought out, they can be very worthwhile for the people who go on them as well as for any clubs and organisations they belong to. There are probably a few individuals who can't see the point of them – and ironically, these may be the people who most need these activities – but I'd say the majority find them enjoyable and useful.

Examiner: What do you think, Marta?

Marta: Well, I think I'd benefit from them personally, but not everyone would be comfortable with activities like these and I don't think they should be forced to take part if they don't want to.

Extract 2

Marta: I'd say it's easy for individuals to feel a bit lost in a large club, and particularly when they first join, especially if they don't already know anyone who belongs. In this situation team-building activities provide opportunities for people to get to know each other better more effectively than simply leaving things to chance, so that when they start joining in club activities, they feel more comfortable. That's not likely to be such a problem for members of smaller clubs, where everyone gets to know everyone else quite quickly.

Examiner: Do you agree, Laura?

Laura: Yes, I do. I think in smaller organisations people tend to get together socially, and maybe don't need things organised for them.

Writing Part 2

An informal letter

1

(Suggested answer)

when the contact needs to be official, formal or serious, e.g. a letter of application, resignation, condolence or complaint

2

(Suggested order)

1 B   2 E   3 D   4 C   5 A

3

1 A asking a friend let him/her stay for a few days
B a holiday rental company confirming payment and reminding the client of conditions
C inviting staff and students to an end-of-term party
D thanking musicians who played at party
E apologising to a customer for damage to a package of books in transit

2 *(Suggested answers)*
A The two people know each other well.
B This is part of a business transaction between the company and the person renting the property.
C The tutor or student who is writing has a friendly relationship with the people involved in the course.
D The party organiser/host was pleased with the music and wants to show his/her appreciation.
E The company is making a polite apology to a customer who has complained.

3 A am looking (leaving out I), put me up, didn't, meet up, I'd, I'll be around, Don't worry, it's, loads of, it'd be good
B no informal features
C to get everyone together, we're asking (people) over, It's, hopefully, shouldn't
D Just a short note (leaving out This is), as well, set the evening up
E no informal features

4

(Suggested answers)

1 (This is) Just to let you know (that) …
2 your holiday that's coming up soon / the holiday you've got coming up
3 will be taken from your credit card
4 the week after you leave
5 I'm very sorry about this
6 We try really hard
7 To start with, I wanted to know about / I asked about
8 If you want / you'd like me to do it for you
9 There's something else we need to think about
10 I can't tell you what to do about this

5

(Suggested answers)

A Good to hear from you – it'll be great to get together when you're over here in November. Unfortunately, we've got people staying at that time, so we won't be able to put you up – sorry.

C Thanks for the/your invitation to the college get-together in June. It sounds great and I'll certainly be there.

6

(Suggested answers)

1 quite informal as this is to a friend
2 Should Stevie go on tour with his classmates or stick with his friends
3 & 4 Students' own answers

7

1 end   2 middle   3 beginning   4 middle   5 end   6 middle

8

a 4 and 9   b 1, 3, 6 and 10   c 2, 3, 5, 7 and 8

Unit 8 Sound and vision

Listening Part 3

2

1 D   2 D   3 D   4 A   5 C   6 A

Track 27

Interviewer: I'm with final-year university student Kate Evans and radio personality Harry Fielding, who've both been involved in university student media organisations. Kate, you joined your university's student newspaper – what was behind that decision?

Kate: Well, a friend invited me to go along and help out on it. Admittedly, I wasn't that enthusiastic initially. I'd been feeling time was running out to decide what to do after graduation and didn't think it would present a possible way forward workwise, despite the paper's great reputation. My friends all had their futures mapped out – and I was panicking about being left high and dry. Luckily, after a few shifts, I discovered I was wrong and could see where the paper could lead.

Interviewer: So, tell us about your experiences of working there.

Kate: Well, I was frightened when I joined – worried it would be a high-powered news room full of serious people. Thankfully, it's pretty relaxed and everyone is really supportive of one another. We're all beginners, slowly building up our know-how. I admit, my interviewing techniques and graphic design skills would benefit greatly from a course, but I think it's a great way to start to learn the ropes.

Interviewer: Student newspapers are increasingly publishing online rather than in print. What's your view on that?

Kate: Well, obviously with print, there's a cost, especially as sourcing greener and more sustainable printing can be expensive. And of course, with online editions, breaking news stories can be instantly included, rather than having to wait for the next print run, which is great for promotion via social media. But with our printed copies, we distribute updates for major stories. Having said that, print circulation figures are still important. It certainly helps to give a student letting company an idea of how many papers we deliver when persuading them to advertise. Without that, we risk losing valuable income.

Interviewer: And Harry, since you graduated, you've worked as a radio sound engineer and presenter. And you started through university student radio.

Harry: Absolutely. I started studying electronic engineering at uni without a specific career in mind. I discovered through another student I bumped into at a party that the university's radio station was the best in the country, so I signed up. I soon found my feet there, worked my way up to being a presenter, and developed my own style. All that provided a great stepping stone for my subsequent career. I also took on the role of station manager for a while – managing budgets, programming – but soon realised that my skills were better used elsewhere.

Interviewer: So for students considering following in your footsteps, how does student radio compare to real-world broadcasting?

Harry: Well, even if radio doesn't seem the right career for you, student radio's good fun – but that doesn't mean you won't have to work hard! But you get far more chances to really push the boundaries of your imagination – a privilege you might not get in professional radio! Obviously, how people listen to radio is changing, with content increasingly delivered digitally – but creating new content, and the technical knowledge to broadcast it still needs to be acquired, and student radio's an excellent start – although you may find your station's kit leaves something to be desired, depending on where you're studying.

Interviewer: So, both of you – how important are student media organisations? Kate?

Kate: Well, I've recently found a post with a national newspaper, working in global news and the arts. But without the experience I've had, it would have been harder to get a foot on the ladder, especially in an industry that depends on connections to get you through the door. And no matter how the material is consumed by young people, whether online or in printed form, we'll always need writers and broadcasters to produce content – that'll never change. I can't see a day coming when that'll be generated by automatic processes.

Interviewer: Harry?

Harry: I now mentor a lot of young people looking for media careers, and if those student media opportunities disappear, it'll be a lot harder for new talent to get the skills they need to break through. It's often said young people don't listen to the radio or read newspapers. They do, but they're consuming the content in non-traditional ways – so we'll always need writers and broadcasters to produce it. And through the media, they engage with local and world affairs – climate change, political matters – and help maintain things like a vibrant creative arts world.

Interviewer: Thanks!

3

1 They both got a lot of experience in their respective fields. Kate has now been offered a job on a national newspaper, and Harry's range of experience has led to work as a mentor in media careers.
2 *(Suggested answer)* They might have found the work they were doing a distraction from focusing on their studies, and also difficult to fit in time-wise.

4

1 running 2 mapped 3 met 4 found 5 worked 6 get 7 provided 8 took 9 following 10 push 11 get

Grammar

Reported speech

1/2

1 How important are student media organisations?
2 I've recently found a post with a national newspaper.
3 We'll always need writers and broadcasters to produce content – that'll never change. I can't see a day coming when that'll be generated by automatic processes.
4 It's often said that young people don't listen to the radio.
5 We'll always need writers and broadcasters to produce content.

2

Track 28

1 So, both of you – how important are student media organisations?
2 Well, I've recently found a post with a national newspaper,
3 We'll always need writers and broadcasters to produce content – that'll never change. I can't see a day coming when that'll be generated by automatic processes.
4 It's often said that young people don't listen to the radio …
5 … they're consuming the content in non-traditional ways – so we'll always need writers and broadcasters to produce it.

3

Track 29

1
Latifa: Have you ever listened to student radio, Jake?
Jake: Yes, I tuned in for the first time yesterday. It was brilliant!
2
Jake: How hard is it to become a journalist, would you say?
Latifa: Well, I think it could be quite difficult.
3
Latifa: What will you do after graduation?
Jake: If I can't get a job, I'll probably go travelling for a while.
4
Jake: What time are you leaving tomorrow?
Latifa: About 10 am.

4

(Suggested answers)
1 Latifa asked Jake if/whether he had ever listened to student radio. Jake said (that) he had tuned in for the first time the day before / the previous day, and it had been brilliant.
2 Jake wondered how hard it was to become a journalist. Latifa thought it could be quite difficult.
3 Latifa wanted to know what Jake would do after graduation. Jake replied that if he couldn't get a job, he would probably go travelling for a while.
4 Jake asked Latifa what time she was leaving the following day. Latifa told him (that) she was leaving at about 10 am.

Vocabulary

Prefixes and suffixes

1

1 unpopular 2 inexperienced 3 inefficient 4 illegal 5 dissatisfied 6 irrelevant 7 imperfect 8 uncertain
Nouns: 1 unpopularity 2 inexperience 3 inefficiency 4 illegality 5 dissatisfaction 6 irrelevance 7 imperfection 8 uncertainty

2

1 disapprove 2 relocate 3 interact 4 misunderstand 5 underestimate 6 reconstruct
Nouns: 1 disapproval 2 relocation 3 interaction 4 misunderstanding 5 underestimation 6 reconstruction

3

1 autobiography 2 co-pilot 3 non-fiction 4 ex-president 5 semi-detached

Reading and Use of English Part 3

2

(Suggested answers)
1 It was a system that added sound and sensations (even simulated motion) in a cinema while a film was running, to match what was on the screen (eg an earthquake) and heighten the viewers' experience.
2 The writer mentions that how people perceive different smells and tastes, for example, can vary widely, so the sprays and drinks provided may not have the desired effect of creating an attractive taste or smell. Also, the equipment may turn out to be quite complex, which might not be very relaxing when watching TV.

3

1 enrich 2 combinations 3 persuasive 4 novelty 5 unforeseen 6 perception(s) 7 subjective 8 complexity

Speaking Part 3

3

1 They address all of them.
2 *(Suggested answers)* They give quite full answers to the topics they address, apart from newspapers, where they don't really address the idea of what changes in behaviour newspapers can bring about.
3 *(Suggested answers)* Yes, they do, but the subject of newspapers is discussed in less depth than the others.
4 Yes – they both contribute fairly equally, without one person dominating, and they each respond to what the other person says.

Track 30

Daniel: So, let's have a look… the first one's celebrities. I guess there's all sorts of stuff they could influence, isn't there? I mean, I don't personally take much notice of what they're up to, but the way they dress, what they're doing and so on is hugely important to some people.

Marta: Mmm, especially young people who might want to copy them – their clothes, things like that. But you do see them using that influence to champion good causes, highlight stuff, you know, which is brilliant and they can have a really positive effect. And I'd say social media is another powerful influence, wouldn't you?

Daniel: Definitely, but not always with such positive outcomes.

Marta: No, I mean, there've been all kinds of movements and ideas promoted on social media that have changed people's thinking and behaviour, sometimes in quite dangerous ways, and they wouldn't have a platform without social media.

Daniel: No, but it's also been a force for good in many ways – it's highlighting things like climate change and so on, that we need to be aware of.

Marta: True. So, then what about environmental groups? I mean, some of those have really caught my attention with their adverts and so on, and made me change my behaviour to try and be more environmentally friendly.

Daniel: I'd agree with that. As for political groups, I've always tended to think people probably naturally belong to one group or another regardless of any publicity they put out, so I'm always surprised during elections when there's a massive change of direction.

Marta: Well, they may have a lot of influence over people's voting choices, but once those choices are made, do those groups continue to influence behaviour? I'm not entirely sure …

Daniel: And maybe, both of those groups exert their influence through other media like TV and radio? Loads of people use the TV news as their main source of information.

Marta: … although, they may have made up their minds about what they think before they tune in. That might determine which programmes they watch. But TV's certainly a powerful platform – and it's so accessible, and does influence what people think, and what they buy.

Daniel: Yeah, and pretty much every house has got a television – and you can watch on a computer if you haven't. But what about radio? I mean, I'm a real radio fan – I listen to loads of new bands on music channels, but I don't know how widespread that is.

Marta: Well, it's the same as TV – you can listen on the move, can't you, although maybe that's a newish concept for older people? But I do think people are influenced by what they hear – they might get live festival tickets and so on based on the music they've heard on the radio – but whether it affects their ideas, I'm not so sure.

Daniel: Well, there's plenty of talk radio alongside the music stuff that could almost certainly do that, but maybe those programmes are catering for a more niche audience. Anyway, we haven't mentioned newspapers.

Marta: Hmm, I'm just not sure how many people read them nowadays, what with so many other sources of information available. But maybe front-page headlines can subconsciously affect your attitude to things.

Daniel: Yeah, you don't even need to read the whole story for that to be the case.

4

I guess, all sorts of, stuff, I mean, things like that, and so on
a lot, loads of, plenty of
almost, pretty, probably
the suffix *-ish* (newish)

7

2 They interact well, each putting forward ideas and negotiating to reach their final decision.

Track 31

Examiner: Now you have about a minute to decide which two of these influences have the greatest effect on people.

Marta: I think we've more or less decided, haven't we?

Daniel: Well, I'm not sure. I mean, we agreed that all of these can be hugely influential in their own ways – but which have the greatest effect? I think we had quite a lot to say about social media.

Marta: Its effects can certainly be extreme – but is it as powerful as TV? We talked quite a bit about that.

Daniel: So would we say that's one of the most powerful? I mean, there are all the news programmes and adverts.

Marta: Plus its accessibility. TVs are everywhere, and radio to a lesser extent.

Daniel: Yeah, we did touch on that. OK?

Marta: So, are we also saying that social media's also more influential than the other things on the list? I mean, for me it is.

Daniel: Me too. So, I think we're agreed.

Marta: Good.

Vocabulary

Reporting verbs

1

1 tells 2 talk/speak 3 discussed 4 saying 5 comment
6 spoke/talked

2

1 tell 2 saying, speak 3 mention 4 expressed 5 says 6 comment
7 told, mention 8 speak

Reading and Use of English Part 6

2

1 a process in which people work together
2 talk about something in depth to sort out possible problems
3 get readers to look at material on your website
4 accept whatever (work) people ask you to do
5 a topic on which people are likely to hold opposing opinions
6 adapt themselves in a particular way
7 made them less attractive
8 thinking in a similar way, having the same approach to things
9 quick to notice something

3

1 b 2 b 3 a 4 a

4

1 B 2 A 3 C 4 D

Grammar

Transitive and intransitive verbs

1

1 allowed, instructed, required, warned
2 convinced, informed, reminded, told

2

1 a intransitive, visit someone's home
b transitive, give a name to (somebody)
2 a intransitive, move very quickly
b transitive, manage (an organisation)
3 a intransitive, succeed in doing something difficult
b transitive, be in charge of (an organisation)
4 a intransitive, depart
b transitive, let (something) remain where it is
5 a intransitive, go to live in a different place
b transitive, change the position of (something)

3

1 assure you 2 tell me 3 gave it to me 4 allow us to
5 introduced me to 6 wish you

Writing Part 2

A proposal

2

1 Yes 2 Yes 3 *(Suggested answers)* I welcome this opportunity, I feel able to make some valuable suggestions, I strongly recommend, an exploration of, this thriving facility consistently provides, showcase, move its focus, encapsulates the modern approach, are bound to be, I hope very much that you take my proposal into consideration

3

(Suggested answers)
1 I suggest conducting street interviews.
2 Children and teenagers would especially appreciate this kind of programme.
3 I am sure/certain/convinced that filming in this way would attract the attention of the audience.
4 A visit to the impressive concert hall currently under construction would also be a good idea.
5 I do hope you find my suggestions useful.

4

1 from 2 to 3 to 4 on 5 with, with 6 to 7 in, in

7 Vocabulary and grammar review

1

1 afford 2 rent 3 earns 4 sell 5 hired 6 lend
7 cost, paying 8 buy

2

1 account 2 exchange 3 because 4 aid 5 place 6 keeping
7 regard 8 behalf

3

(Suggested answers)
1 (While) dealing with his mother's absence, an eleven-year-old boy tries to understand his family and stop it from breaking apart, (all of) which he finds very difficult.
2 A man called Black, whose brain becomes magnetised, unintentionally destroys every tape in a video store, (which is) owned by his best friend. Feeling sorry for the store's most loyal customer, an elderly woman who is losing her memory, Black and his friend set out to remake the lost films, which include / including *The Lion King* and *RoboCop*.

3 In this film, (which is) based on a sci-fi novel by Richard Matheson, a military scientist, played by Will Smith, is left completely alone in New York, which is deserted after a virus has wiped out the human race.

8 Vocabulary and grammar review

1

1 ex-president 2 misunderstand 3 illegal 4 dissatisfied 5 autobiography 6 rebuild 7 irrelevant 8 inefficient

2

1 unpopular 2 inexperienced 3 imperfect 4 uncertain 5 disapprove 6 relocate 7 interact 8 underestimate 9 overestimate

3

(Suggested answers)

1 Roland told Joanna that she mustn't tell / not to tell anyone what she had seen.
2 Clare said it was / had been a surprise seeing Tom last week / the previous week. She said she hadn't seen him since they were / had been at school together.
3 Ben asked Jerry if he should do the shopping that afternoon.
4 The doctor told me that I had to stop smoking if I wanted to get rid of my cough.
5 Bogdan asked me how many languages I could/can speak.

4

1 'What are you doing out so late?'
2 'Do you have / Have you got any plans for tomorrow evening?'
3 'This is the worst programme I've ever seen.'
4 'I'll phone you as soon as I get home.'
5 'I hope I'll be going there tomorrow.'

5

1 promised never to / (that) she would never 2 advised me to apply for that 3 asked (me) if/whether I'd / I had 4 suggested meeting the following / suggested (that) we (should) meet the following 5 warned the motorist not to drink 6 announced that they were getting married

Unit 9 Invention and innovation

Listening Part 1

1

a Disagreement
b Disagreement
c Agreement
d Agreement (but negative)

2

B

Track 32

Woman: What's that you're reading?
Man: An article called, 'Inventions that never made it'. Listen to this: 'In the late 1890s, French artist Jean-Marc Côté said, "by the year 2000, humans won't be living only on land – we will also have settled in the sea, travelling on underwater buses guided by whales." How do people dream up such absurd ideas?
Woman: I don't know, but I can't help but respect anyone who can come up with something so unbelievably inventive. Anyway, it was a very different era then, wasn't it?
Man: Yes, it's certainly not something someone would come up with now. Could you imagine going online tomorrow and seeing some supposedly visionary inventor presenting it as a solution to congestion in cities?
Woman: No, but who are we to criticise?

3

(Suggested answer)

People, specifically the man, can get too excited about new technology which, ultimately, doesn't end up being successful.

Track 33

A few years ago, everyone was convinced that augmented reality glasses were 'the future'. I'm sure that invention must have got a phenomenal amount of investment. Apparently, everyone would be walking around wearing them, or so they said. I clearly remember you excitedly placing an advance order for a pair. And did life undergo a massive transformation? Hardly. So, it might be an idea to exercise a little more caution before doubting someone else's judgement.

4

a AR glasses
b The woman says nothing about the challenges for a company, more about the difficulty for people in knowing what technology.
c 2 c The man

5

Track 34

Woman: What's that you're reading?
Man: An article called, 'Inventions that never made it'. Listen to this: 'In the late 1890s, French artist Jean-Marc Côté said, "by the year 2000, humans won't be living only on land – we will also have settled in the sea, travelling on underwater buses guided by whales." How do people dream up such absurd ideas?
Woman: I don't know, but I can't help but respect anyone who can come up with something so unbelievably inventive. Anyway, it was a very different era then, wasn't it?
Man: Yes, it's certainly not something someone would come up with now. Could you imagine going online tomorrow and seeing some supposedly visionary inventor presenting it as a solution to congestion in cities?
Woman: No, but who are we to criticise? A few years ago, everyone was convinced that augmented reality glasses were 'the future'. I'm sure that invention must have got a phenomenal amount of investment. Apparently, everyone would be walking around wearing them, or so they said. I clearly remember you excitedly placing an advance order for a pair. And did life undergo a massive transformation? Hardly. So, it might be an idea to exercise a little more caution before doubting someone else's judgement.

6

3 C 4 C

Track 35

Woman: By the end of this decade, we'll have been relying on computers for about seventy years, which really isn't that long, historically speaking. In that time, technology has helped us to pretty much reinvent whole societies. I mean, look at how far we've come with smartphones. In the coming year or so, more than half the world's population will be using them. That's widespread, portable and increasingly affordable access to the internet. So why people complain about the pace of technological change with things like that going on, I'll never know.
Man: Are things actually that clear-cut? I'm not sure there's so much to celebrate. What gets me is how everyone around the world is passively watching these technological shifts take effect, blindly accepting the idea that all this innovation doesn't have an off-switch, when, as history shows, it unquestionably does. We need to take responsibility now if we're to gain control of it all, otherwise life could change beyond recognition and not necessarily for the better. Like, we used to just text each other and wait for a response. Today, we instantly know if the other the person has read our message. Is that necessarily a good thing, given that, if they don't reply immediately, we get annoyed about being ignored?

7

5 B 6 C

> **Track 36**
>
> **Man:** Wow, your new fitness app looks fantastic.
>
> **Woman:** Yeah, well, from an aesthetic point of view, it is pretty eye-catching, if that's your type of thing. I love how well integrated all the menu options are: look … it makes devising a training plan for myself so much more straightforward than anything else on the market. It's a little annoying that the trial period only lasts for three days, but I suppose the company was confident enough in the product to know that's plenty of time for someone like me to decide they like it, and pay for a subscription.
>
> **Man:** That's good. It's amazing when you find exactly the right app for yourself, but it is difficult, isn't it? I've no idea how many times I've downloaded one and lost interest within minutes because it's unusable. And although, on the whole, you shouldn't trust them, I'm always getting taken in by those suspiciously flattering reviews most of them get given. Mind you that was actually how I stumbled across my guitar tutorial app – seeing all those five-stars on screen. It's made a huge impact on my playing in that time. I'll have had this phone for two years soon. I bet I'll have been spending more time on this app than any other by the time I upgrade my phone.

8

1 dream up 2 undergo 3 presenting 4 exercise 5 take 6 lost 7 made

Grammar

Future perfect and continuous; *be* + *to* infinitive

1

1 I'll have had 2 be using 3 be living / have settled
4 we'll have been relying on 5 I'll have been spending 6 we're to gain

2

1 We will have left by the time you arrive.
2 My brother will be playing his new video game all evening.
3 In May we will have been learning English for eight years.
4 Come over after 9.00, I'll definitely have finished my work by then.
5 Soon, it will have been six weeks since Angela moved to Argentina.
6 The president is to give a speech later today.

3

1 In ten years' time, we **will be travelling** around in driverless cars, and taxi driving will have ceased to exist as a job.
2 In the future, the majority of the world's students **will do** most of their learning online.
3 By the end of the century, thousands of people **will have been offered** the chance to take a holiday on the moon.
4 It won't be long before most people **will have decided** to switch to a plant-based diet.
5 Correct

Reading and Use of English Part 7

1

Ethical hacker: computer security expert who is employed to simulate an unauthorised attack on a computer network. This is done to test or evaluate its security, so that appropriate defence systems can be put in place that protect the network from a real attack by someone with malicious or criminal intent.
Computational linguist: someone who uses computers to study and analyse models of natural language and speech. One example of a current application of these skills is the development of text-to-speech software, which translates what someone says into digital text (e.g. Siri/Bixby).
Chief listening officer: someone who searches through the internet – particularly social media – to find all instances where their company has been mentioned whether in a positive or negative way. They then share that feedback with the appropriate departments.
Digital overlord: Despite the menacing-sounding job title, this is essentially a website manager who is in charge of monitoring the site's performance, updating registrations and content, and so on.

2

Paragraph 1 Introduction: A personal story about being hacked. *'I'm shaking with fury.' '… Such a thing …'*
Paragraph 2: A friend explains that she hacked the writer's accounts. *'… inviting herself in …' 'Shall I make coffee?'*
Paragraph 3: Description of a person who hacks computers to identify security issues (ethical hackers) for the company to fix. *'… the term is an oxymoron.' '… hackers with far less honourable intentions.'*
Paragraph 4: A further description of ethical hackers and how they differ from the stereotypes. *'Some of them …' '… Hollywood cliché …'*
Paragraph 5: A summary of how much ethical hackers can earn. *'She even seems a little embarrassed to confess that …' '… job-title …'*
Paragraph 6: Summary of why we have ethical hackers *'…ordinariness of their working environment …' '… as high as $10 trillion …'*
Paragraph 7 Conclusion: Explanation of what we should be doing. *'… we should all pay more attention …'*

3

1 F 2 B 3 A 4 G 5 D 6 E (C is not used)

Grammar

Objects, reflexives and reciprocals

1

1 from 2 herself 3 you 4 itself 5 selves 6 themselves 7 another

2

1 I'm sure my programming and coding skills would improve if I had an online tutor to teach **me**.
2 Thank goodness my computer's operating system updates **itself** – I'd never remember to do it otherwise.
3 My dad is one of those people who have almost no technical know-how, yet never blame **themselves** when they have problems with their devices.
4 I'd love it if someone **bought me** a new VR headset for my birthday.
5 My friends and I will always support each **other** unquestioningly, whatever the circumstances.
6 The only way you can guarantee something will be done right it is by doing it **yourself**.

3

1 mother bought a smartphone for her
2 (all) by ourselves makes me
3 constantly arguing with one another
4 to lock myself out of

Vocabulary

Multi-word verbs

1

1 hacked into 2 pops up, lock out 3 logged on 4 scroll through, signing in/on, shutting down 5 filter out

2

a hacked into b shutting down, running out c popping up/pop up
d locked out, log on/in e Scrolling through

action*, *activity*, *event* and *programme

1

1 activity 2 action 3 events 4 programme

2

1 offer varied programmes
2 attending glamorous events
3 take decisive action
4 participating in outdoor activities
5 threatened with legal action
6 commemorate important historic events
7 presenting popular programmes
8 involve myself in criminal activity

Speaking Part 2

3
1 Yes 2 Yes 3 No (She suggests two ways.) 4 Yes 5 Yes 6 Yes

Track 37

Examiner: Now in this part of the test I'm going to give each of you three pictures. I'd like you to talk about two of them on your own for about a minute, and also to answer a question briefly about your partner's pictures. Anna, it's your turn first. Here are your pictures. They show people using technology while studying. I'd like you to compare two of the pictures and say why they might be using that type of technology, and how difficult it would be to study without it.
Anna: OK, so the first picture shows three children in school and they're each wearing a virtual reality something or other – glasses? Or would you call them headsets? Yeah, VR headsets. I'm assuming that they don't actually belong to the children, so presumably they've been provided by the teacher to bring a subject to life in one way or another, like, it could be a geography class and the students might be using them for something along the lines of visiting an interesting landmark or a geographically important part of the world, and being able to see something up close, even if it's only virtually, helps students to understand things that bit better. You obviously couldn't do that without those headsets, but on the whole I think they're just a nice addition to a lesson – you'd be perfectly capable of studying a subject without them.
The second picture is much the same as the first one, in that it also shows someone wearing a headset of some description, but in this case it's a pair of wi-fi headphones, sorry, I mean 'wireless' headphones. The guy in the photo might find that listening to music helps him to – what's the phrase? – blank everything out and just work without distraction. He's also using his – it's not a hundred percent clear whether it's a tablet or a laptop, but I'd imagine he's using that to stream a few songs while working through the study materials on the screen. Overall, I think that, although it wouldn't be impossible to study without this device, it would certainly become a huge amount trickier. It's pretty much the norm, these days.
Examiner: Thank you. Daniel, which type of technology do you think is the most useful for studying?
Daniel: Oh, no question for me, the laptop (or tablet, as Anna said, it could be either). I mean, VR headsets are great, but they are limited in terms of what programs or class materials are currently available on them. With a laptop, you get access to the internet, and what a study resource that is.
Examiner: Now, Daniel, here are your pictures …

4
1 something or other 2 one way or 3 along the lines 4 much the same
5 of some description 6 sorry, I mean 7 what's the phrase?
8 a hundred percent

5
a 6 b 2, 3, 8 c 1, 7 d 4, 5, 6

7

Track 38

Examiner: Now in this part of the test I'm going to give each of you three pictures. I'd like you to talk about two of them on your own for about a minute, and also to answer a question briefly about your partner's pictures. Here are your pictures. They show people using items of technology. I'd like you to compare two of the pictures and say why the technology might be important to these people, and how they might be feeling as they use this technology.

Track 39

Examiner: Now in this part of the test I'm going to give each of you three pictures. I'd like you to talk about two of them on your own for about a minute, and also to answer a question briefly about your partner's pictures. Here are your pictures. They show people using machines as part of their work. I'd like you to compare two of the pictures and say how the machines might help the people to do their work, and how rewarding this work might be.

Reading and Use of English Part 4

1
1 unexpected denial of (any) responsibility 2 put off 3 had no choice but

2
1 tell the difference between 2 to be a comprehensive review of
3 apologised for letting the team 4 a/any doubt in my mind
5 you not phoned, I may/might/could well 6 huge impact on
the way in

Writing Part 1

An essay

3
2 Always tell someone if you're worried about something that happened online. She expresses this in her own words.

4
1 On the whole 2 as such 3 That said 4 as and when
5 It goes without saying that 6 as a consequence of
7 All things considered

5
1 By and large 2 accordingly 3 Having said that
4 at any given point when 5 Needless to say 6 as a result of
7 Ultimately

6
1 Para 3 2 Para 2 3 Para 4 4 Para 1

Unit 10 Learning for life

Starting off

4
- educational contexts – learning environments, e.g. school, college, university, online, etc.
- optimum – most likely to bring success or advantage
- in-person – physically face-to-face
- manner – the way something is done
- catastrophic – absolutely awful
- conformity – behaviour that follows the standards accepted by a group or society
- facilitate – make something possible or easier
- pragmatic – solving problems in a practical and sensible way, instead of by having fixed ideas or theories
- equip – provide

Listening Part 2

2
(Suggested answers)
critical thinking, problem solving, reasoning, research skills, creativity, perseverance, planning, self-discipline, adaptability, initiative, collaboration, etc.

3

Track 40

Hi, everyone. My name is Samia Godin and I'm here to tell you about a project I did with a group of fellow students about the essential skills we'll need to develop as we move further into the 21st century.
Our group all felt that this is a fascinating area of research. If you find anything we mention today of interest, we've put together a bibliography of all the titles we referred to which we can happily provide you with. In a way, our talk is only really meant to summarise our response to that research.
One thing we'll all need, if we're aiming to thrive in the future, is the ability to cope with how quickly everything around us is changing, whether that's the growth of Artificial Intelligence, the endless updates to technology, or, most disturbingly, the climate.
A good number of the studies we read emphasised being conscious of and questioning what we can or can't trust as a reliable source – especially online – and so information literacy is going to be ever more crucial. Obviously, using critical thinking to interpret what we read in class is nothing new, but it'll be vital to reimagine this skill for the 21st-century context.

We can also be expected to be continuingly learning things throughout our lifetimes. Regarding this, there is a belief amongst education academics that self-study is not the best way forward. They all point to collaboration being far more effective for learning, whether this be through group study or working as part a team.

Developing our knowledge, though, is just one part of the puzzle. We also need the skill of remembering what we have learned so we can use it again and again. Obviously, anyone can check a fact online these days, but this is still a small element of learning. Most of what we know comes from long-term memory, and it's this that enables us to develop and build our skills for future use.

Another aspect to consider is where we develop these skills? Whether it's at work or at school it's misguided for students to see their place of study environment as a two-tier structure separating teachers and students. Instead, we should consider ourselves as part of an ecology, with everyone existing interdependently.

So, what criticisms do we have about how students are prepared for the future? The problem is that, so many education systems across the world remain centred on putting students through high-pressure exams Attainment is set above all else, often at the cost of developing student interest or curiosity.

Given there is agreement that what young people desperately need is time to reflect, to understand their own minds, what should education institutions be doing? Well, learning happens most effectively when someone is in a good place, mentally speaking, so surely it's imperative to really focus on student well-being when designing a course or curriculum, rather than presuming that students all have the same ambition to get top grades in every subject?

Now, I'm going to hand over to Chris, who's going to talk about this idea in more detail …

5

1 bibliography 2 climate 3 information literacy 4 collaboration 5 long-term memory 6 ecology 7 attainment 8 well-being

Reading and Use of English Part 1

1

1 eight 2 four 3 before

2

a lateral thinking b wishful thinking c logical thinking d critical thinking

4

The solution to the problem is:
1 Empty the box of drawing pins.
2 Pin the box to the wall.
3 Put the candle upright in the box.
4 Light the candle with a match.

5

creative thinking, flexible thinking

6

1 A 2 B 3 B 4 C 5 D 6 C 7 D 8 A

Speaking Part 4

2

a 4 and 5 b 1 c 3 and 6 d 2

4

They discuss questions 4 and 2.

Track 41

Extract one

Laura: I'd say probably older students, for the simple reason that they're more able to work independently than younger students. This kind of learning only works if students are motivated and interested. For this reason, it works more effectively when students work in pairs or groups. Members of the group can decide what needs to be done and share out the different tasks. Later, they can get back together to report the results of their efforts. I would say that anyone below secondary school age would find this difficult to do successfully.

Lukas: I agree with most of what you say, but I think we should introduce children to this kind of work while they're still in primary school, just to get them used to the idea of managing their own learning. Of course, teachers need to make sure they prepare their students well; that means giving very clear instructions to make sure students know what they're supposed to be doing …

Extract Two

Lukas: I think the main advantage is that students get a programme of study which is specifically designed for them. This approach lets the teacher focus on specific problems or difficulties that the individual student has, as well as adopting a learning style which suits that student. In most class teaching situations, teachers have to cater for a wide range of abilities and learning styles.

Laura: I don't disagree with that, but I think you're only looking at one aspect of education and learning. When students are in classes they're not just absorbing information. They're learning to get on with other people. Some people would say that this is at least as important as academic study.

Reading and Use of English Part 8

3

(Suggested underlining)
1 aimed / differentiate themselves / from / peers
2 drew / sense of determination / existing interest
3 amusement / subsequent outcome / efforts
4 understood / importance / adopting / set routine
5 experienced / gain in proficiency / chance meeting
6 took advantage of / sudden change / self-belief
7 felt relief after / adaptation / physical characteristics
8 paid / close attention / constructive remarks
9 allowed / concerns / their ability / delay / pursuit / ambition
10 convinced / widespread appeal / what they had learnt

4

1 B 2 C 3 A 4 B 5 E 6 A 7 E 8 D 9 C 10 D

Grammar

Expressing ability, possibility and obligation

1

1 ability, past
2 possibility, past
3 obligation, past
4 possibility, future
5 obligation, past
6 obligation, past
7 possibility, future
8 obligation, present

2

1 Both are correct.
a The pressure to finish is from an external source.
b The pressure to finish comes from within the speaker himself/herself.
2 Both are correct.
a I didn't catch a taxi because it wasn't necessary.
b I caught a taxi but it wasn't necessary.
3 Both are correct.
a It isn't necessary for you to go to the lecture.
b You are prohibited from going to the lecture.
4 a incorrect (We cannot use the affirmative *could* [ability] to refer to a single past occasion.)
b correct (We use *managed to* / *succeeded in* + *-ing* or *was able to* to refer to a single past occasion.)
5 Both are correct.
a It is possible for him to stay, and it is quite likely that he wants to.
b It would be possible for him to stay, but he probably doesn't want to.
6 a correct
b incorrect (We do not use *could not* to refer to a future possibility.)

3

1 ~~correct~~ corrected 2 ~~can't~~ couldn't 3 ~~lie~~ have lied 4 ~~could~~ can (This is a definite offer – *could* would suggest it is only a possibility.)
5 ~~would be able to~~ will be able to / can 6 ~~we afford~~ we can afford

Vocabulary

chance*, *occasion*, *opportunity* and *possibility

1

1 opportunity 2 occasion 3 possibility 4 chance

2

1 opportunity 2 occasions 3 opportunity 4 possibility 5 occasion 6 possibility

3

1 chance/opportunity 2 opportunity 3 possibility 4 chance 5 opportunity/chance 6 possibility/chance 7 occasion 8 chance/possibility

4

Examples

1 to visit / of visiting China.
2 be moved to our Paris office.
3 finding out what happened to my grandparents.
4 lose my temper with a colleague.

Writing Part 2

A report

4

a need   b are not   c the main topic

5

(Suggested headings)
1 Introduction   2 The Survey / Methodology   3 Issues
4 Menu   5 Price   6 Furniture   7 Conclusion

6

1 *(Suggested answer)* It starts with an announcement of aims and ends with a general conclusion. It is organised into clear sections with informative headings. It is mostly factual, giving information based on evidence.
2 suggest + noun (suggest ways); suggest + that + *would* clause (suggested that they would be willing…); suggest + *-ing* (suggest implementing price increases)
recommend + *-ing* (recommend improving/providing/offering/repairing/replacing)
3 feel that, report that, conveyed, raised, supported by, there were hardy any complaints that, suggested, considered, feel
4 would be grateful if

7

1 the school principal and the governors' committee
2 five
3 *(Suggested answers)* Introduction/Aim, Town attractions, Educational innovations, Improvements to leisure facilities and social activities, Conclusions and recommendations

8

(Suggested answers)
1 host families   2 computer-assisted learning / e-learning / online study   3 socialise   4 increased opportunities to speak
5 acquire   6 well-qualified / experienced teachers   7 class size
8 leisure activities   9 teaching methods / approaches to teaching
10 independent learning / self-study

9 Vocabulary and grammar review

1

1 programme   2 activity   3 action   4 events   5 action
6 programme   7 event   8 activity

2

1 up   2 into   3 of   4 of   5 out   6 in   7 through   8 to

3

1 won't renew / won't be renewing
2 will have been teaching
3 will have been
4 going to launch / to launch
5 won't/will not have got
6 to be charged
7 will have been waiting
8 will be offering

4

1 myself   2 themselves   3 itself   4 other   5 one   6 him

10 Vocabulary and grammar review

1

1 an equal   2 last   3 historic   4 slight   5 miss, golden   6 real
7 solemn   8 second   9 slim   10 opportunity

2

1 won't have to / won't need to
2 must, didn't have to / didn't need to
3 must / have to, have to / need to
4 needn't / don't need to / don't have to
5 mustn't, 'll have to / need to
6 need to / must / have to
7 needn't
8 don't have to / don't need to

3

1 ~~could~~ can / will be able to   2 correct   3 ~~could~~ can   4 ~~could pass~~ managed to pass / succeeded in passing/ was able to pass
5 ~~could be able to~~ / would be able to   6 ~~couldn't~~ shouldn't / needn't

Unit 11 Globetrotters

Starting off

2

(Possible answers)
Means of transport: cramped, delayed, environmentally friendly, hassle-free, inconvenient, luxurious, scenic, stressful, well-organised
Types of destination: challenging, cosmopolitan, exotic, harsh, hostile, inhospitable, isolated, luxurious, off the beaten track, remote scenic, urban
Types of traveller: adventurous, cautious, enthusiastic, open-minded, resourceful, respectful, uncompromising, well-organised

Listening Part 1

1

1 three   2 different themes   3 A, B or C, twice   4 read the questions and underline the key ideas   5 listen to the whole extract before making your choices

2

(Suggested underlining)
1 woman / travelling by air   2 agree   3 he / travel advice   4 regret/ trip
5 friends / difficulties / travelling / describing / man   6 own experience / woman

3

1 B   2 C   3 A   4 A   5 B   6 C

Track 42

Extract One

Man: You travel huge distances by train, don't you? Why opt for that if it can take far less time by plane? I know there's the environmental aspect …

Woman: Well, I just get sick and tired of having to check in everything but the bare essentials, knowing I won't see my stuff again until we arrive. And there's that feeling of being processed through the airport, nervous you'll be kept waiting. On top of that, there's the lack of space on the plane, with no prospect of being out in the open for hours. And you can spend a fortune for the privilege – although there are bargains out there, if you look.

Man: Well, other means of travel aren't necessarily the solution, are they? I had to change four times on my trip to Edinburgh. The flight would have got me there far quicker, even with putting bags in the hold. Still, I will admit I've learnt to enjoy going to the airport. I now find the process interesting and try not to focus on any of the stuff that's annoying.

Woman: Well, to be honest I wish I didn't find air travel so incredibly stressful – otherwise I might do it more. If only I could adopt your mindset – it'd make some things easier. But I'd miss the views from the train.

Man: Sure …

Extract Two

Woman: You've just returned from a round-the-world trip – that must make you the ultimate go-to person for travel advice!

Man: I'm not sure that confidence is entirely justified! I mean, I saw a lot, but whether I'd recommend someone follow my footsteps – that's debatable. It all depends on the individual and what they're after. Even if they did follow my advice, there's no guarantee they'd experience the same things.

Woman: And would you have done anything differently if you'd realised what lay ahead?

Man: Well, there are a few regrets, I guess. Things didn't go entirely smoothly, travelling alone, although that made me more resourceful, having to make do with what I had. And inevitably I felt lonely at times, missing having a permanent home. But, that came as no surprise – that was the whole point, after all. I made sure I stayed safe the whole way, too – but maybe the downside was that I'd have had more fun if I hadn't been so risk-averse. That said, travelling the world is an adventure however you do it. And if I hadn't done the trip, I wouldn't even be talking to you now!

Woman: So, what'll you do if you get itchy feet again?

Man: Plan another trip!

Extract Three

Woman: So, you nearly got stranded abroad?

Man: Yeah, travelling alone . A 3-day train journey. We'd been told we'd stop for an hour at a station, so people wandered inside to buy stuff. If I'd known what'd happen, I definitely wouldn't have got off – rather ill-advised, looking back! Anyway, I returned to the platform where the train had been, only to find it'd disappeared without a trace, with all my stuff inside. And no sign of my fellow passengers … I was struggling to keep my cool! Anyway, a friendly guard eventually reassured me the train had moved away from the platform – but was due back any moment.

Woman: Scary experience!

Man: Haven't you encountered anything like that?

Woman: Not exactly. I remember arriving by train in a new city abroad. I left everything in the station lockers while I went to explore, then returned to the station – to find it unrecognisable! My locker had disappeared into thin air. Anyway, I managed to get help, in the local language, I'm delighted to say. The staff were lovely, and led me to a back entrance – and the lockers – I'd gone in at the front.

Man: Phew!

Woman: If only I'd stopped to think, instead of panicking! Still, it hasn't put me off …

Vocabulary

Fixed phrases

1

1 h 2 b 3 a 4 e 5 g 6 c 7 d 8 f

2

1 keep your cool 2 whole point of 3 without a trace
4 spend a fortune on, rough it 5 get sick and tired of 6 out in the open

Grammar

Conditionals

1

a 5 b 2 c 4 d 1 e 3

2

(Suggested answers)
1 Because the speaker is talking about a lengthy activity in progress at the time.
2 The first verb (hadn't done) refers to past time, and the second (wouldn't be talking) to the present (it's a mixed conditional)

3

1 hadn't left, wouldn't be wandering
2 wasn't/weren't rushing, would/'d be
3 wasn't/weren't, would/'d probably have reached / probably would have reached
4 were, would/'d carry
5 wouldn't have happened, had/'d been concentrating
6 would/'d like, will/'ll show

4

1 ~~wouldn't~~ won't 2 ~~send~~ would/could send 3 ~~am~~ will be
4 ~~won't~~ wouldn't 5 ~~have travelled~~ travel 6 ~~stand~~ be standing

5

1 can count on you to
2 as/so long as we set
3 be working late tonight unless
4 would not / wouldn't have presented her with
5 would be grateful if you would / you'd / you could
6 had not / hadn't come up

wish* and *If only

1

1 it would, could 2 I hadn't written so many 3 I wasn't / weren't travelling
4 it were / was 5 you would, could do more 6 I'd brought the picnic, could have something

Reading and Use of English Part 5

1

1 T 2 F Read the text quickly to get an idea of its structure and what it is about before dealing with the questions. 3 F The questions are answered in the same order. 4 T

4

1 B 2 C 3 A 4 D 5 A 6 C

Vocabulary

***at*, *in* and *on* to express location**

1

1 in 2 on 3 in 4 On , in , at 5 in 6 at, in 7 in 8 in, in

2

1 ~~of~~ in 2 ~~at~~ on 3 ~~of~~ in 4 ~~at~~ in 5 ~~at~~ on 6 ~~at~~ on 7 ~~at~~ in 8 ~~in~~ on
9 ~~at~~ on 10 ~~to~~ in

Reading and Use of English Part 2

1

1 eight
2 Read the whole text quickly, read before and after each gap.
3 Think about what type of word you need.
4 It is essential: if you spell the word wrongly, you lose the mark.
5 Read through the completed text to make sure your answers make sense.

3

The places can range from luxurious to back-to-basics. The advantages are free accommodation and food, and spectacular views from where you're living. People says it's a once-in-a-lifetime opportunity.

4

1 If 2 away 3 which/that 4 few 5 take 6 more 7 not 8 beyond

6

1 brought 2 not 3 one 4 only 5 away/off 6 at 7 till/until/before
8 less

Speaking Part 1

1

(Suggested answer)
all except 3 and 7

2

1 Laura: 6 Daniel: 4 Marta: 1 or 8
2 Laura and Marta
3 No, because sometimes they're describing reality rather than an imagined situation or event.
4 Marta – wonderful, such a lovely area, fabulous, great, I'd really love that, the chance of a lifetime. She also shows enthusiasm through her intonation.
5 They use their own vocabulary. This shows range of vocabulary, knowledge of synonyms, understanding of the question, confidence with English.

Track 43

Student A

Laura: Well, it depends where to. I'm certainly not afraid of taking risks for a bit of excitement and I get a real buzz from a bit of danger. But it would have to be a journey to somewhere interesting, somewhere that was worth visiting. I wouldn't want to do it just for the excitement.

Student B

Daniel: Well, it certainly helps with the day-to-day problems like buying tickets, getting information and so on. But I'd say it's generally better to try to speak the local language if you can, because then you can get to know people, talk to them on their own terms, and that's when real communication starts happening. On the other hand, you can't learn the language of every country you want to visit, and in those cases English is definitely better than nothing.

Student C

Marta: Normally, I go to Croatia and the Adriatic Sea for a couple of weeks in the summer, which is wonderful, it's such a lovely area, but the chance to go even further afield and have some completely different experiences, well, for example to spend two or three months travelling round Africa, would be fabulous. It'd be great to see some of those places you only normally see on television, for example the Ngorongoro Crater or the Kruger National Park. I'd really love that. It'd be the chance of a lifetime!

Writing Part 2

A review

1

(Suggested underlining)
local people / hotels / help visitors choose / review recommending two hotels in your area / two different types of visitor / what sort of visitor / why

3

Plans A and B are both fine but other ways of organising the review (C) are also possible. The important thing is that the plans cover all the task requirements.

4
Plan C
Para 1: Introduction: why business travellers don't like the same hotels as tourists
Para 2: Rooms and prices in hotel 1 – suits low-budget tourists
Para 3: Other features of hotel 1 – some positive and negative points
Para 4: Features of hotel 2 – suits business travellers
Para 5: Brief rounding off
5
1 However 2 Equally 3 though 4 as 5 both
6 An added attraction is that 7 As 8 together with 9 not only
6
1 compact, moderately priced, elegant, moderately sized
2 clean, airy, basic, luxurious, spacious, well-equipped
3 friendly, helpful, competent, professional
7
1 b (There is a lot of information, but it uses contractions and addresses the reader as 'you'.)
2 using contractions and addressing the reader as 'you'

Unit 12 Our planet

Listening Part 2

1
1 Ross Island
2 scientists conducting research and support staff – key place for studying Antarctica
3 Average temperature of -18 degrees. Lowest temperature recorded of -50 degrees.

Track 44

On the southern side of Ross Island, located around 4,000km south of New Zealand, you'll find McMurdo station, the largest and one of the most remote research facilities on the continent of Antarctica. Each year it serves as an important laboratory and logistical hub for hundreds of scientists from around the world conducting research on and around Ross Island.

Here you will find astrophysicists, biologists, glaciologists and geomorphologists working alongside specialists from numerous other scientific disciplines, all of whom incorporate their daily findings on McMurdo into their research. Over the years, this has contributed to our global understanding of the causes of climate change, as well as helping to shed light on the weather patterns, geology and wildlife of this region.

Since being established in 1955, time and technology have enabled McMurdo to progress from a small military camp of temporary huts to a permanent research station, housing people year-round. Summertime sees the station supporting a summer population of around 1,200 people while, in the winter, McMurdo depends on the remaining people – around 200 civilian support personnel and a few scientists – to keep it going.

Living there is not for the faint-hearted. Those who do choose to live and work there must adapt quickly to the cold climate. It is rare to see the temperature creep above 0 degrees celsius, while the annual mean is minus 18, and the lowest recorded extreme was minus 50 degrees.

3
1 F You have to complete eight sentences.
2 F No more than three words will be missing from each sentence.
3 T
4 F You should read the gapped sentences before you listen.
5 F Write what you think you hear, even if you are not sure. (Your answer may be correct. If left blank, it will always be wrong.)
4
1 seasonal
2 mining camp
3 curiosity
4 maintenance
5 vegetation
6 the military
7 mental strain
8 visibility

Track 45

Hi, I'm Kirsty Steele, and today on the Work2Travel podcast, I want to tell you about how it's possible to get paid to live in Antarctica.

First off, despite what you might assume, there's no shortage of positions you can apply for. There are currently 43 permanent scientific research stations operating year-round in Antarctica, with an additional 50 facilities that run seasonal operations, one of which I was attached to. All stations accommodate people who work and live on-site, so I had the shortest commute of any job I've ever had.

I was eligible to work at McMurdo, a US station on Ross Island. When you first arrive there and see only grey buildings set against the vast, white background of that jaw-droppingly beautiful continent, feel as if you're walking into a mining camp. But once you become part of this hard-working community, you start to appreciate how functional everything is.

I was lucky to join a team I really got on with. Even though our backgrounds couldn't have been more diverse, we worked extremely well together, bonding with each other through our shared circumstances, our occasional homesickness and, most notably, the curiosity that united us and made day-to-day living a real journey into the unknown.

Now, it's not just scientists who live and work in Antarctica. A wide range of crew positions become available as and when people go home after their placements. If you've worked in maintenance at some point, your skills may well be required – mine certainly were. I also know McMurdo's currently short of people on kitchen duties, but aren't likely to be recruiting until the next cycle.

One word of warning – if you are vegan or vegetarian, McMurdo probably isn't the place for you. Don't get me wrong, the canteen food was miles better than I'd been expecting, even though there wasn't a huge amount of variety. But you may need some vitamin tablets, primarily because the only vegetation that can grow there is lichen – the slimy, plant-like stuff growing on rocks.

February is the best month to be at McMurdo. That's when huge cargo deliveries arrive from the US and New Zealand, with a year's worth of supplies and fuel, brought to McMurdo by the military. They join us for a few days of pretty unforgettable parties before heading home again.

The sun sets for the final time in late April and doesn't rise again until August. Winter brings with it continuous darkness, coupled with a constant, biting wind throughout the station, so it's no surprise that there's a high incidence of mental strain affecting most residents as they go about their daily duties.

It's tough when flights home from McMurdo are delayed. Planes can get within minutes of the airfield, only for the pilots to turn back because of visibility issues caused by snowstorms. The runway itself is far from ideal – not least because it's made from compacted snow – but if pilots can't even aim for it properly, their refusal to attempt a landing is understandable.

Vocabulary

Prepositions following verbs
1
1 as 2 on 3 to 4 into 5 to 6 for 7 to 8 with
2
1 ~~to~~ in 2 ~~in~~ on 3 ~~on~~ in 4 ~~in~~ on 5 ~~in~~ on 6 ~~with~~ to 7 ~~in~~ on 8 ~~for~~ to

Reading and Use of English Part 7

1
1 six 2 is one 3 gapped text 4 words, phrases and logical development
4
Sentence 2, with its reference to 'The additional realisation', is incorrect as there is no realisation mentioned in the first paragraph. In sentence 4, there is nothing in the first paragraph that could be logically connected to 'This idea'.
The other two sentences are possible.
5
Students' own answers
6
1 F 2 E 3 B 4 G 5 D 6 C

Grammar

Countable and uncountable nouns
1
1 elephant, plant 2 trees, elephants, years 3 bark, skin, tissue 4 skin, tissue (a skin = the whole covering of an animal, especially used when this covering has been removed from a dead animal; a tissue = a paper handkerchief) 5 Africa, Earth

2
1 a the taste or the drink in general b a cup of coffee
2 a mass of hair b a single strand of hair
3 a the substance b different types of cheese
4 a heaviness b individual pieces of metal used in weight-lifting
5 a the substance b spectacles used to help your eyesight
6 a knowledge, understanding b events or activities
7 a physical activity b sets of questions

3
1 a 2 Ø 3 Ø, the 4 the, a, a 5 the, the, Ø, Ø

4
1 The 2 the 3 the 4 a 5 the 6 Ø 7 a 8 the 9 a 10 the 11 Ø
12 a 13 Ø 14 a

5
1 a suit and tie, a formal occasion
2 the/a job (the job = the particular one we're referring to)
3 the advantages and (the) disadvantages
4 the Internet
5 the homeless
6 ~~A~~ The most important thing
7 ~~a~~ the capital
8 ~~the~~ technology
9 a basic knowledge
10 ~~the~~ a degree, ~~the~~ work in ~~the~~ IT

Vocabulary

Word formation

1
appreciate: appreciation
encourage: encouragement(s)
explain: explanation(s), explication(s)
inspire: inspiration
investigate: investigation(s), investigator(s)
receive: receipt(s), reception(s), receptacle(s), recipient(s), receptionist(s), receiver(s), receptiveness

2
access: access
belief: believe, disbelieve
conversation: converse
determination: determine
equality: equalise
pursuit: pursue

3
access: accessible, inaccessible
activist: active, inactive
account: accountable, unaccountable
community: communal
damage: damaged, damaging, undamaged
honour: honourable, dishonourable, honoured, dishonoured

4
1 first-hand 2 city-dwelling 3 record-breaker 4 outdoor
5 birdfeeder, outside, wildlife

5
first-hand, outside

6
1 play
2 rip
3 time
4 eye
5 narrow
6 work
7 eco, forward
8 high, world

Speaking Part 3

1
1 your partner
2 written prompts
3 three
4 more
5 need not

2
1 forest fires 2 drought 3 deforestation 4 oil spills 5 air pollution
6 overfishing
a *(Suggested answers)* 1 wildfires; bushfires 2 famine; extreme weather; over farming 3 forest clearance 4 oil pollution; water pollution; water contamination; biohazards 5 fossil fuels; smog; air contamination
6 over-consumption other words: flood
b Students' own answers

4
(Suggested answers)
1 They deal with four out of five of the environmental issues in their discussion – which is perfectly acceptable, they don't need to cover all five – but on deforestation and air pollution they don't talk directly about how people's lives are affected. Too much time is spent talking about causes rather than effects, and about the amount of news coverage each issue receives. They are better when detailing the effects of extreme weather and overfishing.
2 They could focus more directly on the question asked by the examiner in the first part of their discussion.

Track 46

Examiner: Now I'd like you to talk about something together for about two minutes. Here are some environmental issues that affect people's lives today. First, you have some time to look at the task.
Now, talk to each other about how these environmental issues affect people's lives today.

Anna: Well, this one's really relevant at the moment because it's been in the news a huge amount over the past few days – deforestation. Apparently, the world is losing its forests at a faster rate than at any time in history. I heard that about 80% of Earth's land animals and plants live in forests, and huge numbers of those may well soon be lost forever.

Lukas: Yes, and still so many people have got this idea that deforestation is limited to a small number of countries and regions, mainly those that have rainforests. Which isn't actually the case at all. OK, let's move on. I'd guess that air pollution gets more widespread recognition in the media. You know, how so many people today have breathing problems as a result of it, it's always on the news.

Anna: Is that something you've noticed? I'd have said the opposite. From what I see, it's becoming less prominent in the news. Maybe that's because of scientists saying air pollution isn't increasing as quickly as it used to, or vehicle emissions and exhaust fumes are supposed to be decreasing as everyone moves towards using electric cars, or whatever.

Lukas: Yeah, but not quickly enough, not by any means.

Anna: Well, exactly. Umm, shall we look at extreme weather? My dad was telling me the other day about how he used to watch the news on TV when he was a kid, and see reports of famine and starvation in particular regions – usually equatorial regions – all caused by drought, with rivers drying up, livestock dying. It was the big warning about climate change and what was to come.

Lukas: Yeah, and now look – extreme weather has blown up and it's the norm pretty much everywhere now. No one can say, 'oh, it's something that happens over there' anymore. Like, there are annual, devastating heatwaves in my country, often leading to forest fires, and they never used to happen anywhere in Europe. People are losing their homes, even their lives. It's like no one ever read the signs.

Anna: And in so many parts of the world, extreme weather leads to problems like poor harvests and crop failure, which means people have no food and have to travel for days, on foot, to refugee camps where they can find food. Too many places have become desert regions where people simply can't live any more.

Lukas: Very true. And next there's overfishing. Well, initially I might say that it's obviously more of a problem for marine life than it is for humans, who seem to be largely focused on destroying the environment for land animals, but that's not the case, is it? We're doing huge damage to the food chain living in our oceans as well.

Anna: Well, exactly. And, yeah, while fewer fish means there's less food available for sea birds or other predators, for example, it's also the case for those communities of people whose diet relies primarily on the fish they catch each day, not to mention, of course, anyone who depends on fishing as a source of income.

Lukas: Yeah, that's a really good point, I hadn't thought of that.

Examiner: Thank you.

5
Yes, they reach agreement. They decide that extreme weather poses the greatest threat.

> **Track 47**
> **Examiner:** Thank you. Now you have about a minute to decide which of the issues poses the greatest long-term threat to people's lives.
> **Anna:** Right, OK. Which one of these five do we think is the biggest threat?
> **Lukas:** It's very difficult to say, isn't it? They all do in one way or another – but perhaps the time scale is different.
> **Anna:** What do you mean?
> **Lukas:** Well, they all affect us now, but in the future some will get worse and some will improve.
> **Anna:** Like what?
> **Lukas:** Well, for example, in the short term, I think air pollution really is at such high levels in so many cities – increasingly high in many cases – and you wonder how anyone would be able to live there without their health suffering more and more each year. But as you mentioned before, vehicles are moving away from petrol and diesel and becoming electric…
> **Anna:** And, at some point we'll inevitably run out of fossil fuels, which means that those levels of air pollution should eventually come down. By that time of course the impact of all those other issues will probably have worsened.
> **Lukas:** You could be right. Umm, so what are we going to decide? Personally, I think extreme weather is going to pose the greatest threat. I don't know about you?
> **Anna:** Yes, I think I agree. I mean, millions of people are going to be displaced from their homelands and forced to migrate in search of a new life.
> **Lukas:** OK, I think that's a pretty convincing argument for extreme weather, right there.

Reading and Use of English Part 3

1
(Suggested answers)
friend: friendship, friendliness, unfriendliness; befriend (unfriend – Facebook); friendly, unfriendly
help: helper, helpfulness, helplessness; helpful, unhelpful, helpless; helpfully, unhelpfully, helplessly
know: knowledge; knowledgeable, knowing, unknowing, unknown, unknowable; knowledgeably, knowingly, unknowingly
live: life, liveliness, livelihood; lively, alive, lifeless
move: movement, removal; remove; moving, unmoved, movable, immovable; movingly, movably, immovably
nation: nationality, nationalist, nationhood; nationalise, denationalise, renationalise; national, international, multinational; nationally, internationally
sense: sensitivity, sensibility, sensitisation, desensitisation; sensitise, desensitise; sensitive, insensitive, sensible, insensible, senseless, sensitised, desensitised; sensitively, insensitively, sensibly, insensibly

2
1 ~~number~~ outnumber 2 ~~humour~~ humorous 3 ~~time~~ daytime/daylight
4 ~~deep~~ depth 5 ~~come~~ upcoming/coming/forthcoming
6 ~~practice~~ impractical 7 ~~advice~~ advisory 8 ~~exist~~ non-existent

3
1 tirelessly 2 likelihood 3 proudly 4 heightened 5 foundations
6 disagreeable 7 injustice(s) 8 overcome

Writing Part 2

A proposal

1
1 F Proposals are normally written for organisations, clubs, colleagues, etc.
2 T
3 F You should support suggestions and recommendations with factual information.
4 T
5 F The style can be less formal if you are writing for colleagues or fellow members of a club.

3
(Suggested answers)
1 In general the question is well answered. Factual information is included, e.g. *The college currently uses twice as much printing paper as it did two years ago. This is despite the fact that all information and study material could be moved to a cloud-based storage system.* 2 Yes. The clear, simple headings help the organisation.

4
1 the college
2 the fact that the college is using twice as much paper as it did two years ago
3 printing documents
4 lights, heaters, computers and other electrical devices
5 leaving on lights, heaters, computers and other electrical devices overnight
6 car park spaces
7 reduction of the number of places in the car park and replacement with bicycle racks
Reference words like these are used to avoid repetition when referring to things or ideas previously mentioned and to make links between sentences.

5
1 will be suggested, could be moved, should be printed, should be required, are (ever) turned off, are (commonly) left, should be reminded, is (widely) acknowledged, be reduced, be replaced, to be used, were implemented
2 *(Suggested answer)* The passive is commonly used in formal contexts. It focuses on the action rather than the person who does the action – this makes the language impersonal, which is appropriate for a text of this kind.
3 a, b, d, f
4 a Use of the recycling bins needs to be encouraged.
b If the air conditioning system was/were replaced, less electricity would be wasted.
c Cannot be changed. The verb has no direct object which could become the subject of a passive verb.
d The roof should have been insulated when the building was constructed.
e Cannot be changed. Neither verb has a direct object.
f At present the problem is not being taken seriously enough.
g Cannot be changed. There is no passive form for the present perfect continuous.

11 Vocabulary and grammar review

1
1 spend a fortune 2 rough it 3 kept waiting 4 sick and tired of
5 the whole point of 6 without a trace 7 keep your cool 8 out in the open

2
1 at 2 at 3 in, at 4 on 5 at/in, on 6 on 7 in 8 at

3
1 not overslept, he would not / wouldn't have
2 had arrived/been on time for
3 were better, she could have applied
4 would be (most/very/extremely) grateful if you
5 had not / hadn't been for Bruno's advice
6 would not / wouldn't be taking part in
7 was not / wasn't / were not / weren't afraid of
8 had got in / made contact

12 Vocabulary and grammar review

1
1 loneliness 2 widely 3 inability 4 oversimplified 5 Apparently
6 handmade 7 clarify 8 carefree

2
1 ~~with~~ in 2 ~~to~~ on 3 ~~in~~ to 4 correct 5 ~~for~~ to 6 ~~for~~ on 7 ~~to~~ on 8 correct

3
1 Ø 2 the 3 a 4 the 5 Ø 6 the 7 Ø 8 the 9 Ø 10 Ø 11 the 12 Ø
13 an 14 Ø 15 Ø 16 the

4
1 hydrocarbon 2 humans 3 matter 4 fuels 5 organism 6 reactions
7 setting 8 requirements 9 product 10 years

Unit 13 A healthy lifestyle

Starting off

1
(Suggested answers)
1 Advantages: alerts you to any problems, e.g. insomnia, so that you attend to them more quickly
Disadvantages: can make you over-concerned and obsessed about your own state of health or sleep patterns
2 Advantages: keeps you mentally alert and physically well
Disadvantages: too much sleep can make you feel groggy and mentally sluggish

3 Advantages: clean air and environment, less stressful life, less traffic
Disadvantages: allergic reactions to plants, venomous spiders and snakes, fewer medical services, smaller hospitals
4 Advantages: more medical services, larger hospitals
Disadvantages: pollution, risk of catching contagious diseases, heavy traffic causing pollution, which can affect asthma sufferers, traffic accidents
5 Advantages: getting a range of vitamins and minerals in food, keeping weight down through avoiding over-consumption of, e.g. fat and sugar
Disadvantages: greater expense and possible lack of availability of healthy food
6 Advantages: prevents childhood diseases, gives immunity to disease, reduces the spread of infectious diseases
Disadvantages: some vaccinations may cause illness in a minority, some people have a fear of needles, some have allergies to vaccinations
7 Advantages: keeps you physically fit, helps keep heart and lungs healthy, helps prevent obesity
Disadvantages: can cause injury and pain – bruises, muscle strain, aches, fractures, blisters, bruises, sprains, etc.
8 Advantages: keeps you fit, gets you out in the fresh air, allows you to grow fresh fruit and vegetables
Disadvantages: physically tiring, can cause injury, e.g., bad back, aches, blisters, bruises, sprains, insect stings, etc.

Listening Part 3

1

1 conversation 2 four 3 six 4 four 5 express the same ideas 6 before

2

1 Possible answers: eg increased stress, longer working hours
2 Dividing the night into two sleeps and eg working in the middle of the night
3 Possible answers: early risers find it hard to stay awake in the evenings, may miss out on social events. Night owls might find it hard to be on time for work, school or college in the mornings.

3

1 C 2 B 3 A 4 D 5 B 6 C

Track 48

Interviewer: Today I'm with authors Karen Nash and Paul Crosby, who're researching the subject of sleep for a book they're writing. Welcome! Karen, did anything particularly strike you during your research?

Karen: Well, getting enough sleep is critical to maintaining good health – it's when the brain does some of its most important work. Anyway, I came across some research on the purpose of dreams – fascinating stuff! I'd thought it was only during restful sleep that dreams occurred, and they were a means of filtering the previous day's events. This research suggested that as our days become predictably similar, we're unready for unexpected circumstances. So the role of weird dreams might be to provide us with suitable responses. The idea really appealed! However, despite the author arguing there was neuroscientific evidence to support it, the jury's still out, sadly, as to whether dreams do perform any useful function or are just a coincidental by-product of sleep, which you may or may not recall later.

Interviewer: Then you discovered an author who'd written extensively about sleep issues.

Karen: Indeed, just when I'd been having bouts of insomnia myself. The author's message was that even though sleep was a perfectly normal thing for our bodies, sometimes we just had to relearn how to do it. I found that comforting, somehow – that changing my sleep patterns was achievable. But I also knew I'd have to work at the solution. The hardest part was applying his rule that rather than lying awake, you should get up and do something calming, whereas I'd just stay in bed. Coincidentally, though, I also took on more daily exercise, and my sleep improved significantly. However, I did relapse later.

Interviewer: And Paul, you looked at sleep patterns of different individuals?

Paul: That's right. While people clearly need different amounts of sleep, it seems they fall into two distinct groups known as chronotypes – what we usually call early risers and night owls. And if you're a night person, there's little you can do to become an early riser. There's also a general acceptance that work or studies have to start early in the morning, whereas owls really need to start later. There's been research to suggest that applies to teenagers, too, but schools aren't very tolerant of late arrivals! And changing that'd require a massive culture shift.

Interviewer: But you've adopted a new sleep pattern – splitting the night into two?

Paul: Mmm, it started at university – staying up late to finish assignments. Then I realised I was much more effective after a nap, before working on into the early hours, when I wasn't disturbed. That inevitably meant having early nights, which though damaging to my social life, removed any worries I had about long-term negative impacts on my health. Anyway, to my relief I came across research indicating that, far from being innovative, this sleep pattern would've been familiar to people centuries ago – until electric lights were developed, in fact – as people had previously slept to pass the dark evenings.

Interviewer: And Karen, you've adopted a similar sleep pattern to Paul.

Karen: Indeed. I'd relapsed into having difficulties sleeping, and got tired of lying awake, and frustrated with feeling I was wasting valuable time, as my mind was so alert. So I decided to accept it. That's removed the stress of wondering whether I'll sleep. I just take what comes, which seems to suit me much better. I did worry that, after working during the night, I wouldn't be able to drift off again, but I've usually fallen into a deep sleep and my productivity's restored to previous levels. It means I forego certain things, like early-evening TV but there's always online catch-up!

Interviewer: So, what do you both feel has been your most important discovery, for the book? Karen?

Karen: Well, everyone's got an expert opinion on sleep, not surprisingly – it's something we've all got in common, as we can't do without it. But that does mean you have to treat some 'evidence' as anecdotal rather than scientifically proven. And people are becoming increasingly exposed to the 'sleep business' that's developing – the promotion of expensive beds as solutions, say. But it seems the more obsessed you are with getting enough sleep, the harder it is to achieve – that was key for me.

Interviewer: Paul?

Paul: I discovered a general lack of awareness about the importance of sleep – as if we can just put it on hold if we're busy. The thing is, it's a bit like breathing – the moment you're aware of it, it gets more difficult to do. But I did also come across useful advice amongst all the theories.

Interviewer: Thanks! And the book'll be published on …

Vocabulary

Prepositions following adjectives

1

1 of 2 to 3 to 4 to 5 of, with 6 with 7 with 8 of

2

1 ~~by~~ to 2 correct 3 ~~for~~ with 4 ~~to~~ for 5 ~~for~~ to 6 ~~for~~ to 7 ~~with~~ of 8 ~~to~~ of

3

1 for 2 of 3 by 4 with 5 against 6 about 7 to 8 in

4

1 of 2 of 3 to 4 to/for 5 with 6 in 7 about 8 at 9 to 10 about/of

Grammar

Ways of contrasting ideas

1

1 However, despite 2 though 3 whereas 4 While 5 even though

2

1 despite, whereas, while, even though
2 None of them – they can also be placed at the beginning.
3 However
4 *(Suggested answers)* although, in spite of (the fact that), (and) yet, Nevertheless, Even so, All the same, Still, On the other hand
5 In sentence 3 *but* could replace *whereas*.
In sentence 5 *although* or *despite / in spite of the fact that* could replace *even though*

3

1 although / even though 2 but 3 whereas/but 4 However 5 Although / Even though

4

Sentence 1: I recognised you as soon as I saw you, in spite of / despite the fact that we'd never met before. / I recognised you as soon as I saw you, in spite of / despite (my) never having met you before.
Sentence 5: In spite of / Despite the fact that I'd been there twice before, I forgot where the post office was. / In spite of / Despite having been there twice before, I forgot where the post office was.

5

1 ~~Despite~~ Although / Even though / Despite the fact that / In spite of the fact that
2 ~~however~~ but / However,
3 ~~However~~ Even though / Although / Despite the fact that / In spite of the fact that
4 ~~Though~~ However,
5 ~~where~~ whereas/but
6 ~~While~~ Although / Even though / Despite the fact that / In spite of the fact that

Reading and Use of English Part 8

1

1 ten 2 before 3 questions or statements 4 all 5 likely

3

(Suggested underlining)
1 determination increased / weren't going well
2 surprised / demanding
3 applied lessons / everyday life
4 compensate for disappointments / outside / sport
5 adopt/ different attitude
6 get over / previous negative sporting experiences
7 liberated by / fresh perspective
8 regrets absence/ aspects of other sports
9 accepted / lack of talent / compromising on dreams
10 doubt/ suitability / character

4

A basketball, football, hockey B rugby C cricket D tennis, football, hockey

5

1 B 2 D 3 D 4 A 5 D 6 B 7 C 8 D 9 A 10 C

Grammar

The language of comparison

1

1 fewer 2 more of 3 by far 4 well 5 more and more 6 far more 7 as ... as 8 a bit less 9 much more 10 nearly as many ... as 11 Most surprisingly 12 as ... as

2

1 nouns, long adjectives, adverbs
2 Less can be an adverb (e.g. People smoke less than they used to.) and may be followed by an adjective or another adverb (e.g. He's less practical than his brother. She works less efficiently than her sister.). Less can also be a determiner followed by an uncountable noun (e.g. We have less money than we thought.).
Fewer is a determiner and is followed by a plural noun (e.g. These days fewer people smoke than in the past.).
3 by far = easily, without any doubt, certainly
4 a bit, a little, slightly or no (I'm feeing a bit / a little / slightly / no better now.)

3

1 Many people earn less money than they did five years ago.
2 Finding a new job was less difficult than / not as difficult as I expected it to be.
3 That was the funniest film I've ever seen.
4 There are fewer unemployed people now than there were ten years ago. / Fewer people are unemployed now than ten years ago.
5 Working conditions aren't as good as they used to be.
6 Petrol is becoming more and more expensive.

4

1 ~~much~~ more / ~~far much~~ much more 2 ~~worst~~ worse 3 ~~like~~ as 4 ~~less~~ fewer 5 ~~harder~~ hardest 6 ~~fewer~~ less 7 ~~difficult even more~~ even more difficult 8 ~~much~~ far / a lot

Speaking Part 2

1

1 F You have to speak about two photos. 2 F You have to answer two questions. 3 T 4 T 5 T 6 F Correct a mistake if you notice you have made one.

2

1 *(Suggested answer)* They are all physical activities which people do to keep fit.

5

(Suggested answers)
1 The woman fulfils the task requirements better than the man, but although she talks coherently about why the activities are popular, she doesn't say how effective they are. She talks about her own personal preferences, which are irrelevant here as they are not part of the task.
The man talks about all three activities instead of selecting two. He doesn't fulfil the requirements of either part of the task he is set, although he does say a little about the qualities needed for rock climbing. Like the woman, he talks about his own personal preferences instead of saying why people participate in the activities.
2 Advice to the woman: Listen carefully to what you are asked to do. Don't be sidetracked into talking about yourself.
Advice to the man: Select two of the photos to talk about. Listen carefully to what you are asked to do. Think for a few seconds before you start to talk. Once you have started talking, try not to pause too often.

Track 49

Marta: OK, I'm going to choose gym exercises and walking, I think, because they seem to me to be quite different. I think gym exercises are becoming more and more popular because people don't have the opportunity to go out into the countryside, especially if they live in a town – so lots of people join a gym because they think that's a good way to keep fit. I think it's to do with time and space and not having the opportunity to walk. Whereas walking is something you can do only if you have access to the countryside – which a lot of people don't have these days. Anyone can join a gym and plan their visits to fit in with their other commitments. Personally, I prefer walking to gym exercises, which I think are dreadfully boring. Walking's more interesting because you get to see the countryside.

Lukas: The three photographs here show very demanding activities. Perhaps the most physically demanding would be either rowing or cycling because you're exercising more parts of the body, but then again for rock climbing you need a certain level of physical fitness. Umm, I've never actually been rock climbing myself, but I know someone who does it regularly and he's very fit. I suppose if I had to choose one activity to help me keep fit, it'd have to be rowing, I think, because it works the muscles in almost every part of your body – especially your arms, legs, back and stomach. I did it a couple of times when I was a kid and I remember it was absolutely exhausting. Cycling on the other hand is an everyday activity you can do at any time – and you don't need anywhere special to do it.

Reading and Use of English Part 3

1

1 eight 2 one 3 yes 4 You can add a prefix or suffix. 5 Correct spelling is essential. 6 Read through the whole text, checking that the completed sentences make sense and are grammatically correct.

2

2 intention; intentional, unintentional; intentionally, unintentionally
3 application, applicant, appliance; applicable, inapplicable; applicably
4 explosion, explosive; explosive; explosively
5 advice, adviser/advisor; advisory, advisable, inadvisable; advisedly
6 knowledge; knowledgeable, knowing, unknowing, known, unknown; knowledgeably, knowingly, unknowingly
7 repetition, repetitiveness; repetitive, repetitious, repeated; repetitively, repeatedly
8 inclusion, inclusiveness; inclusive; inclusively
9 description; descriptive, describable, indescribable; descriptively, indescribably

3

1 beneficial 2 similarities 3 improvements 4 lower 5 inflammation 6 inability 7 loss 8 reduction

Writing Part 2

A letter

1

1 three 2 review 3 (target) reader 4 260 5 sections, heading 6 persuade/convince

2

Yes, it covers all parts of the task.

3

(Suggested answers)
Para 1: introduction – a general statement of the purpose of the letter
Para 2: problems that are worrying club members
Para 3: suggested improvements
Para 4: closing remarks, urging action from the manager

4
Explanations: In the view of members, there are two possible explanations, Firstly, we believe …, Secondly, …
Suggestions: As to what action can be taken, our main suggestions are …, reduced fees could be …, There could also be …, We also believe that …
5
1 concerned about 2 the way it is being run 3 some time
4 noticeably less busy 5 Firstly 6 in the area 7 adjust 8 introduced
9 retired people 10 consider 11 as soon as possible
6
1 representing
2 very modern, using the most recent ideas and methods
3 not able to do what they are supposed to do
4 show their dissatisfaction by leaving or withdrawing their support

Unit 14 A new land

Starting off
2
1 C 2 F 3 B 4 G 5 D 6 A

Track 50
1 I've been here now for about fifteen years. It's a good life, though I work hard, but frankly I miss my country and the town where I grew up and dream of going back. I feel special ties to the place and when I retire I hope to return there to be among my friends and my family.
2 We were utterly fed up with the crime and feeling of insecurity that surrounded us and it was precisely for that reason that we moved away. What really worried us was the effect it might have on the kids going to the local school. We felt it just wasn't worth the risk. On the other hand, it hasn't been easy coping with the language barrier. At least not for us parents. The kids integrated straight away, of course.
3 There's been an ongoing conflict in my country for so many years now, and I'm one of many thousands who became a refugee to escape that. I was only ten when we made it here, and could barely speak a word of the language at the time. I'm in my final year at university now and, yeah, of course I'm proud of what me and my family have achieved since we arrived, but I do often wonder what it would be like to go back there, even just to visit for a while.
4 I love lots of things about my country: the food, the sense of humour, the people, lots of things. Actually, I have to admit it was the climate I couldn't stand any longer. I just found the short grey days and the continual rain totally depressing. Mind you, the heat's sometimes a problem here and then I dream of going home. But that's only the odd day here and there. Mostly it's fine.
5 I guess you could call me a rolling stone, if people still use that expression. I mean, I've been abroad for so long I don't know all the latest slang. You see, unfortunately I'm one of those typical expatriates who spends two years working in this country and three years working in that. I don't think I could ever go back to my home country because, quite honestly, I just wouldn't fit in. I'd be completely out of touch.
6 As a professional ballet dancer there's just no way I could have stayed in my home town. Obviously, you have to be prepared to move abroad if you want to get to the top and there's no point in being in this business unless that's your aim. I've been incredibly lucky, though, and I think everyone needs luck.

Vocabulary
Comment adverbials and intensifying adverbs
1
unfortunately, quite honestly
2
1 Fortunately 2 undoubtedly 3 Generally speaking 4 To be honest
5 Apparently 6 generously 7 Obviously 8 Personally
3
a 1 utterly 2 totally 3 completely 4 incredibly
b 1 absolutely, completely, totally 2 completely, incredibly, utterly
3 totally 4 no other adverb
c They make the adjective more emphatic.
4
1 utterly, absolutely 2 absolutely 3 incredibly, perfectly
4 utterly, completely 5 extremely, incredibly 6 perfectly, absolutely
7 totally, utterly 8 incredibly 9 absolutely

Reading and Use of English Part 6
1
1 four texts and four questions
2 Read the texts carefully before you read the questions to make sure you've understood them. If you do this, you should find the questions easier to answer. If you don't read the texts carefully, you probably won't understand what the questions are referring to.
3 to understand attitudes and opinions and find where they are replicated or not across different texts
3
1 a 2 b 3 a 4 a 5 b 6 a 7 b 8 a
4
1 A 2 D 3 C 4 A

Listening Part 4
1
1 T 2 F You have to choose from eight options. 3 Maybe – you should decide whether this way suits you best or whether you perform better when you deal with both tasks each time you listen. 4 T
2
1 a 272 million
2 b 3.5%
3 c The United States; India
4 (answers from survey)
found a job independently (13%)
to live in their partner's country/for love (11%)
sent by their employer (10%)
to find a better quality of life (8%)
to go to school or university (7%)
to look for adventure/personal challenge (5%)
to simply enjoy living abroad (3%)
to improve language skills (1%)
3
Students' own answers
4
1 E 2 H 3 D 4 A 5 B 6 C 7 F 8 D 9 E 10 G

Track 51
1 Last year, two of my close pals went away together, somewhere completely off the beaten track. They didn't invite me; they'd assumed I'd automatically say 'no'. Understandable, really, I've never been one for adventure. But something inside me must have snapped… I was inspired to discover somewhere with customs and traditions totally unlike those I'm used to, booked a ticket and came over here to live. I'm from a small, sleepy village and felt completely lost initially, even dizzy at times. This is a typical 'big city' and everyone's always rushing around. What's made it so worthwhile is being able to shape a new, adventurous persona for myself. I'll never play things safe again.
2 When I was a kid, I saw this game called Aussie rules football on TV. I became obsessed by it and soon found out as much about it as I could. That led me to learn more about Australia and from an early age I'd decided that I'd come and live here one day. After years of saving, I finally managed to scrape together enough money and flew over here, two weeks ago. So far it's everything I'd hoped for. Well, almost. The apartment block where I'm living is this huge, modern building right in the centre of town, but my studio itself is so cramped. I'm still trying to figure out where to put half my stuff.
3 I suppose I've always been a bit spoilt. Living at home, I never had to bother with any of the chores, as I always knew someone else would eventually do them. Being here, I'm really struggling with having to do all that myself. I've met some interesting people, and hopefully we'll become good friends, but you never know. I do know that I haven't got a great set of qualifications – they don't count for much here, anyway – so I'm taking on a few jobs that might eventually lead to better opportunities. Why I wanted to come here, no one in my family could imagine, but I knew deep down it was time to start standing on my own two feet.
4 Both of my parents are from Malaysia, so perhaps moving here was bound to happen sooner or later. On miserable, damp days, which, frankly, are pretty much guaranteed back home, my mood would always take a turn for the worse. It was that, more than anything, which drove my decision to go, though knowing my grandparents would be here to help me settle in was so reassuring. I'm still finding my way in terms of getting a social life organised, though I haven't really met anyone I share any interests with. Still, gone are the days of being stuck inside, feeling low, so I'm more than happy with life at the moment.

5 At home, my friends and I'd always text each other if we were going to be even five minutes late. Here, when I meet someone at a café and they arrive twenty, thirty minutes late, without even acknowledging that or apologising, I can't help but get annoyed. Like when no one ever tips the staff! But they're little things, really, I couldn't go home now. I was so stressed, working constantly but still having no money and no time for myself, utterly desperate to find somewhere I could get more of both. My sister-in-law used to spend three months each year over here for her job and it was while talking one day that she recommended I try the place out. That conversation? It has completely changed my life.

Grammar

Emphasis

2

1 What's made it so worthwhile is being able to shape a new persona for myself.
2 The apartment block where I live is this huge, modern building right in the centre of town, but my studio itself is so cramped.
3 … hopefully we'll become good friends, but you never know. I do know that I haven't got a great set of qualifications …
4 Why I wanted to come here, no one in my family could imagine.
5 … my mood would always take a turn for the worse. It was that, more than anything, which drove my decision to go.
6 Gone are the days of being stuck inside, feeling low.
7 That conversation? It has completely changed my life.
a Auxiliary verb 3
b *It*- cleft sentence: 5
c Fronting 2, 4, 6, 7
d Reflexive pronoun 2
e *Wh*- cleft sentence: 1

Vocabulary

learn*, *find out* and *know*; *provide*, *offer* and *give

1

1 c 2 a 3 b

2

1 provide 2 offer 3 give

3

1 find out 2 provide 3 find out 4 learn / find out 5 know 6 provide 7 learned / found out 8 provide 9 offer 10 give 11 provided 12 gave

Speaking Part 4

1

1 five
2 subjects connected with the theme in Speaking Part 3
3 are expected to discuss your ideas about the same questions
4 quite long answers

3

1 Laura: grow as a person, broaden your experience of life, a change in your mindset
Daniel: encourage tolerance, stand on your own two feet
2 Laura: open to new possibilities, aptitude for language learning
3 Daniel: relative cost of international travel, long-term effects of pandemics, political instability, climate change

Track 52

Examiner: Laura, how might someone benefit from moving to another country?

Laura: Well, for me, there are many, and the benefits definitely outweigh any disadvantages, without a shadow of doubt. One that immediately springs to mind is the way it helps you grow as a person. Living in another country can broaden your experience of life, make you more understanding of cultural and social differences. Even a short period of time living away – five or six months, say – could bring about a complete change in your mindset – so much so that your outlook on life is changed for ever.

Examiner: And Daniel, do you agree with Laura?

Daniel: Yes, absolutely. It's beyond question that it encourages tolerance, and allows someone to appreciate another culture in a way that they might not or, more likely, would not do otherwise. From my own perspective as a young person, I can imagine it might make someone of my age mature more quickly, become self-sufficient, and better able to stand on their own two feet.

Examiner: Laura, why do some people find the idea of moving to another country more attractive than others do?

Laura: I think people are generally open to new possibilities in life, by and large. But it's undoubtedly a big step to take, and there are so many factors that might seem appealing to some people, but quite intimidating to others. I mean, for one thing, not everyone has the same aptitude for language learning, and if you find that sort of thing difficult, you might be less likely to consider relocating. And I'm inclined to think that someone who is naturally more sociable and confident is more likely to find the whole idea more appealing than someone who is quite shy and reserved. Would you agree with that, Daniel?

Daniel: I'm not sure it's categorically the case that you need have an outgoing personality to move away, but, yeah, on the whole I'd probably go along with that. I suspect that Laura was looking at things from the perspective of someone without any family ties, as I'm sure that would be a factor as well. It's pretty self-evident that the logistics of moving overseas would become more complex with more than one person to consider, and that may well have a huge impact on how attractive someone feels it is.

Examiner: And Daniel, what do you think are the main factors influencing international migration today?

Daniel: Well, I think the relative cost of international travel is perhaps higher than it was a few years ago, so that may well put people off the idea. There's inevitably less of a 'give things a go and come home if it doesn't work out' type of attitude if the cost of relocation means it's just not worth the risk. I'd also suggest that the world may still be experiencing the long-term effects of pandemics, and many people are perhaps more reluctant than before even to jump on a plane and go overseas for a holiday, let alone relocate to another country. But, of course, that's just those who have a choice in the matter – we really can't close our eyes to the fact that there are so many people forced to leave their homelands because of political instability. Or the effects of climate change, although I don't think the real impact of that on migration has even been felt yet.

4

1 can 2 could 3 might, would 4 can, might 5 may

Track 53

1 Living in another country can broaden your experience of life.
2 Even a short period of time living away – five or six months, say – could bring about a complete change in your mindset.
3 … and allows someone to appreciate another culture in a way that they might not or, more likely, would not do otherwise.
4 I can imagine it might make someone of my age mature more quickly …
5 The relative cost of international travel is perhaps higher than it was a few years ago, so that may well put people off the idea.

5

1 without a shadow of doubt 2 It's beyond question 3 categorically
4 It's pretty self-evident

Track 54

1 … the benefits definitely outweigh any disadvantages, without a shadow of doubt.
2 It's beyond question that it encourages tolerance …
3 I'm not sure it's categorically the case that you need have an outgoing personality to move away.
4 It's pretty self-evident that the logistics of moving overseas would become more complex with more than one person to consider …

Reading and Use of English Part 4

1

1 six 2 three 3 word 4 Contractions 5 change 6 same 7 number 8 given

2

The correct answer is b. Answer a is incorrect grammatically; c exceeds the six-word limit; d doesn't use the word given.

3

1 be grateful if you could/would remind
2 in completing the project all by
3 in two minds about studying
4 with a view to relocating permanently

4
1 (well) be holding Katya up/holding up Katya is
2 was not/wasn't until lunchtime / lunch time that
3 does behave even worse
4 Pat is astonishingly intelligent
5 is his love of being/of the/for the outdoors
6 might/may/could have caused the fire was / caused the fire may/might/could have been

Writing Part 1

An essay

1
6, 4, 3, 2, 1, 5, 7

2
(Suggested underlining)
help support immigrants after their arrival / language / culture / work / language classes / local people / familiar with cultural norms and expectations / businesses / schemes / route into employment / two / ways / Immigrants can be supported / reasons / which of the ways / most benefit to migrant communities

5
1 with the result that
2 Consequently
3 During the documentary it was suggested that
4 on the grounds that
5 so what I would suggest is that
6 I entirely agree with the point made during the documentary that
7 To offer some examples
8 it is through these experiences that
9 all of which
10 For this reason, I personally believe that

13 Vocabulary and grammar review

1
1 to 2 for 3 to 4 with 5 at 6 to 7 for 8 to

2
1 ~~however~~ but / dis~~ease, however~~ disease. However,
2 ~~although~~ whereas / but
3 ~~Despite~~ Despite the fact that / ~~Despite he didn't feel~~ Despite not feeling
4 ~~But~~ Although / Even though
5 ~~doctor. Although~~ doctor, although

3
1 not as good as it was
2 have fewer qualified nurses than
3 is more difficult than
4 sooner we get home the
5 didn't / did not earn as much money
6 is no better than / isn't/is not any better than

14 Vocabulary and grammar review

1
1 learned/learnt 2 find out 3 provide 4 know 5 given 6 offered
7 find out 8 learn

2
(Suggested answers)
1 thoughtfully 2 hopefully / almost certainly 3 Actually / To be honest
4 Actually / To be honest 5 quite surprisingly 6 Obviously 7 apparently
8 almost certainly / hopefully

3
1 was more/enough/sufficient time to take
2 that everyone/everybody objected to
3 to do is fill in/out
4 the last thing I want to / will
5 do was (to) take things/it
6 is (doing/the) paperwork that takes (up)

The COMPLETE grammar reference

1 Verb forms to talk about the past

1
1 has injured; fell over; was running
2 I've cut
3 was having; rang
4 had broken; was; would often steal
5 did you get
6 has been playing

2
1 Have you had
2 I didn't sleep
3 I've looked
4 I took
5 I've never had
6 You revised
7 I've failed
8 I've ever taken
9 I've been waiting for
10 You've passed!
11 I really thought
12 I'd failed

3
1 had been copying
2 had been staying
3 had forgotten
4 Have you been exercising
5 have been repairing
6 had been driving
7 have gone

2 Expressing purpose, reason and result

1
1 because
2 Since
3 Because of
4 so that
5 Due to
6 in order to
7 so
8 ✓
9 as
10 ✓

2
1 I'm not going to save all my money just **so** (**that**) I can buy an overpriced flat.
2 I left the house this morning with the intention of buy**ing** a coffee.
3 Very few people turned up to the meeting owing **to** the 7am start time
4 David didn't speak very good English. As a **consequence**, he couldn't really communicate with his partner's parents.
5 I missed my train. **For this** reason, I'm late for work.
6 Fewer people are learning the language, with the result **that** ancient traditions are slowly being lost.
7 I left work early so **as** not to get stuck in traffic.
8 Everyone is moving away because **of** the closure of the coal mines.

3
1 As 2 with 3 of 4 in 5 due 6 Consequently 7 result 8 order

3 *no, none, not*

1
1 **None** / **Not one** of my teammates could offer me a lift to the next game as they all lived on the other side of town.
2 I **can't** find anybody / can find **nobody** to take this chest of drawers away to be recycled.
3 We need to go to the supermarket and buy some milk. There is **none** in the fridge.
4 I went to the bookstore on Friday, but I couldn't find **any** books that I wanted to buy.
5 My family were **not** very pleased when I arrived home without the shopping.
6 The restaurant was awful. We sat down at our table but there were **no** waiters available to take our order.
7 Many classmates of mine were **not** pleased to have to do homework on a Friday night.
8 The train company had hardly **any** information / had ~~**hardly**~~ no information available about the journey.
9 As far as I'm aware there's **no** difference between the two paintings. They're identical.
10 Even though I went to the party, none **of** my so-called friends turned up and I had a terrible time.

The passive

1
1 Interviews for the other top jobs will be held next week.
2 This form has to be seen to be believed. It has been written in pencil.
3 No one has been appointed to replace Ms Kirkby since she was promoted last year.
4 Applicants were asked to send in hand-written letters to accompany their CVs.
5 Your application must be sent as a PDF.
6 Successful applicants will be required to start work on Monday.
7 The name of the new CEO will be announced (by Jeffrey Bowman) at the next board meeting.
8 No one / Nobody with experience could be expected to work for that salary. / Someone with experience couldn't be expected to work for that salary.
2
A city centre mansion worth £5 million **has** finally **been abandoned** by illegal squatters after a week of destruction. Three of the bedroom walls **had been covered** with graffiti and cupboards **had been ripped** apart. Most of the furniture **had been chopped up** and **used** as firewood. The carpets **had been torn up** and the mirrors and windows (**had been**) **smashed**. The damage **has been estimated** (by builders) at more than £1million.
3
1 The term 'amnesia' is used to refer to a partial or complete loss of memory. It is usually a temporary condition which only affects a certain part of a person's experience. Amnesia can be caused by specific medical conditions.
2 We all know that our memory is formed by/from our real experiences. But could a false memory be put into our heads (by someone)? Could we be persuaded that we had experienced something that never actually took place?
3 Our semantic memory is used to store our knowledge of the world. Everyone has this knowledge base, and normally it can be accessed quickly and easily.
4 Our working memory can be thought of as the ability to remember and use a limited amount of information. However, this information is erratic. If you are distracted (by someone), the information can be lost and the task has to be started again.

4 Expressing possibility, probability and certainty

1
1 can't 2 can 3 might 4 should 5 may 6 must 7 every 8 could
9 every 10 might not
2
1 every chance (that) the
2 conceivably give me
3 is bound to break down
4 should have fallen down
5 any chance of it
6 highly unlikely that

5 Verbs followed by *to* + infinitive or the *-ing* form

1
1 to buy 2 to get 3 to win 4 thinking 5 seeing 6 watching
7 to put 8 to buy 9 being
2
1 I suggest taking
2 is helping (to) maintain
3 *correct*
4 I'd consider spending
5 impossible to sleep
6 pretended to understand
7 I remember seeing
8 *correct*

6 Avoiding repetition

1
1 There are only a few slices of cake left. Take **one** while you've got the chance.
2 Because of the snow, all the trains were cancelled. I would have been really angry but I realised that when things like **this** happen, it's better to just relax.
3 She exhibited some wonderful photos, the best of **which** was taken in the townships of South Africa.
4 The best candidates are **those** that show that they have done their homework prior to interview.
5 The fans were chanting for Simons, the man in **whose** ability the crowd always put their faith.
6 She is a baker who knows how to produce some excellent cakes. And **that is** what matters.
7 Having broken mine while climbing a mountain, I really needed a new camera, so I was delighted when my partner gave me **one** as a present.
2
1 so / it would be
2 done so / been
3 So should you
4 so
5 of them
6 ones
7 Either

7 Linking ideas: relative and participle clauses; apposition

1
1 wondering
2 based
3 Having read
4 written
5 specialising
2
1 Walking along the path by the canal, we watched children opening and closing the lock gates to allow boats to pass through. OR Walking along the path by the canal, we watched children who were opening and closing the lock gates to allow boats to pass through.
2 Referring to written notes, the police officer described how she had heard someone screaming at the top of their voice. OR Referring to written notes, the police officer described how she had heard someone who was screaming at the top of their voice.
3 Before moving to Barcelona, Jeff lived near Houston in Texas where he worked in a school teaching English to students from other countries.
4 Built in 1889, the Eiffel Tower has dominated the Paris skyline for over a century, during which (period) it has been repainted 19 times.
5 Bob Marley, whose full name was Robert Nesta Marley, was a Jamaican reggae singer who recorded the best-selling reggae album of all time.

3
2 That's the house **that**/**which**/**Ø** I'd buy if I had enough money.
3 What's the name of that hotel **that**/**which**/**Ø** Mike recommended?
4 What's the name of that hotel **where** we celebrated your birthday?
5 Which is the season **when**/**Ø** most tourists come here?
6 Which is the season **that**/**which** has the best weather?
7 Is it Pete or Jayden **who**/**that** said he couldn't come to the meeting?
8 Is it Pete or Jayden **that**/**who**/**Ø** Ariana's going on holiday with?

8 Reported speech

1
1 stealing
2 on coming
3 to help
4 not to take
5 having
6 to give
2
1 'We're looking for someone with your qualifications.'
2 'You have the right experience for the job.'
3 'You won't have to work at weekends.'
4 'We'll provide you with a company car.'
5 'Employees are allowed to work from home occasionally.'
6 'You can start next Monday.'
3
1 Rob said he'd / he would see me/us the following/next morning.
2 Irina said she hadn't done anything wrong.
3 Steve said we/they could meet at his office.
4 Ahmet said he'd / he had never expected to be there that day.
5 Polly said she and Megan had been there the day before. They had waited for me/us until 7 o'clock.
6 Sacha said (that) Pedro was looking forward to starting his new job the following week.
7 Zoë said I/we could go on holiday with them.
8 Luisa said it had been raining there all night.

Transitive and intransitive verbs

1
1 refused
2 talked
3 lent
4 informed
5 reminded
6 discuss
7 see
2
1 I spoke to someone at the tourist information office and he told **me** that there is a bus we can take to get to the castle.
2 We went into the private room, but the security guard instructed **us** to leave the room immediately.
3 My friend Jason runs **himself** around the park every morning.
4 Your car is blocking the exit and I can't get out – can you move **it** please?
5 Our train is at three o'clock. We need to leave **it** in 30 minutes.
6 Look, I don't care what he said, you can't call **him** that name. It's rude and disrespectful.
7 I found it difficult to make friends at college until my roommate introduced **me** to her friends from the football team.

9 Future perfect and continuous, *be + to* infinitive

1
1 be sipping
2 be attending
3 be relaxing
4 have had
5 have finished
6 will have retired
7 have gained
8 are not to turn over
9 to be announced
10 are to get
2
1 will have become
2 will be eating
3 will have reduced
4 will have increased
5 will be demanding
6 will be choosing

Objects, reflexives and reciprocals

1
1 herself
2 yourself
3 ourselves
4 each other / one another
5 each other / one another
6 themselves
2
1 I've just bought a top-of-the-range iPhone for my gran.
2 I lent my new fibreglass racquet to my tennis partner and she accidently smashed it!
3 They offered a massive increase in salary to us all, in recognition of our contribution to the company.
4 I ordered the up-market presentation set of 'Horrible History' for my children.
5 He got a 'genuine' fake designer handbag for his wife on her birthday.

10 Expressing ability, possibility and obligation

1
1 have to 2 don't need to 3 can 4 don't have to
5 can't 6 mustn't 7 needn't
2
1 can't 2 could have 3 couldn't 4 being able 5 couldn't 6 managed
3
1 needn't have bought
2 mustn't go over / faster than
3 managed to open the window
4 will be able to
5 have to purchase a
6 can't/couldn't have been

11 Conditionals

1
1 could get
2 don't drink
3 would stop
4 can take
5 hadn't been visiting
6 did have
7 train
8 had been concentrating
2
1 If you **hadn't** taken these photographs
2 I'd tell you if I **saw** anything unusual. / **I'll** tell you if I see anything unusual.
3 If I **feel** tired, I usually go to bed early. / If I felt tired I **would go** to bed early.
4 global warming **will** become
5 there **would** still be plenty of oil
3
1 don't / won't usually attack; have
2 keep on; will be promoted
3 hadn't insisted; wouldn't be walking
4 wouldn't get; applied / wouldn't have got; had applied
5 would be running, had kept
6 hadn't improved, would have been ruined
7 had paid, would have been allowed / would be allowed

Conditionals: *wish* and *If only*

1
1 had worked
2 could find
3 wasn't / weren't
4 had told
5 hadn't eaten
6 wouldn't keep
7 would stop
8 hadn't turned down

12 Countable and uncountable nouns

1
1 The **behaviour** of the tourists was disrespectful of the local culture.
2 She had some memorable **experiences** during her gap year in the USA.
3 There wasn't **a** room in the tiny removal van for all his furniture.
4 He did not choose to accept the **advice** from his tutor.
5 BBC News **has** a worldwide reputation for unbiased reporting.
6 ✓

Articles

1
1 Can you buy **Ø** bread and **Ø** milk from **the** shop next to **the** station?
2 I think we should all try to save **the** planet and make **Ø** life better for **Ø** future generations.
3 I spend a lot of **Ø** time looking at **the** sea from **the** balcony of **the** hotel where I'm staying.
4 He really likes **Ø** apples but today he chose **an** orange for lunch.
5 **The** cheapest ferry trip in **the** world is from **Ø** Staten Island to **Ø** Manhattan. It's free!
6 She has **a** brother who goes to **a** different school on **the** other side of town.

13 Ways of contrasting ideas

1
1 though
2 nevertheless
3 whereas
4 on the other hand

2
1 On the ~~other~~ **one** hand … but on the ~~one~~ **other** hand …
2 Even though / Although it was a …
3 ✓
4 In spite **of** the high temperature …
5 ✓
6 despite **being** homeless.

The language of comparison

1
1 as
2 than
3 a lot / a great deal / far / much / even
4 most
5 the more
6 by far / easily

2
1 I'd say that this laptop is by far the ~~better~~ **best** one we've looked at so far.
2 The thing about Julie is that she is not as athletic ~~than~~ as she thinks she is.
3 The ~~long~~ **longer** I live in this city, the more I love it.
4 If you need advice about diet, Ignacio is probably **the** best person to speak to.
5 The neighbour's dog seems quite aggressive at first but he is **more friendly** / **much friendlier** than he first appears.

14 Comment adverbials and intensifying adverbs

1
1 Frankly 2 Personally 3 both 4 incredibly 5 undoubtedly
6 both 7 certainly 8 both

2
1 completely/totally unsuitable
2 far/much more considerate
3 far/much better off
4 easily / by far the most impolite
5 really depressed
6 completely/really/totally amazed

Emphasis

1
1 What I'd really like to do is write stories for children. / What I'd really like to write is stories for children. / It's stories for children that I'd really like to write.
2 What the doctor advised me to do was reduce the amount of sugar I eat. / It was the doctor that advised me to reduce the amount of sugar I eat.
3 It was my best friend who suggested I should apply for a postgraduate degree course. / What my best friend suggested was that I should apply for a postgraduate degree course.
4 It was my father, not my brother, who/that lost his job when the office closed down.
5 It's me who's to blame, not you.
6 What I don't understand is why so many people voted for her. / It's why so many people voted for her that I don't understand.

2
1 At the back of the hall stood a few students chatting.
2 The steak tartar was delicious. But even more delicious was the cheese board.
3 He ordered a bottle of juice and a glass of sparkling water. The sparkling water he gulped down in one go.
4 That she had been jogging was self-evident.
5 Meticulously, he repaired the stitching on his shirt.
6 In front of me crouched a rabid dog ready to attack.

3
1 What I find most annoying is her constant sarcasm.
2 I do hope that she passes her driving test this time.
3 It was on a beach in Thailand that we first met.
4 The reason why / Why he left the party was because he had an argument with his girlfriend.
5 I received a letter from the Prime Minister himself promising to take up our cause.

Multi-word verbs

1
1 between 2 to 3 up 4 together 5 from 6 on

2
1 up 2 over/across 3 on 4 back 5 up 6 up

3
1 being passed over
2 hand in
3 knuckle down
4 see … through
5 take over
6 get off

4
1 on 2 into 3 across 4 in 5 up 6 at

5
1 over 2 away 3 on 4 up 5 out 6 for

6
1 up 2 by 3 in 4 on 5 away 6 up

7
1 on 2 up 3 on 4 off 5 off

8
1 grappling 2 think 3 thrash 4 occurred 5 piece

9
1 through 2 off 3 back 4 out 5 out

10
1 up 2 away 3 up 4 together 5 up / over

WRITING BANK

Part 1: An essay

1
1 2
2 Which of the 2 ways is more effective
3 To help you with ideas
4 No
2
Shopping and food are discussed.
The writer makes use of the first two opinions.
3
Introduction A – it introduces the topic and clearly states which two ways the candidate wants to discuss. B is too direct and provides no context for the reader.
Conclusion B – it clearly summarises the two options discussed in the essay and which would be more beneficial. Conclusion A makes reference to all three 'ways' in the essay question which means that the candidate has not answered the question and would lose marks. The task requires candidates to choose two and then identify the one which is most beneficial.
4
B and C
6
1 Referring forward: This essay will / In the following paragraphs I will / The purpose of this essay is to
2 Sequencing: First of all / To begin with
3 Sequencing: Next / Then / Secondly
4 Expressing opinions: In my opinion / In my view / Personally speaking OR Sequencing: First of all / To begin with
5 Giving reasons for opinions: This is because / The main reason for this is
6 Giving examples: One example of this
7 Referring back: As mentioned earlier
8 Expressing opinions: Personally speaking
8
Model answer
Like many other towns, Weldon has a serious issue with road safety. The situation has become worse over the last few years and several ideas have been suggested to deal with this issue. In my essay, I would like to consider two of these: more car-free zones and better education on road safety.
First of all, we should definitely consider making some roads in the town centre only for pedestrians, because it would be safer for people going in and out of the shops, especially parents with young children, the elderly and people using wheelchairs. We could also consider introducing a car-free zone around primary schools for children's safety. That said, pedestrians would still be at risk when they left these zones because these actions wouldn't improve the quality of people's driving.
For this reason I would say that education is a more effective way of improving road safety. By this, I say we should aim to educate both pedestrians and drivers. We can go into schools to explain to children how to cross the road and use their bicycles safely. In addition, we could have a poster campaign to remind drivers that they need to obey the speed limit and drive carefully. Any drivers caught breaking the rules should be made to attend a course to learn why driving properly is important.
To sum up, although there are many ways we could improve road safety in the town, I personally believe education aimed at drivers and pedestrians from school age upwards would be the most worthwhile.

Part 2: An email/letter

1
1 The local council
2 Formal
3 Your view on whether to cancel music events for teenagers or art exhibitions, with reasons.
2
The art exhibitions
Reasons: The exhibitions are well-attended by people of all ages.
Local artists bring fame to the area.
Sale of art provides income.
3
2, 3, 5, 7, 8
4
A 1, 9 B 6 C 4
5
Para 1–3
Para 2–2
Para 3–5 and 8
Para 4–7
6
1 Informal 2 Informal 3 Formal 4 Informal 5 Formal 6 Formal 7 Informal 8 Formal
8
2 formal, closing 3 informal, opening 4 informal, closing 5 formal opening 6 formal, goodbye 7 informal, opening 8 Informal, opening 9 informal, closing 10 formal closing
9
Model answer
Hi Jacob
Good to hear from you. We are all well over here.
So, you're interested in finding out more about the photography course I did? It was amazing- really practical and well organised. You asked what I found the most useful parts of the course. Well, there were a few. For me, learning how to compose pictures was something new. You know, setting up shots with the right amount of space around them and positioning the object you want to focus on in the best place. Another thing that helped me was the work we did on photographing models. We learnt how to bring out the person's best features and how to position them to show the clothes to their best advantage. I think this is one aspect that will really help when trying to get a job in photography.
Although the course was great, I was not a beginner, but an experienced amateur who wants to become a professional. I have heard that Southgate also does a basic level course and that might be better for you. If you enjoy it, you can move onto the course I did.
You also asked whether the course was good value for money. A few of the other students complained about the cost but I didn't think it was unreasonable at all. It does seem a lot when you have to pay up front, but the course is quite intensive and it covers a lot.
Good luck and let me know if you need anything else.
All the best,

Part 2: A review

1
Describe the shops and facilities, explain one or two features that make the shopping mall special, suggest one improvement
2
1 Yes
2 atmosphere and healthy food
3 Yes. It is written in a neutral tone that would work in a newspaper.
3
1 Unlike 2 much/rather 3 rather 4 more 5 as 6 wide 7 prefer 8 most
4
2 What I liked best were the sound effects.
3 What disappointed me was that I couldn't get to the highest level.
4 It is the quality of the animation that really stands out.
5 Where the designers went wrong was in making the higher levels too difficult.
5
1 absolutely riveting / utterly gripping
2 absolutely breath-taking / totally awesome
3 not of a high standard / not up to scratch
4 extremely user-friendly / beautifully designed / well thought-out
5 absolutely breathtaking / utterly gripping / absolutely riveting / totally awesome
6 absolutely atrocious / shockingly bad
7 absolutely extortionate / excessive to say the least

7
1 Although I enjoyed the film, it was not as good **as** ~~than~~ the other films in the series.
2 What ~~did impress~~ **impressed** me most was the band's performance in a live context.
3 In spite of the restaurant **being** ~~it was~~ crowded, ... / In spite of **the fact that** the restaurant was crowded, ...
4 It was the scenery that stood out the ~~more~~ **most**.
5 Personally, I strongly advise ~~to not buy~~ **against / not buying** the app.
6 If I were you, I **would** avoid this film like the plague.
Model answer
Whenever I get the chance to take a break from work, I like to travel abroad and learn about a different culture. This year, however, I decided to travel around my country by public transport. After so many years of travelling to other countries, I realised that I didn't know my country at all well, so there was a lot to find out!
My first short journey by rail was from Madrid to Segovia with a friend. It was only half an hour away, much quicker than making the journey by car, and with none of the stress of driving or having to find a parking space at the other end.
As soon as the train had gone through the industrial outskirts, we were moving along at high speed through wide open countryside. What I enjoyed most was seeing the farms dotted about, sheep and goats in the fields, and olive trees and vineyards as far as the eye could see. How beautiful, and what a contrast with the noise and pollution of a large city! It was an incredibly relaxing journey, just looking at the changing landscape as the train made its way across the plateau to the city. Once there, we jumped on a local bus to go up to the old centre in order to visit the fantastic UNESCO World Heritage site with its castle and Roman aqueduct.
I highly recommend this way of travelling – and remember, by using public transport and not our cars, we are all reducing our carbon footprint!

Part 2: A report

1
the main activities; which were the most popular activities and why; how the event could be improved; whether or not you would recommend holding the festival again
2
Two: drinks (lack of variety, not enough water), environmental issues
3
Paragraph 1: *Introduction. Report on the camp* is more like the title of the report as a whole, not the first paragraph. *Why I went to camp* is not what the task is asking for and is too informal and personal.
Paragraph 2: *Overall evaluation. Children's opinions on the camp* is OK but sounds less formal. *The camp was great* does not really explain the purpose of the paragraph. It's also very informal.
Paragraph 3: *Most popular activities. The activities that were most enjoyed* is too long and *So what were the best activities?* is very informal and is actually a question.
Paragraph 4: *Recommendations. What we should do differently next time* is too long and *My opinion* is too informal and not really appropriate as it is not really your opinions that the report is asking for but rather those of the children,
4
1 Many of the children enjoyed the arts and crafts activities.
2 The majority of participants preferred the team games.
3 Only a few said they did not enjoy the swimming lessons.
4 Only a small minority felt there were not enough activities
5 ✓
6 A large/considerable/huge/ An enormous number of children participated in the summer camp.
5
1 C iv 2 D iii 3 B i 4 A ii
6
1 In addition 2 particularly 3 also 4. On the other hand
5 due to 6 although 7 Therefore

8
Sample answers
2 The vast majority of people felt the event was well organised.
3 Three quarters believed that the event was not good value for money.
4 Nearly everyone said they had enjoyed the event.
5 About half reported that it was easy to book online.
6 Most people thought there was a good variety of food stalls.
10
Model answer
The course
I attended the College's one-week Introduction to Guitar course from 12th to 19th January. The course took place in the College's Music department from 9am to 1pm each day, with the afternoons left free for participants to practice the morning's lessons.
Overall evaluation of the course
My fellow students and I found the course extremely useful. It provided an excellent introduction to the basics of guitar playing. However, some participants felt some changes to the content and timings may further improve the course.
Strengths
All those who took this course were very impressed by the quality of the teaching. All the tutors were knowledgeable and approachable and most of them had experience as professional musicians. Another strength was the balance between theory and practice, with time being given in the afternoons for us to try out the techniques we had learnt in the mornings. The opportunity to borrow and experiment with professional equipment was much appreciated by all participants.
Point to consider
The course is a very intensive one and was found to be a little too demanding for some of the less experienced students, who felt that they couldn't keep up and became frustrated. Some also expressed a wish to learn some more well-known pop songs rather than focusing so much on music theory.
Recommendations
1 Consider extending the course duration to two weeks and cover one topic per day instead of two.
2 Limit content to the basics. Move the specialist topics to the intermediate course.
3 Include some popular music in the course content.

Part 2: A proposal

1
1 T
2 F (sometimes both are for people in your peer group, such as other students or co-workers)
3 T
4 F (a report focuses on a past or exiting situation whereas a proposal focuses on a future outcome)
2
Why the pool should be re-opened, how it would benefit the town and how costs could be met
3
swimming is healthy, a vital life skill, spend time with family/friends in the fresh air, they won't have to use public transport
4
The pool was closed down in 2005 ...
The costs should be met by the town council, ...
I suggest that half the cost of the redevelopment of the pool is met by the Town Council
A committee should be appointed
Local businesses can be asked for contributions
5
(Suggested answers)
3 The re-opening of the pool has been requested by local people.
4 The profits from the pool will be shared by local businesses.
5 Free swimming lessons should be given to children under the age of ten / Children under the age of ten should be given free swimming lessons.
7 A charity event can be organised to raise money for the renovations / A charity event to raise money for the renovations can be organised.
6
2, 3, 6, 7

8
1 propose/suggest/recommend
2 grounds
3 One
4 could/should
5 more
6 result
7 could/should/can/
10
Model answer
Introduction
The last upgrade to club facilities was the addition of a squash court in 2003. Apart from the weekly pilates class, no new activities have been introduced. As a result, it is felt that changes need to be made to ensure the survival of the club.
The need for change
The number of new members has been declining for the last ten years and a significant number have decided not to renew their membership due to the lack of recent improvements. This has led to a decrease in funds. Nevertheless, remaining members feel that it is only investment in new facilities that will return the club to its former position as the leading club in the area.
Proposed sports and activities
I suggest the introduction of sports which do not require large sums of money, such as karate and yoga, both low-cost activities. It is also proposed that we look for volunteers among the members to organise football and squash teams for children. There will be some expenses involved in buying new equipment, but these will be low compared to other sports.
Benefits of the changes
All the sports proposed are popular with people in the community, and will result in increased income from membership fees, which can be spent on improving the facilities later. Setting up children's teams will also promote a sense of local community pride.
Summary
The introduction of some new low-cost activities and organised children's team sports is recommended, in order to increase the club's income and membership.

SPEAKING BANK

Part 1

1
2 you only talk to the examiner in Part 1
6 your questions will cover several topics
2
Question 1: 5
Question 2: 4
Question 3: 1

Track 55

Examiner: What do you like most about the place you live now?

Julia: Well, there are lots of great things about living here in Brighton. If I had to choose one, it would be living so close to the beach. When I open my window, I can smell the sea air. It's amazing! It's a shame that the sea is too cold to swim in, but I love looking at it.

Examiner: What do you enjoy most about learning English?

Julia: Mmm, let me see … I haven't really thought about it before. I suppose I like being able to translate things for my family and friends and also help out English-speaking tourists who visit my home town. Most of them really appreciate finding someone who can explain things to them in their own language. What else? Well, I guess I enjoy it because compared to other subjects, it really challenges me.

Examiner: Do you ever wish you lived in a different part of the world?

Julia: Sorry, I didn't quite catch that.

Examiner: Do you ever wish you lived in a different part of the world?

3
1 e 2 c 3 f 4 b 5 a 6 f 7 d 8 b 9 b 10 a

4
1 I'd have to say
2 The main reason
3 to be honest
4 If you ask me
5 The other thing is
6 Would you mind repeating that, please
7 On top of that
8 that's a difficult question
Speaker 1 – Question 2
Speaker 2 – Question 8
Speaker 3 – Question 3
Speaker 4 – Question 7

Track 56

1 Well, I'd have to say it's my great grandmother. Not many people are lucky enough to know their grandmother's mother. The main reason I admire her is that she lived through two world wars-although she couldn't remember the first,- and she had such strength of character. She had a hard life but kept on smiling.

2 Not very much, to be honest. It's a bit of a waste of time, if you ask me, especially when you're very busy like I am. The other thing is I actually live really close to most of my friends so I prefer to meet up with them in person. I do have an Instagram account, though, and I occasionally share photos, but not on a regular basis.

3 I'm sorry. Would you mind repeating that, please? I think I'd be good at any kind of work with people and I love travelling so maybe, a tour guide or travel agent, something like that. On top of that I'd like to use my languages in my job if possible because I've spent many years studying them.

4 Well, that's a difficult question. I guess, I'd have to say my favourite place was Budapest. You see, I'm an architecture student and there were so many beautiful buildings to see. I went with a group of fellow students and we enjoyed the nightlife too. One night we took a party cruise on the Danube and it was unforgettable.

5
1 Would you mind repeating that, please?
2 That's a tough question
3 The other thing is
4 On top of that
5 The main reason
6 To be honest
7 I'd have to say
8 if you ask me
6
1 'm a huge fan of
2 are into (sports) in a big way
3 have in common
4 We are fortunate that
5 an Olympic-sized
6 have the same taste in
7 do cover versions of
8 competent musicians
The recorded version would score higher as the candidate demonstrates more advanced-level grammatical and lexical (vocabulary) structures.

Track 57

Well, yes and no. For example, I'm a huge fan of reading while they are into sports in a big way, especially team sports. Actually, the only sport we have in common is swimming. We are fortunate that we have an Olympic-sized pool in our town, and we often hang out there at the weekend. We do all have the same taste in music, though. In fact, some of us play music together. Usually we do cover versions of our favourite groups. If I am honest, we are not very competent musicians, but we enjoy it and that's all that matters.

7
1 cruise 2 great-uncle 3 manual work 4 horror films 5 commuters
6 leap year

Track 58

1 Well, my favourite trip was when I went on a, um, it's like a boat hotel where you visit lots of different places and have entertainment on board.

3 Well, strangely enough, the person who has influenced me most was my, err, the brother of my grandmother.

3 I think I'd be good at, you know, the kind of work you do with your hands as I'm very practical.

4 I can't stand … erm, those films with monsters and ghosts and stuff.

5 The problems with local transport here is that it gets really busy during rush hour, making it difficult for … err, you know, people who need to travel to work in the city every day.

6 I was born in a, a, you know, a year when there is an extra day in February.

8

Sample answers

1 a kind of holiday where the flight, hotel and everything is included
2 your brother's wife or your husband or wife's sister
3 an animal with humps that lives in the desert
4 a person who sets a good example for others and is usually respected
5 a man on his wedding day getting married
6 someone who uses social media to criticise or even persecute other people online

Part 2

1

1 three; two
2 are two; one minute
3 comparing
4 a different
5 one

2

1✓ 2✓ 3✗ 4✗ 5✓ 6✓

3

1 making things
2 Why might they be making these things? How might they be feeling?

Track 59

Examiner: In this part of the test, I'm going to give each of you three pictures. I'd like you to talk about two of them on your own for about a minute, and also to answer a question briefly about your partner's pictures.

Daniel, it's your turn first. Here are your pictures. They show people making things. I'd like you to compare two of the pictures, and say why the people might be making these things and how they might be feeling.

4

Yes, he does.

Track 60

I'd like to talk about the first and third pictures. The first picture shows a potter with his wheel, making a pot from clay. Although it could be his hobby, I think it is more likely that it's his job because he looks like an expert, his pot is pretty professional-looking, and I would guess that he's in his own studio. In contrast, the child in the third picture looks as if she is making a card with her father. It could be something for her mother's birthday or Mother's Day, something like that, or possibly she just enjoys being creative. As for how they are feeling, both of them seem to be concentrating hard and are totally focused on what they are doing, and I would imagine that as a result both are very contented, enjoying the way they can express themselves through their work. Whether you are making something as a hobby or a job, it can be a very rewarding experience.

5

1 appear to 2 Whereas 3 look like 4 may be (2 words) 5 Perhaps
6 on the other hand 7 probably 8 In contrast 9 expect

Track 61

I'm going to talk about the first and second photos. Both photos appear to show people making things as part of their jobs. Whereas the man in the first photo is making something by hand, the men in the other photo look like they are making cars in a factory. The potter may be self-employed. Perhaps he has a workshop at home but in any case, he works independently. The factory workers, on the other hand, are part of an automated process. I would imagine they feel quite differently about their work. The craftsman is probably more satisfied as he is making something unique and using his creativity. In contrast, the factory workers have to follow the employer's design and can't use their own ideas. I expect they find their work more tiring and less enjoyable, but I may be wrong

6

1 The lady in the photo seems **to be** enjoying what she is doing.
2 It looks **as** though they are playing some sort of game.
3 There is **a** possibility that he is doing this as a job.
4 In photo one, they are eating in a restaurant, **whereas in photo two** they are having a picnic outside./ In photo one, they are eating in a restaurant. In photo two, **on the other hand**, they are having a picnic outside.
5 The child in the photo looks ~~like~~ very happy.
6 I **expect** the people in both photos are feeling excited.
7 The man is making something that looks **like** a boat.
8 I think the lady in this photo is **not as happy as** the man in that photo.
9 I would say that they ~~both~~ are **both** feeling tired / I would say that ~~they~~ both **of them** are feeling tired.
10 The activity in this photo is more dangerous ~~that~~ **than** the one in the other photo.

7

Student 1: C
Student 2: A
Student 3: D
Student 4: B

Track 62

1 This photo shows a group of children toasting what look like marshmallows around a campfire. They might be a member of an organisation like the scouts. I think they may have joined to make new friends and have some interesting experiences. What they might enjoy is going camping, being out in the fresh air and having a good time with their friends. The other photo I've chosen shows some old people who look like they belong to a bowling club. I expect they joined this club to keep fit as it is a sport which is not too strenuous for the elderly. They look like they are enjoying themselves taking part in a competition – maybe they like winning. I expect they also enjoy having a drink together afterwards and chatting about their game.

2 I'm going to talk about the second and third photos. Although both of them show people who are members of a club, they are very different. In the second photo, the children may have been enrolled in the club by their parents. They are playing chess, which is not all that much fun for children of that age – say about 8 or 9. Or, possibly their school makes them join after school clubs – in any case, I don't think they chose to join. In contrast, photo three shows older people who have most probably joined this bowling club through choice. At their age, no-one can tell them what to do so they may have decided to join to meet new people and get some exercise.

3 Photos two and three both show children taking part in activities. In photo two the children are scouts at camp, toasting marshmallows on the fire, whereas the children in photo three have joined a chess club at their school. Children join the scouts to take part in different activities and go camping. They enjoy making new friends and getting out of the city. On the other hand, children join a chess club because chess will develop their concentration and thinking. The scouts enjoy being with other children in the fresh air while the chess club members enjoy taking part in competitions and winning prizes.

4 The children in photo two are playing chess so they might be members of their school's chess club. They might have joined this club because chess is a good way for children to develop logic and planning ahead. It is also good for their concentration. In contrast, the older people may have joined the bowls club to relax. The children seem to be enjoying the games they are playing, maybe because they like to compete with others, especially when they win. They probably like interacting with the teacher and learning more about the game. They may even get the chance to take part in tournaments against other schools, which they will enjoy a lot, especially if they win.

8

Yes, she chooses photo 3 and gives reasons why.

Track 63

Examiner: Lola, in which photo do you think the people are benefiting most from the club activity?

Lola: Umm, well, I'd probably have to say the third one because they are older people who probably don't have anything else to do. I mean, they might live alone and need to go to the club to meet others and also to get some exercise, keeping them mentally and physically active. So, yes, I think they are benefiting most.

9

Track 64

Lola: I'd like to talk about the second and third photos. The second photo shows people pushing a car which must have broken down. They could be the passengers from the car, in which case they are helping because they want to get on with their journey. However, they could well be passers-by, who are helping because they feel sorry for the driver who has got stuck. By contrast, in the third photo the younger woman is helping the older one with some kind of exercise. It looks like a gym or fitness centre so I expect the younger woman is helping as part of her job. Both women look happy so I think this help with her exercise is very beneficial to the older one. She may not be able to complete the exercises alone. In the second photo, the help is also fairly vital to the driver to allow them to get their car moving again. Again, I doubt whether the driver would be able to do this on their own.

Examiner: Thank you. Mateo, in which picture do you think the help being given is most important?

Mateo: Well, I would probably have to say the second picture because the driver might not be able to get the car started without their help. The area looks quite remote so there might not be anyone else passing by who could help. The woman in the third photo might be able to do the exercises on her own if she didn't have help.

Part 3

1
1 in print format
2 15
3 two
4 minute
5 follow on logically from
6 two candidates
7 won't

2
How might people benefit from doing the following free-time activities? There are five prompts.

3
Yes, they cover all the options, ask questions and respond to each other.

Track 65

Naomi: OK, where shall we start? What about volunteering for a charity? How might people benefit from doing that, do you think?

Gabriel: Err, well, I suppose it might make them feel good, you know, to be doing something helpful for the community or a particular cause. What do you reckon, Naomi

Naomi: Yes, I'd go along with that. In addition, doing volunteering work can also be useful as a way of getting a paid job later on. It looks good on university applications, too. Shall we move on?

Gabriel: Yes, let's talk about learning something new. What do you think about learning something new?

Naomi: Well, it depends what it is, doesn't it? We all benefit in different ways from learning different things.

Gabriel: Of course. I'm learning to drive at the moment and if I pass my test, I won't have to wait for the bus in the rain anymore!

Naomi: Oh, good luck with that! But I was thinking of other benefits. It keeps your brain active, for one thing.

Gabriel: Which is important for everyone. What about club-based activities?

Naomi: Well, again, I'd say it depends on what kind of club but generally, you get to meet like-minded people and share ideas about whatever it is you're all interested in.

Gabriel: Yes, and for younger people, like voluntary work, being a member of a club can look good on your CV, especially if you hold a position of responsibility.

Naomi: Yes, I suppose that's true. Let's talk about home improvements and gardening. Obviously, the main benefit is living in a nice house and looking at a beautiful garden. Would you agree?

Gabriel: Well, only to a limited extent. Where I come from, having a nice garden is more about showing off to the neighbours. Personally, I have never really understood that or why people care so much about their gardens. But I guess for it makes them happy, right?

Naomi: Right. I'm with you on this one. OK, we only have one left. This is the one we know most about - keeping in touch with friends. Well, the main benefit is having fun, isn't it?

Gabriel: Mmm, possibly …

4
1 Ruby 2 Oliver 3 Ruby

Track 66

Oliver: OK, let's start with family members. The main reason I think is that they genuinely care about the well-being of their relatives. So, for example, when it comes to relationships, our parents want us to be happy and not make stupid mistakes.

Ruby: That's not true at all. I don't think it's a good idea to ask family members for relationship advice. What about friends?

Oliver: Obviously, most people will ask their friends for advice. That's because it is easy – young people probably meet their friends almost every day. Nevertheless, I don't think it's a good idea to rely on friends for advice. Why I say that is they don't have any more experience than we do. They can support us, maybe, but not advise us.

Ruby: You're wrong about that. I would say friends are one of the best people to advise us. I'm not sure why people would ask teachers for advice, unless it is about their studies.

Oliver: It is quite obvious why people would seek advice from professional advisors. They have the experience and knowledge to guide people towards the right decision for them.

Ruby: Possibly in certain circumstances. But you have to be careful of some so-called professional advisors.

Oliver: Well, let's go on to talk about the internet. There are some brilliant websites that can be really helpful but there is also some terrible advice out there.

Ruby: But how are people supposed to know the difference? That's the problem, in my view.

Oliver: The internet is so easy to use and almost everyone has access to it nowadays.

5
Pair A: reach agreement
Pair B: do not reach agreement

Track 67

Pair A

Man: So, I'd say professional advisors are definitely the most useful. I mean, they have to follow certain guidelines and can't give bad advice. Do you agree?

Woman: Well, in most cases, that's true, but not really if it's personal decisions like getting married or something like that.

Man: Well, possibly, but shall we go with it?

Woman: I suppose so and what about the internet for the second one?

Man: Mmm, I'd hesitate to choose the internet. Although it can be useful, it can also do more harm than good if you get on the wrong site.

Woman: That's true. So, what should we choose?

Man: Let's go with family because they are not going to do us any harm.

Woman: OK, I'll go along with that.

Pair B

Woman: Right, what do you think? How about teachers?

Man: Well, as I said earlier, I think that teachers are good for study advice but there are so many things people may need advice about.

Woman: Well, in my experience, teachers – some teachers – anyway, can advise students about all kinds of things. So, professionals then?

Man: Yes, definitely. The only downside is you may have to pay for their advice but they can generally be relied on for good advice.

Woman: Good, we agree on that but what about a second one? The internet, maybe?

Man: No, definitely not. As I said before, getting advice online can do more harm than good. Family or friends?

Woman: Not really because they are too close to you to give impartial advice. No, I'm sticking with teachers.

Man: Well, for me, family comes before teachers.

6
1 I don't 2 ✓ 3 Let's 4 agree to disagree 5 Shall 6 choosing
7 absolutely 8 at all 9 along 10 ✓

7

(Suggested answers)

1 would/'d
2 Let's
3 True/Absolutely/Right/Fine
4 point
5 suppose/guess
6 don't
7 personal/own/humble
8 agree
9 much/way/far
10 minds

Track 68

Woman: OK, shall we start with changing jobs? You'd really need to consider the salary. I mean, you might choose to accept lower pay for a job you found more interesting, but you still need enough to live on.

Man: I agree and I'd add job security. It's not worth giving up a stable job for one that might not last very long.

Woman: That's true and you'd also need to consider the likelihood of being promoted and developing your career. Shall we talk about buying a home?

Man: Well, that's a big decision, isn't it? I think you need to think about how long the house will suit you- so, if your family is going to grow, don't buy a small house, that kind of thing. What do you think?

Woman: Yes, and whether your work might take you away from the area. But also, you need to consider the housing market. Is the house you buy likely to increase or decrease in value in the next few years?

Man: That's a really good point and relates to the next decision, investing money. You have to look at predictions of how your investment will grow in the future.

Woman: Absolutely! And I think with this one, it's a good idea to seek advice from experts because most people haven't got a clue where to invest their money.

Man: Totally and it also depends how much money you're talking about, doesn't it?

Woman: Of course. Shall we move on to choosing what to study? In my opinion, the most important factor is what you're interested in. You have to love the subject or there's no point.

Man: I'm afraid I can't agree with you there. The most important thing to consider is whether the subject you study will lead to a job at the end of it. That's what you're studying for, after all.

Woman: I think we'll have to agree to disagree on that one. Shall we discuss starting a family? What do you think about that?

Man: The main thing is that you can afford to support any children you decide to have and also that you are mature enough to be a parent.

Woman: I can't argue with that. You need a stable home and ideally a reasonable income so you need to consider whether that is in place. That's my opinion, anyway.

Man: Mmm, I tend to agree with you about that.

Examiner: Now you have about one minute to say for which of the things it is most important to make the right decisions.

Man: Well, there are all important decisions, aren't they? But we have to choose two of them. How about investing money? If you get that wrong, it will affect everything else in your life.

Woman: It could do, potentially, but you don't invest money you can't afford to lose, do you? I don't think it is the most important. The same goes for buying a house. If you get it wrong, you could always sell it again or rent it to someone else. Would you agree?

Man: Yes, I suppose so. How about starting a family? Surely that has to be one of the most important.

Woman: Definitely. That has to be one of our choices because it involves children, who will get affected badly if their parents are not mature enough to care for them properly or can't afford to.

Man: Right, so let's choose a second one. Either choosing what to study or changing jobs. What do you think?

Woman: Shall we go with choosing what to study? I mean, you spend 3 or 4 years studying, whereas if you change jobs and it doesn't work out, you can always make another change.

Man: Yes, I'd have to agree with you there.

Part 4

1

1 five 2 follow on from 3 abstract 4 more 5 speculate
6 language only

2

1 topics 2 fine 3 preparation 4 interrupt 5 reply

3

Yes, they do.

Track 69

Examiner: Tom, how important is it for people to have enough leisure time?

Tom: Oh, it's absolutely vital. Why I say that is that people who work too hard can have a lot of problems with their physical and mental health. Not only that, but most people get more enjoyment and happiness from family, friends and activities outside work than from their jobs.

Examiner: What do you think, Mia?

Mia: Well, to be honest, I'm not sure I agree with Tom. I mean, yes, we all need to take time off sometimes but lots of people really enjoy their jobs and get satisfaction from being with colleagues and doing something useful in the community.

Examiner: Mia, what kind of problems may be caused by people not having enough leisure time?

Mia: Well, I would say health problems, primarily. Both physical problems like high blood pressure and heart problems and mental problems like stress.

Examiner: Do you agree, Tom?

Tom: Definitely. Mia has already mentioned mental and physical problems that can result from overwork and another thing is many jobs involve sitting down all day. If people don't get out in the fresh air and get some exercise, they can have all kinds of difficulties with their health. And also, if they don't spend enough time with their family, it can cause problems with relationships.

Examiner: Mia, what do you think is a good work life balance?

Mia: Well, I suppose most people would say of the 24 hours in the day, we should spend about eight hours asleep, eight hours working and the remaining eight hours doing other activities, including leisure activities. I would agree that would be the ideal, but it doesn't always work out that way.

Examiner: What do you think, Tom?

Tom: It sounds a bit too simple, doesn't it? I think it depends on what stage of life you're at. What I mean is when you're young and trying to build up your career, you need to spend more time at work. Then when you start a family, you need to devote yourself to your partner and children.

4

1 B
2 C-the answers focus on describing leisure facilities and the need for them rather than what role the government should play
3 A- the female candidate tries to dominate the conversation and even rudely interrupts the other candidate.

Track 70

Pair 1

Examiner: Elena, do you think people who have to follow rules should help make them?

Elena: Err, well, yes, that would probably be a good idea.

Examiner: Why?

Elena: It just seems fair, really, doesn't it?

Examiner: What do you think, Max?

Max: Yes, I think Elena is right.

Examiner: Why?

Max: Well, like she said, if people have to follow rules, it's fair for them to have a say in making them.

Pair 2

Examiner: What role do you think the government should play in supporting leisure activities?

Jorge: Well, leisure is really important to people, so the government should help pay for it. Like take my local swimming pool. It's really amazing now with all kinds of water chutes and diving boards. The price of admission has gone up a lot though.

Examiner: What do you think, Isabella?

Isabella: Well, I agree with Jorge. Everyone needs leisure facilities. Not just sports centres, but parks, libraries, museums and art galleries. People have different interests so there should be something for everyone. I personally don't think people do enough leisure activities. Most people just watch TV or spend their time on social media, which I think is just making us lazy.

Pair 3

Examiner: Lee, are there any rules you currently have to follow that you would like to change?

Lee: Yes, there are a few, actually. First of all, I don't like having to get home by 11 pm. I think I'm old enough to decide when to come home. And another thing is we are not allowed to have our smartphones in class ….

So Young: Well, of course not. Students would be checking their messages all the time and not listening to the teacher. You can't have that. Anyway, I would change the rules in sports so that men and women can compete against each other. For example, I play tennis and I am better than many men I play against in practice, but I am not allowed to play them in competitions. I think this is extremely sexist and unfair. Also, I hate all the rules when I go to the airport. My hand luggage can only be this size or this weight, and all of that stuff about liquids and so on. What else? Well, …

Examiner: Thank you. Lee, would you say that …

5

1 In general
2 As a rule
3 there are exceptions of course
4 generally speaking
5 Nine times out of ten
6 it's not always the case
7 On the whole
8 not in every case
9 by and large
10 there may be the odd occasion

Track 71

Examiner: Fabio, some people say you should use your head not your heart to make decisions. What do you think?

Fabio: In general, I would say it is better to make important decisions with your head. That means you need to think about whether something is practical or not rather than just considering what you feel like doing. As a rule, I tend to use common sense when I have to decide about something. But, there are exceptions of course. When it comes to love and getting married, for example, you obviously need to be guided by your heart more than your head.

Examiner: What about you, Leah?

Leah: Well, generally speaking I am a person who tends to go with my heart rather than my head. For example, I'm quite spontaneous and take a lot of risks. Nine times out of ten, my heart makes good decisions, which is probably why I continue to do things this way, but it's not always the case.

Examiner: Leah, do you think it is important to get your family's approval when making a decision?

Leah: On the whole, I would say, yes. Things will be much easier if you have your family on your side. They'll be more likely to support and help you if they approve of what you're doing. So, yes, it is important but not in every case. I don't think you should give up your dreams if others don't agree with them.

Examiner: Do you agree, Fabio?

Fabio: Well, yes, by and large, I agree with Leah. Most of the time I try to convince my family that what I want to do is a good idea. I do value their support, but there may be the odd occasion when you need to do something they are not really on board with. Hopefully, they will come around to your way of thinking later.

6

Generalising	Making exceptions
In general As a rule Generally speaking Nine times out of ten On the whole By and large	there are exceptions of course it's not always the case not in every case there may be the odd occasion

8

Track 72

Examiner: How important do you think it is for vocational training to be available for young people who need it?

Student 1: I would say it's extremely important because not everyone is suited to a university education. Many people prefer practical subjects which are more directly linked to a job, such as hairdressing or plumbing. The trouble is that in many countries, academic studies are considered more important but, in my view, it is vital for young people to receive training to prepare them for jobs.

Student 2: I would agree with all that. In fact, I'd go further and suggest that some practical skills for jobs should be taught in schools. And I think it would be great to have presentations from people who work in different fields, so that school children can learn about what skills are needed for each job, what the positives and negatives are, and so on. That way students have more information about which careers suit them or not.

Examiner: Some people say that family matters more than friends. What is your opinion?

Student 2: Let me see. That's not an easy question to answer because both family and friends matter a lot. Overall, though, if I were forced to choose, I'd have to agree that family is more important. That's because there are constant in your life, whereas friends might come and go. Your parents and grandparents, in particular, really do have your best interests at heart, right?

Examiner: Do you agree?

Student 1: I'm not sure I do. I think it depends on who you are. For some people, friends are the people who understand them the most and they have problems communicating with their family. I think your age matters here too. I'd say that that as a rule, young people value their friends more than their family, especially during adolescence. But then you have children and everything changes.

Examiner: Do you think parents should limit the amount of time their children spend online?

Student 1: Yes. By and large, I think parents should restrict children's access to the internet, but it depends on the age of the child and how responsible he or she is. The main thing is that parents should not just leave their children to explore the internet on their own. They should teach them about the potential dangers and what they can do to stay safe online.

Student 2: I think you make some good points, but for me the question is who decides what the limits are. I think the government or doctors should study the effects of children spending time online and make recommendations or rules. That way, it's the same for all families and kids can't complain that their friends get more time online than they do.

Examiner: Is it best to make sports compulsory for school students?

Student 2: I haven't really thought about that before, to be honest. Erm, we all know that sports are good for children – and adults too, of course – but if they are compulsory, it could, in the long run, make people less active. What I mean is, if you are forced to do something, you might end up hating that thing so once you are no longer obliged to do it, you will stop. So, I'd say making sports fun is a more useful approach.

Student 1: I have to disagree here. I think sports in schools should be compulsory to maintain a healthy population. Our population is getting more and more unhealthy and I think a lot of this is due to lack of regular exercise. Perhaps to make sports more fun, schools could offer more variety. I mean, not everyone enjoys competitive sports, so maybe offering things like yoga or dance classes would be a good idea. So yes, I would make sports obligatory.

Acknowledgements

The authors and publishers would like to thank the following contributors:

The COMPLETE Grammar reference: Sarah Greet
Writing and Speaking Bank: Claire Wijayatilake
Additional Writing tasks: Bridget Bloom

The authors and publishers are grateful for the following for reviewing the material during the writing process: Charlotte Aldis, Carole Allsop, Dan Beardshaw, Bridget Bloom, Jo Kent, Meredith Levy, Angela McCarthy, Sarah Taylor and Helen Tiliounie.

The authors and publishers acknowledge the following sources of copyright material and are grateful for the permissions granted. While every effort has been made, it has not always been possible to identify the sources of all the material used, or to trace all copyright holders. If any omissions are brought to our notice, we will be happy to include the appropriate acknowledgements on reprinting and in the next update to the digital edition, as applicable.

Key: U = Unit, R = Review, SB = Speaking Bank.

Text

U1: The Guardian for the text adapted from 'Love it, hate it, can't do without it – teenagers reveal all on family life' by Teenage special Family, *The Guardian*, 12.12.2015. Copyright © 2021 Guardian News & Media Limited. Reproduced with permission; **U3:** Holly Baxter/The Independent for the text adapted from 'What it's like to live with Synaesthesia, by Holly Baxter, *The Independent*, 13.06.2016. Copyright © 2016 Independent Digital News & Media Ltd. Reproduced with permission; **U5:** The Guardian for the text adapted from 'Into the valleys: an off-road cycle ride through south Wales' by Jack Thurston, *The Guardian*, 01.05.2021. Copyright © 2021 Guardian News & Media Limited. Reproduced with permission; **U12:** Mya-Rose Craig for the text on 'The Dramatic Life – so far – of Birdgirl', represented by Claire Conrad at Janklow & Nesbit. Reproduced with kind permission;

Photography

The following images have been sourced from Getty Images.

U1: Povozniuk/iStock/Getty Images Plus; Asia-Pacific Images Studio/E+; Flashpop/DigitalVision; Stephen Zeigler/The Image Bank; Vladimir Vladimirov/E+; Mike Harrington/Stone; monkeybusinessimages/iStock/Getty Images Plus; Thomas Barwick/Stone; Uwe Krejci/DigitalVision; Image Source; FG Trade/E+; DMEPhotography/iStock/Getty Images Plus; SolStock/E+; JGI/Jamie Grill/Tetra images; Catherine McQueen/Moment; **U2:** Favour Nnebedum/EyeEm; d3sign/Moment; Jacobs Stock Photography Ltd/DigitalVision; SensorSpot/E+; Inti St Clair/Tetra images; Edwin Tan/iStock/Getty Images Plus; Juanmonino/E+; eclipse_images/E+; Westend61; Mykyta Dolmatov/iStock/Getty Images Plus; Maskot; BananaStock; Mint Images/Mint Images RF; Comstock/Stockbyte; kate_sept2004/E+; Szepy/iStock/Getty Images Plus; filo/DigitalVision Vectors; **U3:** Chris Madden/Moment;Maja Hitij/Getty Images Entertainment; Rosdiana Ciaravolo/Getty Images Entertainment; Jeff Vespa/WireImage; Paras Griffin/Getty Images Entertainment; Pablo Blazquez Dominguez/Getty Images News; Monica Schipper/FilmMagic; Emmanuel Dunand/AFP; VI-Images/Getty Images Sport; ViewStock/View Stock; Saowakhon Brown/Moment; huseyintuncer/iStock/Getty Images Plus; Pakin Songmor/Moment; Fred Stein Archive/Archive Photos; Sean Gladwell/Moment; nadia_bormotova/iStock/Getty Images Plus; Tomwang112/iStock/Getty Images Plus; John Coletti/The Image Bank; Halfdark/fstop; The Real Tokyo Life/Moment; **U4:** Willie B. Thomas/Stone; Morsa Images/DigitalVision; Halfdark/fStop; CreativeDJ/iStock/Getty Images Plus; Philippe Roy/Image Source; LordHenriVoton/E+; Tom Werner/DigitalVision; Tom Werner/Stone; 10'000 Hours/DigitalVision; Luis Alvarez/DigitalVision; Hiraman/E+; Doug Armand/Stone; Maskot; Edwin Remsberg/The Image Bank; fanjianhua/Moment; **U5:** Andreas Rentz/Bongarts; joggiebotma/iStock/Getty Images Plus; James Strachan/Photodisc; scotto72/iStock/Getty Images Plus; Justin Paget/Stone; Kmatta/Moment; Visoot Uthairam/Moment; Thomas Barwick/Stone; Matthew Micah Wright/The Image Bank; Cavan Images; Rick Doyle/Corbis Documentary; monkeybusinessimages/iStock/Getty Images Plus; **U6:** Westend61; Dan Totilca/iStock/Getty Images Plus; J_art/Moment; EgnisMoore/iStock/Getty Images Plus; isaxar/iStock/Getty Images Plus; Mint Images RF; Nastasic/E+; Ben Pipe Photography/Image Source; alvarez/E+; Keep It 100/DigitalVision; Sam Edwards/OJO Images; Nutthaseth Vanchaichana/EyeEm; HEX; kali9/E+; AntonioGuillem/iStock/Getty Images Plus; Thomas Barwick/DigitalVision; **U7:** stevecoleimages/E+; Hill Street Studios/DigitalVision; Silvrshootr/E+; Westend61; izusek/E+; vorDa/E+; SangHyunPaek/iStock/Getty Images Plus; Mint Images RF; Sorrasak Jar Tinyo/Moment; franckreporter/E+; South_agency/E+; **U8:** ULTRA.F/Photodisc; mgkaya/E+; Westend61; d3sign/Moment; Veerapong Boonporn/EyeEm; clu/iStock/Getty Images Plus; georgeclerk/E+; Oscar Wong/Moment; Jakkapan Jabjainai/EyeEm; vm/E+; littleny/iStock Editorial; Witthaya Prasongsin/Moment; Alistair Berg/DigitalVision; Ignatiev/iStock/Getty Images Plus; Richard Drury/Stone; millann/iStock/Getty Images Plus; Billy Hustace/Corbis Documentary; Wayne Eastep/The Image Bank; Rob Tilley/Corbis Documentary; **U9:** Reg Speller/Hulton Archive; Fox Photos/Hulton Archive; JGalione/E+; Maskot; hobo_018/E+; Puay Ng/EyeEm; Zuraisham Salleh/E+; SDI Productions/E+; Peter Muller/Image Source; Carles Navarro Parcerisas/Moment; FG Trade/E+; SDI Productions/E+; Westend61; Sladic/E+; Comstock/Stockbyte; **U10:** Carol Yepes/Moment; skynesher/E+; monkeybusinessimages/iStock/Getty Images Plus; Luis Alvarez/DigitalVision; Clerkenwell/Vetta; donlucius/iStock/Getty Images Plus; LIgorko/iStock/Getty Images Plus; Steve Wisbauer/Photodisc; shironosov/iStock/Getty Images Plus; ferrantraite/E+; Andersen Ross Photography Inc/DigitalVision; Amir Mukhtar/Moment; Raf Willems/Corbis; Byba Sepit/DigitalVision; recep-bg/E+; Simon Potter/Image Source;

PeopleImages/iStock/Getty Images Plus; FG Trade/E+; John M Lund Photography Inc/Stone; imaginima/iStock/Getty Images Plus; Roy Mehta/DigitalVision; Jure Gasparic/EyeEm; ferrantraite/iStock/Getty Images Plus; Angela940/iStock/Getty Images Plus; **U11:** Mlenny/iStock/Getty Images Plus; ke/iStock/Getty Images Plus; Roberto Moiola/Sysaworld/Moment; ersler/iStock/Getty Images Plus; tommaso79/iStock/Getty Images Plus; EXTREME-PHOTOGRAPHER/E+; FluxFactory/E+; Stefan Cristian Cioata/Moment; kolderal/Moment; R A Kearton/Moment; georgeclerk/iStock/Getty Images Plus; Wangwukong/Stone; feng xu/Moment; Global_Pics/iStock Unreleased; Image Source; **U12:** Andrew Peacock/Stone; David Merron Photography/Moment; Mint Images/Art Wolfe/Mint Images RF; John Brown/Photodisc; Jeff R Clow/Moment; Chad Springer/Image Source; guenterguni/E+; Alexander Joe/AFP; Miguel Sotomayor/Moment; kristianbell/RooM; Mint Images/Mint Images RF; Martin Harvey/The Image Bank; Westend61; pastie/iStock/Getty Images Plus; LeoPatrizi/E+; MarioGuti/E+; mbbirdy/E+; Sergiy Trofimov; Photography/Moment; Eloi_Omella/E+; **U13:** Tara Moore/Stone; Mike Harrington/DigitalVision; d3sign/Moment; Westend61; 10'000 Hours/DigitalVision; ShotPrime/Moment; Peter Dazeley/The Image Bank; svetikd/E+; technotr/E+; isitsharp/E+; Burcu Atalay; Tankut/Moment; Claudia Totir/Moment; Jenner Images/Moment; Juanmonino/E+; Taiyou Nomachi/DigitalVision; Buena Vista Images/Stone; vgajic/E+; Torwai Suebsri/EyeEm; Ben Queenborough/Photodisc; Bernd Vogel/Corbis; **U14:** FatCamera/E+; Smile/Stone; FatCamera/iStock/Getty Images Plus; 10'000 Hours/DigitalVision; Oscar Wong/Moment; Klaus Vedfelt/DigitalVision; Catherine Falls Commercial/Moment; Marco Bottigelli/Moment; Klaus Vedfelt/DigitalVision; Flashpop/DigitalVision; Monty Rakusen/Image Source; _laurent/E+; shomos uddin/Moment; SpB: Kathrin Ziegler/Stone; Monty Rakusen/Image Source; Jules Ingall/Moment; filmstudio/E+; Hans Neleman/Stone; Photo_Concepts/Image Source; MoMo Productions/DigitalVision; Jordan Siemens/Stone; Sean Anthony Eddy/E+;

The following photographs are sourced from other sources/libraries.

U6: 123rf **U9:** The Picture Art Collection/Alamy Stock Photo; **U12:** Mya Rose/Claire Conrad at Janklow & Nesbit.

Cover photography by Moyo Studio/E+/Getty Images; BackyardProduction/iStock/Getty Images Plus.

Audio

Audio production by Leon Chambers.

Typesetting

Typeset by Hyphen S.A.

The COMPLETE grammar reference videos

Audio production by Daniel Strauss
Video production by QBS